CMS
Fall 2018

On the Web | www.cmstudies.org

Archival News
Professional Notes
In Focus
Conference Reports
Author Postscripts

JCMS: Journal of Cinema and Media Studies is published for the Society for Cinema and Media Studies by the University of Texas Press.

JCMS: Journal of Cinema and Media Studies (ISSN 2578-4900, e-ISSN 2578-4919) is published quarterly in Fall (November), Winter (February), Spring (May), and Summer (August) by the University of Texas Press, Journals Division, 3001 Lake Austin Blvd. Ste 2200, Austin, TX 78703-4210. Subscription rates are $264/year for institutions and $60/year for individuals. PERIODICALS POSTAGE PAID at Austin, Texas, and additional mailing offices. POSTMASTER: Send address changes to JCMS, University of Texas Press, PO Box 7819, Austin, TX 78713-7819.

JCMS is published in cooperation with the Society for Cinema and Media Studies; members of the society receive the journal as one of the benefits of membership. For further information on membership, see inside back cover of this issue. All business inquiries (subscriptions, advertisements, and change-of-address notices) should be addressed to the Journals Division, University of Texas Press, PO Box 7819, Austin, TX 78713-7819. All views or conclusions are those of the authors of the articles and not necessarily those of the editorial staff, the University of Texas Press, the University of Texas at Austin, or the Society for Cinema and Media Studies. For ordering information, visit our website: https://utpress.utexas.edu. Domestic and non-US claims for missing issues must be received within 90 days of the publication date. Issues returned "undeliverable" are available for reshipment at cost of new shipment. To process a claim please see our claims form at the UT Press website.

This journal is a member of CELJ, the Conference of Editors of Learned Journals. It is indexed in *Academic Search Premier*, *Arts and Humanities Citation Index*, *Film Literature Index*, *IBR (International Bibliography of Book Reviews)*, *IBZ (International Bibliography of Periodical Literature)*, *International Index to Film Periodicals*, and *MLA Bibliography* and abstracted in *Academic Search Premier* and *Extended Academic Abstracts*.

JCMS is available electronically: current content through Project Muse, a full archive through JSTOR, and back issues through ProQuest, Ebsco, and Gale/Cengage Inc.

Living in a World without Sun: Jacques Cousteau, *Homo aquaticus*, and the Dream of Dwelling Undersea

by JON CRYLEN

Abstract: This article examines Jacques-Yves Cousteau's 1960s concept of *Homo aquaticus* in relation to three documentaries. A utopian variant of *Homo sapiens* that Cousteau forecast would evolve to live and work undersea, *Homo aquaticus* also appeared at a time when Western nations regarded the sea primarily as an exploitable resource. Cousteau's films give expression to this idea aesthetically, in the undersea life they depict and in the array of diving technologies and underwater habitats they showcase, apparatuses that extended human reach underwater. By emphasizing Cousteau's vanguard figure of the underwater man, this article shifts scholarly focus from Cousteau's celebrity, his conservationist stances, and his films' representations of wildlife to a central paradox of his early films: a poetic vision of freedom from the surface that is bound to a project of ocean domination.

"I think there will be a conscious and deliberate evolution of *Homo aquaticus*, spurred by human intelligence rather than the slow blind natural adaptation of species. We are now moving toward an alteration of human anatomy to give man almost unlimited freedom underwater."[1] So Jacques-Yves Cousteau told a baffled audience of ocean scientists at the World Congress on Underwater Activities in London in October 1962. Although Cousteau based his claim on American scientists' research into surgically implantable artificial gills that would allow divers, like fish, to regenerate the oxygen in their blood without breathing air, his ultimate vision was of "future generations born in underwater villages, finally adapting to the environment so that no surgery will be necessary to permit them to live and breathe underwater."[2] In other words, Cousteau believed that the human body would evolve to perform organically functions for which it had hitherto relied on prostheses.

1 Qtd. in Brad Matsen, *Jacques Cousteau: The Sea King* (New York: Pantheon, 2009), 160–161.

2 Jacques-Yves Cousteau, "Ocean-Bottom Homes for Skin Divers," *Popular Mechanics* 120, no. 1 (July 1963): 183.

Jon Crylen is an independent scholar. He has taught film studies at the University of Iowa and Coe College and is completing a book manuscript titled "Ocean Movies: Representing the Undersea World in the Anthropocene."

Although Cousteau's dream of a race of surgically and later evolutionarily enhanced water people who live and work undersea remains unfulfilled, both his films and television shows and the diving technologies that enabled him to make them—the Aqua-Lung he developed with Émile Gagnan, as well as his fleet of submersibles and undersea habitats along the continental shelf—were instrumental in shaping popular ideas of what human life undersea might be like. Not only is "undersea film" synonymous with Cousteau, the aquatic life he epitomized in his media work influenced countless subsequent films of ocean space, including both documentaries and fiction films by the likes of James Cameron, Luc Besson, Al Giddings, Wes Anderson, and Cousteau's own progeny, who continue to advance the late captain's conservationist attitudes toward the ocean.

More an avatar of conquest than of conservation, however, *Homo aquaticus* was conceived of at a time when Western industrial nations increasingly turned to the ocean, the "inner space" covering more than 70 percent of the earth's surface, to solve the problems posed by the terrestrial limits to growth. They viewed the ocean as a potentially endless treasure trove of food and fuel and even as a dumping ground for nuclear waste. As John F. Kennedy put it in his March 29, 1961, letter to the US Senate: "Knowledge of the oceans is more than a matter of curiosity. Our very survival may hinge upon it."[3] Noting the military necessity of mapping the seafloor to maintain strategic advantage over the Soviet Union, Kennedy expressed what would for another decade remain dominant sentiments concerning the uses of the sea, advocating for the ability of the ocean's bounty of food and minerals to meet a growing population's needs and the possibility of predicting—even controlling—weather and climate by studying the ocean's influence on the atmosphere.

Cousteau, for his part, boldly predicted a full-fledged domestication of ocean space that, along with the alteration of the human body that he envisioned, would generate an absolute freedom from the earth's surface and thus radically transform human values. "In ten years," he predicted, "there will be permanent homes and workshops at the bottom of the sea where men can stay for three months at a time, mining, drilling for oil, coal, tin, other materials, and farming seafood and raising sea cattle. . . . More important than the huge space and wealth, they will draw new thoughts and creativity from a whole new world. And hopefully we may enter an era that deserves the title, civilization."[4] Indeed, when Cousteau asked the divers of Conshelf I, the first of three underwater habitat experiments he spearheaded, for their impressions of life underwater, one responded that "everything is moral down here"—a reply that Cousteau would invoke a quarter century later, noting that his divers had traversed a "kind of moral gateway that made them see national and tribal disputes as ridiculous, as something mankind must learn to leave behind."[5] The permanent technical expansion of humans' reach into the earth's inner space would, Cousteau thought,

3 John F. Kennedy, "Letter to the President of the Senate on Increasing the National Effort in Oceanography," March 29, 1961, http://www.presidency.ucsb.edu/ws/index.php?pid=8034.

4 Qtd. in Axel Madsen, *Cousteau: An Unauthorized Biography* (New York: Beaufort Books, 1986), 127.

5 Qtd. in Madsen, *Cousteau*, 128.

bring about a veritable sea change in human consciousness, albeit one that in the 1950s and 1960s espoused only a limited environmental stewardship.

In this article, I treat *Homo aquaticus* as less a fully fledged futurist concept pertaining to human evolution than a general midcentury image of what underwater life and work could be that Cousteau's early movies helped to shape. These films include *The Silent World* (*Le monde du silence*; Jacques-Yves Cousteau and Louis Malle, 1956), *World without Sun* (*Le monde sans soleil*; Jacques-Yves Cousteau, 1964), and *Conshelf Adventure* (Philippe Cousteau, 1966), the latter two of which documented Cousteau's Conshelf II and III underwater habitat experiments, respectively. Drawing on several of Cousteau's writings, I discuss *Homo aquaticus* in three registers vis-à-vis these films: their aesthetics, the undersea life they depict, and the array of technologies deployed by their human subjects. These technologies extended man's physical reach underwater by allowing him—almost always him, both in discourse and in practice—to breathe at depth without being tethered to the surface. They included the Aqua-Lung (the first commercially successful scuba apparatus) and a fleet of mini-submersibles that used the famous mother ship *Calypso* as a base: the SP-350, or *soucoupe plongeante* (diving saucer), and its smaller siblings, the SP-500 Sea Fleas. They also included Cousteau's underwater habitats along the continental shelf, bases where saturation divers could live and work for potentially unlimited periods of time, doing mining, farming, construction and repair, or scientific research in a range of fields. Together these technologies conspired to create an image of freedom from the surface—a freedom that, per Cousteau, would transform human values and bring about a more utopic existence on planet Earth (or, as Arthur C. Clarke is reputed to have called it, planet Ocean).[6] The paradox here is that this image of a new man, however poetically conceived in Cousteau's hands, was bound up with the period project of exploiting the sea economically, such that whatever utopian transformations of the human Cousteau's movies either depict or allow viewers to experience vicariously are underwritten by projects of ocean conquest that we now understand to be and to have been ecologically destructive.[7]

Additionally, and unsurprisingly given that ocean science of this period (at least, in the West) was dominated by Caucasian men, *Homo aquaticus* marks a white male ideal, one that, furthermore and insofar as recreational diving became a major postwar leisure pursuit, is found primarily among the affluent.[8] Indeed, as a proto-posthumanist

6 The quotation attributed to Clarke—"How inappropriate it is to call this planet Earth when it is quite clearly Ocean"—is, as Stefan Helmreich notes, ubiquitous in writing about the sea but impossible to actually source. See Helmreich, "From Spaceship Earth to Google Ocean: Planetary Icons, Indexes, and Infrastructures," *Social Research* 78, no. 4 (2011): 1216–1217.

7 As a descriptor of a prosthetic human subject who is coextensive with marine technologies and exists in various, changeable combinations with them, *Homo aquaticus* correlates with the philosopher Bernard Stiegler's idea that humans are essentially technical beings who have coevolved with their appurtenances. See Stiegler, *Technics and Time, 1: The Fault of Epimetheus*, trans. Richard Beardsworth and George Collins (Stanford, CA: Stanford University Press, 1998).

8 On the midcentury gender bias in the marine sciences, particularly against women at sea, consider that the famed marine biologist and conservationist Sylvia Earle was the lone woman among seventy men on a National Science Foundation–funded expedition to the Indian Ocean; similarly, the storied deep-submergence vehicle *Alvin*, commissioned in 1964, took no female passengers until 1977. Regarding racial diversity, as the African American marine geologist Evan Forde put it in 1981: "I've never met another Black oceanographer." See Wallace White, "Her Deepness," *New Yorker*, July 3, 1989, https://www.newyorker.com/magazine/1989/07/03/deepness; Kathleen

figure, *Homo aquaticus* is perhaps best understood as exclusionary—a symbol of an economically and socially elite minority of men who, loosed from their biological chains, could leave everyone else behind.[9] In the visual culture of the 1950s and 1960s, oceanauts—or aquanauts, or frogmen, or men-fish, other common names for amphibious man—are almost always white males, and their technologically enhanced bodies stand in stark contrast to the bodies of women and native others underwater. The latter bodies are notably technology-free—for instance, the Weeki Wachee mermaids of Silver Springs, Florida, and the models in Bruce Mozert's photographs, both of which I discuss toward the end of this article. Unencumbered by technical supplements, these women appear at one with the natural space of the sea. In this respect they seem to signify an ideal, unattainable state of unity with aquatic space to which men can only aspire.

By prioritizing Cousteau's vanguard figure of the underwater man, I depart from the scholarly tendency to frame Cousteau's work in terms of his celebrity, his conservationist stances and those stances' limitations, and his representations and treatment of wildlife. Nonetheless, various scholars' claims inform my argument. Graham Huggan, for instance, divides Cousteau's career into three phases: scientific, exploratory, and conservationist. I have limited myself primarily to this first phase, which for Huggan lasts from the 1940s through the mid-1960s, relates to Cousteau's efforts to colonize the seafloor, and includes both the Aqua-Lung's invention and Cousteau's pronouncements about future man.[10] For Cynthia Chris, *The Undersea World* affirms Western hegemony over the seas through its episodes' narratives of exploration and discovery, a charge that equally applies to the three films discussed here. Chris also calls attention to the more objectionable activities depicted in *The Silent World*: the *Calypso* crew's dynamiting of a coral reef to collect dead specimens and their "revenge" killing of a few sharks for feasting on a baby whale that the ship's propeller chopped up.[11] While I do not discuss Cousteau's treatment of animals here, I share Chris's view (also Huggan's) that the early Cousteau movies are anything but environmentally friendly. Finally, Nicole Starosielski situates Cousteau's movies amid general cultural trends that configured the ocean in terms of exploitable resources and domesticated it for its ideal inhabitants: the white American family.[12] While I

Crane, *Sea Legs: Tales of a Woman Oceanographer* (Boulder, CO: Westview Press, 2003), 296; and "Evan Forde: Deep Sea Scientist," *Ebony Jr!* 8, no. 10 (April 1981): 8.

9 As the critic Joel Dinerstein puts it vis-à-vis techno-utopians, such as Ray Kurzweil, who believe genetic engineering, bio- and nanotechnology, and robotics will enable humans to transcend their bodily limits, "the *post*human is an escape from the *pan*human." Dinerstein, "Technology and Its Discontents: On the Verge of the Posthuman," in *Rewiring the 'Nation': The Place of Technology in American Studies*, ed. Carolyn de la Peña and Siva Vaidhyanathan (Baltimore: Johns Hopkins University Press, 2007), 16.

10 The exploratory phase is roughly contemporaneous with *The Undersea World of Jacques Cousteau*, which aired on ABC from 1968 to 1976. This slightly overlaps with his conservationist phase, which for Huggan encompasses Cousteau's television work from the early 1970s until his death in 1997, as well as his activities with the Cousteau Society, which he created with his two sons in 1973. Graham Huggan, *Nature's Saviours: Celebrity Conservationists in the Television Age* (New York: Routledge, 2013), 67–69.

11 Cynthia Chris, *Watching Wildlife* (Minneapolis: University of Minnesota Press, 2006), 41–42, 56–57.

12 Nicole Starosielski, "Beyond Fluidity: A Cultural History of Cinema under Water," in *Ecocinema Theory and Practice*, ed. Stephen Rust, Salma Monani, and Sean Cubitt (New York: Routledge, 2013), 159–163.

concur with Starosielski's major point that movies of the postwar period idealize the sea as a place for white bodies, I also revise the distinction she makes between ocean exploitation and ocean domestication movies. In my discussion of Cousteau's films and the vision of ocean-dwelling humans they promulgate, I show that exploitation and domestication are continuous projects.[13]

An Aesthetic of Freedom Undersea. As a visual idea, the life aquatic, *Homo aquaticus*, finds expression not only in the activities of the camera-wielding aquanauts or undersea habitat dwellers depicted on-screen in Cousteau's movies but also in the films' aesthetics—the lyrical, free-floating, and seemingly subjectless camera movements that penetrate aquatic space from inside it. The general view here is that of a participant in the aquatic scene, a perspective that embodies possibilities of spatial orientation and movement impossible on land, as in the images of vertical descent down the water column that begin *The Silent World* (see Figure 1). Cousteau's roving undersea images, which move with a fluidity unusual for handheld cameras, appear as dazzling invitations to viewers to imagine themselves, too, inhabiting undersea space.

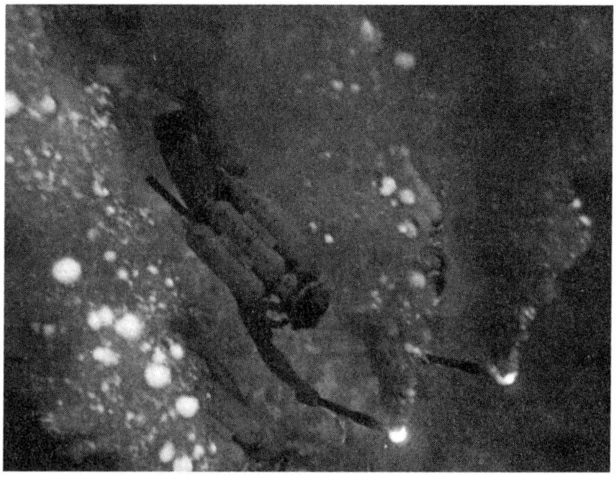

Figure 1. Aqua-Lung divers descend by torchlight into the blue in *The Silent World* (Columbia Pictures, 1956).

With no shortage of awe, Rudolf Arnheim highlighted these very qualities in a 1966 essay on the state of film art:

> Cousteau's film creates fascination not simply as an extension of our visual knowledge obtained by the documentary presentation of an unexplored area of our earth. These most authentically realistic pictures reveal a world of profound mystery, a darkness momentarily lifted by flashes of unnatural light, a complete suspension of the familiar vertical and horizontal coordinates of space. Spatial orientation is upset also by the weightlessness of these animals and

13 Other than the foregoing accounts, English-language scholarship on Cousteau's films is scarce, with the vast majority of discussion of his work appearing in popular biographies. A few exceptions: Janine Marchessault has analyzed *The Silent World* in relation to Roland Barthes's critique of Jules Verne's reduction of the natural world to a space of "conventional, bourgeois imagining." Gregg Mitman has briefly remarked on *The Silent World*'s opening in relation to the popular mid-twentieth-century discourse that framed outer space and the ocean ("inner space") as the two poles of the scientific unknown. Finally, the 2012 meeting of the Society for Cinema and Media Studies in Boston featured a panel on Cousteau's films titled "Regarding Jacques Cousteau, Regarding the World"; participants included Marchessault, James Leo Cahill, Jason Zuzga, and Jennifer Fay. See Janine Marchessault, "Invisible Ecologies: Cousteau's Camera and Ocean Wonders," *Media-N: Journal of the New Media Caucus* 11, no. 2 (2015), http://median.newmediacaucus.org/caa-conference-edition-2015-new-york/invisible-ecologies-cousteaus-cameras-and-ocean-wonders; and Gregg Mitman, *Reel Nature: America's Romance with Wildlife on Film* (Seattle: University of Washington Press, 1999), 174.

> dehumanized humans, floating up and down without effort, emerging from nowhere and disappearing into nothingness, constantly in motion without any recognizable purpose, and totally indifferent to each other. There is an overwhelming display of dazzling color and intricate motion, tied to no experience we ever had and performed for the discernible benefit of nobody. There are innumerable monstrous variations of faces and bodies as we know them, passing by with the matter-of-factness of herring or perch, in a profound silence, most unnatural for such visual commotion and rioting color, and interrupted only by noises nobody ever heard.[14]

Arnheim's agenda here is not to sing the wonders of distant reality as *World without Sun* reveals it to be. Typically, he praises aspects of the film that conform to a purely aesthetic idea of what cinema should do—namely, "interpret the ghostliness of the visible world by means of authentic appearances drawn directly from that world."[15] What stands out in this passage, however, is not only the wondrous groundlessness Arnheim describes but also the apparent uselessness of the dazzling world on display, the "motion without any recognizable purpose . . . performed for the discernible benefit of nobody." Such descriptions suggest a world defiantly at odds with the means-ends nature of the era's resource-based environmental thought. In this respect they cast the world of *Homo aquaticus* as utopian, as a world in which things are valued for more than their usefulness or the ways they might be exploited (even if underwater man's work often was exploitative).

As Arnheim indicates, splendorous colors were essential to the wonder associated with Cousteau's films—although in this respect they were hardly unique among films of the period that showcased marine environments. Filmmakers had attempted to film the ocean in color as early as *The Uninvited Guest* (Ralph Ince, 1924), which included a two-strip Technicolor sequence. And although in cinema of the 1930s and 1940s a colorful ocean appears almost exclusively in animation—notably in a spate of Disney's Silly Symphonies and culminating in *Pinocchio* (Ben Sharpsteen and Hamilton Luske, 1940), when Pinocchio and Jiminy Cricket search the ocean floor for Monstro the whale—the early 1950s witnessed several Technicolor features with sequences shot undersea, mostly in the limpid waters of the Caribbean or the Gulf of Mexico.[16]

Significantly, many of the eye-popping color images of marine life in Cousteau's and other films of the period are actually false to their environs. Consequently, they show the world as not even marine animals, regardless of the biophysics of vision of particular species, can normally see it. The "overwhelming display of dazzling . . . rioting color" that so delights Arnheim can be produced only via artificial light. Without

14 Rudolf Arnheim, "Art Today and the Film," *Art Journal* 25, no. 3 (Spring 1966): 243–244.

15 Arnheim, "Art Today and the Film," 244.

16 The Silly Symphonies in question are *King Neptune* (Burt Gillett, 1932), *Water Babies* (Wilfred Jackson, 1935), *Merbabies* (Rudolf Ising and Vernon Stallings, 1938), *The Whalers* (David Hand and Dick Heumer, 1938), and *Sea Scouts* (Dick Lundy, 1939). The live-action color features that preceded *The Silent World* include 20th Century Fox's *Beneath the 12-Mile Reef* (Robert D. Webb, 1953); Disney's *20,000 Leagues under the Sea* (Richard Fleischer, 1954); RKO's *Underwater!* (John Sturges, 1955) and *The Sea around Us* (Irwin Allen, 1953); and Hans Hass's documentary *Unternehmen Xarifa* (*Under the Caribbean*, 1954).

artificial illumination, everything undersea below a certain, very shallow depth appears lost in a blue-green haze. This is because water absorbs higher frequencies of light, or the warmer colors of the visible spectrum, at shallower depths than it does the lower frequencies, which penetrate farthest—blue in particular. (The most transparent seawater appears blue from the surface because the least-absorbed color is the one the water reflects.) Artificial white light becomes necessary even a short distance below the surface to restore the warmer end of the spectrum, and Cousteau plays with the effect of its limited range in a scene in *The Silent World* when his divers descend to 247 feet with floodlights, illuminating parts of corals but not others, such that the objects we see shift briefly into dazzling, warm relief before receding into the tranquil blue (see Figure 2). The transience of colors is further emphasized in a later sequence that notes that the dazzling colors of fish taken as specimens quickly fade at the surface. In the nighttime and *soucoupe* deep-dive sequences in *World without Sun*, these vibrant colors emerge from a perpetual night where, Cousteau tells us, non-bioluminescent light has never before shone.

Figure 2. Artificial light illuminates a coral reef in *The Silent World* (Columbia Pictures, 1956).

The use of artificial light is of more than mere aesthetic consequence. In addition to lighting shots and conveying for viewers the spectacular environs that were a part of underwater man's stream of experience, artificial light was central to efforts to research and plans to engineer the deep-ocean environment, which would be the work of *Homo aquaticus*. *World without Sun* shows the collection of specimens and nighttime and deepwater observation of marine life with the help of floodlights—work that in the context of the film appears to serve only a disinterested science of nebulous purpose. Artificial light, however, would also be used in attempts to simulate photosynthesis in aphotic (lightless) waters, which Cousteau's oceanauts attempted to do in Conshelf III to "boost the food productivity of the sea."[17] Additionally, it would be essential to deepwater construction and maintenance work. As Cousteau writes in his book *Window in the Sea*, "Even in the dark waters beyond 300 feet, and with the aid of artificial light, vision was the necessary factor in showing man could, for example, set up an oil-well head."[18] Indeed, the final section of *Conshelf Adventure* depicts the saturation divers engaged in a wellhead repair exercise; the narrator tells us that oceanauts' success would mark "a giant leap forward in man's economic occupation of the seafloor." Dazzling aesthetic effects become continuous with the scientific study and economic conquest of undersea space.

17 Jacques-Yves Cousteau, *Window in the Sea* (New York: World Publishing Co., 1973), 73.

18 Cousteau, *Window in the Sea*, 43.

Although artificial light could illuminate the environs in which *Homo aquaticus* lived and worked and marks the ocean as a place of overwhelming visual splendor in Cousteau's movies, the key technology for the aesthetic of freedom the movies indulge in was the Aqua-Lung, which Cousteau invented with his compatriot Émile Gagnan in 1943 and which became the first commercially successful scuba apparatus. Indeed, the prized idea of being freed from the surface—swimming and breathing without tethers—seems unthinkable without scuba gear. And because scuba helped bring about the advent of recreational diving in Europe and the United States, it also gave the aesthetics of Cousteau's movies a correlative with the direct human experience of undersea space.

The Aqua-Lung was the first widely used device that freed *Homo aquaticus* from air hoses and safety lines that might entangle him or break, ensuring, per Cousteau, that his "safety was in freedom."[19] Yet the diver-cinematographer (emblematized by Jacques's son Philippe, who shot eleven of the thirty-six episodes of *The Undersea World*) not only had to be trained on how to properly and safely use the scuba apparatus but also had to know how to contend with the potentially fatal dangers associated with using it. These many dangers included nitrogen narcosis and decompression sickness ("the bends"), both of which *The Silent World* dramatizes. In an early sequence, one of Cousteau's divers narrates a scene in which his diving partner suffers from both of these maladies, setting free the lobsters he has just caught and twirling a piece of coral around his index finger before suddenly—and perilously—removing his mouthpiece. This behavior, we learn, is the result of nitrogen narcosis, a pleasant, drunken sensation caused by the increased solubility of gases in bodily tissues under pressure. Its effects, which diving manuals tend to liken to one strong alcoholic drink for the first 100 feet and another for every subsequent 33 feet (or one atmosphere of pressure), are easily reversed by ascent, but afflicted divers may forget this and endanger themselves—just as the diver in the sequence does. Drunk and low on oxygen, he ascends from a depth of 150 feet without decompressing, rising to the surface with a pain in his knee. The cause: the bends, which occurs when gases dissolve into bodily tissues under pressure and reemerge as bubbles upon too-quick depressurization. (The syndrome gets its nickname because bending the joints can alleviate localized joint pain, the most common symptom.) Divers afflicted by the bends must typically spend time in a recompression chamber—shown in *The Silent World* as a sort of coffin tube into which the claustrophobic diver reluctantly slips.

These twin dangers affect both the work we see depicted in Cousteau's movies and the films' visual aesthetic. Regarding "the rapture of the deep," his phrase for nitrogen narcosis, Cousteau imposed an absolute depth limit of 300 feet—and 250 feet on working dives—on his crew members after one of them lost consciousness and drowned at 396 feet.[20] Cinematographically, this depth limit put a floor (rather than ceiling) on the kinds of spaces that the cameramen among Cousteau's crew could film. In addition, the cameramen had to incorporate techniques for preventing the

19 "Those Incredible Diving Machines," *The Undersea World of Jacques Cousteau*, first broadcast March 10, 1970, by ABC, directed by Philippe Cousteau and written by Marshall Flaum.

20 David M. Owen, *A Manual for Free-Divers Using Compressed Air* (New York: Pergamon Press, 1955), 32–33.

bends into their cinematic practice. It was essential that they, like the other aquanauts, use dive tables to prevent its onset, adhering to standardized limits on descent rate, exposure time at deepest depth, and ascent rate, which may be continuous or staggered (including stops at various specified depths along a diving shot line with the assistance of depth-gauge wristwatches). In addition, they had to make sure they had a sufficient air supply to account for both exposure time and all needed decompression stops. Consequently, the imagery that conveys an impression of total freedom from the surface is actually rather limited, its possibilities restricted by the diver's overriding need to manage the risks associated with the marine environment.

Because scuba views have become so prevalent, we might easily lose sight of their novelty for film viewers in the 1950s—and an important part of their novelty would have been operational. In the book version of *The Silent World*, Cousteau notes that the Aqua-Lung—and, by extension, what I am calling a visual aesthetic of freedom from the surface—was, like so many other "successful" technologies, built on a bedrock of failed, even dangerous, experiments. Previously, Cousteau tried diving with a makeshift device consisting of a gas canister full of soda lime (used to absorb carbon dioxide), a bottle of pure oxygen, and a motorbike inner tube. This apparatus twice induced oxygen poisoning, causing Cousteau to convulse, lose consciousness, and nearly drown. Another apparatus, the Fernez, consisted of a surface pump and a pipe through which it pushed a constant, pressurized airflow, but the pipe broke, and had Cousteau not realized this and closed his glottis, he would have breathed surface air, which at his depth of two atmospheres would have caused the water pressure to collapse his lungs.[21] Beyond these failures, the research and techniques that went into the Aqua-Lung place it—and the idea of a free-diving human—in a longer history of what the English diving technician Robert H. Davis, a contemporary of Cousteau, called "breathing in irrespirable atmospheres."[22] The prosthetic breathing that extends humans' reach underwater grows from the techniques and materials deployed in other spaces—in mining, on battlefields, and at high altitudes. Indeed, Cousteau, a failed pilot, sought a self-contained mechanism of a similar type as "the demand system used in the oxygen masks of high-altitude fliers."[23] When he met Gagnan, the latter was developing a demand valve to transfer cooking gas into automobile motors to compensate for the lack of available petroleum during the war—a problem he regarded as similar to Cousteau's. We should therefore regard Cousteau's balletic imagery not simply as a product of scuba gear but also as a visual byproduct of diverse efforts to enable the human to breathe—and therefore act—within spaces where biology alone will not permit it.

Undersea Vehicles: Scooters, the *Soucoupe*, and the Sea Fleas. Although the Aqua-Lung defines the Cousteau visual aesthetic of freedom and offers spectators a corollary for *Homo aquaticus*'s experience of his environment, the views it afforded were complemented by those a set of untethered, battery-powered underwater vehicles

21 J. Y. Cousteau, with Frédéric Dumas, *The Silent World* (New York: Harper & Brothers, 1953), 16–19.

22 Robert H. Davis, *Breathing in Irrespirable Atmospheres* (London: Saint Catherine Press, 1947).

23 Cousteau, *Silent World*, 19.

could provide. These vehicles were designed to extend divers' reach underwater without compromising the mobility and surface freedom the Aqua-Lung offered; in Cousteau's movies, they are both widely showcased on-screen and used off-screen to shoot the footage we see. One such vehicle was a camera scooter on which sat a camera in a watertight tube affixed to an antivibration mount; the device allowed cameramen to "slip and slide and race about" after the denizens of the deep.[24] Steering with their bodies, the camera operators could create spectacular traveling shots that barrel through the aquatic medium at speeds and with a range of mobility typically reserved for marine animals. *The Silent World* showcases such views in several sequences, notably during a spectacular montage of racing porpoises, which intercuts underwater views from among and alongside the porpoises with surface shots from the deck of the *Calypso* and with aerial views from the *Calypso* helicopter, as well as in a later sequence in which the camera, mounted on the scooter, darts along the seafloor, through schools of fish, and along the edges of reefs. Then, more distastefully, the seabed becomes "a parking lot" (Cousteau's English narration), where a diver parks his scooter to hitch a ride on the back of an apparently distressed sea turtle as though it were a fairground attraction.

Cousteau's fleet of saucers promised freedom from the surface while eliminating the environmental risks scuba divers faced (e.g., the bends, nitrogen narcosis). These vehicles included the *soucoupe plongeante*, which he debuted for audiences in *World without Sun*, and its smaller companions, the Sea Fleas. Like the scooter, these are best understood as technologies that extend the reach of divers beyond depths, distances, and diving time limitations permitted by skin diving, albeit without sacrificing the Aqua-Lung user's independence from the surface. And although they were designed to preserve free divers' mobility, the views these submersibles offer are less acrobatic than those created by the scooters and less balletic than those of scuba divers. Gone is the scooter's whizzing along dips and rises of the reefs and the seafloor, and gone is the Aqua-Lung diver's ability to languidly spin in space, his camera upending the familiar terrestrial coordinates of up and down, left and right. But what these apparatuses trade in terms of mobility and their visual interaction with space, they gain in vertical movement, opening the world below the depth limit Cousteau imposed on his divers to both *Homo aquaticus* and movie audiences.

The *soucoupe*, later christened *Denise*, was designed to reach depths as great as one thousand feet, a limit to which Cousteau on multiple times descended, including in the climax of *World without Sun*. (If the diving saucer's vertical exploits in this sequence seem exceptional, it is doubtless because Cousteau's narration makes no mention of other, deeper dives, among them William Beebe and Otis Barton's half-mile dives in their Bathysphere and the Bathyscaph *Trieste*'s seven-mile plunge to the bottom of the Mariana Trench in 1959.) Named because its disc shape resembled a comic book UFO, this "strange crustacean" included swiveling twin propulsion jets on the bow that gave it a freer range of motion than propellers and rudders would, and it could travel at speeds of up to two knots (about 2.3 miles per hour).[25] Designed to house two

24 Cousteau, *Window in the Sea*, 58.

25 Narrator Rod Serling dubs the saucer a "strange crustacean" in "Those Incredible Diving Machines."

divers, it could sustain them for twenty-four hours with its carbon dioxide scrubbers and rebreathing system; it also included a hand lever that allowed the pilots to jettison ballast and ascend to the surface if the vessel incurred damage. As if in keeping with Cousteau's project of domesticating the sea, the *soucoupe* featured a cushioned interior that made it a model of luxuriant decadence compared to the cramped and unpadded submersibles such as Beebe's and gave it the familiarity of terrestrial transit. As Massachusetts Institute of Technology (MIT) engineering professor Harold E. Edgerton observed, "Being in the saucer is no different from being in an automobile, except that we are more comfortable and loll on our mattresses like Romans at a banquet."[26] A strobe camera and synchronized light were mounted on struts extending from the bow along with a floodlight for the film camera, which remained inside the saucer to allow for reloading. Clearly regarding these as the craft's sine qua nons, Cousteau describes *Denise* as "a giant undersea camera with men inside," one that "extends to them the privilege of seeing the marine underworld with their own eyes and"—here referring to the craft's hydraulic claw in a way that links vision with more tactile manipulation—"even of plucking specimens from regions far beyond reach of a diver's hand."[27]

World without Sun opts to poetically defamiliarize the *soucoupe* and does not make any of the vehicle's capacities clear at the outset. In the first shot of the film, we make the saucer out only as a strange shadow craft propelling itself toward the camera and then sailing overhead like a manta ray. The camera takes pursuit, rising above the craft, revealing the hatch, and hovering over it as the film's title appears on-screen (see Figure 3). As the credits roll, a montage ensues, cutting to shots of either side of the strange vessel, showing off the jet nozzles, and finally drifting in on the portholes from the front before cutting to the interior to reveal Cousteau, who flicks on the lights and checks the various gauges, introducing us to the technology aboard. Only after the credits does Cousteau's narration commence, explaining what this device is and what it works for, as the diving saucer parks in its garage—an onion-shaped, open-bottomed steel shell where technicians hoist

Figure 3. First shots of the *soucoupe* in *World without Sun* (Columbia Pictures, 1964).

26 Edgerton's automobile comparison anticipates a chase sequence in the James Bond film *The Spy Who Loved Me* (Lewis Gilbert, 1977), in which Bond's Lotus Esprit turns into a submarine. Qtd. in Matsen, *Jacques Cousteau*, 52.

27 Cousteau, *World without Sun*, 171.

the saucer on a winch, place grates beneath it to hold it in place, and prepare it for the next dive.

The *soucoupe*'s possibilities for visualization become clear only in the film's final sequence: a nighttime plunge to one thousand feet. The sequence showcases strange life forms that themselves may never have seen white light—depicting the Frenchmen as no less alien to the world they inhabit than it is to them—while also demonstrating the craft's ability to withstand crushing pressure. Here, for the first time, Cousteau opens up the world below the three-hundred-foot depth limit he imposed on his Aqua-Lung divers to his viewers.

The demonstrations of these devices as well as the footage shot aboard them gives us a sense of the kinds of views they can offer on account of their velocity and mobility, the power of their lighting rigs, their ability to get close to objects (because the saucer shape prevented snagging) and into tight quarters, and the depths to which they can descend. Indeed, besides changes in underwater cinematographic technologies over the past half century, such as the implementation of faster film stocks, IMAX film cameras, and high-ISO digital and high definition video cameras, depth is arguably the major difference between the cinematic views Cousteau's and other manned submersibles provide of undersea space (although for many viewers this is necessarily a trivial difference, as it is difficult to gauge depth from visual cues in sunlit images and all but impossible in aphotic ones). But as the *soucoupe*'s research uses should indicate, the same functional capacities that enabled Cousteau's scooters and saucers to produce smoothly gliding, seemingly unfettered cinematic views of an often stunning marine environment were tied to scientific and, later, military attempts to visualize that same environment so as to better measure, calculate, and control it—to "handle" or "grasp" it, as it were, as an extension of seeing it.[28]

Daily Life Undersea. Although the Aqua-Lung and Cousteau's various submarine vehicles were essential to conveying both an impression of life undersea—how one would move through space and what one would see down there—actually living there only became possible with Cousteau's three habitats along the continental shelf. Indeed, for Cousteau, these dwellings marked *Homo aquaticus*'s proper birth. Conshelf I (1962), stationed near Marseilles, placed two divers in a small, 33-foot-deep habitat (named Diogenes) for a week. Conshelf II (1963), the subject of *World without Sun*, was more of a hamlet. Established along the Roman Reef (Sha'ab Rumi) in the Red Sea near Port Sudan, it consisted of two habitats—one at 33 feet that housed five divers for four weeks (the Starfish House) and another at 98 feet that two divers occupied for one week (the Deep Cabin)—as well as a garage near the shallower habitat to accommodate the *soucoupe*. Conshelf III (1965), finally, submitted six divers to three weeks at 328 feet in a habitat near Nice, where Cousteau's surface crew observed them as they worked on a mock oil well; Cousteau's TV documentary *Conshelf Adventure* chronicles this experiment. Placed to obviate the need for decompression when

28 Thinking it might fill a gap among the capabilities of its other undersea research vessels, the US Naval Electronics Laboratory (NEL) leased *Denise* from Cousteau after Conshelf II, using it on twenty-one dives between 1964 and 1965 to test its utility for biological, geological, and physical oceanographic research. The navy's uses for *Denise* are the subject of the NEL's short film *Oceanographic Research with the Cousteau Diving Saucer* (1966).

returning from extreme depths, the Conshelf habitats enabled oceanauts to swim and work for longer periods of time and at greater depth without the burden of having to surface. In other words, they greatly extended the distances over which saturation divers could viably farm the seabed and mine it for oil, gas, and other resources, and extended the periods of uninterrupted time they could devote to these tasks.[29]

Along with demonstrating the nature of underwater work and portraying the marine environment in lyrical fashion, Cousteau's two habitat movies address the mental and psychical changes men undergo in their submarine environment as well as the everyday activities that occupy them in their underwater homes. As in *World without Sun*, oceanauts chain-smoke Gauloises, drink copious amounts of wine, and even keep a pet parrot, much as they might surface-side, but life undersea is "upside down." In *World without Sun*, for instance, Cousteau informs the viewer that down in the Starfish House, wounds "heal almost overnight, but beards almost stop growing." Additionally, for the oceanauts, a general disorientation sets in. "One cannot remember whether we're inside the aquarium or outside it," Cousteau remarks—a thought reinforced by windows that offer the inhabitants picturesque views of divers and fish.[30]

Writing about the unfilmed Conshelf I experiment, Cousteau notes that his divers' minds drifted away from surface concerns—a psychological transformation that *World without Sun* also illustrates. By their third day underwater, he states, the Conshelf I divers no longer read, watched TV, or listened to the radio; they also began to develop an independent sense of time. As Albert Falco, one of the mission's oceanauts, put it, "I don't care what happens on the surface. . . . Time has no meaning. I know what day it is, because they tell me, but I could not care less."[31] Likewise, in *World without Sun*, Cousteau remarks that intrusions from topside divers disturb the oceanauts, who "have crossed to a new way of life. Their sense of time becomes hazy. They neglect the clock and the calendar. They shut off the radio and turn to tape recordings." Their dependence on topside divers irritates them, says Cousteau, who promises the viewer that future undersea stations will operate independent of the surface, although without indicating exactly how an autonomous undersea habitat could be achieved.

Finally, Cousteau suggests that *Homo aquaticus* possesses greater mental acuity than his earthbound cousin. A strange moment in *Conshelf Adventure* depicts the oceanauts taking intelligence tests to measure whether atmospheric pressure and the mixture of gases they breathe have affected their cognitive abilities at 328 feet below sea level.

29 The habitats also enabled them to experience underwater space with greater leisure. As the oceanaut Albert Falco wrote in his diary during the Conshelf I experiment: "This is the first time in 20 years of diving . . . that I have the time to see. The seaweeds, for example, are absolutely fantastic, particularly at night if one takes a searchlight. The bottom is alive with sea horses, sea anemones, shrimps and fish laying eggs. It is as though we are really present at the birth of fish." Qtd. in Cousteau, "Ocean-Bottom Homes," 182.

30 Starosielski, who distinguishes ocean exploitation films from ocean domestication movies, asserts that the former stress the "immersive and potentially overwhelming aspects of underwater scenes," whereas the latter, emblematized by *World without Sun* and sundry fiction films of the 1960s, "marked a return to the positioning of a viewer in [John Ernest] Williamson films" of the 1910s–1930s, which were shot from inside a submersible steel camera booth he dubbed the "photosphere": "one could view conflict safely from behind a glass window." *World without Sun*, however, blurs the distinction between exploitation and domestication in terms of both Conshelf II's purpose and the copresence of immersive views and views through a window. Starosielski, "Beyond Fluidity," 161.

31 Qtd. in Cousteau, "Ocean-Bottom Homes," 183.

Mysteriously, they score higher IQs than they did at the surface, a feat the project psychologist attributes to the "motivation and total concentration" induced by the divers' environment. The overall picture of underwater man that emerges here is not a radically different, biologically altered human being but one who has undergone subtle environmental adaptations and grown oblivious to life above the waves.

In contrast to such 1950s and 1960s television programs as *Sea Hunt* (syndicated, 1958–1961), *Diver Dan* (syndicated, 1960–1963), *Flipper* (NBC, 1964–1967), and *Voyage to the Bottom of the Sea* (ABC, 1964–1968), shows that brought the ocean into the home in family-friendly fashion, Cousteau's version of undersea life squares somewhat oddly with domestic life above water. In part, this difference owes to the strangeness of aquatic life as related in Cousteau's written and cinematic accounts, both of which reveal an uncanny tension between the familiar and unfamiliar rarely found in other undersea-themed media of the period. But the highly technologized nature of Cousteau's undersea habitats also inscribes daily life underwater within a rigid, mostly preordained set of social arrangements. Undersea habitats require oceanauts to live and work in a predictable, regulated fashion and under constant monitoring to ensure that the operations undersea proceed smoothly and safely. Such regulation and surveillance were particularly important given that the habitats were experimental; truly self-sustaining undersea habitats were not (and are not) feasible.

In *World without Sun*, the hierarchical nature of undersea life is illustrated by a diagram of the habitat Cousteau doodles for the viewer early in the film; it depicts *Calypso* at the surface, the Starfish House below it, and the Deep Cabin deeper below, implying certain chains of dependence and command. Ships, as Langdon Winner notes, are classic examples of the view that technologies mandate certain social arrangements, particularly authoritarian ones; he specifically cites Plato, who claims in the *Republic* that the state should be run like a ship, with the philosopher-king presiding over his subjects like a captain over an obedient crew.[32] And in *World without Sun*, the *Calypso* functions as an implicit control center for all of the activities that occur in and about the habitats below. The ship's crew, led by Cousteau, dictates, monitors, and responds to the actions of the oceanauts below, although in somewhat distant fashion. Using intermittent television and radio communication, its divers make contact with the undersea dwellers mostly to bring Starfish House crocks full of fresh supplies. Likewise, the inhabitants of Starfish House monitor the goings-on in Deep Cabin and replenish their soda lime on a regular basis. It is telling of the relations in the film that Cousteau, the leader of the Conshelf expedition and ship captain, is also the only subject who traverses the full vertical distance from surface to the deepest depth depicted in the film, spending most of the film off-screen aboard *Calypso* (the superior position from which he presumably narrates the movie) but also riding the *soucoupe* down to one thousand feet—much deeper than the Deep Cabin's inhabitants ever descend. If the undersea habitats have an analogue with ordinary life on land, it is not a suburban household in which the window onto the sea resembles the television

32 Langdon Winner, *The Whale and the Reactor: A Search for Limits in an Age of High Technology* (Chicago: University of Chicago Press, 1986), 32; Plato, *Republic* 488e–489d.

screen.[33] Rather, they resemble a company town, wherein all residents work for one employer that underwrites and regulates their social and political lives.

Although *World without Sun* allows viewers to glimpse the hierarchical relations that as a practical necessity govern undersea life, it also tends to efface technological politics by poetically withholding context. The habitats seem given; we see none of the work of their construction and are given little sense of how they have come to occupy the seafloor, how long they have been there, and how long they will remain (even though we know Cousteau's oceanauts are to spend one month and one week in the Starfish House and Deep Cabin, respectively). Likewise, Conshelf II's broader economic and political implications are hard to discern in *World without Sun*. Through the narration, we learn the names of the scientists involved as well as some of the work they do, but we do not learn that Conshelf II was in part funded by the French national petroleum industry to locate suitable drilling sites or the film's Sudanese location (mentioned only midway through opening credits).[34] Cousteau conceals this information in the interest of lyricism—eliding what might seem an unsavory connection to Europeans' historical colonization and economic exploitation of the African continent (although in the case of Sudan, the link would have been to British rather than French colonialism).[35] The closest the film comes to acknowledging a link between undersea conquest and European colonialism is when Cousteau observes that the worldwide continental shelf is larger than Africa—leading one to wonder about the ethics of dominating it.[36]

Mechanical Perception Underwater. So far I have focused on cinematic views of undersea space, the exploratory technologies that construct those views, and the image of submarine space that Cousteau's films construct. For film spectators, movie cameras and the diving technologies that could carry them were essential means of exposure to the undersea world that oceanauts dwelled in, the oceanauts' activities there, and the oceanauts' visual experience of that world. Indeed, these were views spectators could imagine themselves one day experiencing directly if, indeed, civilization were to move undersea—a possibility explored in contemporary fiction films such as *The Underwater City* (Frank McDonald, 1962), *Captain Nemo and the Underwater City* (James Hill, 1969), and *Hello Down There* (Jack Arnold and Ricou Browning, 1969). But for Cousteau and *Homo aquaticus* generally, film cameras were one means of mechanical perception and visualization among many, and not necessarily a privileged one. They were means of extending the human ability to see and therefore map, measure, and ultimately exploit an aquatic environment that, because of its physical inaccessibility and nontransparency as well as the limits an aquatic medium imposes on biological sight, resists easy intelligibility. Seawater absorbs, refracts, and scatters light, causing a general fog undersea as particles of salt, sand, and minerals bounce light off one

33 Starosielski makes this comparison in "Beyond Fluidity," 160–161.

34 Madsen, *Cousteau*, 129.

35 As Cousteau told reporters at the film's December 1964 American premiere: "We never even identify the locale as the Red Sea. As soon as you are specific, the poetry disappears." Qtd. in Madsen, *Cousteau*, 135.

36 *Conshelf Adventure* is more direct about these arrangements. More akin to the US Navy's films about its three SEALAB underwater habitat experiments (1964–1969), it keeps poetics to a minimum and focuses on conveying hard facts about the Conshelf III mission.

another's surfaces. Its general condition is turbidity, which varies only in intensity. Physiologically, human eyes have not evolved to see underwater, and technical compensations distort optical space. As Cousteau writes in *Window in the Sea*, "Our eyes are complex apparatuses which have been specifically engineered for the reception and interpretation of light traveling through air."[37] When our corneas make contact with water, we see poorly because our eyes refract light traveling through air quite differently than they do light traveling through water. Diving masks, at minimum, become necessary to create separation between our eyes and the water so that our corneas have a chance to properly focus light through air—although these also warp the field of view. Placing a flat surface between air and water magnifies everything we see by one-third, making objects appear closer than they are; tunnel vision and distortions in peripheral sight become other problems.[38]

Indirect vision becomes a necessary, though often imperfect, supplement to human vision underwater. Most of the equipment must not only solve such optical problems as registering intelligible images in low-light conditions and compensating for the magnification caused by light's refraction underwater but also remain watertight under extreme pressures and resist corrosion from the saltwater. For Cousteau, the most important imaging supplements to human vision were underwater television, specialized strobe photographic equipment, and a variety of sonar technologies, the latter two of which Harold Edgerton designed with the aid of colleagues at the Woods Hole Oceanographic Institution. Underwater television, which had a range of applications, could be used along with a remote-operated film camera to observe and record marine life independently of human observers—especially animals that withdraw from humans or hide in their presence. In *World without Sun*, the oceanauts demonstrate such a setup, which allows them to watch the television monitors from their underwater base and trigger the camera to record when anything of interest transpires. More important, underwater television was necessary to managing the habitats, because it allowed humans in one place to observe humans from another at a distance, typically in conjunction with radio communication. In *World without Sun*'s Conshelf II experiment, we see that the two members of the Deep Cabin, the one-week habitat at about one hundred feet, were under constant televisual supervision from the main base, the thirty-two-foot-deep Starfish House. In Conshelf III, shown in *Conshelf Adventure*, underwater television was used to observe the oceanauts' mock oil rig repair exercise from the surface and thus report on the efficiency of their work at depth.

Edgerton's main contributions to Cousteau's explorations were to build automatic electronic flashes and waterproof cameras that photographed the seafloor and the ocean's deep scattering layer (DSL) (a focus of Cousteau's interest in the early 1950s), as well as sonar equipment that would enable them to measure the depth to which

37 Cousteau, *Window in the Sea*, 6.

38 Cousteau notes that flat faceplates shrink the field of peripheral vision from "more than 180° to less than 80°." He further notes that spherical lenses, such as those used in cameras to correct underwater refraction and magnification, are not feasible in masks, as each eye would see a different image. Cousteau, *Window in the Sea*, 27.

to lower the camera equipment—work of definite scientific value.[39] Recruited by the National Geographic Society in 1952 to work for Cousteau, Edgerton worked with him throughout the 1950s, appearing in *The Silent World* in a segment that documents his flash camera's use, snapping flash pictures of the DSL at fifteen-second intervals for three hours.[40] Cousteau notes that he and Edgerton had used the flash camera to take more than twenty-five thousand pictures of various sea bottoms at that point; the film shows several of their images of the DSL, which "resemble starry skies," showing the occasional bioluminescent fish. Edgerton also contributed two synchronized cameras and a strobe to a self-righting, deep-sea camera sled Cousteau built called the *Troika*. Cousteau and crew used the sled for photographing stereo images of the Mid-Atlantic Ridge, which they presented in 1959 at the First International Congress on Oceanography in New York. One image, which depicted "pillows of lava newly extruded from the center of the earth," offered evidence for the then-contentious theory of continental drift.[41] Another revealed that the sandy base of a seven-thousand-foot-deep seamount was rippled like a desert, demonstrating the strength of deep-sea currents. The *Calypso* crew also fitted the sled with a movie camera containing one thousand feet of 16mm film, shooting images as deep as sixteen thousand feet with the strobe's help.[42]

Placing the cameras near the DSL required the use of sonar—a sort of picturing with sound. Sonar works by sending a sound signal toward a surface and measuring the time it takes for the sound to return to the source to calculate distance. As a locating and mapping device, it substitutes for strictly visual technologies as a sort of sonic prosthesis for the human eye—allowing humans to "see" and act on a space that the light-scattering, absorbing, and refracting properties of seawater obscure. Edgerton designed three such sounding technologies: a "pinger," which measured the distance from ocean surface to ocean floor; a "boomer," which penetrated the bottom of the seafloor to find things beneath it; and a "fish," a side-scan device that could locate objects protruding up from the seafloor.[43] In *The Silent World*, Cousteau demonstrates the pinger at work as it produces a continuous, side-scrolling image of the ocean floor in real time, revealing also the DSL when Cousteau cranks up the pinger's sensitivity dial (see Figure 4). This technology enabled Edgerton and Cousteau to picture unimageable space to establish coordinates for camera and lighting placement from afar and produce scientifically significant images of the seafloor and the DSL.

39 Besides his sonar innovations, Edgerton contributed to marine imaging in two key ways. He developed a time-lapse system abetted by strobe lights so as to capture the movements of marine animals that move too slowly for humans to normally perceive. Additionally, he contributed to shadow photography in mid-1980s, photographing tiny marine animals by placing them directly on the film's emulsion and exposing them with a small electronic flash, which revealed their interior structures.

40 The DSL is essentially a false bottom consisting of a range of marine animals that swim between 1,000 and 1,500 feet deep during the day and rise at night to feed.

41 Cousteau, *Window in the Sea*, 56.

42 Cousteau, *Window in the Sea*, 54–57.

43 More than a hundred of Edgerton's sonar images, as well as technical writing about their creation, appear in Harold E. Edgerton, *Sonar Images* (Englewood Cliffs, NJ: Prentice-Hall, 1986).

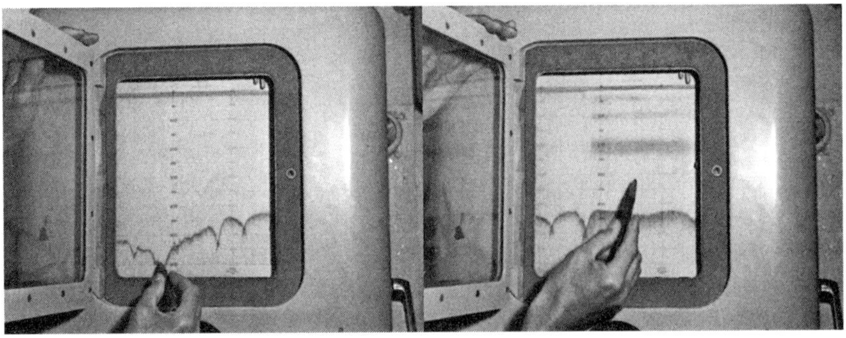

Figure 4. Sonar images of the ocean bottom (left) and of the sea's deep-scattering layer (right) made using the Edgerton pinger. Screen grabs from *The Silent World* (Columbia Pictures, 1956).

Other technologies Cousteau used to supplement direct vision included holography, which involved making 3-D movies and photographs using laser beams, and an "owl-eye" photomultiplier attached to the *soucoupe* that could take pictures using as little as one photon of light, which it could multiply by as many as eighty thousand photons, enabling *Denise*'s occupants to "see in the dark as if it were daylight."[44] In a speculative vein, Cousteau suggests a "mirage photo system" that sits "at the very edge of modern possibilities"—an apparatus too costly to permit practical development.[45] It would illuminate objects up to 130 feet away, compensating for light scattering and allowing the camera to block out scattered light and isolate light reflected directly back from the object photographed. Mounted on the *soucoupe*, it would effectively enable the divers to overcome environmental obstacles to visualization and to photograph objects and animals from a distance when getting up close would disturb an animal, pose a hazard to the vessel, or simply be spatially unfeasible. Although Cousteau remains silent about the longer-range effects of using these technologies to visualize and therefore comprehend ocean space, they, like the other forms of indirect vision, open up new possibilities for hands-on mastery and manipulation of the marine environment.

Toward a Nontechnical Human Undersea. Although I have to this point related some of the technological, perceptual, and physiological ways that *Homo aquaticus* was constituted, I now address *Homo aquaticus* in relation to race and gender. The world of oceanauts, explorers, frogmen, and men-fish is almost exclusively white and male. In both Cousteau's films and other popular undersea media of this period (and into the present), the aquanauts at the vanguard of ocean exploration are almost exclusively white men, as were their real-world counterparts in oceanography and recreational diving. The only woman we see in Cousteau's films before *The Undersea World* is his wife, Simone, who appears for a few seconds on a two-way television screen in *World without Sun*. Moreover, Cousteau's technically enhanced *Homo aquaticus* stands in stark contrast to women and nonwhite native others whose bodies in popular American media of the period inhabit the sea with evidently no technical help whatsoever—as

44 Cousteau, *Window in the Sea*, 104.

45 Cousteau, *Window in the Sea*, 107.

though their bodies were naturally suited to aquatic space. We seldom see women or people of color wearing scuba gear or even diving masks in film and media of the postwar decades, and nonwhite male oceanographers were a rare occurrence in the United States and Europe, as scientific professions have historically excluded women and people of color.[46] To be sure, gaunt Cousteau and his pasty crew hardly project the rugged masculinity characteristic of ocean explorers in postwar popular culture—such as Lloyd Bridges in *Sea Hunt*, Kirk Douglas's harpooner in *20,000 Leagues under the Sea* (Richard Fleischer, 1954), or the title character of the children's show *Diver Dan*. But their eccentric world is no less exclusionary for not conforming to stereotypes of white male adventurers.

Idealizations of people of color as more "of nature" than whites is a familiar trope in undersea filmmaking, particularly in the decades before Cousteau. We see this notably in John Ernest Williamson's "photosphere" movies, such as *30 Leagues under the Sea* (1914) and his autobiographical *With Williamson beneath the Sea* (1932), with their displays of Bahamian divers fetching coins, hoisting corals, and fighting sharks, as if these activities were second nature to them. By contrast, the white divers who appear in these movies inevitably wear metal helmets and suits, as though they are strangers on a distant planet habitable only by a mysterious other. In one scene of *With Williamson*, a Bahamian nicknamed Cinderella takes a diving helmet on and off underwater, at once playing peekaboo with Williamson's young daughter through the photosphere window and seeming to say he can do without this strange device. Nicole Starosielski persuasively argues of the imperialist dimension of such display that the ocean is a fluid space where racial others can "evade established structures of colonial power."[47] That these others can freely navigate the seas without the technology needed by white explorers from European and American imperial powers testifies to their independence from those powers. It also suggests that a freedom from advanced technologies is what it would take for Western powers to seize the ocean realm. For Cousteau to fantasize about a new man with total freedom from the surface and eventually the biological capacity to live undersea is of a piece with taking the other's place, with making the ocean an extension of Western land bases, and snuffing out all pockets of anticolonial resistance.[48]

If ethnic others' apparent belonging to the sea marks Western nations' lack of mastery over it, women's seemingly "natural" alignment with the underwater world is more closely allied with the project of domesticating it. Indeed, much of the women-in-water imagery of the postwar decades suggests a future in which the aquatic realm has already been tamed. Bruce Mozert's 1950s underwater photographs from Silver

46 A significant exception is Lotte Hass, a mainstay in the films of her husband Hans Hass, an Austrian contemporary of Cousteau's whose films and undersea research merit further study.

47 Starosielski, "Beyond Fluidity," 155.

48 Though a familiar cinematic trope, the idea that racial others are "naturally" aquatic while white bodies are technologized undersea has a much longer history. As James Delbourgo shows, for instance, European travelers marveled at indigenous divers' ability to remain at great depth for long durations as early as the sixteenth century, and they exploited these divers' abilities in violent relationships that frequently bordered on and sometimes included slavery. See James Delbourgo, "Divers Things: Collecting the World under Water," *History of Science* 49, no. 2 (2011): 149–185.

Springs, Florida, for instance, depict women engaged in middle-class leisure activities common to the surface: ballet, archery, watching television, sunbathing, and, self-reflexively, photography.[49] It is as if Mozert were imaging how suburban American women would spend their time if they could dwell or vacation underwater.[50]

The pivotal figure here is the mermaid—understood as woman on the order of competitive-swimmer-turned-leading-lady Esther Williams rather than the more familiar half fish with a female torso.[51] Mixing traditional female beauty with remarkable athletic prowess, the mermaid was best exemplified by the "aquabelles" at Weeki Wachee Springs, whose underwater theater was arguably Florida's premier tourist attraction in the quarter century before Disney World opened in 1971.[52] Crucial to the mermaid image is the apparent absence of diving technologies. Esther Williams dons little other than her bathing suit; Mozert's subjects typically dress and pose as if in a terrestrial setting. At Weeki Wachee, where shows took place entirely underwater, the mermaids would sometimes breathe from concealed compressed air hoses in between stunts. However, they would also need to be able to hold their breath for long periods of time—forty-five seconds at the very least—while doing their flips and dives and bracing themselves against the frigid water. Despite the physical demands involved for the performers, the point was for their work to appear effortless. As Kokai writes, the shows were "about the taming of nature, the ability for certain special kinds of humans to survive and thrive in an inhospitable environment and for it to look 'natural.'"[53] In this sense, the mermaids' shows have much in common with Cousteau's ideal of undersea exploration, except that for Cousteau the fantastic end point would be for certain humans to colonize the ocean in a manner that not only looked natural but also, as their biology overtook technology, actually was.

Conclusion. This article has addressed Jacques Cousteau's utopian notion of *Homo aquaticus* in relation to his 1950s and 1960s documentaries, treating it not as a fully elaborated posthumanist idea (which it was not) but rather as a set of issues—of aesthetics, technology, and perception—that arise when human bodies interact with the marine environment and that together shaped the midcentury image of life undersea. Technologies such as the Aqua-Lung, Cousteau's fleet of mini-submersibles, and the Conshelf underwater habitats extended human reach into the ocean by allowing humans to breathe and move freely underwater without tethers to the surface. They also gave rise to new ways of perceiving and physically engaging with the world, as

49 Mozert's photographs are collected in Gary Monroe, *Silver Springs: The Underwater Photography of Bruce Mozert* (Gainesville: University Press of Florida, 1998).

50 For examples of such, see Gary Monroe, "The Life Aquatic with Bruce Mozert," *Smithsonian*, May 2008, https://www.smithsonianmag.com/travel/the-life-aquatic-with-bruce-mozert-38188395.

51 See Jennifer A. Kokai, "Weeki Wachee Girls and Buccaneer Boys: The Evolution of Mermaids, Gender, and 'Man versus Nature' Tourism," *Theatre History Studies* 31 (2011): 69–71.

52 Weeki Wachee Springs was founded by Newt Perry, a Hollywood "human fish" known for performing underwater tricks in newsreels. On the park, see Kokai, "Weeki Wachee Girls"; Lu Vickers and Bonnie Georgiadis, *Weeki Wachee Mermaids: Thirty Years of Underwater Photography* (Gainesville: University Press of Florida, 2012); and Maryann Pelland and Dan Pelland, *Weeki Wachee Springs* (Chicago: Arcadia Publishing, 2006).

53 Kokai, "Weeki Wachee Girls," 78–79.

reflected in the balletic visual aesthetic of the underwater sequences in Cousteau's movies—an aesthetic that relates ambivalently to the project of ocean conquest that his exploratory technologies served. This balletic aesthetic finds a further corollary in the dramatic experiential changes Cousteau's divers claimed to undergo while living underwater, changes that included a transformed sense of time. In addition, the Aqua-Lung in particular gave rise to new techniques for filmmakers to learn. Producing cinematic views became a problem not only of adequate lighting, transparent waters, and waterproofing cameras but also of monitoring air supplies and following strict procedures to prevent such potentially deadly maladies as decompression sickness and nitrogen narcosis.

Machinery of indirect vision accompanied these exploratory technologies. Underwater television, strobe cameras, and sonar imaging enabled Cousteau and crew to overcome the limits that the aquatic medium imposes on biological sight; in the case of strobe cameras and sonar, they even allowed the crew to "see" farther than exploratory technologies allowed them to travel. Being able to visualize ocean space over great distances went hand in hand with gaining knowledge about it and consequently controlling and exploiting it, whether that meant establishing stable undersea habitats or drilling for oil. The purpose of these imaging technologies—as well as other, speculative ones—was to render a turbid and mostly lightless environment completely transparent and thus infinitely useful for human ends. For these technologies to open the vast marine frontier to potentially boundless exploitation put Cousteau's research in line with prevailing postwar Western sentiments toward the sea—that it was an enormous treasure chest waiting to be plundered—and at odds with the marine conservationism that Cousteau would eventually espouse.[54]

The political dimension of the technologies Cousteau deployed in this period is not limited to their merely being placed in the service of ocean conquest (a politics of use); there is also the matter of the social, economic, and environmental arrangements inherent to them. In the first place, we must assume that the various visual and exploratory technologies Cousteau uses—machinery that is extremely sophisticated—are each made from a thick weave of interests, materials, techniques, actors, forms of expertise, and flows of capital. Additionally, despite the rhetoric of "freedom" with which Cousteau surrounds his technologies, some of them, such as the undersea habitats, can only ever be deployed pragmatically within a fixed, centralized, and hierarchical social arrangement—even if such a top-down structure is loosely imposed. The playful, poetic nature of Cousteau's films obscures the hierarchical arrangements within which the oceanauts live, just as it conceals the Conshelf missions' purpose: to plan undersea farms and prospect for oil.

54 Cousteau's contradictory attitudes are perhaps best represented at the end of "Those Incredible Diving Machines," when his voice-over moves quickly from exploitation to stewardship: "Soon, most of the mysteries of the sea will be revealed to us, and we will see that the ocean is but an immense extension of man's own world: a province of our own environment. We will have to farm it, mine it, and harness its energies." And then: "But we must remember to protect its integrity and its harmony as we make this great voyage of discovery into a once mysterious but still beautiful world. . . . We must learn to protect and to love the sea for the sea sustains life. That is our greatest resource and treasure."

Finally, the perceptual and technological changes described above implicitly belong to white bodies alone—white male bodies in particular. Read against earlier undersea imagery of native bodies underwater, Cousteau's movies convey a sense of what scholar Joel Dinerstein calls "an escape from the *pan*human": a sort of white flight into cyborg bodies uncontaminated by racial difference.[55] Born of an inability to come to terms with the human as "*a multiethnic, multicultural, multigenetic construction created through centuries of contact and acculturation*," this escape from otherness takes the paradoxical form of beating otherness at its own game: inhabiting the fluid space of the sea more dexterously than could other bodies and thus converting it from a space of difference to one of continuity with the industrialized West.[56]

Homo aquaticus as a concept linked explicitly to ocean habitation would disappear from the Cousteau universe as Cousteau gave up the idea of ocean colonization in favor of conservation. Still, the idea of a human being who might overcome his or her biological limits persists in films and media clearly influenced by Cousteau. Aesthetically, Luc Besson's all-underwater documentary *Atlantis* (1991) takes up the dizzying and kinetic camera movements we see throughout Cousteau's films as the cameramen engage with marine life, exploring the possibilities of movement and perception that the ocean realm opens up. Narratively, *Homo aquaticus* surfaces in Besson's *The Big Blue* (*Le grande bleu*, 1988) and James Cameron's *The Abyss* (1989). The former film concerns a champion free diver (i.e., someone who dives without scuba) who, in the fantastic conclusion, plunges to a record depth of four hundred feet and swims away into the darkness with a dolphin, convinced as he is that life is better undersea than on land. In *The Abyss*, the protagonist, played by Ed Harris, plunges to the bottom of the sea breathing a helmet full of liquid oxygen, which allows him to survive more than four miles of vertical pressure and disarm a sunken nuclear warhead. Although different from Cousteau's artificial gill, the liquid breathing apparatus is based on real experimental technologies and offers an image of what a solo, nonsubmersible descent to the deep sea might be like. Additionally, *Homo aquaticus* persists in prose fiction. Peter Watts's novel *Starfish*, for instance, concerns a group of deep-sea power-plant workers whose bodies have been surgically altered to withstand their environment's extremes.[57] In a dystopian twist, these workers are not vanguard figures of humanity's ever-extending planetary reach but social outcasts from the overpopulated world above. And Hugh Nissenson's *The Song of the Earth* features a character who explicitly invokes Cousteau's concept: "I could design humin beings to live under water: *Homo aquaticus*. It's not so far-fetched. I could give them gills and webbed hands and feet. Tough, scaly skin. Why, they could visually communicate with each other under water by changing their skin color at will, in individually colored patches all over their bodies, like squid."[58] While these examples may not all be consistent with Cousteau's precise vision of divers with surgically implanted gills

55 Dinerstein, "Technology and Its Discontents," 16.

56 Dinerstein, "Technology and Its Discontents," 37.

57 Peter Watts, *Starfish* (New York: Tor Books, 1999).

58 Hugh Nissenson, *The Song of the Earth* (Chapel Hill, NC: Algonquin Books, 2001), 222.

and humans who biologically evolve to live and breathe underwater, they all speak to the core idea of human bodies that can more fully inhabit the sea with a minimum of technical appurtenances, even if that idea no longer corresponds to a vision of a real-world future. *

I wish to thank Paula Amad, Steve Choe, and the anonymous JCMS *reviewers for their detailed comments on earlier versions of this article.*

SCMS

From the Question of Soul to a *Carnival of Souls*: The Truncated Road Film, Gothic Automobiles, and Dangerous Women Drivers

by KIMBERLEY MONTEYNE

Abstract: This article argues for a revision of conceptual and historical mappings of the American road film through a rereading of Herk Harvey's cult classic *Carnival of Souls* (1962) and the era's slew of highway safety productions, related literature, and institutional practice. It suggests that the genre of the road film began with a trio of movies in the early 1960s, including *Psycho* (1960) and *The Haunting* (1963), as well as Harvey's film, which exposed and dramatized historical anxieties about the "dangers" of women appropriating the freedoms and pleasures of the open road connected to car culture.

The Road Film Reconsidered. *Carnival of Souls* (Herk Harvey, 1962) begins with a high-speed drag race—a carload of carefree young girls tear through the rural roadways of a small Kansas town while pursued by another automobile. The contest ends in disaster when the car containing the young women careens over the side of a bridge and plunges into the river below. As the lone survivor, Mary (Candace Hilligoss), stumbles from the depths of the watery crash, a narrative of macabre and eerie events begins to unfold. Viewers are subsequently invited on another journey, a road trip to Utah with Mary, in which the boundaries between life and death begin to disintegrate as the protagonist is inexplicably drawn toward an abandoned amusement pavilion at the side of the road. In the final moments of the film, it becomes apparent that Mary did not survive the accident and that the pavilion is a den of terrifying dead souls. Ultimately, the viewer understands that she has been following the perambulations of a ghost. At this point *Carnival of Souls* returns once again to the site of the horrific crash at the bottom of the river as the camera reveals the carload of dead girls, including Mary, dredged from the water.

Surprisingly, critics and historians have all but ignored the film's interest in the dangers of the open road and the perils of female drivers. For instance, an essay devoted to this B horror movie published in the anthology *Crash Cinema: Representation*

Kimberley Monteyne teaches at the University of British Columbia. She is the author of Hip Hop on Film: Performance Culture, Urban Space, and Genre Transformation in the 1980s *(University Press of Mississippi, 2013) and the in-progress manuscript "The Pleasures of Public Health."*

in Film, expressly concerned with the relationship between automobile accidents and motion pictures, has little to say about the film's engagement with car culture.[1] Instead, James Riley suggests that the production straddles the spaces between high and low culture—trashy drive-in film and European art-house cinema—while at the same time frustrating audience expectations of the traditional horror genre though its emphasis on stasis over action, as well as coldness and detachment over gore and sensual appeal. Riley does note how the film's icily spectral protagonist Mary "subverts patriarchal mastery within the film" because she refuses to be absorbed into conventional spaces of male-dominated culture, including the church and courtship rituals.[2] Yet it seems to me an oversight not to directly connect this unusual depiction of female subjectivity with the film's appropriation of car culture and, more specifically, the dangers of highway travel—especially given the context of the essay in a volume dedicated to the cathartic and terrifying power symbolized by the automobile collision.

It is also surprising that *Carnival of Souls* has been written out of nearly every major study of the road film because, as this article argues, the film—a justifiably celebrated cult favorite—and its female driver-protagonist Mary Henry are crucial to an emergent history of cars in cinema. Moreover, Harvey's film is not alone in its concerns and thematic content. It is bookended by two other productions, *Psycho* (Alfred Hitchcock, 1960) and *The Haunting* (Robert Wise, 1963), which feature female drivers who "take the wheel" and attempt to engage with the space of the open road. Considering this trio together reveals and clarifies postwar attitudes about gender, mobility, and car culture, making these issues central to a full definition and productive understanding of the genre of the road film.

The release of these productions coincided with a dramatic increase in car ownership; nearly 80 percent of all US families owned cars by 1960—a substantial increase from less than half the population in the immediate postwar period. In the face of this world of prolific car culture, David Laderman suggests that the genre of the road film centers on driving (or movement on roads by other means), the interstate highway, and an imagery of vast expanses seen from the open road. Such features correlate with an intense desire to escape conventional culture and life choices, and as a result, "highways symbolize the potential of venturing beyond the familiarity of home, whether on a whim or as a planned excursion" and "freedom becomes rediscovered as movement across open space."[3] Although Laderman admirably explores the integral relationship between cars and film technology from the beginning of cinema, he actually dates the arrival of the road film to the late 1960s, with *Bonnie and Clyde* (Arthur Penn, 1967) and *Easy Rider* (Dennis Hopper, 1969). Laderman does admit that "most road movies . . . retain a traditional sexist hierarchy that privileges the white heterosexual male, in terms of narrative and visual point of view," and he addresses the representation of women in such films as *Bonnie and Clyde* and *Two-Lane Blacktop* (Monte

1 James Riley, "'Have You No Respect? Do You Feel No Reverence?': Narrative and Critical Subversion in Herk Harvey's *Carnival of Souls*," in *Crash Cinema: Representation in Film*, ed. Mark Goodall, Jill Good, and Will Godfrey (Newcastle, UK: Cambridge Scholars Publishing, 2007), 14–24.

2 Riley, "'Have You No Respect?,'" 20.

3 David Laderman, *Driving Visions: Exploring the Road Movie* (Austin: University of Texas Press, 2002), 14–15.

Hellman, 1971), but he does not offer a sustained critique of gender and mobility in the genre.[4] *Psycho*, *Carnival of Souls*, and *The Haunting* are never mentioned in the book. These titles are also entirely omitted in the popular volume *100 Road Movies*, and they do not appear in Devin Orgeron's expansive discussion *Road Movies: From Muybridge and Méliès to Lynch and Kiarostami*, save for one sentence that mentions *Psycho* in passing.[5] An earlier anthology, *The Road Movie Book*, omits the films discussed in this article as well, except for a brief remark outside of the scope of the genre in which *Psycho* is somewhat sensationally noted for initiating the "cult of the maniac."[6] Laderman chalks up the privileging of masculine subjectivity in the road film to a historical impulse inherent in Hollywood cinema itself; active desires and movement tend to be linked to male characters, and women tend to be associated with erotic contemplation and narrative stasis.[7] It is not my intention here to question this assumption, but it is curious that film scholars do not look for more instances in which women claim the pleasures of the open road aside from the one obvious example, *Thelma and Louise*, which is treated as an anomaly in the genre.[8] Acknowledging these earlier films—*Psycho*, *Carnival of Souls*, and *The Haunting*—as formative texts for the genre troubles the basic premise that the road movie arises from a male-centered countercultural sphere.

Psycho, *Carnival of Souls*, and, to a lesser degree, *The Haunting* represent a special type of truncated road film concerned with the possibilities and ultimately the "horrors" of women at the wheel in the postwar era. Even at the outset of the automobile's entry into civilian life in the early twentieth century, car ownership and usage were heavily policed by gender boundaries. Electric-powered cars for driving short local distances were initially marketed toward women, while men were understood to be the primary consumers of gasoline-powered automobiles, which could travel long distances and traverse state boundaries effortlessly.[9] The former (which generally had a maximum driving distance of twenty-five miles per charge) offered apparent freedom but in fact merely buttressed and made increasingly efficient women's perambulations within a

4 Laderman, *Driving Visions*, 20.

5 Jason Wood, *100 Road Movies* (London: British Film Institute, 2007). See also Devin Orgeron, *Road Movies: From Muybridge and Méliès to Lynch and Kiarostami* (New York: Palgrave Macmillan, 2008).

6 Steven Cohan and Ina Rae Hark, eds., *The Road Movie Book* (London: Routledge, 1997), 167.

7 Laderman, *Driving Visions*, 20.

8 Fortunately, scholarship on the road film is beginning to take shape in a more dynamic direction. See Katie Mills, *The Road Story and the Rebel: Moving through Film, Fiction, and Television* (Carbondale: Southern Illinois University Press, 2006). This excellent volume offers a welcome corrective that employs an interdisciplinary approach to "fill in missing information about women and minority contributors to the road genre" (3). However, the author's focus on locating the productive spaces of the genre (particularly in relation to mobility) for subcultural groups and underrepresented populations shifts her interest in women and car culture in road films toward very different social and cultural intersections than those explored in this essay. See also Bernice Murphy, *The Highway Horror Film* (Basingstoke, UK: Palgrave Macmillan, 2014). Murphy examines the overlooked connections among cars, the road film, and horror in this fascinating work, but the overview nature of her volume prevents a deep analysis of the films investigated here, and most significantly, the author does not make gender a central concern of her project.

9 Martin Wachs, "The Automobile and Gender: An Historical Perspective," in *Women's Travel Issues: Proceedings from the Second National Conference* (Baltimore, 1996), 99–108, conference funded by the Federal Highway Administration and organized by the Drachman Institute of the University of Arizona in cooperation with Morgan State University. Although women were not precluded from owning gasoline-powered cars, their ability to perform the mechanical skills required for the maintenance of such vehicles increasingly came under scrutiny.

circumscribed area related to domestic work and social duties.[10] When cars were first introduced for a mass market, male critics worried about wives and mothers taking the freedoms afforded by motor travel too far; a jaunt around the neighborhood to pick up bread and visit the neighbors was fine, but an interstate road trip helmed by a female driver was increasingly viewed with suspicion and derision.[11] Since its introduction to the American market, the automobile has become intimately, profoundly wed to social life in the United States, symbolizing notions of class mobility, the increasing importance of youth culture, and especially anxiety about the changing role of women. Truncated road films like *Psycho*, *The Haunting*, and *Carnival of Souls* reflect this latter anxiety, especially because the urbanization processes of the early 1960s brought significantly more women drivers onto the roadways.[12] These productions begin with all the promise of the road film—new adventures, brighter tomorrows, different relationships—and, indeed, initially present viewers with a number of cinematic attributes associated with these generic qualities. However, the motivation for narrative and spatial growth associated with this type of cinema becomes hijacked by a social imperative to punish women (especially women drivers) who seek freedom from conventional social roles. The truncated road film neatly combines all the historical anxieties related to nonconformist and socially threatening female identities that negate, either willingly or unwittingly, the conventional feminine roles of wife and mother and presents them in the figure of the solitary and unmarried female driver.

This convenient trope of the lone female motorist who operates outside of conventional cultural parameters is also related to two distinct facets of American postwar road culture: the specter of the distracted female driver who ostensibly put other motorists (perhaps even society itself) in danger and an anxiety over the fragility of the physical body when involved in highway accidents. (Notably, women's bodies have historically been put in the service of representing material vulnerability more frequently than male bodies.) These concerns informed the truncated road film as well as a slew of highway safety features, including *Anatomy of an Accident* (LeRoy Prinz, 1961) and *Signal 30* (Richard Wayman, 1959). This article, therefore, later detours into the territory of nontheatrical cinema to examine the contemporaneous representation of women in car safety films, because taken together, these productions reveal an ambivalent view of female subjectivity operating within the male-defined parameters of

10 Virginia Scharff, *Taking the Wheel: Women and the Coming of the Motor Age* (New York: Free Press, 1991), 35–44.

11 Scharff, *Taking the Wheel*, 35–50. The author points out that early critics of female motorists brought together two preexisting tropes about women's limitations and social roles. On the one hand, women were understood to be most properly suited to the home, or at least to staying put in established, regimented, and scrutinized social spaces, and on the other hand, women were thought to lack any aptitude for mechanical expertise. Thus, gasoline-powered cars, which could take women away from their husbands, family, friends, and domestic duties, could be presented as unsuitable for women drivers because they required mechanical skills for smoother operation and maintenance that women ostensibly did not have. This prohibition against women performing mechanical tasks neatly solved the problem of gasoline-powered cars offering women freedoms that conventional culture was not ready for them to possess.

12 Katherine J. Parkin, *Women at the Wheel: A Century of Buying, Driving, and Fixing Cars* (Philadelphia: University of Pennsylvania Press), 2017, xviii. Parkin notes that "increasing suburbanization, greater affordability and accessibility of the car, and women's growing public responsibilities all led to increasing numbers of women drivers, and by 1963, the ratio of male-to-female licensed drivers stood at 60:40."

automobile culture across fictional and education films. In this broad terrain, women are simultaneously the most significant threat to road safety and the social order, and, fatefully, the most convenient bearer of physical trauma and bodily destruction.

Psycho, *Carnival of Souls*, and *The Haunting* all display this dialectical representation of women through automobile culture, which is in fact aligned with more general tropes of the horror genre. The horror genre often focuses on the physical and psychological deterioration of the female body while exploring social anxieties around female empowerment and autonomy. Commonly, the trope of the absent or bad mother (or conversely the overbearing mother) is the root of American postwar horror films, while women usually outnumber men as victims in these productions.[13] Thus, the genre presents an ambivalent mechanism in which women precipitate horror by failing to align with dominant patriarchal values and are simultaneously the primary victims punished for such transgressions. This generic pattern sets in motion the possibility for women to resist assimilation into conventional cultural roles at the same time it orchestrates excessive punishment of such desires. The three films discussed here could certainly be described as horror films and explored in this more general vein, particularly in relation to conspicuously absent mothers (in *Psycho* and *The Haunting*) or entire familial structures (in *Carnival of Souls*), and the woeful failure of protagonists to successfully align themselves with normative expectations of female identity.

Therefore, this article examines the neglected intersection of gender, highway travel, and ultimately violence, and the ways in which space is contracted and movement contained within the narrative of *Psycho*, *Carnival of Souls*, and *The Haunting*. The journey out onto the motorway opened up via the hallmarks of the road-film genre is progressively curtailed in all three films as cinematic space increasingly conforms to the demands of the gothic genre. Indeed, narrative space is inverted or condensed through a "gothicization" of the cinematic environment to confine and punish the female protagonist's desire for independence, relegating her to a specific place or space (e.g., the forgotten motel, abandoned den of dead souls, haunted house). Although a concise definition of the gothic is difficult to pin down, most scholars agree that the genre of literature (and its translation into cinema) insists on a particular evocation of space and atmosphere. The road film's emphasis on mobility, freedom, escape, and wide-open vistas would seem to defy the very foundation of a gothic sensibility—space that is enclosed, condensed, or convoluted, accompanied by a sense of vision that is dark, partial, and given over to inward reflection.[14] Yet when women "take the wheel" in truncated road films, it is precisely these gothic conventions that most accurately describe the journeys our protagonists endure.

Automobiles are sites of terror or hauntings in these films and ultimately they become portals that deliver women to death or insanity. Such representations seem impossibly at odds with the presentation of cars in contemporary advertising culture

13 Barbara Creed, *The Monstrous Feminine: Film, Feminism, Psychoanalysis* (London: Routledge, 1993).

14 Catherine Spooner, *Contemporary Gothic* (London: Reaktion Books, 2006), 18. Spooner emphasizes physical containment and entrapment in gothic literary texts as a primary feature of the genre, represented by "labyrinth underground vaults and torture chambers . . . secret passages and attics." See also Gregory Pepetone, *Gothic Perspectives on the American Experience* (New York: Peter Lang, 2006), 15. The author provides a list of gothic attributes or elements, which include disorientation, primeval forests, dungeons, labyrinths, and vortices.

of the 1960s, where smiling ladies entice buyers (presumably men) into an eroticized relationship with the ultimate postwar commodity. Such images outwardly represent all of the freedoms and indulgences that American postwar plentitude offered—easy and safe interstate travel, abundant disposable income to take leisurely daytrips, and a tidy correlation between road travel and pleasure. That is not to say that the country remained oblivious to the roadside carnage that accompanied increased highway travel, as evidenced by the proliferation of automobile safety films throughout the decade. Two shockingly frank road safety films, *Mechanized Death* (Richard Wayman, 1961) and *Safety Belt for Susie* (Pat Shields, 1962) terrified high school students in the early 1960s, just a short while after the aforementioned *Signal 30* hailed the arrival of the very first American road safety productions complete with actual footage from fatal car accidents.[15] Women sometimes appeared as drivers in car advertisements rather than merely erotic accoutrements. Wives and mothers represented potential consumers for new automobile models in the early 1960s, and as the decade progressed, manufacturers tried to appeal to women drivers in increasingly diverse ways—from presenting color and texture choices in terms of matching fashion accessories to emphasizing the practical aspects of family transportation by motorcar. The automobile industry's attitude toward capturing the market of female drivers is marked by a profound ambivalence. Although the dawn of the motorist era bifurcated car ownership along gender lines wedded to the type (and longevity) of energy that powered individual vehicles, Michelle Tolini has shown that immediate postwar automotive marketing campaigns sought to capture both male and female buyers through a sophisticated mode of presentation, which offered something for everyone. Women were encouraged to appreciate the aesthetics of a particular model, while men were directed toward the vehicle's performance. Options such as interior fabrics and color schemes were marketed as choices best left to the wife, fashion magazines ran glamorous advertising for upscale car models, and haute couture apparel figured predominantly in several automobile campaigns.[16] On the less spectacular side, Chevrolet produced a series of advertisements in the early 1960s that highlighted the economical aspects of the ill-fated Corvair for female motorists (see Figure 1), and the historians Ellen J. Gerl and Craig L. Davis have attested that *Woman's Day* magazine was never able to persuade the big manufacturers to spend their advertising dollars with the publication despite the long-running column "Women at the Wheel," which first appeared in 1964.[17]

15 Ken Smith, *Mental Hygiene: Classroom Films, 1945–1970* (New York: Blast Books, 1999), 73–82.

16 Michelle Tolini, "Mistress vs. Wife: The Realization of the American Dream in 1950's Automobile Advertising" (MA thesis, Fashion Institute of Technology, 1998), 15–24. See also Mark Kennedy, "Exhibition Links Cars and Fashion," *Wilmington (DE) Morning Star*, July 10, 1997. This article covers an exhibit at New York's Fashion Institute of Technology, *Driving Fashion: Automobile Fabrics of the 1950s*, cocurated by Tolini, who states in the article: "Detroit soon learned that eye-catching styling—even more than automatic transmission or power steering—was the way to win buyers. Auto designers studied the color, designs and fabrics of fashionable clothing to keep current." Summing up the thrust of the show, Kennedy notes: "The exhibit—which uses, swatches, advertising and photographs—makes clear that the automobile industry's new emphasis on styling, color, texture and fabric was marketed with women in mind."

17 Ellen J. Gerl and Craig L. Davis, "Selling Detroit on Women: Woman's Day and Auto Advertising, 1964–82," *Journalism History* 38, no. 4 (Winter 2013): 209–220.

Figure 1. Corvair marketed to women on the basis of thrift and practicality (1960).

Figure 2. Ford Mustang collaborates with cosmetic manufacturer Tussy to produce a line of makeup to match a woman's car (1966).

Of course, nothing speaks to the anxiety over women drivers at midcentury more than advertising from the decade, which features the perverse practice of situating a woman erotically draped over the hood or trunk of a newly minted "hot rod" rather than placing her (relatively) safely inside it. Such an external position suggests the undoing of female subjectivity on two fronts: both violence—being thrown from or onto a car—and a rather obvious conflation of woman and car as aesthetic and sexual object. The 1966 advertising campaign for Mustang's collaboration with Tussy cosmetics (see Figure 2), though a few years after *Carnival of Souls*, clearly underlines both.[18]

The Automobile as Gothic Portal. A deep ambivalence toward female drivers in the postwar era combined with concerns over the connection between car travel and the potential unmooring of traditional roles for women are unmistakably the forces that structure the trio of films I have outlined as initial instances of truncated road films. Like Mary Henry, *Psycho*'s Marion Crane (Janet Leigh), is unmarried, has a career, and turns to automobile travel to escape an impossible situation. After she steals $40,000 to secure a future with her lover (who insists that he cannot marry her because he is impoverished), Marion attempts to flee with the cash in her car. The promise of the open road does not bring freedom or positive new experiences, however. Rather, it delivers Marion to one of the most terrifying places ever imagined in film—the Bates Motel and the home of "Mother"—Norman Bates's (Anthony Perkins) murderous alter ego. For Eleanor Lance, a middle-aged spinster and the protagonist of Wise's adaptation of Shirley Jackson's novel *The Haunting of Hill House*, a car trip to a grand, sprawling manor for a weekend of paranormal investigation promises intrigue, romance, new acquaintances, and an escape from her unbearable, dreary life of familial obligations and servitude. Unfortunately, the journey and its destination only further unsettle Eleanor's delicate mental state. When she attempts to flee Hill

18 Several of these advertisements are archived on the website Mustang Attitude (http://www.mustangattitude.com).

House in her automobile, the car seems to become possessed by supernatural forces and drives into a tree, killing her instantly.[19]

All three women—Mary, Marion, and Eleanor—fail to secure the traditional gender roles of wife, mother, and homemaker. Mary apparently has no desire for familial or romantic attachments; conversely, Marion desperately desires such conventional status—she steals money and risks her job, reputation, and presumably jail time to have a chance at married life. Eleanor's estrangement from traditional social coupling poignantly arises from an excess of familial attachment. She has missed out on a chance at marriage, growing old and letting her "eligible" years slip away because she has dutifully taken on the role of full-time caregiver for her invalid mother. This is significant because single, unmarried women would have been viewed as particularly useless, and possibly even dangerous, in the early 1960s. Although women had dutifully trotted out of the home to take over manufacturing jobs during the war, there was an effort underfoot to rigidly reimpose a public-private split that relegated women to the domestic sphere. This division was an essential element of imagined postwar stability, which invoked the home as a cathartic, cleansing space capable of bracketing off the chaos of public life. It was women's duty to play the role of domestic guardian and establish a balanced, tranquil society in the face of increasingly fragmented corporate and industrial structures. Illinois governor Adlai Stevenson specifically described this situation in his infamous address to Sylvia Plath's graduating class at Smith College in 1955. His notorious attack on women's rights and social roles was later reprinted in *Women's Home Companion*. Women were implored to keep their men "purposeful" and "whole" as well as to "frustrate the crushing and corrupting effects of specialization, to integrate means and ends, to develop that balanced tension of mind and spirit which can properly be called 'integrity.'"[20] Such a monumental task, however, was to be conducted largely "in the living-room with a baby in your lap or in the kitchen with a can opener in your hand."[21] Further, a 1962 Gallup poll charged with determining the identity of the average American woman focused solely on the housewife.[22] Stephanie Coontz notes that not only was the housewife central to the idealized American social structure presented in this study and accompanying *Saturday Evening Post* article, but also all other identities—"'[o]ld maids,' divorced women, childless women, and working mothers"—were

19 Marc Jancovich, *Rational Fears: American Horror in the 1950s* (Manchester, UK: Manchester University Press, 1996), 285–302. The author discusses Hitchcock's *Psycho* and Jackson's novel *The Haunting of Hill House* (1959) together as postwar horror narratives driven by the split between a desire for independence and individuation, and the need for integration and filiation, with respect to both the mother-child dyad and its reverberations in the larger social order. I am not the first to bring attention to the similarities between the plight of Eleanor and Marion in their struggles with various facets of patriarchal expectations, yet this earlier work does not view the car as a significant part (or even, indeed, a part) of this process.

20 Adlai Stevenson, "A Purpose for Modern Women," *Women's Home Companion*, September 1955, 30–31. This is a reprint of the author's commencement address at Smith College, 1955.

21 Stevenson, "Purpose for Modern Women." See also Stephanie Coontz, *A Strange Stirring: The Feminine Mystique and the American Woman at the Dawn of the 1960s* (New York: Basic Books, 2011), 1–18. The author describes in detail how the early 1960s conceived of "normal" female identity wholly in terms of marriage, domestic duties, and child rearing.

22 Coontz, *Strange Stirring*, 1.

construed as both extreme and unusual.[23] Mary, Marion, and Eleanor, as childless, unmarried women, are likewise presented as social problems. Moreover, some critics have also discussed Eleanor (in Jackson's novel) within a queer framework, and it would not be a stretch to ascribe a queer sensibility to Mary—a character who is as terrified of male authority as she is repulsed by the sexual advances of a male neighbor.[24] Their journeys could be understood as a desire to sidestep male authority and a path that would allow them to take up a queer identity or relationship specifically challenging normative heterosexual identity. The desire for an excessive or aberrant autonomy, whatever the motivation, is specifically mapped onto the character's relationship to the car and road travel itself. It is this dangerous and threatening female subjectivity that acts as a catalyst for the transformation of cinematic space, which reroutes the road film and forces a detour into the gothic genre.

This article focuses the bulk of its attention on *Carnival of Souls* because it is the most jarring and relentless example of a truncated road film, which continually seeks to reduce the expansive spatial properties of the road film by inverting, contracting, and indeed "gothicizing" cinematic space. As previously noted, the film is bookended by a car accident. When we return to the initial collision site at the end of the film with newly imparted knowledge of Mary's spectral state, it entirely reorients the way we understand our experience of the narrative. Thus, the accident functions as a framing device, which ultimately destabilizes all the plot information previously offered to the viewer. The narrative of the film is contained, and ultimately structured, by paranoid imagery of cars out of control at the hands of young women.[25]

Anecdotal accounts suggest that the idea for *Carnival of Souls* was prompted by Harvey's vision from a car window when the director came upon the marvelously dilapidated Saltair Pavilion on a highway excursion through Utah.[26] Thus, it is not surprising that the film is largely focalized around the automobile and even through its windows, the latter functioning as variable and repetitive framing devices and sites of vision. The film's spontaneous birth from this vision also explains the unnerving recurrence of shots in which the protagonist repeatedly returns to the pavilion—her call toward death—by car (see Figure 3).

In these shots the archaic and ominous leisure palace is entirely framed by the windshield. Mary approaches the structure in her vehicle, and the sense of movement as the pavilion comes into view is exactly that of a slow-moving car, as indeed the

23 Coontz, *Strange Stirring*, 1. The author writes: "The homemakers in the *Saturday Evening Post* article may have thought they were *choosing* to defer to their husbands, but they actually had few alternatives. Many states still had 'head and master' laws, affirming that the wife was subject to her husband. And the expectation that husbands had the right to control what their wives did or even read was widespread" (5).

24 See George E. Haggerty, *Queer Gothic* (Urbana: University of Illinois Press), 2006, 131–150.

25 Lawrence A. Waltz, "Mary Henry's Journey from Owl Creek Bridge," *Literature Film Quarterly* 23, no. 4 (1995): 262–265.

26 Tom Weaver, *Return of the B Science Fiction and Horror Heroes: The Mutant Melding of Two Volumes of Classic Interviews* (Jefferson, NC: McFarland, 1999), 128. In response to the question "How did you come up with the idea to make *Carnival of Souls*?" Harvey responds: "I was on location in California shooting an industrial film for Centron, and decided to travel home by car. Driving back, I was passing Salt Lake, and I saw for the first time an abandoned amusement park called Saltair. . . . Well, with the sun setting and with the lake in the background, this was the weirdest-looking place I'd ever seen *[laughs]*!"

camera was positioned inside an automobile. The spectator, along with Mary, is doomed to endlessly repeat the director's initial roadside vision until our protagonist finally surrenders to the call of the pavilion, abandons her car, and disappears into the world of the dead. She leaves only the trace of her footprints behind in the sand and ultimately is seen as a beautiful corpse, revealed by the transition back to the site of the initial car crash.

Shot construction, editing, and camera placement all underscore the centrality of the car as the primary and dominant perspective for the entire film. After a shot of Mary stumbling to the shore with authorities dragging the water in search of the submerged vehicle behind her, there is a sudden cut to the accident site (presumably a few days later) featuring Mary—now well dressed, perfectly coiffed, and wearing heels—traversing the same bridge (see Figure 4). As the apparent survivor moves toward a car parked on the bridge at the location of the collision, there is a swift cut to a perspective from the interior of the automobile and Mary comes into view. The first time our protagonist is presented as a conventional female Hollywood film character, she is framed by the car windshield, with dashboard and steering wheel clearly visible in the shot, and the ominous bridge stretching out in the distance.

Figure 3. The Saltair Pavilion framed through the car windshield multiple times throughout *Carnival of Souls* (Herts-Lion International Corp., 1962).

Figure 4. Mary "reborn" after the accident: perfectly coiffed and framed from within the car, bridge in the background, in *Carnival of Souls* (Herts-Lion International Corp., 1962).

Even though we have seen Mary's face during the initial car race, there is no indication in this opening sequence that we are meeting the star of the film, and our subsequent glimpse of her—sullied, soaking wet, and struggling from the depths of the river—obscures a clear view of her facial features. This presentation certainly defies classical

Hollywood expectations of introducing a female film protagonist. Thus, the spectator's initial image of Candace Hilligoss as a clearly recognizable lead actress is produced from, and contained by, the confines of the car's interior space. In this sequence the mise-en-scène suggests a very forceful connection between conventional female subjectivity (Mary strolling on the bridge in demure dress and heels), the act of driving (the steering wheel), and the perils of women appropriating the freedom offered by cars (the odious bridge), all neatly enclosed within the parameters of the glass windshield.

Carnival of Souls also skillfully employs graphic and sound matches to suggest the centrality of the car in relation to Mary's desires and her ability to make choices that are not dependent on men. In other words, the car is initially presented in the film as a symbol of freedom attached to the concept of sheer mobility. For instance, when Mary enters the stationary car on the bridge in the scene described earlier, there is a cut to a close-up of her hand reaching for the keys to start the engine. This image is quickly replaced by a shot revealing her hand grasping for an organ draw knob as she skillfully plays an enormous instrument in what we later learn is an organ production workshop. Such a transition suggests that as she takes control of her career (she aspires to be a church organist), Mary appropriates the freedoms offered by the automobile to facilitate independent life choices.[27]

We subsequently learn that Mary is leaving Kansas to start her life over after the terrible accident, taking a job as a church organist in Utah. After Mary's practice session at the Kansas organ factory ends, a conversation between the master builder and his worker ensues in which they discuss the budding organist's "peculiar nature." The two men surmise that the young woman is "behaving strangely," and the carpenter resumes his work at the circular saw, creating a loud repetitive hum. In the next shot we return to the bridge, where Mary drives her car over the wooden planks of the structure, creating a loud drone unmistakably similar to the "whir" of the circular saw heard just moments before. These two sounds are joined nearly seamlessly on the soundtrack, linking the creation of the organ—the source of Mary's livelihood—and the initial revolutions of the car wheel that begin the organist's second journey. Both sound and image initially reinforce the centrality of the car to Mary's fragile sense of autonomy—a relationship that unravels as the film progresses.

In fact, not long after Mary drives away from the horror of the car accident toward what is presumably a desire for a fresh start in Utah, we first realize that something is terribly amiss. Herk Harvey's terrifying visage trimmed in ghoulish white paint emerges to hover on the plane of glass, terrorizing the young blonde from the threshold of the driver-side window. Before the presence of the alarming ghoul signals that Mary's "escape" to the open road has become a gothic narrative, however, that journey closely adheres to the conventions of the road film. We see the car traverse the motorway while the camera travels upward to reveal a vast expanse of highway topography, with trees and embankments flanking the roadway and a mountain rising up in the

27 Julie Brown, "*Carnival of Souls* and the Organs of Horror," in *Music in the Horror Film: Listening to Fear*, ed. Neil Lerner (New York: Routledge, 2010), 1–20. The author notes that Mary Henry is constructed as a "projection of male fears of castration" in the conjunction of organ playing (a stereotypically male activity or profession) and car operation suggested by this sequence in the film (11–12).

distance—then a sign reading Welcome to Utah and Please Drive Carefully makes an appearance as Mary hurtles past and the dimming light signals that night is falling.

These fleeting images of highway signage may seem insignificant to the contemporary viewer. However, as postwar culture grappled with the increasing commodification of all aspects of social life, the untrammeled wilderness stretching out from the edges of the interstate was also unclaimed and its fate uncertain. Debates over the future of this liminal space became infused with anxieties related to the tension between two conflicting tenets of American identity: the promise of unparalleled (and unspoiled) natural beauty and the protection and encouragement of free enterprise.[28] The national regulation of outdoor advertising and signage along highway roads was first proposed as an amendment to the Federal-Aid Highway Act in 1955 but was ultimately rejected.[29] In 1958 the Federal-Aid Highway Act included a segment (section 131) on the regulation of roadside advertising for the national highway system.[30] While debates in this relatively new arena of consideration were primarily waged as a struggle between the rights of individual states versus the reach of federal legislation, legal discourse inevitably engaged with dark and frightening aspects of highway culture, such as the forty thousand deaths per year on US roadways and fears that fire and splinters from billboards along defense highways posed a risk during wartime attack.[31] The potential commodification of interstate motorists' view from the windshield was fraught with worries about safety: would properly placed highway signs reduce collisions or would road signage distract drivers, causing accidents?

Distraction was clearly a major concern. Because women historically were more closely associated with a susceptibility to the surface pleasures and seductive nature of commodity advertising than men, would they be a greater risk for dangerous driver distraction in this bricolage of wilderness and graphic signage? As Andreas Huyssen has convincingly argued, women have always been more closely identified with pulp fiction, mass culture, and, in turn, images and the surface pleasures of advertising. He writes of this feminized trope that "the lure of mass culture, after all, has traditionally been described as losing oneself in dreams and delusions."[32] In this context, women drivers would have been construed as a far riskier type of driver, with the potential for being given over to fantasies, delusions, and distractions on the interstate. Driving long

28 William John Martin Jr. and David E. Nelson, "Outdoor Advertising Control along the Interstate Highway System," *California Law Review* 46, no. 5 (December 1958): 796–827. Martin and Nelson note that even though there appears to be tension between altruistic desires to protect natural environments by reducing roadside signage and the furthering of outright capitalist enterprise, the former was also marked by entrepreneurial forces. On the nature of debates about the fate of interstate roadway advertising in the late 1950s, the authors remark: "The final regulatory scheme is the denouement of conflicting economic, social, and legal arguments presented to Congress by such disparate groups as roadside business associations, garden clubs, trade union councils, and nurserymen's associations. Roughly, these organizations can be divided into those with a financial interest in outdoor advertising and those with public spirited or a financial interest in beautifying the nation's highways" (796).

29 Martin and Nelson, "Outdoor Advertising," 796.

30 Martin and Nelson, "Outdoor Advertising," 796.

31 Martin and Nelson, "Outdoor Advertising," 815. For a discussion of roadway safety and highway signage, see also Morton L. Price, "Billboard Regulation along the Interstate Highway System," *University of Kansas Law Review* 8, no. 1 (October 1959): 81–109.

32 Andreas Huyssen, *After the Great Divide: Modernism, Mass Culture, Postmodernism* (Bloomington: Indiana University Press, 1986), 55.

distances not only produces a dreamlike state of being; the possibility of destructive results related to surface pleasures and distractions historically associated with female readers and viewers is suggested.

Even women drivers joined by companions were charged with a higher incidence of distracted and dangerous habits. Jean Lee, female motorist and director of the American Academy of Safe Drivers, outlined the numerous faults of her fellow female drivers in 1954, including following fashion trends that were adverse to safe driving, being overanxious, and having a tendency toward distracting chatter: "A woman driver, especially if she's travelling with other women, gets to gabbing and forgets to watch the road."[33] However, just a few years prior, a major investigation by the American Automobile Association (AAA) strongly indicated that female drivers actually had fewer accidents than men.[34] Today, the misogynist myth of distractibility as a distinctly feminine trait continues. An online article from CBS News, which reported data from a study undertaken at Kansas State University, found that "female drivers are involved in more crashes at intersections and more collisions with pedestrians, *perhaps* due to distractions."[35] Numerous articles citing a recent influential study by the AAA Foundation for Traffic Safety tend to grossly misconstrue the actual data presented in the findings and perpetuate the myth of the distracted female motorist. According to table 5 of the AAA Foundation report, "Percent of Recorded Teenage Clips in Which Electronic Device Use by Drivers and Other Distracted Driver Behaviors Were Observed, by Sex of Driver," the overall percentage of distracted behavior observed in video clips of teen drivers was 15.1 percent, while the rate for teenaged female drivers was only 15.6 percent—hardly an alarming confirmation of the reputed danger of female distractibility.[36] Harvey's film demonstrates this persistent myth—a female driver operating outside of male companionship and guidance allows her feminine traits to fully take over, succumbing to the terrifying reverie of ghoulish demons as she is fully distracted and absorbed into a dreamlike state by the imagery in front of her.

As the signage on the Utah billboard fades out, a close-up of Mary comes into view with high-contrast lighting completely obscuring one side of her face. When an

33 "Women Drivers," *The Day* (New London, CN), August 23, 1954. Lee also admonishes the female driver for wearing garments that are too tight or too loose, jewelry that is apt to get caught, and heels that are too high and interfere with the safe operation of a vehicle.

34 "Women Drivers—How Do They Compare with Men," *Spokesman Review*, June 23, 1953. The AAA study of 1952 noted that men have 2.8 accidents per 1 million miles, whereas women have only 1.7 in the same distance. In 1952 men were responsible for 92.5 percent of fatal accidents but accounted for 73 percent of the nation's 51 million drivers.

35 "Are Young Female Drivers Any Safer than Males?" *CBS News*, August 27, 2014, http://www.cbsnews.com/news/are-young-female-drivers-any-safer-than-males (my emphasis). See also Nicholas Bakalar, "Profiling the Distracted Driver: Young, Female and Solo," *New York Times*, March 31, 2015. Bakalar cites a slightly more alarming statistic of cell phone use at 63 percent higher for female drivers than their male counterparts, from one survey conducted at an intersection in Texas over a period of several months. Yet other reports cite cell phone use or distracted driving at similar levels for men and women. What is clear is that statistical evidence based on gender varies greatly between reports from different countries and US regions. However, what remains constant is the glee with which headlines proclaim a link between women and negative behavior patterns associated with driving.

36 See Arthur H. Goodwin, Robert D. Foss, Stephanie S. Harrell, and Natalie P. O'Brien, *Distracted Driving among Newly Licensed Teen Drivers* (AAA Foundation for Traffic Safety, UNC Highway Safety Research Center, March 2012), 14.

interior automobile light exposes her entire visage—a seemingly enormous steering wheel in the young woman's hands—eerie and ominous organ music becomes audible.[37] The spectator is alerted to the fact that the music is diegetic by an extended close-up of Mary's hands frantically attempting to manipulate the radio dial in vain efforts to stop the omnipresent spooky melody. A too-big steering wheel made all the more ridiculously large in relation to the driver through camera placement, as well as her inability to manage the radio dials, all indicate that Mary cannot control the car. The ghoul, given the title of "the man" in the opening credits, repeatedly "haunts" the automobile. He reveals himself in the passenger window before spectacularly appearing nearly full figure in the road ahead of the car, at which point the justifiably terrified driver veers off the highway into some shallow water (see Figure 5).

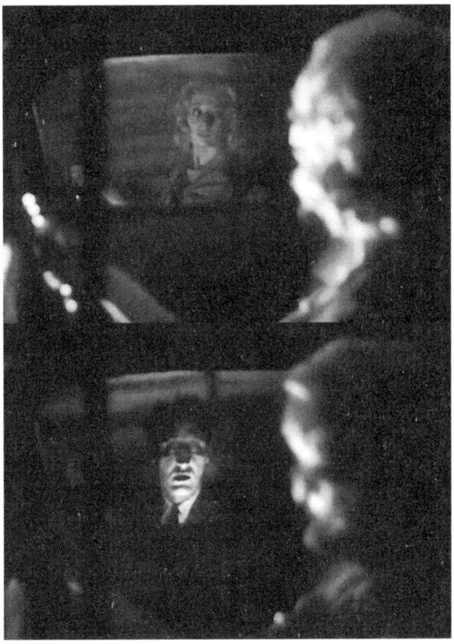

Figure 5. Mary's reflection in the driver-side window quickly replaced by Herk Harvey's terrifying ghoul "the man" in *Carnival of Souls* (Herts-Lion International Corp., 1962).

In just a few short minutes Mary has been presented as the protagonist of a road journey—her desires fused with the freedoms offered by the car and the open road—only to be emphatically stripped of such autonomy by the sudden appearance of the director of the film in the guise of a ghoulish figure who functions to run the car off the highway. The road trip has been reborn as a gothic journey in these moments, and automobile space is now connected to Mary's inner psyche and vision rather than to the approaching vista. Even when a view of the open road in front of the car is offered, it does not signify expansiveness, other opportunities, or anything new "out there"—the promise of the road film. It is not a vision that opens up or out onto anything; we are not shown the promise of a new town or the beauty of a cresting hillside. Here, the vista from the windshield offers only opaque blackness as the figure of Harvey materializes. It is not a translucent darkness suggestive of actual vision in nighttime driving—hazy and shadowy outlines, or contrasting sharp, bright lights and road-sign reflectors—but rather the view suggests that actual, objective vision is cut off, blinded by the inner eye of Mary's psyche (see Figure 6).

Likewise, in *Psycho*, Marion's car assumes the function of a gothic portal early on in the film as she attempts to leave Phoenix with the stolen money. We would assume such a road trip might mean entertaining dreams of a better (i.e., married)

37 For a lucid and comprehensive discussion of the pervasive use of organ music in *Carnival of Souls*, see Brown, "Carnival of Souls and the Organs of Horror." See also Faye E. Riley, "Centron, an Industrial/Educational Film Studio, 1947–1981: A Microhistory" (PhD diss., University of Kansas, 1996), 57.

Figure 6. The road trip reborn as gothic journey—a view of "the man" replaces the vista of expansive topography glimpsed at the outset of the road trip from Mary's front windshield in *Carnival of Souls* (Herts-Lion International Corp., 1962).

future. However, in the space of the automobile interior anxieties are amplified and made audible for the film spectator as Marion imagines her punishment for the transgression she has committed—a measure of "her soft fine flesh"—so eloquently described by Robin Wood as "hideously disproportionate to the crime."[38] Eleanor Lance also enters into a fantastical, distracted state of enclosed reverie while driving toward her doomed fate at Hill House, and the entire journey is accompanied by unsettling music as well as a voice-over in which she muses about possible futures—becoming a new person and living in a different home. However, as Eleanor nears the sprawling manor, her reflections become much more sinister, culminating in the possibility that she might "drive on and on until the wheels of the car are worn to nothing" as she approaches "the end of the world." As in *Carnival of Souls*, when a woman takes the wheel in *Psycho* and *The Haunting* to control her situation, assert autonomy, and crawl out from under the weight of patriarchal expectations of docility, patience, and passivity, the perspective from the car she occupies tends to focus on the interior rather than the exterior experience or the view outward. The female motorist's anxiety and interiority spill out and seemingly fill up the entire vehicle.

In a later sequence in *Carnival of Souls* the car not only completely closes up to become a site of reflection for interior psychic imaginings and terror but also literally demobilizes the protagonist. After Mary's haunting by "the man" becomes too much for her to bear, she resolves to set out on yet another road trip and leave her new home even though she has only just arrived. However, this time the journey is drastically and permanently curtailed as the car simply breaks down and acts as a foil to her plans. Determined to flee, she brings the halting vehicle to a garage in hopes of a quick repair and a hasty departure. What happens next is perhaps the most unnerving and confusing sequence in the film. Mary elects to stay in her car as mechanics hoist the automobile onto a hydraulic lift, during which time she apparently falls asleep. When she is subsequently awoken by the sounds of a creaking door and foreboding footsteps, Mary falls from the car and takes flight from the garage on foot. We see her feet and

38 Robin Wood, *Hitchcock's Films Revisited* (New York: Columbia University Press, 1989), 145.

legs from behind in a low-angle shot. An abrupt change in camera placement shows Mary running on the sidewalk behind a row of stationary cars. The moving camera is located behind the parked vehicles, and their slanted position reveals intermittent views of Mary's body through multiple car windows as the camera travels alongside. This view fuses camera placement and movement with a mise-en-scène of parked automobiles that is suggestive of the essential shutter mechanism of the motion picture camera, which makes the illusion of movement possible. Such a turn offers yet another point in the film at which cinematic vision is dramatically wedded to the car. A haunted pedestrian journey then unfolds in which Mary is nearly run down by a vehicle, then terrorized by a busload of ghouls after seeking an alternate escape route.

Finally, our terrified protagonist ends up in the office of a psychiatrist named Dr. Samuels and proceeds to declare her anxious secrets. As she begins her confession—"I don't belong in the world. Something separates me from other people"—the doctor's chair is turned away from Mary, permitting only the top portion of his head to be seen. When Mary finishes her anguished declaration and implores, "Doctor, you've got to tell me what to do!," the chair slowly swivels around to reveal not the seemingly benevolent Dr. Samuels but "the man"—the ghoulish Harvey! At this point there is a quick and jarring cut back to the interior of the car still in the garage and of Mary inside screaming with her head resting on the wheel. The escape was only illusory, and the car has once again become a site of gothic enclosure—fully immobilized and wholly given over to hauntings and delusional imaginings while also trapping the protagonist in a terrifying dream.

As a point of comparison, in *The Haunting* Eleanor Lance's car seems to actually kill her, or at least it is possessed by a supernatural entity that uses the car as a weapon, and *Psycho* ominously weds automobile imagery to the smug expression of the film's killer after he dispenses with its female protagonist. The latter's most significant and haunting images are usually understood to be the infamous shower sequence—a flesh-flaying assault on the viewer that arguably transformed the contours of the horror genre and film language itself. What is just as important here, however, are the images in which Norman, after violently murdering Marion, drives her car to the edge of a secluded swamp to banish the thing for good. The stark white Ford, with Marion's lifeless body in the trunk, is brought to the brink of a marshy opening in the earth to be swallowed up forever, and the automobile's descent is paused by the recalcitrance of the thick earth for a few tense seconds before submitting to its (temporary) fate. Norman's unnerving smirk as the car resumes its downward journey might be read as his pleasure in murder and in getting away with it, yet it is also suggestive of another culturally and historically significant factor—the permanent and decisive undoing of the relationship between a woman on the run and her accomplice, the car. The violence done to Marion—the erasure of her desire and subjectivity—are emphatically linked to a separation between the plucky secretary from Phoenix and the mobility suggested by her newly acquired automobile, which so boldly promised a proactive avenue and radical change for a seemingly hopeless situation. In truncated road movies cars no longer offer escape and the limitless possibilities connected with conventional road films and their male drivers but are instead completely enclosed portals that reflect, refract, and condense the anxieties of female motorists. Moreover, the automobile also becomes a literal, albeit temporary, tomb for Marion and Mary as the steel skins encase and hide fragile inert bodies until they are unearthed from their respective watery graves by the authorities. For female motorists in these instances, the road film closes up, is transformed by a gothic sensibility, and ultimately brings only death.

The Educational Film and Car Culture. It would be too neat (though incredibly tempting) to suggest that Herk Harvey himself is imploring female drivers to get off the road in *Carnival of Souls*. However, as Bernice Murphy points out, the production sometimes resembles a highway safety film, the likes of which famously careened toward increasingly repellant and gory subject matter in an attempt to scare young drivers "safe" when screened in high schools.[39] Indeed, Harvey was an industrial filmmaker who worked for Centron Films—based in Lawrence, Kansas—a company that specialized in both educational and industrial productions, with clients ranging from John Deere to the American Medical Association. Harvey did not make highway safety films himself, but as an educational filmmaker he was likely aware of their aesthetics and trend toward realistic roadside carnage at the time *Carnival of Souls* was produced. The director was also involved in other nontheatrical films featuring car culture, such as *None for the Road* (Herk Harvey, 1957), which illuminated the dangers of drunk driving for college students, and even *Star 34* (Herk Harvey and Arthur H. Wolf, 1954), a production highlighting the natural beauty and historical interest of Kansas. In fact, *None for the Road* can be thought of as a type of automobile safety film. Although it does not focus on dangerous driving per se (outside of alcohol consumption) or depict bloody roadside carnage, it does follow the story of three young couples out on a date who dance, consume alcohol, and use motorcars for transportation.

The film is relevant to this discussion because it grafts gendered social characteristics and psychology onto the act of driving, a correlation that binds together educational movies about car culture and truncated road films in the early 1960s. Only the male characters in *None for the Road* are given last names and identifiable personality characteristics: Jerry Landon, an overconfident, obnoxious drunk who is described by the film's white-coat-clad scientist-narrator as "an all-out type"; Keith Stephens, a "conservative type" who consumes only a moderate amount of alcohol (four beers!); and the only sensible one of the bunch, Dan Parker, who abstains in favor of ginger ale. All three couples rely on their respective males to drive home after the evening's revelries draw to a close, and the fates of the girls in their company are determined by the behavior of their companions. A degree of autonomy is given to one female character, since Jerry's girl recognizes that her date is too inebriated to drive, and she attempts to ride home with someone else. Unfortunately, the girl's desire to get home safely is thwarted by her decision to ride with Keith, the moderate drinker, who flips his car, causing a fatal accident.

None for the Road, a Young America Films release, spends a good deal of time presenting a typical social situation involving young people. The production implies that men do the driving, and the interest of the film is directed at identifying how differing "types" of masculine personalities perform in relation to patterns of alcohol

39 Murphy, *Highway Horror Film*, 81–90.

consumption and driving. Women are merely the victims of gendered circumstance, not the subject of study. The authenticity of the situation depicted here is actually supported by a contemporaneous report from the Allstate Insurance Corporation—*The High School Student and the Automobile: A Study of the Relationships between Scholastic Records of High School Students and Their Use of the Family Car, Conducted at Niles Township High School, Skokie, Illinois (May, 1959)*. Allstate's report revealed that the "number of high school girls who drive extensively turned out to be so small as to be insignificant to the survey."[40] Male socialization and typology are revealed in attitudes toward driving and automobile culture according to the logic of *None for the Road*. Apparently, young women and girls hardly drove in the postwar era, so the impact of driving on their social "type" or development is left out of the film.[41] However, as I mentioned at the outset of this article, by the early 1960s female drivers began to significantly increase in number, according to the ratio of male to female driver's licenses in the United States. This sharp increase in female drivers clearly resulted in a generalized anxiety about women on the road and the potential for social transgression that driving might permit. The truncated road film, unlike *None for the Road*, underscores the social typology of women who chose to get behind the wheel and explores their deviancy through the act of driving.

Star 34, produced by Centron, also showcases driving as a gendered activity and presents its sweeping travelogue of the picturesque state of Kansas—the thirty-fourth state to be admitted to the Union—in the form of a road trip. City folk Bill (Herk Harvey) and Mary Asher (Shirley Rae) must travel to the Sunflower State as a precondition for receiving an inheritance and are so enraptured by the raw beauty and historical interest of the region that they decide to relocate there. Even though the film ostensibly functions only to advertise the positive merits of Kansas, it still retains traces of the social guidance productions made by Centron and their competitor Coronet Films because it defines normal social behavior along gender lines. Moreover, it does so through the form of a road trip and the expectations of car culture. As the couple, described by the film's narrator as "normal young people," prepare for their journey, we learn that Mary is "a typical helpful female" who "has the solution to the packing while Bill, the male of the species, loads the car." A shot from inside the automobile reveals Bill at the wheel, Mary in the passenger seat, and a vast expanse of road stretching out from the windshield as the journey begins. Kansas materializes in the form of billowing wheat fields, strangely beautiful rock formations, and an abundance of parks and pools. This early Centron production powerfully establishes "normal" behavior at the outset of the film in relation to gender-specific activities connected with automobile travel, and here the cinematic travelogue is focalized through an

40 Edward A. Tenney, *The Highway Jungle: The Story of the Public Safety Movement and the Failure of "Driver Education" in the Public Schools* (New York: Exposition Press, 1962), 99–100. Allstate conducted a further, more extensive study on the same subject in 1960: *A Teenage Pattern: A Study of 20,000 High School Students and the Inter-Relationships of Their Grades, Cars, and Jobs*. In this survey, according to Tenney, girls figure as dangerous accomplices of the automobile and part-time job, functioning to distract young men from their scholastic obligations. He writes: "The question of how many boys fail to capitalize on their potential because they have succumbed to the lure of girl-plus-car-plus-job is a social question which the Allstate study makes no attempt to answer."

41 "Women Drivers." This article notes that female motorists account for 27 percent of all US drivers.

exceptionally conventional view of gender relations and social activities dramatically wedded to the road trip.

The previously mentioned highway safety film *Signal 30* also dramatizes anxieties related to women's participation in postwar car culture. This infamous production intended to scare drivers into heeding traffic rules and using common sense by depicting the gruesome aftermath of roadside accidents. Accompanying documentary footage of twisted steel, severed limbs, and mutilated torsos freshly pressed into tree trunks is a voice-over that relates facts about the identity of the victims—young football stars, husbands, and children.[42] Strikingly, the only sequences that provide what appears to be synchronous audio of the drivers and passengers after the collision are ones in which there are female victims. Anguished screams and hysterical gasps are heard as female victims are revealed to viewers. Each accident in *Signal 30* is treated as a distinct narrative event, and the vignettes of carnage are introduced in one of two ways—either with a straightforward explanation of the traffic violation that caused such horrific suffering or a more theatrically suggestive tagline. For instance, one accident involving a husband and wife is introduced with "Death sometimes plays an overture of torture." In this sequence an audio recording of a female victim moaning "Oh my legs, oh no my legs, oh my legs" interrupts the factual voice-over narration and dramatic orchestral soundtrack as the camera surveys the wreck. In a later accident involving four women, the narrator asks at the outset, "What is the price to be paid for failure to yield right of way or violating a stop sign?" Of course, by now we know that the answer is surely a gruesome, unthinkable death, and here an extended audio of undecipherable cries and moans from a woman who "dies only a few hours later" accompanies nearly the entire grisly scene.

Even if these were, by unlikely chance, the only accidents for which the filmmaker was able to obtain synchronous audio after the collision, it would be hard to ignore the fact that suffering is overwhelmingly represented in this film through a depiction of the female body in agony. Women's unbearable screams provide a seemingly universal touch point for all pain experienced collectively. Although male victims are indeed filmed, they remain stoically silent. Thus, women emerge as the victims, the hurt ones, and the spectator can relate to their suffering in a more immediate and physical way because the production engages both sight and sound in portraying their misfortunes. Pain is, of course, an overwhelmingly difficult experience to represent. A largely "unsharable" experience, physical pain is mobilized and represented in a complex manner here—one that fuses the car as object and weapon and the spectacularization of female suffering as normal and natural in these narrative events. The film is not so much concerned with specific gendered behavior and driving per se, as all drivers are admonished for a "callous defiance of the law," but it is notable for the ways it allows the suffering of women to represent the pain and tragedy of all roadside victims. Physical vulnerability to the dangers of interstate travel is overwhelmingly associated with

42 Ken Smith, *Mental Hygiene: Classroom Films, 1945–1970* (New York: Blast Books, 1999), 79. The director Richard Wayman had a police scanner installed in his vehicle to quickly alert him to nearby collision sites. Wayman filmed the unfolding roadside carnage and this footage, along with other images captured at accident sites by Ohio state troopers, was assembled to create *Signal 30*.

women in this film, as their sounds supplement the images with heartrending cries, again evoking the car as a gothic portal that traps and expresses feminized trauma.

Anatomy of an Accident, another highway safety film, presents women as an impediment to safe driving on two fronts. A technically proficient and inventive narrative, this film, like *Carnival of Souls*, is told from the perspective of a spectral entity. John (David Wayne), an employee of the Bell Telephone Company, dies in a car accident while transporting his family to Grandma's on a Sunday afternoon. The specter replays events leading up to the crash, and we learn that he was involved in driver safety classes for the corporation. In an early scene, John presents an illustrative placard to his wife to be used for the class. A lone male driver peers out of his windshield in the poster, and the interactive lesson includes adhesive words, which can be placed in his outlying vision to indicate distractions. "Sleep" and "vacation" make a predictable appearance, yet other words inexplicably emerge in relation to the exercise, such as "blonde" and "redhead," indicating that women, their very presence even in a virtual manner, bring the possibility of distracted driving and danger (see Figure 7).

The accident, which robs a family of their patriarch, is also blamed on the (too-slow) driving of a female motorist: a self-righteous cranky spinster (Irene Tedrow) replete with thick black glasses and a soft-spoken sidekick whose plodding speed and indecisive steering are the cause of not one but two accidents in the film (see Figure 8, Tedrow on right)! Tedrow was a character actress who made her career playing obstinate older women for comic effect—busybodies, unwelcome aunts, meddling widows, and crabby librarians. Casting Tedrow yokes this character to a litany of stereotypes about difficult older women and suggests that female drivers represent a category of dangerous women unnecessary to the road and perhaps to society itself. While John was transporting his household for important family business, the spinsters, "inconsiderate Sunday drivers" according to Helen, John's wife, were merely out taking up valuable roadway space, disrupting vehicular and indeed social patterns, ultimately causing death and the destruction of the nuclear family. Great pains are taken to paint Tedrow's character as selfish, arrogant, and inconsiderate. In response to her companion's query as to why she did not heed a roadway stop sign, she replies, "I was gonna stop, only when I saw that open place I slid in quick before anybody else did." The spinster stereotype, an unattached older woman who historically thwarts "proper" heteronormative social constructs, is here conflated with the menace of the female driver who also operates outside of conventional social relationships and spaces. This

Figure 7. Illustrative placard featuring common driver distractions including blondes and redheads from *Anatomy of an Accident* (produced by Jerry Fairbanks, Bell System, 1961).

Figure 8. The spinster (Irene Tedrow, right), as bothersome and lethal motorist in *Anatomy of an Accident* (produced by Jerry Fairbanks, Bell System, 1961).

socially threatening woman is rendered as a bothersome, thoughtless (and ultimately deadly) female motorist.

Driving—how one does it, where, and why—is represented as intimately related to processes of socialization and identity formation during the late 1950s and into the next decade, as I have shown in my examination of film culture from this era. However, these ideas actually took root after World War I, when the progressive ideals espoused by educational reformer John Dewey flourished. His philosophy was sharply defined in a tract written by one of his proponents, Dr. George E. Payne, who grandiosely stated: "We have come to regard education purely with reference to its effect on some form of behavior of the individual. We no longer look upon the function of education as being that of giving information about arithmetic, geography, and the like, but as a means of securing to the individual the right sort of social action, and of developing in the individual the right kinds of feelings, attitudes, points of view, and ideals."[43] Education became more focused on producing socially desirable citizens instead of merely transmitting standardized rote information, and this turn heavily emphasized safety in a broad sense. In the same volume, for instance, Payne proposed that accident prevention education could simply be inserted into nearly every existing discipline in the current school curriculum. The morbid publication presents these arithmetic problems as suitable for seventh grade:

> 1. If there are 700,000 people in St. Louis and 510 of them are killed by accident, how many would be left. What per cent [*sic*] are killed?
> 2. One hundred people are killed by automobiles and 37 by street cars. If four times the number killed by automobiles are killed in other ways, how many people will be left out of a population of 700,000? What percent would be killed?[44]

When the reformist waves of Progressive Era values transformed American education, it became heavily invested in the promotion of safety as an ideal attribute and measurement of a well-adjusted citizenry. Safety emerged as the most important civic virtue for educational reformers, and driver education became yet another way the

43 E. George Payne, *Education in Accident Prevention: A Treatise Showing How Accident Prevention May Be Made a Part of Regular School Instruction without the Addition of Another Subject to the Curriculum* (Chicago: Lyons and Carnahan, 1919), 19–20.

44 Payne, *Education in Accident Prevention*, 87–88.

ideal citizen could be "produced"; the alarming fact of increasing driver fatalities coinciding with the steady rise in automobile travel seemed to easily dovetail with these edifying goals. Indeed, the need for driver education in the school system would have appeared as a natural and indeed necessary extension of Progressive education ideals, connecting teachable practical skills with lessons about social responsibility and moral behavior.[45] The films discussed in this article extend this connection on several fronts and bring female motorists to the fore by linking gendered social expectations and deviant behavior with motor skills and roadway practices.

By the end of World War II, the tenets of Progressive education were somewhat transformed to meet the needs of postwar America by focusing on practical life skills as well as social adjustment. This new incarnation of Progressive education, labeled "life adjustment," quickly came under scrutiny from critics such as Edward A. Tenney, who vigorously argued that driver education in the United States was a failure precisely *because* it was conceived of as part of the "life adjustment" thrust of public school education, which emphasized the inculcation of a sense of civic duty and shared values over the transmission of information. In this framework driving was understood to be a social activity, not just a practical one, and led to a corresponding theory of driver education in which "good people don't have accidents and . . . bad people do."[46] Tenney goes on to state that, according to this "science of driver education,"

> [a]ccidents are caused by bad people being bad, and safety is created by good people being good. Those who have right attitudes live safely and usually die of old age; those with wrong attitudes live recklessly and often die prematurely. . . . Safe driving allegedly illustrates a person's charity, benevolence, and good will toward everybody. It represents the high-water mark of civilization, for it symbolizes the co-operative, noncompetitive spirit. A spiritually educated driver never contests the right of way but yields it humbly. . . . The primary problem is a problem of soul, of right attitude.[47]

Mary "takes the wheel" in Harvey's film, and we move from a problem of "soul"—an exploration of her social type, attitude, and spirituality—to a *Carnival of Souls*, a gothic fairground spectacle in which Mary's desire for independence from conventional social roles is finally laid to rest, consumed by a hoard of zombielike creatures dancing in a dilapidated pleasure palace. Throughout the film Mary rebuffs every representation of patriarchal culture that seeks to control her—the church, a lascivious neighbor, and a male doctor (a figure not unlike Dr. Charles Wentworth, the physiologist who narrates *None for the Road*). She uses the car to cross state boundaries and exercise autonomy. Thus, the car becomes a symbol of her alterity to the normative state of gendered social relations and her inability to be absorbed into the patriarchal social order. Given the centrality of automobiles to the practical subversion of male authority and

45 Payne, "An Experiment in Education in Accident Prevention," *Elementary School Journal* 20, no. 5 (January 1920): 352–358. As early as 1920, car accident statistics appear in sample work and exercises undertaken by school-aged children in *Elementary School Journal*.

46 Tenney, *Highway Jungle*, 68.

47 Tenney, *Highway Jungle*, 68.

social spaces in *Carnival of Souls*, and the contemporary emphasis on car culture as a marker of social type and character, it is difficult not to see the film as anything but a treatise on what happens when women "take the wheel." They die, as indicated by the carload of dead girls revealed at the end of the film. When our spectral protagonist endeavors to exceed the limited roles allocated to women within the social order, the initial pleasures associated with the open road soon evaporate as she is pulled closer and closer toward the ghastly pavilion and her true state—death and submission to the forces of patriarchy. Mary is met by a bevy of terrifying ghouls waiting to entertain her at the pavilion, as well as the macabre Harvey himself, the director of the film. He literally runs Mary off the road with his antics, waiting to receive his victim and offer her a final dance before her exile from automobile travel and her deadly expulsion from the social order.[48] *

48 Initial audiences of the film may not have been aware that the director also played the central ghoul. However, this fact is well publicized in contemporary sources on the film.

Malthus at the Movies: Science, Cinema, and Activism around *Z.P.G.* and *Soylent Green*

by JESSE OLSZYNKO-GRYN and PATRICK ELLIS

Abstract: This article investigates cinema's engagement with the Malthusian movement to control global overpopulation in the long 1960s. It examines the contested production and reception of *Z.P.G.: Zero Population Growth* (Michael Campus, 1972) and *Soylent Green* (Richard Fleischer, 1973) to shed new light on the nexus of science, activism, and the media. It argues that the history of the movement, usually reconstructed as an elite scientific and political discourse, cannot be fully understood without also taking into account mass-market entertainment.

The Science-Activism-Media Nexus. In the early 1970s, two Hollywood films portrayed the coming millennium as desperately overcrowded and polluted, fast running out of resources and space. Both *Z.P.G.: Zero Population Growth* (Michael Campus, 1972) and *Soylent Green* (Richard Fleischer, 1973) were products of the "Malthusian moment," a brief peak in the late 1960s and early 1970s of environmental concerns with world population growth and its control, but they also differed in significant ways.[1] *Z.P.G.* imagined a totalitarian state that banned childbirth on penalty of death, fared as poorly at the box office as with critics, and became embroiled in a major fracas with the grassroots organization Zero Population Growth (ZPG). *Soylent Green* envisioned a powerful corporation that perpetuated mass cannibalism, performed well at the box office, and generally satisfied activists as a politically neutered, if passably ecological, "message" film.

Although Malthusian environmentalism was as much about birth control as the biosphere, scholars have generally framed both films in terms less of reproductive politics than of environmentalism. As early as 1978, Joan Dean's influential

1 See Thomas Robertson, *The Malthusian Moment: Global Population Growth and the Birth of American Environmentalism* (New Brunswick, NJ: Rutgers University Press, 2012).

Jesse Olszynko-Gryn is a Chancellor's Fellow and lecturer at the University of Strathclyde. His first book, A Woman's Right to Know: A History of Pregnancy Testing in Britain, *recovers the contested rise of a little-studied technology from around 1900 to the present day. Patrick Ellis is a Marion L. Brittain Postdoctoral Fellow at the Georgia Institute of Technology. His book* Aeroscopics: Media Archaeology of the Bird's-Eye View *provides a history of aerial vision in the era before commonplace flight.*

essay on science fiction cinema, "Between *2001* and *Star Wars*," established *Z.P.G.* and *Soylent Green* as part of a Hollywood cycle of decidedly terrestrial and often ecologically themed dystopian films.[2] Dean argues that during this period, overcrowding and resource depletion became central to Hollywood as nuclear fears temporarily subsided and were largely displaced by new anxieties—around Watergate, Vietnam, and the oil crisis.[3] Now widely regarded as the first film to explicitly mention the greenhouse effect, *Soylent Green* has subsequently been embraced both within and beyond the academy as a prescient cautionary tale.[4] *Z.P.G.*, in contrast, has "fallen into obscurity . . . unclaimed, unloved and abandoned, even by genre fans."[5]

Histories of population control, meanwhile, have tended to privilege the somewhat rarefied intellectual discourses of scientific and political elites. Mass communication and public perception receive little more than passing commentary in these histories, if they are mentioned at all.[6] This is a major oversight for the analysis of a movement that was fundamentally about reaching a large proportion of the world's population. But approaches are starting to change, and recent accounts have foregrounded the circulation of iconic images in environmentalism as well as the use of educational films in sex education, birth control, and family planning.[7] Media scholars have given cinema and television a starring role in revisionist histories of the sexual revolution, and historians of reproduction have made communication more central to their accounts as well.[8] Science, activism, and the moving image have also been coming

2 Joan F. Dean, "Between *2001* and *Star Wars*," *Journal of Popular Film and Television* 7, no. 1 (1978): 32–41; David A. Kirby, *Lab Coats in Hollywood: Science, Scientists, and Cinema* (Cambridge, MA: MIT Press, 2010), 172–173.

3 James Chapman and Nicholas J. Cull, *Projecting Tomorrow: Science Fiction and Popular Cinema* (London: I. B. Tauris, 2013), 5.

4 See Noreena Hertz, *The Silent Takeover: Global Capitalism and the Death of Democracy* (New York: Free Press, 2001), 236–237; Stephen Rust, "Hollywood and Climate Change," in *Ecocinema Theory and Practice*, ed. Stephen Rust, Salma Monani, and Sean Cubitt (London: Routledge, 2013), 191–211.

5 James Leggott, "ZPG: Zero Population Growth," *Science Fiction Film and Television* 3, no. 2 (2010): 335–338, 335.

6 The major histories are Matthew Connelly, *Fatal Misconception: The Struggle to Control World Population* (Cambridge, MA: Harvard University Press, 2008); Derek S. Hoff, *The Stork and the State: The Population Debate and Policy Making in US History* (Chicago: University of Chicago Press, 2012); Robertson, *Malthusian Moment*; Alison Bashford, *Global Population: History, Geopolitics, and Life on Earth* (New York: Columbia University Press, 2014); and Carole R. McCann, *Figuring the Population Bomb: Gender and Demography in the Mid-Twentieth Century* (Seattle: University of Washington Press, 2017).

7 Elisabet Björklund, *The Most Delicate Subject: A History of Sex Education Films in Sweden* (Lund: University of Lund Publications, 2012); Manon Parry, *Broadcasting Birth Control: Mass Media and Family Planning* (New Brunswick, NJ: Rutgers University Press, 2013); Birgit Schneider and Thomas Nocke, eds., *Image Politics of Climate Change: Visualizations, Imaginations, Documentations* (Bielefeld, Germany: Transcript, 2014); Finis Dunaway, *Seeing Green: The Use and Abuse of American Environmental Images* (Chicago: University of Chicago Press, 2015).

8 See Eric Schaeffer, ed., *Sex Scene: Media and the Sexual Revolution* (Durham, NC: Duke University Press, 2014); Nick Hopwood, Peter Murray Jones, Lauren Kassell, and Jim Secord, "Introduction: Communicating Reproduction," *Bulletin of the History of Medicine* 89, no. 3 (2015): 379–404; Jesse Olszynko-Gryn and Patrick Ellis, "'A Machine for Recreating Life': An Introduction to Reproduction on Film," *British Journal for the History of Science* 50, no. 3 (2017): 383–409.

together in histories of the antinuclear movement's engagement with nuclear-disaster cinema and television.[9]

Taking cinema as the example, in this article we investigate the science-activism-media nexus in the case of Malthusian thinking about global population and its control in the early 1970s. We show how film and fiction were not downstream of elite scientific and political discourses. They did not simply mirror these discourses but were produced and consumed, from screenplay to screening, through a process of negotiation and contestation. As we shall see, ZPG the organization fought back against *Z.P.G.* the movie, and the explicitly anti-Catholic, pro-contraception message of the book adapted for *Soylent Green* was lost in the production process. But first, we take a step back to consider more broadly how Malthusians engaged with different genres and forms of mass communication in the long 1960s.

Malthusians and Mass Communication in the Long 1960s. The long 1960s, a politically tumultuous period from the mid-1950s to the mid-1970s, was marked by a deepening crisis in scientific authority.[10] It also saw a confluence of science fiction's expository techniques and ecology's concern with the near, extrapolated future.[11] Not only did professional science fiction writers forecast ecological doom; prominent ecologists also fictionalized their own predictions. Take Rachel Carson's *Silent Spring* (1962) and Paul Ehrlich's *The Population Bomb* (1968), the two most influential books of American environmentalism. *Silent Spring*, above all concerned with the effect of pesticides on birds, contributed to the ban on DDT a decade after its publication. But from a literary perspective, its enduring success is today partly attributed to Carson's affective blend of science fact and fiction, especially in her book's memorable preface, "A Fable for Tomorrow."[12] At the time, however, Carson's rhetorical strategy left her vulnerable to attack. A marine biologist by training, she risked undermining her own scientific authority by penning evocative, fictionalized prose. Agricultural scientists dismissed *Silent Spring* as science fiction on par with *The Twilight Zone*, while other experts openly disagreed with Carson's data.[13]

9 Deron Overpeck, "'Remember! It's Only a Movie!': Expectations and Receptions of *The Day After* (1983)," *Historical Journal of Film, Radio and Television* 32, no. 2 (2012): 267–292; Daniel Cordle, "'That's Going to Happen to Us. It Is': Threads and the Imagination of Nuclear Disaster on 1980s Television," *Journal of British Cinema and Television* 10, no. 1 (2013): 71–92; Tony Shaw, "'Rotten to the Core': Exposing America's Energy-Media Complex in *The China Syndrome*," *Cinema Journal* 52, no. 2 (2013): 93–113.

10 Jon Agar, "What Happened in the Sixties?," *British Journal for the History of Science* 41, no. 4 (2008): 567–600.

11 Karlheinz Steinmüller, "Science Fiction and Science in the Twentieth Century," in *Companion to Science in the Twentieth Century*, ed. John Krige and Dominique Pestre (London: Routledge, 1997), 339–360.

12 M. Jimmie Killingsworth and Jacqueline S. Palmer, "Silent Spring and Science Fiction: An Essay in the History and Rhetoric of Narrative," in *And No Birds Sing: Rhetorical Analyses of Rachel Carson's "Silent Spring,"* ed. Craig Waddell (Carbondale: Southern Illinois University Press, 2000), 174–204; Lisa H. Sideris, "Fact and Fiction, Fear and Wonder: The Legacy of Rachel Carson," *Soundings* 91, nos. 3–4 (2008): 335–369; Joshua David Bellin, "Us or Them! Silent Spring and the 'Big Bug' Films of the 1950s," *Extrapolation* 50, no. 1 (2009): 145–168.

13 Gary Kroll, "The 'Silent Springs' of Rachel Carson: Mass Media and the Origins of Modern Environmentalism," *Public Understanding of Science* 10, no. 4 (2001): 403–420, 418; Mark Hamilton Lytle, *The Gentle Subversive: Rachel Carson, "Silent Spring," and the Rise of the Environmental Movement* (Oxford: Oxford University Press, 2007), 173.

Ehrlich's best seller was published in paperback by the Sierra Club, a well-established environmental group, in partnership with Ballantine Books, known for publishing politically engaged science fiction alongside serious nonfiction dealing with social issues such as contraception, nuclear energy, and the environment.[14] A butterfly ecologist with no formal training in demography, Ehrlich, too, invited criticism by presenting readers of *The Population Bomb* with not one but three fictitious "doomsday scenarios" variously combining mass famine, plague, and nuclear war.[15] Ehrlich later regretted the use of these scenarios as the "biggest tactical error in *The Bomb*" because it enabled critics to cite their "failure to occur" as a "failure of prediction."[16] But as others have noted, it was the book's "tragic apocalyptic inflection" that "produced both its phenomenal success and enduring scandal."[17]

The mobilization of science fiction was part of a broader educational strategy widely adopted not only by individual authors but also by organizations such as ZPG. Cofounded by Ehrlich in 1968, the same year *The Population Bomb* was published, ZPG was headquartered in Palo Alto, California, where Ehrlich taught at Stanford.[18] From January 1970, the charismatic professor effectively used his many appearances on Johnny Carson's *The Tonight Show* to promote both his book and the organization.[19] By 1971, ZPG had grown to thirty-five thousand members in more than four hundred local and state chapters, mainly along the academic corridors of the Northeast and countercultural California.[20] A political lobbying force with catchy slogans including "Stop Heir Pollution" and "Make Love, Not Babies," ZPG distributed newsletters and organized letter-writing campaigns.[21] It also edited and supported the publication of an anthology of science fiction short stories devoted to overpopulation, *Voyages: Scenarios for a Ship Called Earth* (1971).[22]

Also published by Ballantine and showcasing such luminaries as J. G. Ballard, Ray Bradbury, and Doris Lessing, *Voyages* contained a comprehensive paratext to encourage readers' deeper engagement.[23] Paul and his wife, Anne Ehrlich, provided the introduction; a sample letter was included at the back to promote activism; and didactic introductory material and scholarly bibliographies framed each section. ZPG not only invited readers

14 Kenneth C. Davis, *Two-Bit Culture: The Paperbacking of America* (Boston: Houghton Mifflin, 1984), 331.

15 Paul R. Ehrlich, *The Population Bomb* (New York: Ballantine, 1968), 72.

16 Paul R. Ehrlich and Anne H. Ehrlich, "The Population Bomb Revisited," *Electronic Journal of Sustainable Development* 1, no. 3 (2009): 63–71, 67. For a contemporaneous critique of ecological doomsayers, including Carson and Ehrlich, see John Maddox, *The Doomsday Syndrome* (London: Professional Library, 1972).

17 Greg Garrard, *Ecocriticism*, 2nd ed. (New York: Routledge, 2012), 109.

18 "ZPG: A New Movement Challenges the U.S. to Stop Growing," *Life*, April 17, 1970, 32–37; Shirley L. Radl, "Zero Population Growth, Inc.: Past, Present, and Future," *Biological Conservation* 3, no. 1 (1970): 71–72; Wade Greene, "The Militant Malthusians," *Saturday Review*, March 11, 1972, 40–49.

19 Paul Sabin, *The Bet: Paul Ehrlich, Julian Simon, and Our Gamble over Earth's Future* (New Haven, CT: Yale University Press, 2013), 1–2.

20 Hoff, *Stork and the State*, 179, 320.

21 Hoff, *Stork and the State*, 180.

22 Rob Sauer, ed., *Voyages: Scenarios for a Ship Called Earth* (New York: Ballantine, 1971).

23 See Jon Adams, "Real Problems with Fictional Cases," in *How Well Do Facts Travel? The Dissemination of Reliable Knowledge*, ed. Peter Howlett and Mary S. Morgan (Cambridge: Cambridge University Press, 2011), 167–192.

to take the dystopian futures imagined in *Voyages* as seriously as demographers' forecasts but also instructed its members on how to use the book—as "a tool for ZPG."[24] An essay in the *ZPG National Reporter* directed members to confirm the book's availability in shops and ensure that it was displayed prominently; then ("for the brazen") they could forge the anthologist's signature in the local copies of the book; and finally, it encouraged them to "Write a book review. Get one written. Get one published."[25] But the printed word could go only so far, so zero populationists also set their sights on the moving image.

As the 1960s wore on, activists opposed to mainstream culture made "underground" movies of their own and "New Hollywood" directors fêted outlaws and misfits as the new, countercultural antiheroes.[26] Network television, in contrast, was more resistant to change. It was, after all, "an invited guest into American homes," as CBS repeatedly put it in its dealings with *The Smothers Brothers Comedy Hour*, a satirical variety show that was relentlessly censored and ultimately canceled by the network.[27] Frustrated by television's conservatism, some members of ZPG playfully reimagined what its content might look like if they were in control. For example, in "Towards New Images," her essay for the February 1972 issue of the *ZPG National Reporter*, Ellen Peck lamented that daytime television's "birth rate" rivaled "that of Latin America!"[28] Peck, who was a leading advocate of the "childfree" movement, singled out an advertisement for Pampers diapers in which "several children stand over a crib and discuss Pampers, [and] one child comments, 'I'm going to tell my mommy I want a new baby brother, too.'" She argued that the product on offer was not diapers, but rather children, and rewrote the commercial as follows:

> Unobjectionable Pampers Commercial (30 sec.)
>
> Girl: Hello, I'm Judy Singer. I'm president of my town's chapter of Zero Population Growth. For our country's sake—and for our children's sake—I hope you won't have more than two children. If there should be a new baby at your house, though, I'd like to suggest you try new recycled-paper Pampers, because (shows Pampers) they have an outer absorbent layer that keeps babies dryer.[29]

Peck's fantasy rewrite gives us a sense of ZPG's stake not only in the fate of the biosphere but also in women's reproductive choices and the reproductive narratives

24 "Using Voyages," *ZPG National Reporter*, September 1971, 14.

25 "Using Voyages," 14.

26 David E. James, "'The Movies Are a Revolution': Film and the Counterculture," in *Imagine Nation: The American Counterculture of the 1960s and '70s*, ed. Peter Braunstein and Michael William Doyle (New York: Routledge, 2002), 275–303; Thomas Elsaesser, Alexander Horwath, and Noel King, eds., *The Last Great American Picture Show: New Hollywood in the 1970s* (Amsterdam: Amsterdam University Press, 2004).

27 See Steven Alan Carr, "On the Edge of Tastelessness: CBS, the Smothers Brothers and the Struggle for Control," *Cinema Journal* 31, no. 4 (1992): 3–24, 4.

28 Ellen Peck, "Towards New Images," *ZPG National Reporter*, February 1972, 8.

29 Peck, "Towards New Images," 9. On Peck and childfree activism: Jenna Healey, "Rejecting Reproduction: The National Organization for Non-Parents and Childfree Activism in 1970s America," *Journal of Women's History* 28, no. 1 (2016): 131–156.

purveyed on screen. But with the important exception of Ehrlich's appearances on *The Tonight Show*, ZPG was unable to exert any control over the content of television. Like other grassroots organizations, however, it was able to make short, educational movies.

Produced in 1972 by ZPG's Population Education Project in collaboration with Southern University of Illinois at Carbondale, *World Population!* dramatically depicted the history and future of human population growth as dots (each representing one million people) multiplying on a world map. A short animated film, it originally circulated on 16mm film for a rental fee of $3.[30] A revised version came out on VHS in 1989, and the "Millennium edition" has been viewed millions of times since it was first uploaded to YouTube in 2007.[31] A further updated 2015 edition uses GIS software to place the dots and includes language tracks in Arabic, English, French, Hindi, Mandarin, and Spanish.[32] Although not the first film to thematize overpopulation, it has proved one of the most enduring.

More than a decade before the making of ZPG's classic "dot" film, millions of Americans tuned in to "The Population Explosion" (1959), an award-winning installment of *CBS Reports*.[33] Canada's National Film Board produced *People by the Billions* (1960) and *Population Explosion* (1967), and the Ford Foundation's National Educational Television (NET, later replaced by PBS) broadcast the six-part series *The Population Problem* in 1965. *The Squeeze* (1964), a short experimental film about overpopulation by time-lapse pioneer Hilary Harris, won a Golden Gate Award for best fiction at the San Francisco Film Festival in 1964. And most famously, the Population Council commissioned Walt Disney's *Family Planning* (1967), a ten-minute color cartoon starring Donald Duck that cost $300,000 to produce.[34] Intended for "men and women of reproductive age in the developing countries of Asia, Africa, and Latin America," the council distributed 16mm and 35mm prints of the film in over twenty languages for "showings to small groups in the field and to larger audiences in commercial motion-picture houses and via television."[35]

During roughly the same period, fictionalized narratives about overpopulation and population control also flourished. A thriving subgenre of science fiction, subsequently dubbed demographic-dystopian, or "demodystopian," was not only published in paperback but also broadcast on radio and television.[36] Following Malthusian episodes

30 See Elaine M. Murphy, "Teaching about Population," *American Biology Teacher* 39, no. 9 (1977): 539–541.

31 *World Population*, millennium ed. (Population Connection, 2000), YouTube video, 7:31, posted by Bob Gumbrecht, September 21, 2007, https://www.youtube.com/watch?v=4BbkQiQyaYc.

32 World Population Video, 5:46, Population Education, A Program of Population Connection, accessed April 9, 2018, https://populationeducation.org/curriculum-and-resources/world-population-video/.

33 Carole R. McCann, "Figuring the Population Explosion: Demography in the Mid-Twentieth Century," *Feminist Media Histories* 3, no. 3 (2017): 30–56.

34 Parry, *Broadcasting Birth Control*, 1, 89–90.

35 "The Population Council: The Disney Film on Family Planning," *Studies in Family Planning* 1, no. 26 (1968), unpaginated.

36 Andreu Domingo, "Demodystopias: Prospects of Demographic Hell," *Population and Development Review* 34, no. 4 (2008): 725–745. For a somewhat different and longer view of cinema's engagement with demography, see Justin Sully, "Cinema and Demography," *Screen* 16, no. 1 (2015): 133–141; Sully, "On the Cultural Projection of Population Crisis: The Case of *The Omega Man*," *Criticism* 58, no. 1 (2016): 87–113.

of radio's *Exploring Tomorrow* (1958) and television's *ABC Stage 67* (1966) and *Star Trek* (1969), *ABC Movie of the Week* aired *The Last Child* on October 5, 1971, just three months before *Z.P.G.* opened nationwide.[37] Set in New York "sometime in the not too distant future," the made-for-TV movie follows a young couple's attempt to save their unborn child from state-administered abortion by fleeing the overpopulated police state America has become to Canada, where population control laws are more lenient.[38] The narrative structure of defiantly reproductive heroes on the run from draconian authorities, as well as the conservative (profamily, antiabortion) subtext of *The Last Child*, was soon echoed in *Z.P.G.*, the first demodystopian film to be seen not on television, in domestic privacy, but in cinemas across the nation. The name of the film, identical to that of Ehrlich's organization, brought *Z.P.G.* into direct conflict with ZPG.

ZPG versus *Z.P.G.* In contrast to the typically private or family-oriented experience of television viewing, going to the movies is a public activity with a long and turbulent history of political protest, often against particularly controversial films, directors, or genres.[39] Although thematically very similar to *The Last Child*, *Z.P.G.* (the film) uniquely attracted the attention of ZPG (the group) for two main reasons. First, its theatrical release created the space for a direct, public confrontation that television lacked. Second, and more important, the identical name guaranteed that Ehrlich's organization would take notice.[40] Indeed, the filmmakers may have been strategically trying to trade on the growing public awareness of the term "zero population growth," which had earlier appeared on the cover of *Life* magazine.[41]

The film began not as *Z.P.G.*, but as *The First of January*, an original screenplay by Max Ehrlich (no relation to Paul) and Frank De Felitta.[42] In 1971, the screenplay was made into *Z.P.G.* by first-time director Michael Campus and simultaneously adapted into a novel, *The Edict*, by Max Ehrlich. Published as a film tie-in paperback by Bantam and in hardcover for Nelson Doubleday's Science Fiction Book Club, *The Edict* was ominously (and reproductively) dedicated:

37 See Michael Smith, "The Short Life of a Dark Prophecy: The Rise and Fall of the 'Population Bomb' Crisis, 1965–1975," in *Fear Itself: Enemies Real and Imagined in American Culture*, ed. Nancy Lusignan Schultz (West Lafayette, IN: Purdue University Press, 1998), 331–354.

38 Michael McKenna, *The ABC Movie of the Week: Big Movies for the Small Screen* (Lanham, MD: Scarecrow Press, 2013), 69. See further Douglas Gomery, "Television, Hollywood, and the Development of Movies Made-for-Television," in *Regarding Television: Critical Approaches—An Anthology*, ed. E. Ann Kaplan (Los Angeles: University Publications of America, 1983), 120–129.

39 Charles Lyons, *The New Censors: Movies and the Culture Wars* (Philadelphia: Temple University Press, 1997); Samantha Barbas, "The Political Spectator: Censorship, Protest and the Moviegoing Experience, 1912–1922," *Film History* 11, no. 2 (1999): 217–229.

40 Berkeley sociologist and demographer Kingsley Davis is generally credited with coining the term in 1967. See Davis, "Population Policy: Will Current Programs Succeed?," *Science* 158, no. 3802 (1967): 730–739; and Davis, "Zero Population Growth: The Goal and the Means," *Daedalus* 102, no. 4 (1973): 15–30.

41 *Life*, April 17, 1970.

42 An award-winning screenwriter, De Felitta later accused director Michael Campus of hiring an English hack "to rewrite the script" and blamed the hack for making his "serious story on overpopulation" into a "comedic . . . disaster." See Frank Appelbaum, "Audrey Rose: The Author Frank De Felitta interviewed," *Films and Filming* 24, no. 2 (1977): 22–24.

> To our children . . .
> And their children . . .
> And their children's children.
> If any.[43]

Although distributed by Paramount, *Z.P.G.* was produced by Edgar Miles Bronfman, an heir to the Bronfman distillery empire of the US Prohibition era.[44] After briefly serving as MGM's chair, this wealthy businessman and philanthropist founded Sagittarius Productions "to make movies for domestic television and foreign theatrical release."[45] Although filmed cheaply in Copenhagen, *Z.P.G.* was intended for domestic theatrical release. It starred Geraldine Chaplin—daughter of Charlie Chaplin and Oona O'Neill—and Oliver Reed, the highly regarded actor who by that time was a notorious alcoholic, taking films indiscriminately "to pay the bills for Broome Hall," his extravagant mansion in Surrey.[46]

In the winter of 1971, the freelance journalist Fradley Garner interviewed Campus in Denmark for *Ecology Today*, a recently launched monthly magazine out of Connecticut. Garner's summary of the plot carried consistently to the final version and gives a flavor of how the film was promoted in an environmental context, with a doomy telegraphic relay of plot points:

> It is the year 2000, somewhere on this planet. Deaths are clicking off sluggishly. War and disease no longer maintain an ecological balance. World population is increasing at a staggering rate. The crisis is clear and imminent.
>
> In a massive conference room, the world leaders assemble to deal with the nightmare of overpopulation. After furious argument, they return to their own countries to issue the decree: As of the First of January no children may be born for 30 years. The penalty for having a child is death.
>
> The world is plunged into gloom but adjusts swiftly. Babies then in hospitals everywhere are stamped with a sign on their foreheads ["BE": Before Edict] to show they were conceived or born before the deadly decree.
>
> Dolls are sold to women as substitutes for children. The dolls are computerized to make them lifelike. Women are programmed by the State to accept the dolls as their own flesh and blood.
>
> Some women cannot make the adjustment. Carole McNeil (Geraldine Chaplin) resists [with] her husband Russ (Oliver Reed). . . . She decides to have a child, to risk death to keep the cycle of human life going.[47]

43 Max Ehrlich, *The Edict* (New York: Bantam, 1972).

44 Peter C. Newman, *The Bronfman Dynasty: The Rothchilds of the New World* (Toronto: McClelland and Stewart, 1978).

45 Fred Goodman, *Fortune's Fool: Edgar Bronfman Jr., Warner Music, and an Industry in Crisis* (New York: Simon and Schuster, 2010), 21.

46 John Brosnan, *Future Tense: The Cinema of Science Fiction* (London: Macdonald and Jane, 1978), 201; Robert Sellers, *What Fresh Lunacy Is This? The Authorized Biography of Oliver Reed* (London: Constable, 2013), 200–201.

47 Fradley Garner, "The First of January: An Interview by Fradley Garner," *Ecology Today*, January 11, 1972, 3–6, 44–46. Today Campus is best known for his second film, *The Mack* (1973), a "Blaxploitation" classic: Novotny

A crucial turning point, not mentioned by Garner, comes when Carole decides not to go through with a routine postcoital "electronic abortion," but opts for pregnancy in direct defiance of the edict (see Figure 1). The summary continues:

> Throughout her pregnancy Carole wanders about her bewildering world, until the day she moves into an abandoned civil defense bomb shelter in the basement of their home to await the birth of their child.
>
> The neighbors become aware of the child and jealously report Carole to the authorities. She and her family must flee, and they do so under the city through a labyrinth of tunnels, to the open sea, now a polluted disaster, and cross it in search of a new world. They are cast ashore on an island . . . not knowing if they will live or die.[48]

Garner then cautions that the reader can "shrug it off as so much celluloid sci-fi, if you want. But then you pretty well have to dismiss biologist Paul R. Ehrlich's book . . . and ignore the considered opinions of other scientists who checked every turn of the script."[49]

Regularly citing *The Population Bomb* as his inspiration, Campus repeatedly insisted that *Z.P.G.* "is not science fiction, it is science fact."[50] He further claimed that a team of scientists from New York, Los Angeles, and Copenhagen had determined that a United Nations edict against childbearing was the most plausible outcome of overpopulation.[51] At first activists welcomed Campus's interest in directing a film about overpopulation, but support began to waver after a special advance screening was provided for the upper levels of ZPG's leadership, including Paul Ehrlich.

On February 8, 1972, a "Special Report" on *Z.P.G.* was issued as part of the "ZPG Fortnightly Report," a newsletter distributed among chapter heads. At this stage, the film was seen as "basically positive" so long as "a prologue and/or epilogue can be added to set the picture in a positive context"—and so long as ZPG could receive 5 percent of the film's earnings for use of the name (estimated before release to equal minimally, $115,000, or almost $750,000 dollars today).[52] Paul and Anne Ehrlich met with Campus to discuss these issues and to see about offering an "endorsement" of the film. In sum, ZPG's initial interest in *Z.P.G.* had as much to do with marketing and fund-raising (a basic necessity of all grassroots organizations) as with communicating their core message to a mass audience.

Although ZPG was cautiously optimistic that Campus "sincerely tried to make a film that will present the urgency of population stabilization to a mass of unconcerned

---

Lawrence, *Blaxploitation Films of the 1970s: Blackness and Genre* (New York: Routledge, 2008), 62–77; David Walker, Andrew J. Rausch, and Chris Watson, eds., *Reflections on Blaxploitation: Actors and Directors Speak* (Lanham, MD: Scarecrow Press, 2009), 16–23.

48 Garner, "First of January," 3–4.

49 Garner, "First of January," 5.

50 Garner, "First of January," 6.

51 Garner, "First of January," 44. Poul Christian Matthiessen, a leading Danish demographer, is the only scientist formally credited as a technical adviser on the film.

52 Hal E. Seielstad, "Special Report on Film ZPG," February 8, 1972, Paul Ehrlich Papers, Department of Special Collections and University Archives, Stanford University, Stanford, CA (SC0223).

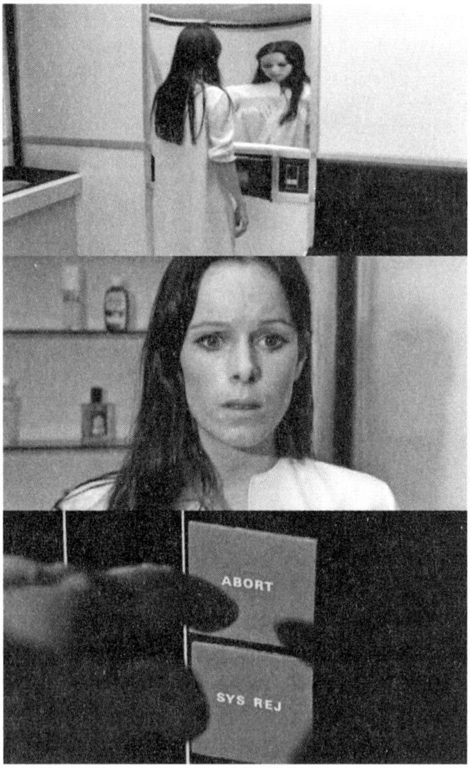

Figure 1. Consecutive screen shots of the contemplated abortion scene in *Z.P.G.* (Paramount, 1972), a dramatic turning point in the reproductive narrative of the film. The novel explains that the "electronic aborting device . . . had replaced the Pill, since by using it there wasn't the remotest possibility of any unpleasant side effects." Ehrlich, *Edict*, 68.

apathetic citizens," *Z.P.G.* also subtly threatened to undermine ZPG's previously unchallenged sense of ownership over the use and meaning of the phrase "zero population growth."[53] Higher-ups fretted: "If we threaten a lawsuit to block use of the ZPG name Paramount may just change the name back to 'The First of January' or 'The Edict,' the two previous names and carry on without us."[54] Worse, "they might also fight the lawsuit and win, proving 'ZPG' is public domain."[55] *Z.P.G.* preoccupied the main, Palo Alto branch of ZPG for several months. An epilogue was scripted, submitted to Paramount, and subsequently rejected for length. Despite repeated pleas, Paramount refused to negotiate over a ZPG-scripted supplement. ZPG then filed suit against the corporation for royalties and over the use of their name, but the Superior Court of San Francisco rejected the suit, noting that zero population growth was a concept and demographic goal before it was an advocacy group.[56]

In mid-February, ZPG leaders finally admitted they had no control over the content or name of the film and changed tactics. Going on "crisis alert," they "urgently" requested the "assistance" of rank-and-file members "to help save our name from gross misuse."[57] In practice, this meant getting ZPG's "side of the story to *every film critic* in the country" to turn "what will already be a poor review . . . into an utterly damaging one."[58] From ZPG's perspective, the main sticking point was the gross discrepancies between the method of population control officially endorsed by Ehrlich's group and that portrayed

53 Seielstad, "Special Report," 2.

54 Seielstad, "Special Report," 2.

55 Seielstad, "Special Report," 2.

56 News of the Superior Court's ruling was covered in many regional newspapers; see, for instance, *Tucson Daily Citizen*, April 4, 1972, 22.

57 "Zero Population Growth Crisis Alert," February 17, 1972, Paul Ehrlich Papers (SC0223).

58 "Zero Population Growth Crisis Alert."

in Campus's film. Whereas ZPG officially advocated "personal responsibility for voluntarily restricting child birth," *Z.P.G.* confronted audiences with "government decrees enforced by pain of death." Understandably, ZPG leaders worried that any association with *Z.P.G.* would be "very damaging to our image."[59]

Z.P.G. does seem to have confounded the group's message. Upon the film's release in San Francisco, ZPG members canvassed audiences before and after a screening, having viewers fill out a survey to assess the extent of the confusion caused by its plot and title. Volunteers asked a variety of questions, including, "What does the concept of 'zero population growth' mean to you?"[60] The results were not reassuring (see Table 1).

As Table 1 demonstrates, the ratio of people who ticked the desired information about the organization's goals—convincing people that they should have no more than two children—fell from around three-quarters to just one-third after respondents had seen the film. The number of people who believed, erroneously, that "zero population growth" meant that people should have "no children at all" more than doubled, from eighteen to thirty-eight. Realizing the extent of its public relations trouble, ZPG mobilized. Members were asked to send protest letters to the presidents of Paramount and Gulf & Western (the conglomerate that owned Paramount until 1994), and the embattled organization sent press releases to "all of the nation's movie critics," petitioned newspapers to boycott advertisements for the film, published a list of venues planning to screen the film, and held rallies at some of the more than 175 cinemas at which the film opened (see Figure 2).[61]

Table 1. Cinemagoers' responses to the question "What does the concept of 'zero population growth' mean to you?" before and after a screening of *Z.P.G.*

Answer	Before	After
People should have no children at all	18	38
People should have no more than two children	79	23
People should have as many children as they want	5	7
Not sure	4	11
Total	106	79

As it happened, ZPG's campaign targeted a film that fared as poorly at the box office as with critics. Although few critics appeared to respond to ZPG's plea, *Variety* did append a note about the debacle to their negative review: "A genuinely serious topic is handled so poorly that real-life orgs concerned with population growth are openly

59 "Zero Population Growth Crisis Alert," 1.

60 "'Z.P.G.' Film Survey" and "Board of Directors Monthly Report," December 1972, Paul Ehrlich Papers (SC0223).

61 Hal Seielstad, "Zealot Paramount Gambles," *ZPG National Reporter*, April 1972, 3. To open on 175 screens suggests studio confidence in the picture: 175 is only half as many as Paramount booked for *The Godfather* (Francis Ford Coppola, 1972), but seven times as many as for *The Poseidon Adventure* (Ronald Neame, 1972).

debunking it."[62] Other media sources focused on the confusion over the title and the lawsuit surrounding it. The *Los Angeles Herald-Examiner* ran the headline, "'ZPG' Film Title Hit by Protest."[63] And *Box Office* wryly commented: "With the new PG rating attached to it, Paramount's 'Z.P.G.' (not to be confused with Columbia's 'X, Y & Zee' [a contemporaneous Elizabeth Taylor picture]) is bound to instigate puns and some amount of confusion."[64]

Figure 2. Accompanying the paradoxical tagline—"The time is tomorrow and there's no time left"—the poster for *Z.P.G.* (Paramount, 1972) includes a cluster of vignettes from the film. Against the backdrop of a crowded planet, the bell-bottomed protagonists resist apprehension by a giant dome; a living child is being pointed to while a robot child is thrown; above, drones circle. These images are a visual précis of the film.

When the film opened at the Astoria in London, England, the medical journalist Donald Gould advised "serious minded" readers of *New Scientist*, a magazine he had previously edited, to make a donation to Oxfam instead of spending their money on the "appalling imitation of a melodrama."[65] Everywhere, negative reviews used reproductive metaphors against the film. *Cue: The Weekly Magazine of New York Life* was the most direct, stating plainly, "The film is a miscarriage."[66] Beyond the film's focus on the issue of procreation, Campus may have invited this trope during his press tour by repeatedly comparing his film to his progeny: "The picture is my child. I have given birth to it. If the eyes are too close together; its nose too bent and it makes too much noise. I am sorry. I hope people will look past its bleamishes [*sic*] and get into what I am trying to say."[67]

The underwhelming response must have come as a relief to ZPG. But despite its commercial and critical failure, the film had precipitated an identity crisis for the activist organization. "What's in a name?" asked ZPG in its fortnightly report to the board of directors: "There is a steady trickle of letters coming in recommending that we abandon the ZPG name and choose something more positive. Since the advent

62 Review of *Z.P.G.* in *Variety*, April 18, 1972, Z.P.G. production file, Margaret Herrick Library, Academy of Motion Picture Arts and Sciences, Beverly Hills, CA.

63 "'ZPG' Film Title Hit by Protest," *Los Angeles Herald-Examiner*, March 29, 1972, B-5.

64 Review of *Z.P.G.* in *Box Office*, May 1, 1972, *Z.P.G.* production file, Margaret Herrick Library.

65 Donald Gould, "Cinema: Zero Population Growth," *New Scientist*, May 25, 1972, 459.

66 "*Z.P.G.*" review, *Cue*, May 27, 1972, clipping files, Z.P.G. production file, Margaret Herrick Library.

67 "His Is Social Conscious Film: *Z.P.G.* Director Blasts 'Entertaining' Movies," *Los Angeles Herald-Examiner*, May 14, 1972.

of the movie that trickle has notably increased. I think the suggestion has merit and deserves some thought from all of you. It is the kind of decision that needs at least six months to implement. Some people are weary of being called zero populationists."[68] Professor Wendy Hearst of New York University wrote to ZPG in April 1972: "Dear people, oh, I was up yesterday at a demonstration at the Gulf and Western Building in New York, protesting the Paramount movie titled you know what. When I came away, I began to give some thought to the current situation, and ended up absolutely furious at the organization."[69] She went on to request that ZPG change its name.

The organization eventually did change its name, to Population Connection, "America's voice of population stabilization," but not until 2002.[70] The film, meanwhile, continued to attract ridicule, not least for its misleading title, and gradually fell into obscurity.[71] Although today *Z.P.G.* is largely dismissed as a forgettable B movie, it provoked a significant public-image crisis for ZPG in the early 1970s, compelling both mobilization and soul searching in the group's leadership and rank and file. In the next section we turn to *Soylent Green*, a more commercially successful film that was well received by campaigners. And yet, as we shall see, it was no less an object of contestation and negotiation at the nexus of science, activism, and the media than was *Z.P.G.*

From Contraception to Cannibalism. Whereas *Z.P.G.* has fallen into obscurity, *Soylent Green* has risen to attain "a reputation somewhere between cult and canonical."[72] The film is loosely based on the prolific science fiction author Harry Harrison's best-known work, *Make Room! Make Room!* (1966), the novel Paul Ehrlich endorsed in 1971 as "the most effective fictional treatment of the consequences of the population explosion that I have ever come across."[73] Harrison would later date his interest in overpopulation to a chance encounter—in the New York borough of Queens in the late 1940s—with a member of the Indian Communist Party: "Harry, you will starve with your writing. If you want to make a lot of money, I'll tell you what you can do: go to India and sell them rubber contraceptives."[74]

In the early 1960s, determined to write a realistic novel about the near, extrapolated future, Harrison went "to the specialists, the demographers and the petrologists and agronomists, and read a great number of thick books." All told, he spent five years in

68 "Board of Directors Double Fortnightly Report," April 1–30, 1972, Paul Ehrlich Papers (SC0223).

69 Wendy Hearst to ZPG, April 13, 1972, Paul Ehrlich Papers (SC0223).

70 Roy Beck and Leon Kolankiewicz, "The Environmental Movement's Retreat from Advocating U.S. Population Stabilization (1970–1998): A First Draft of History," *Journal of Policy History* 12, no. 1 (2000): 123–156; Pamela Ann McMullin Messier, "Dissonance in the Population Environment Movement over the Politics of Immigration: Shifting Paradigms of Discourse vis-à-vis Individual Rights and Societal Goals" (PhD diss., University of Southern California, 2006).

71 Brosnan, *Future Tense*, 201; Gene Wright, *The Science Fiction Image: The Illustrated Encyclopedia of Science Fiction in Film, Television, Radio and the Theatre* (London: Columbus, 1983), 281.

72 Leggott, "ZPG," 335.

73 Thomas M. Disch, ed., *The Ruins of Earth: An Anthology of Stories of the Immediate Future* (New York: Berkley, 1971), 116.

74 Harry Harrison, *Harry Harrison! Harry Harrison!* (New York: Tor, 2014), 271.

preparation, "just digging out the material to make an intelligent estimate of what life would be like in the year 2000 AD. At this time there were no popular nonfiction books on the dangers of overpopulation, overconsumption, pollution and allied problems. But there was a great deal of speculation in the scientific journals that interested me greatly."[75] Quoting from former president Dwight D. Eisenhower's 1959 statement on the US government's position on birth control ("not our business"), a prologue suggests that by 1999, "this country will need more than 100 per cent of the planet's resources to maintain our current living standards," then asks, "In which case, what will the world be like?"[76]

The concern with overpopulation is evident throughout the book. The story begins on a "hot day in August in the year 1999" in a New York City that is "populated as no other city has ever been in the history of the world," and concludes at the turn of the millennium as a screen in Times Square announces that the population of the United States has reached 344 million.[77] Alan Aldridge's psychedelic cover art (for Penguin) depicts human sardines packed in a tin coffin, and a bibliography at the back directs readers to specialist journals (*Population Studies*, *Population Bulletin*) and academic books on overpopulation and contraception. As with *The Edict*, Harrison's novel is also ominously dedicated:

> *To*
> TODD *and* MOIRA
> *For your sakes, children,*
> *I hope this proves to be a work of fiction.*[78]

The didactic message of *Make Room* is made explicit in a lengthy Socratic dialogue between the conspicuously Jewish character, Solomon Kahn (Sol Roth in the movie), and Shirl Greene, the naïve Irish-Catholic love interest of the central protagonist, detective Andrew Rusch:

> "You heard about the Emergency Bill? It's been schmeared all over TV for the last week."
>
> "Is that the one they call the Baby-killer Bill?"
>
> "They?" Sol shouted, scrubbing angrily at the boot. "Who are they? A bunch of bums, that's what. People with their minds in the Middle Ages and their feet in a rut. In other words—bums."
>
> "But, Sol—you can't force people to practice something they don't believe in. A lot of them still think that it has something to do with killing babies."
>
> "So they think wrong. Am I to blame because the world is full of fatheads?

75 Harry Harrison, "The Beginning of the Affair," in *Hell's Cartographers: Some Personal Histories of Science Fiction Writers*, ed. Brian W. Aldiss and Harry Harrison (London: Weidenfeld and Nicolson, 1975), 76–95, 92.

76 On Eisenhower's opposition to birth control provision: Donald T. Critchlow, *Intended Consequences: Birth Control, Abortion, and the Federal Government in Modern America* (New York: Oxford University Press, 1999), 41–45.

77 Harry Harrison, *Make Room! Make Room!* (New York: Doubleday, 1966), 9, 222.

78 Original emphasis. In 1966, *Make Room* was simultaneously published in hardcover in the United States by Doubleday and serialized in *Impulse*, a British monthly collection of science fiction stories. Penguin and Berkley Medallion released mass-market paperback editions in 1967. For the complete publication history, see Paul Tomlinson, *Harry Harrison: An Annotated Bibliography* (Holicong, PA: Wildside Press, 2002).

> You know well enough that birth control has nothing to do with killing babies. In fact it saves them. Which is the bigger crime—letting kids die of disease and starvation or seeing that the unwanted ones don't get born in the first place?"
>
> "Putting it that way sounds different. But aren't you forgetting about natural law? Isn't birth control a violation of that?"
>
> "Darling, the history of medicine is the history of the violation of natural law. The Church—and that includes the Protestant as well as the Catholic—tried to stop the use of anesthetics because it was natural law for a woman to have pain while giving birth. And it was natural law for people to die of sickness. And natural law that the body not be cut open and repaired. . . . *Everything* was against natural law once, and now birth control has got to join the rest. Because all of our troubles today come from the fact that there are too many people in the world."
>
> "That's too simple, Sol. Things aren't really that black and white . . ."
>
> "Oh yes they are, no one wants to admit it, that's all. Look, we live in a lousy world today and our troubles come from only one reason. Too goddamn many people."[79]

Kahn, the mouthpiece for Harrison's views, goes on to explain—as much to readers as to Greene—that for most of human history, people "bred like flies and died like flies. . . . That's why there never used to be a population problem. The whole world used to be one big Mexico, breeding and dying and just staying about even."[80] According to Kahn, this natural state of equilibrium persisted until the arrival of modern medicine: "Death control arrived. . . . People are still being fed into the world just as fast—they're just not being taken out of it at the same rate. . . . So the population doubles and doubles—and keeps on doubling at a quicker rate all the time. We got a plague of people who are living longer. Less people have to be born, that's the answer. We got death control—we got to match it with birth control."[81] The rant goes on and on. When Greene continues to equate contraception with "killing babies," an exasperated Kahn, now shouting, explains the "ovarian derby": "Does anyone give a damn about the millions of sperm that don't make it? The answer is no. So what are all the complicated rhythm charts, devices, pills, caps and drugs that are used for birth control? Nothing but ways of seeing that *one* other sperm doesn't make it either. So where do the babies come in? I don't see any babies."[82] The extended expository discussion—including a disquisition, over soup, on the Lippes Loop intrauterine device—was unusually explicit and provocative for science fiction.[83] And yet, published two years before *The Population Bomb* and *Humanae Vitae*, Pope Paul VI's encyclical "on the regulation of

79 Harrison, *Make Room*, 172–173.

80 Harrison, *Make Room*, 173.

81 Harrison, *Make Room*, 173. On the idea of modern medicine as "death control" that needed to be balanced by "birth control," see George Weisz and Jesse Olszynko-Gryn, "The Theory of Epidemiologic Transition: The Origins of a Citation Classic," *Journal of the History of Medicine and Allied Sciences* 65, no. 3 (2010): 287–326.

82 Harrison, *Make Room*, 174.

83 On abortion in 1960s science fiction writing, see Palmer Rampell, "The Science Fiction of *Roe v. Wade*," *ELH* 85, no. 1 (2018): 221–252.

birth," *Make Room* did not make a splash.[84] On the contrary, as Harrison later mused, the novel "came out too early and vanished with a dull whiffling sound."[85] Interest, however, was revived in the early 1970s—by the Malthusian craze triggered by *The Population Bomb* and, more specifically, by the efforts of actor Charlton Heston to bring the book to screen.

Today Heston is remembered not only for his many iconic roles, including Moses in *The Ten Commandments* (Cecil B. DeMille, 1956) and the marooned astronaut in *Planet of the Apes* (Franklin J. Schaffner, 1968), but also as "Hollywood's most prominent conservative," whose lifetime of political activism culminated in his presidency of the National Rifle Association.[86] In the 1950s and 1960s, Heston had used his celebrity status to support civil rights and Lyndon Johnson's arts programs, but in the early 1970s, he became disillusioned with the Democrats and decisively rejected the political and cultural radicalism of the Left.[87] Heston was particularly concerned with overpopulation, a then-bipartisan issue supported not only by left-wing environmentalists but also by Republican conservationists and conservative anti-immigration activists.[88] According to Heston's biographer, *Soylent Green* was "the only film that Heston made with the express purpose of advancing a political message. The fact that it was a movie about the population boom illustrates how important Heston perceived the issue to be."[89]

Heston was able to push Harrison's novel into production at MGM, but only after the commercial success of *Skyjacked* (John Guillermin, 1972), in which he starred.[90] Initially, he and producer Walter Seltzer invested their own money to have a screenplay written, but MGM was "wary of tackling . . . over-population—no doubt for fear of stepping on religious toes."[91] As Harrison later discovered, the studio had been eyeing his book "as a possible film" for some years, but only "when a cannibalism twist was added" with Stanley Greenberg's script did they give it the green light (see Figure 3).[92]

Variety provided a pithy synopsis of *Soylent Green* upon its release in 1973, one which suggests what were then the most pertinent of the perceived anxieties represented in the film:

84 Harrison, *Make Room*, 174. See Alana Harris, ed., *The Schism of '68: Catholicism, Contraception and "Humanae Vitae" in Europe, 1945–1975* (Basingstoke, UK: Palgrave Macmillan, 2018).

85 Harrison, "Beginning of the Affair," 93.

86 See, for example, Amy C. Chambers, "The Evolution of *Planet of the Apes*: Science, Religion, and 1960s Cinema," *Journal of Religion and Popular Culture* 28, nos. 2–3 (2016): 107–122.

87 Emilie Raymond, *From My Cold, Dead Hands: Charlton Heston and American Politics* (Lexington: University of Kentucky Press, 2006), 1.

88 Robert D. Lifset, "In Search of Republican Environmentalists," *Reviews in American History* 36, no. 1 (2008): 117–125; Sabin, *The Bet*, 189–197; Sebastian Normandin and Sean A. Valles, "How a Network of Conservationists and Population Control Activists Created the Contemporary US Anti-Immigration Movement," *Endeavour* 39, no. 2 (2015): 95–105.

89 Raymond, *From My Cold, Dead Hands*, 223.

90 Charlton Heston, *In the Arena: An Autobiography* (New York: Simon and Schuster, 1995), 476.

91 Brosnan, *Future Tense*, 200. See Dennis Fischer, *Science Fiction Film Directors, 1895–1998* (London: McFarland, 2000), 196.

92 Harrison, "Beginning of the Affair," 93.

> The year is 2022, the setting N.Y. City, where millions of overpopulated residents exist in a smog-insulated police state . . . where real food is a luxury item. [Charlton] Heston is a detective [named Thorn] assigned to the assassination murder of industrialist Joseph Cotton, who has discovered the shocking fact that the Soylent Corp. . . . is no longer capable of making synthetic food from the dying sea. The substitute—the reconstituted bodies of the dead.[93]

Here we have the final, cannibalistic revelation of the film. The oft-quoted line, "Soylent Green is people!," which Charlton Heston's character ends the film bellowing, is a Swiftian answer to the Malthusian question, albeit without the satirical intent.[94]

As others have noted, Harrison's "condemnation of the Catholic Church's policy on contraception resulting in too many people being born" did not make it into the film.[95] On the contrary, the overtly Malthusian message of the book steadily diminished in prominence during the adaptation process, which also shifted the original operating title of the film from *Make Room*, after the book, and meant to signify overcrowding, to banal science fiction staples indicating only millennial anxiety, namely *9/99* and later *Thorn: 2022*. There followed a period of ambivalence about the color of the soy-lentil plankton crackers after which the film is named: *Soylent Red* became *Soylent Blue* before finally becoming *Soylent Green*.[96]

As late as August 1972, the script still featured a police researcher saying, "The sea can be revitalized . . . we can enforce birth control," but that line did not make it in to the final version.[97] All aspects of human reproduction were subject to Hollywood censorship from the creation of the Production Code Administration in 1934, but such prohibitions had largely abated by 1972.[98] Contraception may have remained unusually controversial, but it is not entirely clear why birth control was removed from the script. It is possible, as one critic presumed in 1978, that MGM did not want to offend Catholics.[99] But it may also be that the studio did not want to draw attention to a conspicuous flaw in *Soylent Green*'s logic, namely that contraception would always be a far more obvious and plausible form of population control than "breeding [people] like cattle for food," as Heston wails in the film's climax.

Harrison, for one, was appalled by the script, which, he claimed, "transmogrified, denigrated, and degutted the novel from which it had been taken."[100] On set,

93 Review of *Soylent Green* in *Variety*, April 18, 1973, 22.

94 See Jonathan Swift, *A Modest Proposal and Other Writings* (London: Penguin, 2009).

95 Fischer, *Science Fiction Film Directors*, 195.

96 For the food context, see Warren Belasco, "Algae Burgers for a Hungry World? The Rise and Fall of Chlorella Cuisine," *Technology and Culture* 38, no. 3 (1997): 608–634.

97 *Soylent Green* script, August 10, 1972, Charlton Heston papers, Margaret Herrick Library.

98 See David A. Kirby, "Regulating Cinematic Stories about Reproduction: Pregnancy, Childbirth, Abortion and Movie Censorship in the US, 1930–1958," *British Journal for the History of Science* 50, no. 3 (2017): 451–472.

99 Brosnan, *Future Tense*, 200.

100 Harry Harrison, "A Cannibalized Novel Becomes *Soylent Green*," in *Omni's Screen Flights / Screen Fantasies: The Future according to Science Fiction Cinema*, ed. Danny Pearly (New York: Doubleday, 1984), 143–146, 143.

Figure 3. Unlike many science fiction films of the 1970s, the poster for *Soylent Green* (MGM, 1973) pictures not an advanced transportation infrastructure but the future of riot control. The "scoop" trucks shown here are meant to disperse the angry, hungry, overpopulated mob. Thorn (Heston) flees the scoops, but his neckerchief, the only green in the poster apart from the title, is the albatross around his neck, standing for his knowledge of the cannibalism that is Soylent Green.

he "propagandized everyone in sight, from grips to actors, by giving them copies of the original book."[101] Despite all this, and despite Heston's active support of family planning organizations, *Soylent Green* presented audiences with a defanged version of *Make Room*. Instead of Catholicism and contraception, we have euthanasia and cannibalism: "[T]hat old sf cliché, the suicide parlor. Something *I* would never do," and "[I]diotic cannibal-crackers (not in the book)," lamented Harrison.[102] The frenetic montage sequence that begins the film, which traces American history through increasingly urbanized and polluted landscapes, contains the clearest image of environmental crisis. Tellingly, it was produced by Chuck Braverman, a young experimental filmmaker whose influential short film, *American Time Capsule*, had debuted on *Smothers Brothers* in 1967.[103] But overall, *Soylent Green* failed to visually portray overpopulation. The crowd scenes, as numerous critics have remarked, were "especially disappointing"; there just "weren't enough people" (see Figure 4).[104]

The plot device of a corporate conspiracy to conceal the true nature of Soylent Green crackers did, however, resonate with contemporaneous anxieties about the American diet and corruption in the food industry. When *Soylent Green* was in production, Ralph Nader and his "Raiders," a group of college students and young

101 Harrison also had plastic bags removed from view in the name of realism; plastic, he explained, "is a petroleum product and all the world's petroleum had been used up by this time. The bags were instantly whisked away": Harrison, "Cannibalized Novel," 144.

102 Harrison, "Cannibalized Novel," 145.

103 Mitchell Stephens, *The Rise of the Image, the Fall of the Word* (Oxford: Oxford University Press, 1999), 136–137.

104 Barry Keith Grant, *100 Science Fiction Films* (Houndsmills, UK: Palgrave Macmillan, 2013), 143–144; Craig W. Anderson, *Science Fiction Films of the Seventies* (Jefferson, NC: McFarland), 53. Vivian Sobchack, in her classic history of American science fiction films, argued that *Soylent Green* was "at its visual best when convincing us that small things (a tomato, running tap water) are wondrous and strange." See Sobchack, *Screening Space: The American Science Fiction Film* (New Brunswick, NJ: Rutgers University Press, 1987), 131.

lawyers, had recently published *The Chemical Feast* (1970), a tract on food additives and sourcing, and *Whistle-Blowing* (1972), a conference report that popularized the titular neologism.[105] From food adulteration to the social responsibility of insiders to denounce the corrupt organizations they worked for, *Soylent Green* engaged with themes that were very much in the air at the time and specifically associated with Nader's project.

Heston's character, Detective Thorn, who discovers the secret that "Soylent Green is people," is a police insider, a thorn in the side of a system that perpetrates mass cannibalism. In early iterations of the script, the film did not simply end with the revelation of cannibalism. One draft had New York's Governor Santini reading out a televised confession: "Those responsible for the unfortunate excesses must be punished. However our only recourse now is to reveal to the people the measures we have taken to nourish them and to protect them. Gentlemen—the time has come to tell the truth!"[106] In another draft, Heston highlighted the line "Food was food before our scientific magicians polluted the water, poisoned the soil, decimated the plant and animal life," writing in the margins, "is this a hair preachy?? Talk instead about how good it used to be, instead of Nader polemic, which we hear so much of."[107]

Figure 4. Screen shots from *Soylent Green* (MGM, 1973); of the establishing shot of New York City, 2022, and of the main crowd scene, a food riot shot through the greenish haze of pollution. Filmed from a barely elevated height, the shot more evocative of an ordinarily bustling marketplace than of a demographic apocalypse.

In contrast to *Z.P.G.*, *Soylent Green* had "an excellent budget" (around $4 million), "big name stars" (Heston and Edward G. Robinson), and a seasoned director (Richard Fleischer, who had previously directed *20,000 Leagues under the Sea* [1954] and *Fantastic Voyage* [1966]), and it proved

105 James S. Turner, ed., *The Chemical Feast: The Ralph Nader Study Group Report on Food Protection and the Food and Drug Administration* (New York: Grossman, 1970); Ralph Nader, Peter J. Petkas, and Kate Blackwell, eds., *Whistle Blowing: The Report of the Conference on Professional Responsibility* (New York: Grossman, 1972). See further Daniel Horowitz, *The Anxieties of Affluence: Critiques of American Consumer Culture, 1939–1979* (Boston: University of Massachusetts Press), 162–202.

106 *Soylent Green* script, June 21, 1972, Margaret Herrick Library.

107 *Soylent Green* script. Heston's bipartisan engagement with environmentalism later expanded beyond the specific issue of population to include soil conservation and renewable energy: Raymond, *From My Cold, Dead Hands*, 222–223.

a moneymaker and a crowd pleaser.[108] Newly organized genre fans awarded *Soylent Green* the first Nebula Award for best script in 1974 and the second Saturn Award for best science fiction film in 1975.[109] In contrast to the uproar over *Z.P.G.*, experts and activists were largely satisfied with the film. A generally positive review in *New Scientist* argued that although *Soylent Green* "never really meets the wider issue of overpopulation head-on," it nonetheless has a "tight and sophisticated script" and was an "enjoyable thriller."[110]

Frank R. Bowerman, an environmental engineer with the Los Angeles solid waste program and technical consultant on *Soylent Green*, personally endorsed the "science-fact suspense film" he had worked on:

> I am of the firm conviction that uncontrolled population expansion and its concomitant pollution of the air and the seas is the gravest problem facing mankind. . . . Essentially *Soylent Green* plays a murder melodrama against the background of the burgeoning population. . . . I am involved [with *Soylent Green*] because I fervently believe that action must be taken now to control the unbridled explosion of human beings. . . . There is still time to reverse the trend. With action. The alternative is that *Soylent Green* will be more than a warning. It could become the epitaph for mankind's gravestone.[111]

In his positive appraisal of *Soylent Green*, Bowerman was typical of many scientific experts who in the 1970s enthusiastically lent their authority to cautionary, ecologically themed films about the future to promote political action in the present.[112] Heston, too, remained "very proud of the film and delighted by its success."[113] Even Harrison was half-pleased with *Soylent Green*, which he conceded had "delivered" the message of his book by showing "what the world will be like if we continue in our insane manner to pollute and overpopulate Spaceship Earth."[114]

Reviews in the mainstream press were more ambivalent, however. Influential critic Rex Reed joked in the *New York Daily News* that viewers who did not see the end coming had "flunked Cannibalism 101."[115] Writing for *Time* magazine, Jay Cocks called the film "intermittently interesting," and *New York Times* critic A. H. Weiler wrote: "*Soylent Green* projects essentially simple, muscular melodrama a good deal more effectively than it does the potential of man's seemingly witless destruction of the

108 Anderson, *Science Fiction Films of the Seventies*, 53; Brosnan, *Future Tense*, 205. See also John Douglas Eames, The *MGM Story: The Complete History of Fifty Roaring Years* (London: Octopus, 1975), 366.

109 *Soylent* was also nominated for, but did not win, the Hugo.

110 Keith Howes, review of *Soylent Green* in *New Scientist*, July 5, 1973, 38.

111 Frank Bowerman, "Right on Target," in *MGM Soylent Green Pressbook*, 1973, *Soylent Green* production file, Margaret Herrick Library.

112 Kirby, *Lab Coats in Hollywood*, 172–173.

113 Heston, *In the Arena*, 477.

114 Harrison, "A Cannibalized Novel," 146. On the then-current spaceship earth metaphor, see Sabine Höhler, *Spaceship Earth in the Environmental Age* (London: Pickering and Chatto, 2015).

115 Paul Meehan, *Tech-Noir: The Fusion of Science Fiction and Film Noir* (Jefferson, NC: McFarland, 2008), 138.

Earth's resources."[116] Referring to the downgraded status of the future's women as "furniture," novelist Penelope Gilliatt vented in the *New Yorker*: "The latest Fleischer infection is called 'Soylent Green,' set in the year 2022, and starring scorn for women's lib and virtuous points for antipollution and soil conservation."[117]

Although unafraid of sex and violence, not to mention euthanasia and cannibalism, *Soylent Green* lacked any reference to contraception. As a result, later viewers came to regard it as a film more about climate change than overpopulation. Above all, it is associated with the famous and now largely decontextualized catchphrase, "Soylent Green is people!" In the 1990s, spoofs on *Saturday Night Live* and *The Simpsons* introduced a younger generation to the "cult" film, and today we can not only buy T-shirts and mock crackers but also drink a meal replacement product named Soylent (if we dare).[118] A remake has been rumored for years, and changing tastes have shifted the film's status toward the "best remembered" of the 1970s dystopian science fiction films.[119] Although largely disconnected from its origins in the Malthusian moment, *Soylent Green* has gained new contexts and so become newly relevant and differently meaningful.

Follow the Popcorn. In reconstructing the production and reception of the two Hollywood films most directly indebted to Paul Ehrlich's *The Population Bomb*, our goal has been to extend the historical understanding of population control beyond the high-level intellectual and political discourses thus far privileged by historians of the Malthusian moment. Taking cinema as the example, we have argued that fictionalized and filmed scenarios were constitutive of public debates around population, birth control, and the biosphere. As such they should be an essential part of the story. In so doing, we have followed the popcorn to a different kind of story about the nexus of science, countercultural activism, and mass communication in the long 1960s.

From the mid-1950s through the mid-1970s, scientists became politicized campaigners while student protesters turned campuses and laboratories into "theatres of demonstration."[120] At the confluence of human reproduction and environmentalism, both controversial fields in their own right, population control emerged as one of the most contested areas of research and engagement. As we have demonstrated in this article, it was not only campuses and laboratories but also movie sets and cinemas that became hotly disputed sites of activism as experts and activists alike engaged in public

116 Jay Cocks, "Cinema: Quick Cuts," *Time*, April 30, 1973; A. H. Weiler, "Screen: *Soylent Green*," *New York Times*, April 20, 1973.

117 Penelope Gilliatt, "Hungry?," *New Yorker*, April 28, 1973. On the film's controversial portrayal of women as "furniture," see, for example, Delia González de Reufels, "The End of the American Way of Life: Overpopulation and Its Consequences in *Soylent Green* and *Logan's Run*," in *Reality Unbound: New Departures in Science Fiction Cinema*, ed. Aidan Power, Delia González de Reufels, Rasmus Greiner, and Winfried Pauleit (Berlin: Bertz & Fischer, 2017), 34–55.

118 Meehan, *Tech-Noir*, 138.

119 M. Keith Booker, *Historical Dictionary of Science Fiction* (Lanham, MD: Scarecrow Press, 2010), 249–250. See also Alan L. Gansberg, *Little Caesar: A Biography of Edward G. Robinson* (Lanham, MD: Scarecrow Press, 2004), 257.

120 Agar, "What Happened," 583.

struggles over the control of knowledge about the planet's future, its presentation as fact or fiction, and the very meaning of "zero population growth." Although *Soylent Green* did not provoke a fracas, it was no less an object of negotiation, contestation, and compromise among scientists, activists, and filmmakers than was *Z.P.G.*

When thinking about the science-activism-media nexus in the Malthusian moment, it is important to recall that *Z.P.G.* and *Soylent Green* were conceived, scripted, and produced in years that saw the consolidation and mainstreaming of an ecological movement that culminated in the creation of the US Environmental Protection Agency (1970) and the first Earth Day (1972).[121] This brief, intense period was just as crucial for public debates and legislative reforms around women's reproductive rights. *Z.P.G.* came out in 1972, the same year that the Supreme Court extended the right to birth control to unmarried people and reversed the last of the state laws against contraception.[122] By then several states had already legalized abortion. *Soylent Green* came out in 1973, the same year that the Court delivered its landmark decision on abortion in *Roe v. Wade*.[123] Both films, then, were as much a product of these heady years that liberalized access to contraception and abortion as they were of the heyday of American environmentalism.

As we have shown for both *Z.P.G.* and *Soylent Green*, unless one follows the popcorn, even to a mediocre or downright bad film that failed to make a lasting impression, one cannot adequately understand the Malthusian moment. Grassroots activism around population control was about more than elite intellectual and political discourses. As we have argued in this article, fictionalized and filmed scenarios played a constitutive role in environmental and reproductive activism, and also in the imperative of both movements to reach a large number of people. This makes mass-market fiction, both on paper and on celluloid, a privileged site of contestation.

Fictional scenarios extended activism's engagement with mass communication in the Malthusian moment. But this is not a general rule. In the 1980s, for example, television and video—not cinema—were the mass media of choice for antinuclear and antiabortion activists.[124] When it comes to the always-contested production of scientific (and medical) authority, the specificity of the medium—from 16mm film to digital video—matters. It matters because different media engender different forms of engagement that can, in turn, lead to different outcomes. Today, we still read books, watch movies, and listen to radio, but social media and the internet increasingly structure our public debates, activist campaigns, and social movements.[125] Beyond

121 J. Brooks Flippen, *Nixon and the Environment* (Albuquerque: University of New Mexico Press, 2000); Adam Rome, *The Genius of Earth Day: How a 1970 Teach-In Unexpectedly Made the First Green Generation* (New York: Hill and Wang, 2013).

122 John W. Johnson, Griswold v. Connecticut: *Birth Control and the Constitutional Right to Privacy* (Lawrence: University of Press of Kansas, 2005).

123 David J. Garrow, *Liberty and Sexuality: The Right to Privacy and the Making of* Roe v. Wade (Berkeley: University of California Press, 1994).

124 Rosalind Pollack Petchesky, "Fetal Images: The Power of Visual Culture in the Politics of Reproduction," *Feminist Studies* 13, no. 2 (1987): 263–292.

125 For a review of how the internet and social media structure climate change debates, see Mike S. Schäfer, "Online Communication on Climate Change and Climate Politics: A Literature Review," *Wiley Interdisciplinary Reviews: Climate Change* 3, no. 6 (2012): 527–543.

the Malthusian moment, a closer examination of the nexus of science, activism, and communication would do much to enrich the historical understanding of related fields—from abortion, in vitro fertilization, and stem-cell research to nuclear power, fracking, and climate change. *

This article began with a public screening and discussion of Soylent Green *in Cambridge as part of the Wellcome-funded Generation to Reproduction project. We thank the Wellcome [088708] (JOG) and Social Sciences and Humanities Research Council of Canada (PE) for their support, and Salim Al-Gailani, Helen Curry, Caitjan Gainty, Sabine Höhler, Nick Hopwood, David A. Kirby, Thomas Laqueur, Tom Robertson, Mark Sandberg, and two anonymous reviewers for their comments on drafts.*

The Makings of a Contradictory Franchise: Revolutionary Melodrama and Cynicism in *The Hunger Games*

by JOE TOMPKINS

Abstract: This article examines *The Hunger Games* franchise (*THG*) as a case study for how capitalist media cynically mobilize revolutionary desire as a commercial strategy. It integrates ideology critique and media-industry analysis to examine *THG* as a melodramatic fantasy that, on the one hand, bids spectators to enjoy the act of desiring class revolution in the films while, on the other hand, deploying various textual and paratextual strategies that invite audiences to be cynical about such desire. As such, *THG* epitomizes the contradictions of spectacular "revolution": asking viewers to simultaneously buy into and deconstruct the mediated pleasures of class war.

Marx and Engels begin *The Communist Manifesto* by arguing: "The history of all hitherto existing society is the history of class struggles. Freeman and slave, patrician and plebeian, lord and serf, guild-master and journeyman, in a word, oppressor and oppressed. . . . Society as a whole is more and more splitting up into two great hostile camps, into two great classes directly facing each other—Bourgeoisie and Proletariat."[1] In depicting the most general framework for class analysis, Marx and Engels reconfigure the history of social relations into a "more or less veiled civil war, raging within existing society, up to the point where that war breaks out into open revolution, and where the violent overthrow of the bourgeoisie lays the foundation for the sway of the proletariat."[2]

A similar ur-narrative plays out in the blockbuster franchise *The Hunger Games* (*THG*), a transmedia production consisting of four films based on the novelistic trilogy of the same name by Suzanne Collins. Distributed by Lionsgate, the films are explicitly about class struggle and popular rebellion. They take place in the futuristic dystopia of Panem, a postapocalyptic plutocracy where a not-so-veiled

1 Karl Marx and Frederick Engels, "The Communist Manifesto," in *Karl Marx: Selected Writings*, ed. David McLellan (London: Oxford University Press, 1977), 222.

2 Marx and Engels, "Communist Manifesto," 230.

Joe Tompkins is coeditor of Film Criticism *and assistant professor of communication arts at Allegheny College, where he teaches critical media studies.*

civil war looms between a lavishly rich Capitol and its outlying districts, each in varying states of poverty, where people work to extract resources for Panem's elite and starve in the process. Ruled by the despotic leader President Snow, the Capitol and its destitute territories mirror the actualities of global capital, as plutocrats preside over vast inequalities of wealth and brutal forms of apartheid. In dialectical fashion, the districts struggle to resist the power of the Capitol while the Capitol strives to subjugate the revolutionary power of the districts, and this antagonism persists amid glaring oppression and a militarized police force that masquerades under the Orwellian guise of peacekeeping.

At the heart of this struggle is the titular "Hunger Games," a televised death match between twenty-four teenage "tributes," all hailing from the districts and locked into a survivalist competition that hinges on equal parts brand recognition, brutal violence, and audience approval. The ostensible purpose of the Games is ceremonial: to commemorate The Dark Days, an erstwhile rebellion wherein the poorer districts tried, and failed, to overthrow the Capitol, forcing the revolutionary vanguard underground in the seemingly abandoned District 13. But the Games' true function is symbolic violence in the guise of entertainment, a ritualistic reminder of the sheer power of the Capitol and the futility of rebelling against it. In short, the Games exist to keep class conflict at bay, or, to paraphrase Guy Debord, to manifest a social relationship mediated by spectacle.[3]

Naturally, this same spectacle also makes for blockbuster entertainment, an ironic hallmark given the films' penchant for self-reflexivity, whence the horizon of media power turns back on itself to become its own integrated object.[4] As Sady Doyle puts it in relation to *THG*, the franchise basically is what it critiques. Not only do the films invite us "to abhor the idea that people would watch children fight to the death . . . [while] showing us riveting scenes of children fighting to the death"; *Mockingjay—Part 1* (Francis Lawrence, 2014) in particular "asks us to be skeptical of 'revolutionary' media and celebrity, while giving us a 'revolutionary' blockbuster fronted by Jennifer Lawrence."[5] Indeed, much like Lawrence's star power, the sign value of her character, Katniss Everdeen, is shown to be synonymous with her screen presence: once embedded among the rebels, Katniss effectively stars in their propaganda videos. So deployed, Katniss becomes the Mockingjay, an iconic symbol for both the revolution and the franchise.

The upshot of this allegorical twist is a generally "smart" blockbuster that mirrors the promotional realities of our own media-saturated culture.[6] As the propagandistic

3 Guy Debord, *Society of the Spectacle*, https://www.marxists.org/reference/archive/debord/society.htm.

4 Debord describes the "integrated spectacle" as the highest stage of a spectacular society in which the spectacle has "integrated itself into reality to the same extent as it was describing it." Guy Debord, *Comments on the Society of the Spectacle* (London: Verso, 1998), 9.

5 Sady Doyle, "Mockingjay's Contradictory Revolution," *In These Times,* November 24, 2014, http://inthesetimes.com/article/17397/mockingjay_review.

6 See, for example, Danny Leigh, "The Hunger Games: Mockingjay—Part 2: 'A Smart Blockbuster,'" *Financial Times*, November 19, 2015, https://www.ft.com/content/88ac0bbe-8ed1-11e5-a549-b89a1dfede9b?mhq5j=e6; Ben Sachs, "*Mockingjay—Part 1* Is the Most Cynical *Hunger Games* Yet," *Chicago Reader*, November 27, 2014, https://www.chicagoreader.com/chicago/the-hunger-games-mockingjay-part-1-francis-lawrence-jennifer-lawrence-suzanne-collins/Content?oid=15739300.

maneuvers in *Mockingjay—Part 1*, for instance, appear to reflect the commercial publicity for the films (or is it the other way around?), the franchise invites us to see through the power of public images by, in effect, thematizing that power in the context of class war. This war is then redoubled in the films' online promotional materials, where it assumes the form of social media marketing, viral videos, and celebrity intertexts—all of which end up recentering the role of media power as part of *THG*'s commercial appeal.

Indeed, it is as if the films and their marketing extensions were saying, "We know that you know that blockbusters about class revolution are really nothing more than commercial hype, but precisely because you know this—because you're too smart to succumb to the promotional charms of the films—you can knowingly indulge their publicity." Against this backdrop, the spectacle of class war is made to fit blockbuster hype, or, what is the same thing, the films' depiction of class war is made to shore up a highly integrated commodity system in which, as Debord might say, the reflexive reality of media "no longer confronts the spectacle as something alien" but as part of the very reality that it spectacularly depicts.[7] Far from subverting the power of blockbuster media, this gesture arguably reinforces it.

At the same time, *THG* unfolds according to a melodramatic story line that, in similarly reflexive fashion, dramatizes the system of class relations that precipitate a spectacular society. Much like *The Communist Manifesto*, in fact, *THG* tells the story of an entrenched class system that is composed of ruling and oppressed classes, and it does so, also like the *Manifesto*, from the melodramatic viewpoint of the oppressed. That perspective, in turn, helps to authenticate the call to revolutionary action by locating moral virtue with the rebels and villainy with the rulers while also dramatically heightening the back-and-forth clash between "two great hostile camps," "two great classes directly facing each other."[8] No doubt that clash takes on a markedly different form in *THG* when compared to the *Manifesto*—more "cyber-feudal," perhaps, than capitalist—but it still recalls the "simplified class antagonisms" of Marx and Engels's famous work, the stark dichotomies of which make it easy for the reader to identify class villainy and desire its defeat.[9] Hence "where the violent overthrow of the bourgeoisie lays the foundation for the sway of the proletariat" in the *Manifesto*, the violent overthrow of the Capitol lays the foundation for the revolutionary sway of the districts in *THG*. And where both texts represent class suffering to motivate revolutionary desire, both also foretell how the suffering victims will eventually overcome the regimes of class despotism.[10]

7 Debord, *Comments on the Society of the Spectacle*, 9.

8 Marx and Engels, "Communist Manifesto," 222.

9 Both Mark Fisher and Daniel Zamora have argued that *THG* represents a class system that is more "cyber-feudal" than capitalist, which is to say a system that expropriates wealth by "extraeconomic" means (e.g., military, political) rather than through the mediation of the market. Mark Fisher, "Dystopia Now," *Mark Fisher ReBlog* (blog), http://markfisherreblog.tumblr.com/post/39217506447/dystopia-now; Daniel Zamora, "Rebel without a Cause," *Jacobin*, January 4, 2016, https://www.jacobinmag.com/2016/01/hunger-games-review-capitalism-revolution-mockingjay-suzanne-collins. Marx and Engels refer to their own "simplified class antagonisms" in "Communist Manifesto," 222.

10 Marx and Engels, "Communist Manifesto," 222.

All together, this dynamic of media reflexivity and revolutionary melodrama finds expression in a Hollywood blockbuster that affords viewers the chance to confirm their own savvy relationship to spectacular revolution by calling attention to the very apparatus of publicity that renders that spectacle a branded commodity. In accordance with the logics of reflexivity, *THG* supplies a "morality tale about the dangers of a political system where the wealthy dominate," only to couch that tale in a viral marketing scheme that revolves around—and asks us to identify with—a spectacular "Capitolist" system.[11] Accordingly, the franchise gives us a way to see through this setup—to be in the know, as it were—to cultivate an attitude of cynical awareness with respect to its own blockbuster-entertainment status. The result is a branded media space that bids spectators to enjoy the act of desiring class revolt while at the same time *not* taking that desire too seriously—staging an experience of militant class war that reflexively piques our very awareness of its fantasy construction.

The following sections aim to delineate that process, first by exploring the melodramatic structure that appeals to revolutionary desire in the films and second by examining the (para)textual techniques that invite audiences to be cynical of such desire in the realm of consumption. I argue that consumers are ultimately positioned to engage *THG*'s fantasy of class revolution ironically, in the process of reflexively seeing through it.

Revolutionary Melodrama and the Dictatorship of Class. As a way of organizing revolutionary desire in the films, *THG* constructs a melodramatic worldview that approaches the problem of class structure through the moral binaries of victims and villains, pathos and action, and spectacular scenes of suffering that cry out for retribution.[12] This mode of representation relies on spectacular exploits of revolutionary heroes who convey the "good" of class rebellion while inviting audiences to feel sympathy for the oppressed victims.

In schematic terms, *THG*'s class melodrama begins in the context of the Games. Here career tributes hailing from the wealthier districts (i.e., Districts 1, 2, and 4) enjoy the superior training and abundant resources of elite academies, which put them at a tremendous advantage during the competition. To the spectator, these tributes, who typically volunteer for the Games, appear positively evil in their desire for the kill, and they collude with one another once the contest begins to monopolize the limited cache of weapons, food, and water (the "cornucopia"). Meanwhile, tributes hailing from the poorer districts (Districts 10–12) enter the Games reluctantly, because their poverty makes them less likely to survive the contest. Nonetheless, families have the option to receive extra rations of grain and oil ("tesserae") in exchange for additional entries in

11 Steven Zeitchik, "What 'The Hunger Games' Really Means," *Los Angeles Times*, March 24, 2012, http://articles.latimes.com/2012/mar/24/entertainment/la-et-hunger-politics-20120324. For more on the logics of mediated reflexivity, see Mark Andrejevic, "Reflexivity," in *Keywords for Media Studies*, ed. Laurie Ouellette and Jonathan Gray (New York: New York University Press, 2017).

12 This formulation synthesizes arguments about melodrama made in Linda Williams, *Playing the Race Card: Melodramas of Black and White from Uncle Tom to O. J. Simpson* (Princeton, NJ: Princeton University Press, 2001); Christine Gledhill, introduction to *Home Is Where the Heart Is: Studies in Melodrama and the Woman's Film* (London: British Film Institute, 1987); and Elisabeth Anker, *Orgies of Feeling: Melodrama and the Politics of Freedom* (Durham, NC: Duke University Press, 2014).

the "reaping," where tributes are selected by lottery. This system applies to all twelve districts, but the poorest families are most likely to exchange reaping entries for food, so they have a greater chance of being selected for the Games. These circumstances underscore the class divide that propels the competition, and they disclose a world where "pitting every district against the others" is a way of maintaining class structure.[13]

This structure becomes even clearer in the context of District 12, the poorest of the thirteen districts, where occupants work all day to mine coal for the Capitol and Katniss spends her time hunting game to avoid starvation. Against this backdrop, the destitution of the districts is juxtaposed to the wealth of the Capitol, where Panem's richest and most powerful citizens spend their days "decorating their bodies" and "waiting for a new shipment of tributes to roll in and die for their entertainment."[14] When Katniss finally arrives at the Capitol in the run-up to the first Games, she is awestruck by the "oddly dressed people with bizarre hair and painted faces" whose extravagant resources confirm that they have "never missed a meal."[15] As her character puts it in the first book, a single "tribute meal," which appears "at the press of a button" in the Capitol, would take Katniss and her family "days of hunting and gathering . . . and even then it would be a poor substitution for the Capitol version."[16]

By the same token, when Katniss and Peeta Mallark (Josh Hutcherson) attend a dinner party at the Presidential Palace in the opening scenes of *Catching Fire* (Francis Lawrence, 2013), the ostentatious decorations and extravagant food spread make it abundantly clear to them (and the spectator) that not everyone suffers like the people in the districts. At one point, two "Capitol people" enjoin Katniss and Peeta to eat more luscious cuisine, even though, as Peeta says, he cannot stomach another bite. The partygoers respond with a lavender elixir that is meant to induce vomiting: "Drink it," they say, "it makes you sick . . . so you can go on eating!" Katniss's horror-struck reaction, narrated in the book, captures the stark class dynamic at hand: "All I can think of are the emaciated bodies of the children at our kitchen table as my mother prescribes what the parents can't give. More food . . . And here in the Capitol they're vomiting for the pleasure of filling their bellies again and again. Not from some illness of body or mind, not from spoiled food. It's what everyone does at a party. Expected. Part of the fun."[17] Thus while both tributes (and the audience) have firsthand knowledge of people starving in the districts, residents of the Capitol are shown purposefully wasting food for enjoyment—indeed, they are so overrun with sustenance that they are literally puking it up! But because spectators are located in the same contradictory position of Katniss and Peeta as they bear witness to this grotesque scenario, we, too, are afforded their class-conscious perspective of coming to realize that the true "evil" of the Games is on display here, in the routine practices of Panem's upper crust, who glibly waste foodstuffs otherwise denied to (and provided by) the poor.

13 Suzanne Collins, *The Hunger Games* (New York: Scholastic Press, 2008), 19.

14 Collins, *Hunger Games*, 61.

15 Collins, *Hunger Games*, 56.

16 Collins, *Hunger Games*, 65.

17 Suzanne Collins, *Catching Fire* (New York: Scholastic Press, 2009), 80.

Overall, this class dichotomy winds up rehearsing a melodramatic contradiction that captures not only the divergent experiences of class privilege on display in the Capitol but also the underlying relations of class domination that underwrite the Games. To wit, those relations are inscribed at the very heart of the competition, but they also call attention to a long-running trope within the tradition of revolutionary melodrama by which, according to Elisabeth Anker, "human actions are often dictated by social position" and "individual characters are often the metonymic substitute for economic or social classes."[18] This method of characterization goes a long way toward explaining Katniss's resentment toward the Capitol's "delicacies," but it also helps to underscore how the animating tension of *THG*—the class conflict between the Capitol and the districts—can be interpreted to reveal something significant (possibly even subversive) about the real-life society that produced it.

As Peter Bloom sums up this view in the *Washington Post*, "*The Hunger Games* has tapped a certain zeitgeist of global Rebellion"; its "themes of popular uprising are particularly relevant in light of the current civil unrest happening across the world."[19] Although these themes, Bloom says, take the form of "an adolescent rebellion" against "an 'evil' authority figure," they nonetheless substantiate the argument that *THG* "has tapped the real anger of many, on both the left and right, who see a world emerging composed of the 'haves' and 'have nots' ruled by a privileged elite and their police forces." No doubt this anger transcends the dramatic conflict of the Games, but it also signals the degree to which *THG*'s portrait of class war stages a popular desire that corresponds to the fight against oligarchy in the films. Whether we interpret that conflict allegorically—say, as the coded expression of anticapitalist ideals, aristocratic privilege, a "cautionary tale about Big Government," a feminist rebuke of patriarchal rule, or a series of "life lessons for surviving environmental apocalypse"—it is clear that the world of *THG* is a world that appears to give expression to popular desire for radical change even though, as Bloom would have it, that expression falls short of giving us an actual blueprint for real-life revolution.[20]

Still, the point of the films is arguably not to teach audiences how revolutions happen or how radical political praxis actually works (if it is, they most certainly fail) but to construct a fantasy space in which spectators can both desire the end of class rule (at least on screen) and take satisfaction in the resultant spectacle of revolution before them. Yet the dominant critical approach, exemplified by Bloom, has been

18 Elisabeth Anker, "Left Melodrama," *Contemporary Political Theory* 11, no. 2 (2012): 136.

19 Bloom, "Why the Message of the Hunger Games Films Is Dangerous," *Washington Post*, December 14, 2014, https://www.washingtonpost.com/posteverything/wp/2014/12/15/why-the-message-of-the-hunger-games-films-is-dangerous/?utm_term=.a7178138e7c1.

20 Respectively, these interpretive schemes derive from Mike Doherty, "What Occupy Can Learn from the *Hunger Games*," *Salon*, January 8, 2012, http://www.salon.com/2012/01/08/what_occupy_can_learn_from_the_hunger_games; Zamora, "Rebel without a Cause"; *Fox and Friends Weekend*, "Is 'Hunger Games' a Cautionary Tale about Big Government?," *Fox News Channel*, March 24, 2012, http://video.foxnews.com/v/1527269439001/is-hunger-games-a-cautionary-tale-about-big-government/?#sp=show-clips; Katy Waldman, "Why *Mockingjay* Is the 'End of Men' Movie of the Year," *Slate*, November 25, 2014, http://www.slate.com/blogs/browbeat/2014/11/25/mockingjay_and_feminism_the_new_hunger_games_movie_envisions_a_future_where.html; and Paige Smith Orloff, "Five 'Hunger Games' Lessons for Surviving the Environmental Apocalypse," *On Earth*, March 22, 2012, http://archive.onearth.org/article/five-hunger-games-lessons-surviving-environmental-apocalypse.

to sort through the films' cultural and political connotations in an attempt to answer the basic symptomatic-interpretive question: What do these films really signify about our cultural-historical moment? What are their true meanings, if not "adolescent" rebellion? In the next section, I move away from that problematic to address a different set of questions: namely, What is the nature of the fantasy space that permits such readings to take shape in the first place? What is the aesthetic mode that makes this kind of symptomatic critique possible and thus provides the basic fantasy coordinates whereby we might come to understand *THG* as a political allegory?

Left Melodrama. The answer, in short, is left melodrama: a theoretical category that has been developed by Elisabeth Anker to describe how revolutionary desire is rhetorically formed through the narrative and thematic tropes of melodramatic political discourse. Left melodrama takes shape, Anker says, when the standard melodramatic tropes of villainy and victimhood, pathos and action, good and evil, are articulated in a "left" political perspective such that the two become fused to "dramatically interrogate oppressive social structures and unequal relations of power."[21] Thus, according to Anker, "[l]eft melodrama's appeal derives from the moral clarity it confers on the complex powers organizing politics and subjectivity, from its ability to identify the victims of these powers . . . from the virtuous power it bestows upon conditions of subjugation, and in the case of [revolutionary ideology] . . . from the assurance it offers that heroic emancipation can conquer the villainous source of oppression."[22] In other words, left melodrama's appeal derives from the revolutionary picture that it paints for political subjects: a world divided into victims and villains, good and evil, where the sufferings of the former are dialectically linked to the oppressive actions of the latter, and where spectacular scenes of unjust suffering bestow "virtuous power" on the oppressed and generate hostility toward the oppressor.

It follows that this particular mode of melodrama, which Anker argues is endemic to revolutionary contexts, and more generally incorporates the structure of feeling common to all melodrama (i.e., the feeling for good and evil, victims and villains, virtuous suffering and heroic overcoming), does so as a way to stage scenes of unjust victimization that might affectively channel audience identification with "the people."[23] As Anker says: "Melodramas encourage visceral responses in their readers and audiences by depicting wrenching and perilous situations that aim to generate affective connections to victims and the heroes who rescue them. Using a morally polarizing worldview, melodramas signify goodness in the suffering of victims, and signify evil in the cruel ferocity of antagonists. The victim's injury at the core of the

21 Anker, *Orgies of Feeling*, 29.

22 Anker, *Orgies of Feeling*, 204.

23 Anker notes that the link between melodrama and revolution is well established: "Jean-Jacques Rousseau invented the term *mélodrame* and posthumously inspired melodramatic critiques of unjust authority and class inequality in revolutionary France. . . . One French melodramatist even claimed that his plays organized the 1848 revolution. After the Bolshevik revolution, Soviet leftists created and subsidized a particularly expressionist form of melodramatic theater and film and proclaimed melodrama to be the most effective cultural form to explain revolutionary ideology"; Anker, *Orgies of Feeling*, 210–211.

narrative divides the world and demands retribution or redemption as response."[24] In this sense, the rhetorical fulcrum of left melodrama is the way it moralizes (while dramatizing) unequal socioeconomic relations, "connecting poverty with virtue and wealth with venality."[25] In this, left melodrama allies itself with critiques of inequality (cinematic or otherwise) that infuse the conventional melodramatic formation of "pathos and action" with class-revolutionary implications.[26]

Left Melodrama and *THG*. In the world of *THG*, this critique materializes by way of the hierarchy between the Capitol and the districts, as well as the victim-heroes who experience its oppressive violence. Recall, for instance, the spectacle of "vomiting for pleasure" at the Presidential Palace; here Panem's class division is presented in such a way that audiences are encouraged to share Katniss's disdain for "the Capitol people" (the characters who most outrageously embody that divide), and her disdain imparts a sense of "moral clarity" with respect to that opposition. Indeed, as the luxuries of the Capitol, where "food appears at the press of a button," are juxtaposed to the hardships of District 12, where "starvation's not an uncommon fate" and the "miners are sent into blatantly dangerous work sites," a class system is revealed in which "the poor get the worst of it" and "the people who rule" do so while donning "coal pressured into pearls [*sic*] by [District 12's] weighty existence. Beauty that arose out of pain."[27] Such dichotomies "encourage visceral responses in their audiences by depicting wrenching and perilous situations that aim to generate affective connections to victims and the heroes who rescue them."[28] In line with the tenets of left melodrama, then, these situations culminate in "big sensation scenes" that offer the "feeling for, if not the actual reality of, justice."[29]

At the center of this structure is Katniss, the revolutionary hero with whom spectators are meant to identify and share in the feeling of righteous "payback" once the wrongs of class rule are eventually righted. Her role is both formal and affective in that her character functions to articulate (for the audience) clear moral boundaries between the Capitol and the districts while also helping underscore the virtuous standpoint of those who suffer from that divide. The counterpart to that suffering is, of course, President Snow, who, like Katniss, serves to embody the wider forces of class conflict in the films but whose melodramatic character goes even further in motivating revolutionary sentiment. When Snow firebombs a hospital in *Mockingjay—Part 1*, for example, Katniss is melodramatically too late to save the victims. After surveying the wreckage, she delivers a fiery "propo" (a propaganda piece) that conveys the melodramatic perspective of those who suffer from the Capitol's military power.

24 Anker, "Left Melodrama," 136.

25 Anker, *Orgies of Feeling*, 212.

26 Linda Williams describes melodrama's penchant for "pathos and action" in terms of the "suffering of innocent victims *and* the exploits of brave heroes or monstrous criminals," which have the capacity to elicit "moral truths." See Williams, *Playing the Race Card*, 19.

27 These quotes derive, respectively, from Collins, *Hunger Games*, 65 and 28; and Collins, *Catching Fire*, 131 and 365.

28 Anker, "Left Melodrama," 136.

29 Williams, *Playing the Race Card*, 24.

With ashes still smoldering in the background, Katniss turns to Cressida's camera and proclaims: "I have a message for President Snow: You can torture us and bomb us and burn our districts to the ground. But do you see that? Fire is catching. And if we burn, you burn with us!" Shortly after the propo airs, rebels in District 7 lure a team of Peacekeepers to a makeshift death trap. The sequencing implies that Katniss's speech inspired the insurrection, but it also serves to illustrate the cycle of pathos and action that structures the narrative. Here, the suffering of the districts (the site of pathos) is spectacularly shown in contrast to the ferocity of the Capitol (the site of evil), and that spectacle in turn functions to legitimate the actions of revolutionary heroes. What develops at the narrative level is a melodramatic diagnosis of mass victimization that traces the violence of class power back to a categorically evil villain (Snow), who is then shown to inflict interminable harm on a multitude of victims, who must then perform their own rescue by overthrowing that villain (Snow) and the regime of class power he represents (the Capitol).

Such scenes are key to the story line, but they also accord with earlier canonical versions of left melodrama like *The Communist Manifesto*, which, Anker argues, work to maintain the feeling of virtue by articulating revolutionary heroism to social victimization and by melding the dynamics of social change into the binary opposition of oppressor and oppressed.[30] Indeed, much like the *Manifesto*, *THG* is organized in a way that "moves" the crowd (if not the spectator) to revolutionary desire at the moment "when class struggle nears the decisive hour."[31] In the course of this "movement," which takes an explicitly anticapitalist direction in Marx and Engels, the same sensibility of "victimization and virtue, pathos for the suffering of others, and detailed spectacles of unjust persecution" comes to the fore.[32] In the *Manifesto*, that sensibility becomes the sharpest as the text "illuminates class oppression by molding historical relations into stark binaries, detailing the unjust suffering of the proletariat, promising the triumph of heroism, highlighting the moral righteousness of the oppressed and employing all of these tropes with the aim to affectively motivate its reader into revolutionary action."[33]

In a similar fashion, *THG* aims to motivate revolutionary desire in the spectator by insisting that the "rightness" of the districts will eventually prevail and that the collision between the classes will ultimately end in victory for the revolution. Despite the fictitious nature of this appeal, the portrait of left melodrama that unfolds thus arguably performs analogous rhetorical and affective work to that of the *Manifesto*. Indeed, it echoes the *melos* of Marx's other great canonical text, *Capital*, apropos of which, Jane Gaines has argued, "[t]he labor/capital dichotomy suggests characters acting out a scenario. Wylie Sypher reminds us that *Capital* is rife with personifications of economic concepts, his examples being 'our friend moneybags' and 'dead labor, vampire-like.' The author of *Capital* admits as much and encourages our seeing economic theory as human drama (among other things) when he says that 'the characters who appear

30 Anker, *Orgies of Feeling*, 211.

31 Marx and Engels, "Communist Manifesto," 229.

32 Anker, *Orgies of Feeling*, 29.

33 Anker, *Orgies of Feeling*, 211.

on the economic stage are merely personifications of economic relations.'"[34] Thus, we might consider Marx's theory of contradiction in terms of characters like the "puffed up capitalist" and the "cowering worker"—two "personifications of economic relations" that function, as Gaines says, to "encapsulate conflict and instill the kind of pride that can swell the ranks of malcontents."[35] Gaines sums up this formulation in a passage that could just as well be used to describe the conflict between President Snow and Katniss Everdeen: "In melodrama, the rhythmic alternation works in such a way that the destinies of oppressor and victim are connected (although neither can see this connection and both continue to believe in their separateness). We, the readers of *Capital*, like the melodrama audience, see the pattern of injustice laid out before us, and we are appalled."[36]

In much the same way *THG* invites the audience to "see the pattern of injustice laid out before us" and be appalled by the "destinies" of its two main characters, oppressor and victim. In *Mockingjay—Part 2* (Francis Lawrence, 2015), this alternation crystallizes in the concluding moments of the film when Snow, now captured and facing imminent execution, reveals to Katniss that both have been "played for fools" by the rebel leader Alma Coin. As he tells Katniss: "My failure . . . was being so slow to grasp Coin's plan. To let the Capitol and districts destroy one another, and then step in to take power . . . But I wasn't watching Coin. I was watching you, Mockingjay. And you were watching me. I'm afraid we have both been played for fools." At this moment, the destinies of oppressor and victim become clear: Snow's status as the evil enemy dissolves, while the broader system of class domination, which has been usurped by Coin, remains. Although appearing to champion the revolution, Coin has revealed herself to be a class tyrant in the same vein as Snow—to have deviously pitted the Capitol and the districts against each other in order to clear her own path to despotic power. Thus, the final film suggests that the back-and-forth melodramatic cycle of class war will continue so long as the tyrannical conditions of class domination remain.

This helps explain why Katniss kills Coin at the end of *Mockingjay*. Because Coin intends to host one final Hunger Games involving the children of the Capitol, Katniss is made to realize that her personal quest to overthrow the class dictatorship embodied by Snow must not end with his execution; rather, it has to end the very system of class rule that Coin intends to perpetuate. For this reason, Katniss risks her own heroic status as the Mockingjay to stop it, eventually killing Coin in order to negate the power of the new regime and thereby bring forth a utopian Capitol-less (i.e., classless) society. Of course, the facile nature of this conclusion fails to smooth over the contradictions manifested in the happy ending.

Once Katniss kills Coin, she is summarily exiled to District 12, where she rehabilitates in a pastoral countryside, marrying Peeta and having their children. Here, the films diverge from the books, where, rather dolefully, Katniss acknowledges that "it is impossible to take pleasure in anything," and that life with Peeta and their

34 Jane Gaines, "The Melos in Marxist Theory," in *The Hidden Foundation: Cinema and the Questions of Class*, ed. David E. James and Rick Berg (Minneapolis: University of Minnesota Press, 1996), 59.

35 Gaines, "Melos in Marxist Theory," 59.

36 Gaines, "Melos in Marxist Theory," 60.

children, while "peaceful," is also "a little tedious," but "there are much worse Games to play."[37] By contrast, the filmic epilogue seems to suggest that Katniss is at peace in her newfound domestic arrangement, living in a world beyond class politics, having forsaken the revolutionary cause for the joys of married life. Yet more than one critic has pointed out that this ending feels "compulsory" and "tonally inconsistent with everything that came before it";[38] indeed, it does little to mitigate the revolutionary sentiments that structure the narrative as a whole, and thus ends up accentuating the "cracks" in the ideological outcome—cracks that sharpen the "internal criticism" of films as revolutionary melodrama.[39] Failing to deliver on the promise of revolution, in other words, the ending leaves us unsatisfied, longing for a world that will never come (at least not at the movies).

But still, the epilogue does little to undercut the broader portrait of class revolt that *THG* represents: a world where Katniss is the Great Savior who inspires the oppressed masses to act—the one whose heroic presence serves as an affective channel for the suffering of "the people" and whose revolutionary exploits yield a spectacle of inequality that conveys a deeper sense of melodramatic justice. As Katniss asserts on the eve of the final battle in *Mockingjay—Part 2*: "We all have one enemy, and that's President Snow. He corrupts everyone and everything. He turns the best of us against each other. Stop killing for him! Tonight, turn your weapons to the Capitol. Turn your weapons to Snow!" Like the propo scene before it, this climactic inducement to class war typifies the way that *THG* melodramatically configures its contradictory portrait of class revolution: on the one hand, it constructs a clear moral contrast between an evil villain (Snow) and the masses of victims who vividly suffer his cruelty; on the other hand, it suggests the main obstacle to defeating that villain is the regime of class power he represents (the Capitol). Thus, Katniss's injunction to "turn your weapons to the Capitol, turn your weapons to Snow" can be read backward to imply that class rule is bigger than individual villains, and that the real tyranny depicted in *THG* is the despotic system of class hierarchy itself.

The Reflexivity of Media Power. Because that system appears in spectacular form in the films, that is, in relation to a propaganda machine that represents the dictatorship of class power as something of an ideological problem as much as a problem of individual villains, *THG* supplies the grounds for its own self-reflexive critique. Indeed, where the propaganda battle between the Capitol and the districts that comes to the fore in *Mockingjay—Part 1* serves to heighten the melodrama of revolution in the films, it also suggests a way of resisting class oppression. As that film makes clear, the only

37 Suzanne Collins, *Mockingjay* (New York, Scholastic Press, 2010), 388.

38 Roger Ebert, "The Hunger Games: Mockingjay—Part 2," RogerEbert.com, November 20, 2015, http://www.rogerebert.com/reviews/the-hunger-games-mockingjay---part-2-2015; Kenneth Turan, "Jennifer Lawrence and 'The Hunger Games' Deserved a Better Ending than 'Mockingjay—Part 2,'" *Los Angeles Times*, November 8, 2015, http://www.latimes.com/entertainment/movies/la-et-mn-hunger-games-review-20151119-column.html.

39 At best, we might say that the epilogue renders *Mockingjay—Part 2* an "incoherent text" in the sense elaborated by Jean-Luc Comolli and Paul Narboni in their famous essay on category "E" films, in which "an internal criticism . . . cracks the film apart at the scenes." See Comolli and Narboni, "Cinema/Ideology/Criticism," in *Screen Reader 1: Cinema/Ideology/Politics* (London: SEFT, 1977), 7.

way to win the war between the classes is to commandeer the system of propaganda that disseminates political ideas about it. And so the film spends much time uncovering how that system works.

In the districts, for example, the constant presence of video screens and entertainment clips is intended to sustain the dictatorship of class by transmitting the Capitol's propaganda, including its publicity of the Games. Meanwhile, the rebels in the districts maintain a knowing distance from this official discourse, even producing their own propos to rally Panem citizens to the cause of revolution. The upshot of this tit-for-tat media war is a melodramatic critique of the "evils" of media power that also renders the films themselves susceptible to a certain kind of cynicism. That is, while the setup harbors the potential to situate the power of media within the broader terrain of class struggle—to demonstrate the media's imbrication with external class interests—the invitation to the audience is not so much to seize control of that power as to participate self-consciously in it, that is, to see through the spectacle so as to playfully indulge in its obvious fakery.

Hence the enjoyment to be had when we watch media spin doctors manipulate popular opinion by transforming Katniss into the star of the Games in the first film: because the celebrity image that results—the "girl on fire"—is the same one used by Lionsgate in its own publicity for the films, we are led to assume the position of "insiders" who are savvy to the very same media maneuvers that go into making *THG* a blockbuster success. Indeed, we're invited to see through the contrivance in order to take greater (cynical) pleasure in it. With respect to *THG*'s tongue-in-cheek portrayal of media celebrity in particular, films like *Mockingjay—Part 1* rely heavily on our self-reflexive knowledge of the ways in which media power operates. From that perspective, the films and their paratexts foreground the constructed nature of media images so as to establish a sense of cynical, savvy distance that ultimately works to preserve, by exposing, the artifice behind the hype.

Seeing through the Games. *THG*'s reflexive depiction of media celebrity begins with the first film, *The Hunger Games*, by portraying the Games themselves as a massively shared media spectacle that, crucially, *everyone* perceives as a massively shared media spectacle; and by accentuating the highly orchestrated media maneuvers that go into crafting celebrity personas, *The Hunger Games* reflexively caters to a savvy media audience that is already familiar with the constructed nature of televised reality. In particular, the films reveal how "prep teams" remake ordinary people (Katniss and Peeta) into glorified media stars who are then "cast" to perform the appropriate role. In turn, the characters are compelled to adopt their constructed media personas to attract loyal fans, or "sponsors," who will then pay for the survival items they need during the Games. With the help of their experienced, media-savvy mentor Haymitch Abernathy (Woody Harrelson), Katniss and Peeta are carefully staged, costumed, and made up to play "star-crossed lovers" as the Lover Boy and the Girl on Fire—two characters that, ironically enough, represent the same roles their real-life counterparts (Jennifer Lawrence and Josh Hutcherson) are cast to play in the films.

The result is a form of savvy critique that corresponds to the actual strategies of reality television dating shows, which, as Dana Cloud has argued, routinely foreground their constructed nature so as to ironically "bribe" viewers into making investments in the world of mediated romance.[40] As Cloud describes this practice in relation to *The Bachelor*, for example, the fact that viewers actually recognize the show's sappy, artificial character helps to reinforce its fantasy appeal. Indeed, *The Bachelor* "wins viewers to participation in an ideological discourse by tempting them not only with the fantasy, in this case, of mythic romance, but also with the pleasures of the reaction against taking the fantasy seriously."[41] In this sense, shows like *The Bachelor*, which transparently foreground their mythic status, afford viewers the dual pleasure of seeing through the fantasy and indulging in it, "producing investment through disinvestment," which augments the (ego) enjoyment to be had in its ideological structure.[42] The fact that viewers know full well that the fiction is a "fake" only serves to enhance our own savvy relationship to it: because the possibility for enjoyment lies in our very awareness of its illusory character, the fiction is maintained only because "better knowledge" sustains it.[43]

By the same token, *THG* affords its viewers the chance to confirm their own savvy skepticism with regard to the ideological devices of media power by presenting its own fantasy world in a way that spectators are encouraged to "invest through disinvestment": to adopt the cynical attitude of taking pleasure in "seeing through" the media so as not to be fooled. For example, in *Mockingjay—Part 1*, once Katniss becomes established among the rebels in District 13, she becomes the star of their propaganda videos. At the same time, Peeta is brainwashed and forced to perform for the Capitol's propaganda, leading to a propo war that further underscores the contrived, calculated character of media representation. When Plutarch (the commander of the rebel forces in District 13) devises a series of propos for Katniss on a Hollywood-style soundstage (see Figure 1), her performance falls flat, at which point Plutarch enlists Katniss's

Figure 1. Katniss on the soundstage in *Mockingjay—Part 1* (Lionsgate Films, 2014)

40 Dana Cloud, "The Irony Bribe and Reality Television: Investment and Detachment in *The Bachelor*," *Critical Studies in Media Communication* 27, no. 5 (2010): 413–437. See also Katherine Sender, *The Makeover: Reality Television and Reflexive Audiences* (New York University Press, 2012).

41 Cloud, "Irony Bribe," 413.

42 Cloud, "Irony Bribe," 415.

43 For more on the way "knowledge chains us to illusion," see Robert Pfaller, *On the Pleasure Principle in Culture: Illusions without Owners* (London: Verso, 2014), 94–95.

former "prep team" to proceed with the task of rebooting her celebrity image for the cause of revolution. Following an extended lesson in spin-doctoring by Plutarch, Katniss emerges as the revolutionary icon—the Mockingjay—whose same symbolic usage appears all over the film's promotional posters (see Figure 2).

In this sense, the films both critique and become propaganda at the same time, hailing viewers as both cynically aware of the media machinations before them and thus better able to apprehend those machinations as an object of consumer enjoyment. These scenes thereby invite audiences to side with the films' revolutionary heroes, but on the grounds that we know full well their quest to upend class rule is merely the stuff of Hollywood fantasy: that the melodrama of revolution is all the more enjoyable when it's not taken seriously—when the apparatus of entertainment self-reflexively enjoins our own ironic investment in its manufactured character.

Figure 2. The Mockingjay image that appears on the film's promotional posters.

Promotional Cynicism. With respect to that investment, *THG* extends the cynical pleasures of mediated reflexivity by way of a highly marketable series of cultural products. Beyond the books and films, the franchise encompasses a host of ancillary materials that run the gamut from soundtracks to action figures to board games to happy meals to clothing lines to makeup collections and theme-park attractions. But perhaps the most remarkable series of promotional paratexts are those that clearly express the brand's revolutionary ethos.

Most notably, four online marketing campaigns make up *THG*'s "revolutionary" brand extensions. The films' distributor Lionsgate used these extensions during the staggered release of the films, and each one continues to serve as a promotional reference point for expanding the franchise into new digital territory. That territory includes: (1) Facebook groups that encourage fans to become District "mayors" and "recruiters" of other fans; (2) a website called Capitol Couture that takes the form of a fake fashion magazine patterned after real-life style publications like *Dior* and *Ocean Drive* (and which was curated, no less, by a self-described "Capitolist" and *New York Times* fashion contributor, Monica Corcoran Harel); (3) a YouTube channel dubbed Capitol TV that, during the time of films' theatrical runs, updated users regularly with short-form propos and now supplies an archive of official and fan-generated content for the franchise; and (4) the official website, TheCapitol.pn, which initially permitted access to "hidden locations" inside the Capitol, serving as the de facto social media hub for the franchise.[44] All told, these platforms serve not only to market the films and their ancillary products but also to provide a set of roles and goals by which users can immerse themselves in *THG*'s engrossing brand of class-antagonistic warfare.

Lionsgate first employed these strategies in the months leading up to the debut of *The Hunger Games* (Gary Ross, 2012). It began by assigning separate Twitter hashtags to various marketing events with the intention of making them go viral. For example, #HungerGames100 prompted fans to collectively piece together an online movie poster by digitally "hunting" for fragments across various partner sites. Meanwhile, MTV debuted a "sneak peak" that allowed Lionsgate to launch #WhatsMyDistrict, leading fans from the teaser trailer to the "secret" website, TheCapitol.pn, where visitors would be prompted to register their Facebook and Twitter accounts in order to be assigned a district affiliation. Once assigned, each "citizen" was granted a Capitol TV link with a unique URL, which they could then circulate to be elected as "mayors" of their respective districts. Fans were thus incentivized to keep abreast of the latest news and marketing events, and Lionsgate was able to release new information (under the user profile @TheCapitolpn) once previous updates had gone sufficiently viral.[45]

Lionsgate also relied on traditional forms of movie marketing (including eighty thousand movie posters, three thousand billboards, and fifty magazine covers), but those forms of publicity were widely propagated by same social media platforms that addressed users as active participants in the course of promotion. As *THG*'s digital media strategist Danielle DePalma explained to the trade press at the time: "Fans really became this self-policing ecosystem. . . . They created a ton of social buzz and got everyone really excited."[46] Consequently, marketers like DePalma had a way to sponge off fans' social-media networks in order to generate more hype for the franchise.[47]

This tactic occasioned a great deal of commentary when it first debuted. The *New York Times* hailed DePalma's work as part of a "new promotional paradigm"—"the digital hard sell"—which accordingly "used social media and a blizzard of other inexpensive yet effective online techniques to pull off what may be the marketer's ultimate trick: persuading fans to persuade each other."[48] In other words, the trick was to get fans to enhance the value of the *THG* brand through their own participatory labor. Not ironically, that appeal took the form of Capitol propaganda, a move that

44 The URLs for these sites are as follows: Facebook, https://www.facebook.com/thehungergamesmovie/posts/284136098286739; Capitol Couture, http://capitolcouture.pn; Capitol TV, https://www.youtube.com/channel/UCjvqqA-Eogozfm244OhUESw; and TheCapitol.pn (which incidentally comes with its own internet country code, the "pn"), http://www.thecapitol.pn.

45 Brooks Barnes, "How 'Hunger Games' Built Up Must-See Fever," *New York Times*, March 18, 2012, http://www.nytimes.com/2012/03/19/business/media/how-hunger-games-built-up-must-see-fever.html?_r=0.

46 Quoted in Ari Karpel, "Inside 'The Hunger Games' Social Media Machine," *Fast Company*, April 9, 2012, http://www.fastcocreate.com/1680467/inside-the-hunger-games-social-media-machine.

47 For a more detailed examination of this process, see Paul Grainge and Catherine Johnson, *Promotional Screen Industries* (New York: Routledge, 2015), 160–170.

48 Barnes, "How 'Hunger Games' Built Up Must-See Fever."

reportedly "helped the campaign avoid overt product placement, which tend to turn off fans, and instead let them pretend as if they were living within the environment of the story."[49] With that pretense in mind, Lionsgate took to adopting the role of propagandist by echoing the fictional perspective of the Capitol's own "punitive forms of entertainment."[50] Augmenting this approach were websites like Panem Propaganda, where users could participate in one of the "largest online communities of *Hunger Games* fans" under the auspices of the "Ministry of Propaganda." The site operated in conjunction with the megaretailer Amazon and advertised "a place where you never have to leave Panem" but can buy and browse *THG* merchandise under the watchful eye of the Capitol, "the heart and soul of Panem."

Along the same lines, TheCapitol.pn housed the "Citizen Information Terminal," a registration feature by which fans could file their own personal information online to receive customized "public service announcements" from "the official Panem government." Similarly, the YouTube channel Capitol TV supplied a medium for "mandatory viewing" by means of which fans could watch a bevy of marketing materials that had been repurposed by Lionsgate but appeared as information "officially sanctioned by the Capitol for the consumption of District citizens." Likewise, fans could visit Capitol Couture (see Figure 3), the faux fashion magazine that hailed visitors as Panem citizens eager to catch up on the latest fashion trends of the Games. The site even featured "cover stories" profiling real-life designers Alexander McQueen and Christian Dior as if they were citizens of the Capitol, and it gave promotional space to cosmetics brands like CoverGirl and China Glaze, which both introduced *Catching Fire* product lines to coincide with the film's release. In keeping with the Capitol perspective, those tie-ins were accompanied by detailed instructions for "how to transform oneself into a style-crazed citizen"; the overall effect, one industry observer noted, was "a bit provocative, suggesting the Capitol's extreme wealth and

Figure 3. The website Capitol Couture (http://capitolcouture.pn).

49 Marc Graser, "Lionsgate's Tim Palen Crafts Stylish Universe for 'Hunger Games: Catching Fire,'" *Variety*, October 29, 2013, http://variety.com/2013/biz/news/lionsgates-tim-palen-crafts-stylish-universe-for-hunger-games-catching-fire-1200772931/.

50 *Variety* noted that author Suzanne Collins was "thrilled with the work of Tim Palen and his marketing team," saying, "It's appropriately disturbing and thought-provoking how the campaign promotes [the films] while simultaneously promoting the Capitol's punitive forms of entertainment"; quoted in Marc Graser, "Suzanne Collins Breaks Silence to Support 'The Hunger Games: Catching Fire,'" *Variety*, October 29, 2013, http://variety.com/2013/film/news/suzanne-collins-breaks-silence-to-support-the-hunger-games-catching-fire-1200775202/.

frivolity satirized in Collins's book is much closer to our own world than we might want to think."[51]

Indeed, these sites self-reflexively blurred the lines between fictional entertainment and real-life publicity, not for the purpose of spreading class-consciousness but by enticing users into a mode of savvy participation that allowed Lionsgate to spread its properties across "multiple delivery channels for the purpose of creating a unified and coordinated entertainment experience."[52] Notably, that experience reflected the ruling-class perspective of the Capitol, just as it addressed its participants as self-consciously aware of the kinds of crass consumerism at work in the films. To the extent that websites like Capitol Couture and Capitol TV thus staged the luxuries of the Capitol as a proxy for media-savvy enjoyment, they also encouraged a kind of cynical distance—of "knowing" but still "doing it"—which put fans in the position of being able to simultaneously buy into and deconstruct the pleasures of conspicuous brand consumption.

The Propo Wars Go Viral. In the run-up to *Mockingjay—Part 1*, that position found equal resonance in the viral marketing campaign that was launched five months prior to the film's November 2014 debut. Following the reappearance of TheCapitol.pn in June, the website released the "District Heroes Collection," a series of propaganda posters spotlighting individual representatives from seven districts. Each representative was dressed in a manner intended to reflect the region's respective industries, and each photo accompanied a nationalistic slogan such as "Our future is in your hands" and "Panem today, Panem tomorrow, Panem forever" (see Figures 4 and 5). In fictional terms, the posters were meant to emphasize the districts' loyalty to the Capitol, but in terms of promotional strategy, they self-reflexively anticipated the clash of media power dramatized in the film.

Figure 4. The Capitol's propaganda poster for District 9, the "grain district."

Soon after the posters went viral, TheCapitol.pn released a succession of teaser trailers to accompany the print-propaganda push. These trailers featured an enthroned President Snow addressing the citizens of Panem and warning that if

51 Adam B. Vary, "Five Things You Should Know about the Curious New Marketing Campaign for 'The Hunger Games: Catching Fire,'" *BuzzFeed*, August 23, 2013, https://www.buzzfeed.com/adambvary/things-you-should-know-about-hunger-games-marketing-campaign?utm_term=.uw5gPrrK7#.ioBL3OOqz.

52 Henry Jenkins, "Transmedia Storytelling 101," *Confessions of an Aca-Fan*, March 22, 2007, http://henryjenkins.org/2007/03/transmedia_storytelling_101.html.

they were to betray the Capitol and join the rebels in District 13, they would face harsh repercussions.

In the first of these trailers, Snow sits atop his throne against an all-white backdrop, delivering a monologue intercut with the title cards "unity," "prosperity," and "sacrifice."[53] As the music soars, Snow's speech veers from grandiose to menacing, as he reminds his viewers (i.e., district citizens): "Your hard work feeds us [in the Capitol], and in return we feed and protect you. But if you resist the system, you starve yourself. If you fight against it, it is you who will bleed." The camera zooms out to reveal an ominous scene: Peeta Mallark, who was previously taken hostage at the end of *Catching Fire*, is shown standing at Snow's side. The video concludes with the triumphant slogan: "Panem today, Panem tomorrow, Panem forever!"

Figure 5. The Capitol's propaganda poster for District 6, the "transportation district."

In the second video, released two weeks later, Snow's "Unity" address begins in much the same way: Snow is seated on top of his white throne and flanked once again by Peeta but also by a bevvy of Peacekeeper soldiers and another captive tribute, Johanna Mason.[54] Once Snow begins delivering his message of "Panem speaking with one voice," however, the video abruptly gives way to a moment of static, followed by the surreptitious appearance of District 13's resident hacker, Beetee (Jeffrey Wright). As his face becomes clear, Beetee furtively clues viewers into the fact that "this is pirate transmission from District 13 . . . with a message: the Mockingjay lives!" The seditious dispatch is meant to disrupt the Capitol's misinformation campaign, but it also nicely encapsulates Lionsgate's publicity tactic for the films—utilizing fictional propaganda to promote the actual business of the franchise.

Eventually, the propo wars give way to a full-frontal attack on TheCapitol.pn—first, with the 2014 debut of District13.co.in (as in Alma "Coin"), which was launched in the runup to *Mockingjay—Part 1* and enjoined users to "take down the Capitol" by "hacking its mainframe and exposing their lies." In practice, this meant fans had to crisscross different social media platforms in order to unlock "secret case files" on "revolutionary heroes" (e.g., Katniss, Peeta, Beetee) and then "distribute" those case files using their own social media channels (i.e., sharing them on Facebook, Twitter,

53 The Hunger Games, "President Snow's Panem Address #1—'Together as One,'" YouTube video, 1:12, June 25, 2014, https://www.youtube.com/watch?v=7dCB2U9lX48.

54 The Hunger Games, "President Snow's Panem Address #2—'Unity'" YouTube video, 0:52, July 9, 2014, https://www.youtube.com/watch?v=k4e-qJdEAXo.

Tumblr, and Google+). In fantasy, this also meant that users, too, could participate in the District 13 media wars by helping the rebels overtake the Capitol's online proxy, TheCapitol.pn.

This mission wasn't complete, however, until Lionsgate dispatched the promotional materials for *Mockingjay—Part 2* one year later. With the release of that film, Lionsgate effectively completed the viral "takeover" of the Capitol's online propaganda machine by announcing via Twitter that "TheCapitol.pn has been overtaken" and that the new site, Revolution.pn, featuring a caped Katniss Everdeen standing atop a monumental three-finger salute, would allow users to "stand with us" in the fight against the Capitol. In bold letters, the site proclaims: "There is no turning back. Together we will stand. Together we will fight" (see Figure 6); in this way, Revolution.pn marks a triumphant shift in the tenor of *THG* propaganda: where the online promotions once enjoined fans to adopt the perspective of the Capitol, it now, in accordance with the trajectory of the films, encouraged fans to "join the revolution" and "stand with the Mockingjay." And indeed, they could do this by registering their personal information online as "pillars of Panem" so that they might ultimately participate in "the revolution" by "distributing" (i.e., liking, sharing, or reblogging) online publicity for the franchise.

Accordingly, Revolution.pn completes the online cycle of reflexive media promotion begun by the Twitter campaigns #HungerGames100 and #WhatsMyDistrict. By aiming to commit fans to "build our communities and learn to thrive together" under the *THG* brand, Revolution.pn continues Lionsgate's marketing mission of enclosing this fan community within the promotional confines of a media spectacle that aspires to be the premier model of revolutionary, blockbuster entertainment. Just as that spectacle appears to fulfill that very mission by providing a commercial space for fans to affirm their own devotion to the franchise—to "stand with the Mockingjay," as it were—it also enacts a savvy media message that assures us, in no uncertain terms: "the revolution lives."

Locating the Real Enjoyment of Revolutionary Desire. So how do we make sense of this call for revolution in the form of interactive blockbuster promotion? What is the ultimate meaning of *THG*'s fantasy frames? Certainly its commercial paratexts make use of the idea of revolution as franchise fodder, but perhaps this sort of "bribe" is not just a matter of reflexive marketing. Perhaps it's more akin to the sorts of culture-industry products that were identified nearly a century ago by Siegfried Kracauer, when he described the "stupid and unreal film fantasies [that] are the *daydreams of society*, in which its actual reality comes to the fore and its otherwise repressed wishes take on form."[55] In such fantasies "real" desires get staged even as we, the viewers, know very well that these daydreams are fake.

Of course, those desires remain implicated in the sorts of commercial schemes that go into staging a Hollywood blockbuster about class revolution. But this fact should

55 Siegfried Kracauer, "Little Shopgirls Go to the Movies," in *The Mass Ornament: Weimar Essays*, ed. and trans. Thomas Levin (Cambridge, MA: Harvard University Press, 1995), 292.

Figure 6. The site Revolution.PN summons visitors to "stand with" the revolution.

not commit us to the cynical orientation of *THG*'s more savvy paratexts, in which people appear to desire a fictional revolution that is nonetheless transparent to them. This savvy cynicism, which is echoed in the symptomatic critiques of *THG* as a melodramatic distortion of "real" social conditions, seems to disavow a more fruitful, less cynical approach: namely, that "everything we are allowed to approach by way of reality remains rooted in fantasy," and that, accordingly, far from being taken in by unreal film fantasies, we should attempt to traverse them—to confront the underlying reasons for our enjoyment in these revolutionary fictions.[56]

As I have suggested, this traversal happens not by being smarter than the films we intend to criticize or by reflexively buying into a media franchise that promotes revolution as a catalyst for cultural consumption. Rather, it happens by taking franchises like *THG* more seriously than they take themselves, by *overidentifying* with their revolutionary melodramas and responding as if they really mean what they say. This overidentification happens not in some naïve sense of being duped by the fictional representation of screen revolution, but by pushing beyond the cynical injunction to avoid being taken in by the spectacle. To overidentify, in other words, is to call attention to the act of desiring revolution which sustains itself through fantasy—taking it more literally than it takes itself—in order to force an engagement with "the Real of our desire that announces itself in the dream."[57] Indeed, if blockbusters about class revolution perform their ultimate ideological function—maintaining business as usual—by encouraging our cynical distance from those underlying fantasies, the truly subversive thing is not to disregard the dream but to stick to the desire that sustains it.[58]

56 Jacques Lacan, *Seminar of Jacques Lacan, Book XX: Encore, 1972–1973*, trans. Bruce Fink (New York: Norton, 1998), 95; cf. Slavoj Žižek, *The Plague of Fantasies* (London: Verso, 1997).

57 Slavoj Žižek, *The Sublime Object of Ideology* (London: Verso, 1989), 48.

58 Žižek, *Plague of Fantasies*, 29.

No doubt cynical ideology bids us to evade this desire by imagining that we are somehow at a distance from the "unreal" film fantasies before us. But the problem is not that we are unable to grasp this picture, or that we lack the critical wherewithal to map its symptomatic distortion in Hollywood films. The problem is that we are all the time presented with spectacular fantasies of class revolution, yet we don't take them seriously enough. Particularly in the era of generalized media reflexivity, when promotional cynicism directs us to see through commercialized forms of class rebellion as nothing more than fantasy, we are indeed, all the time, made conscious of the fundamental antagonisms that structure our society, yet we carry on according to a capitalist media system that bids us to live out the dream of revolution as mere entertainment. *

(Dis)locating Spain: Performance Intertextualities in Pedro Almodóvar's *Todo sobre mi madre*

by Duncan Wheeler

Abstract: Building on Tim Bergfelder's distinction between reputedly "open" Hollywood films and "culturally specific" European fare, this article focuses on the production and reception of Pedro Almodóvar's *Todo sobre mi madre* (*All about My Mother*, 1999). Critics have pinpointed intertextual references but have assumed that the Spanish filmmaker draws on "universal" texts to make a "culturally specific" vision legible for international audiences. The binaries on which such a model is predicated do not withstand close cinematic or sociohistorical scrutiny. *Todo sobre mi madre* conveys distinct meanings in Spain as compared to the international arena; this is not exclusively, or even necessarily predominantly, the result of autochthonous reference points; it is also due to the contingencies of reception when Hollywood films are translated out of their domestic habitat. Tracing some of these journeys and identifying various interpretive communities will develop understanding of Almodóvar's craft and commercial success, and also help contextualize and potentially reconcile some of the frequently embittered battles between Spanish and Anglo-American critics over the right to define and describe his cinematic output.

In an article titled "Rethinking European Film Studies," Tim Bergfelder deconstructs a series of well-established and frequently interiorized binary oppositions. Specific attention is paid to the ostensible divide between "universal" Hollywood texts and "culturally specific" European art-house fare: "In contrast to the 'open' American film, the closed textuality of European films (and of nationally popular genres in particular) is perceived to demand a culturally competent viewer, which simultaneously denies access to mass audiences in other countries who do not share or acquire the same competence."[1] Furthermore, "as European films are mostly treated as discrete cultural phenomena, transnational

1 Tim Bergfelder, "National, Transnational or Supernational Cinema? Rethinking European Film Studies," *Media, Culture & Society* 27, no. 3 (2005): 315–330.

Duncan Wheeler is professor of Spanish studies at the University of Leeds. A published translator and author of two monographs and over thirty peer-reviewed articles and chapters, he writes regularly for media outlets (including The Guardian *and* Times Literary Supplement*) and is the Hispanic studies editor for* Modern Language Review.

modes of reception are frequently ignored."[2] This article seeks to address this critical deficit in relation to Pedro Almodóvar's *Todo sobre mi madre* (1999), often considered his finest cinematic achievement. It has become axiomatic to the point of cliché to foreground intertextuality in scholarship on this Oscar-winning film, with commentators frequently departing from the premise that the Spanish filmmaker drew on "universal" texts to make a "culturally specific" vision legible for international audiences.[3] I suggest, however, that this heuristic model is predicated on a series of binaries that do not always withstand close cinematic or sociohistorical scrutiny. In the first section, I trace the transfusion of North American texts into the accented vernacular before, in the second, moving on to a discussion of how and why the actors and characters that inhabit Almodóvar's on-screen Barcelona self-consciously reference prior performances. This paves the way for the third and final section, in which I argue that not all palimpsests are afforded equal visibility, a bone of contention in the frequently embittered battles between Spanish and Anglo-American critics staking their claims for ownership of a filmmaker who, for better or worse, has come to embody "a one-man national cinema."[4] As well as offering a more holistic appreciation of *Todo sobre mi madre* than has been available, I demonstrate how and why the film provides a perhaps unique opportunity to critically reassess the currency of potentially redundant classificatory systems.

Hollywood Abroad: *All about Eve* and *A Streetcar Named Desire*. As Hilary Radner notes, "Hollywood classical films provide a bank of images and stories that constitute a source of cultural and intellectual capital for movies within an international market."[5] This does not, however, imply that films mean the same things in different places; if an openness that facilitates the transposition of North American filmmaking into the vernacular is key to their universality, it issues a methodological as well as a commercial threat to the pristine identity and survival of ostensibly pure national cinemas. In the words of Mark Glancy: "As the study of British cinema has proceeded apace over the past few decades, film scholars and critics have usually conceived of it as a separate and distinct entity from Hollywood. . . . However, it is not necessary to define British cinema solely in relation to film production, filmmakers or even films. It can also include audiences and their cinema-going habits, experiences and preferences."[6] The translation of this approach is germane to the

2 Bergfelder, "National, Transnational or Supernational Cinema?," 325.

3 See, for example, María Asunción Gómez, "Todo sobre actrices: La reinscripción de *All about Eve* en *Todo sobre mi madre* de Pedro Almodóvar," *Letras peninsulares* 16, no. 1 (2003): 277–290; Linda Craig, "From National to Transnational in Pedro Almodóvar's *All about My Mother*," *Transnational Cinemas* 1, no. 2 (2010): 161–174; Cristina Manzano, "*Todo sobre mi madre*," in *Las películas de Almodóvar*, ed. Antonio Castro (Madrid: Ediciones JC, 2010), 211–226; and Vilma Navarro-Daniels, "Tejiendo nuevas identidades: La red metaficcional y intertextual en *Todo sobre mi madre* de Pedro Almodóvar," *Ciberletras: Revista de crítica literaria y de cultura* 7 (2002): n.p.

4 Thomas Elsaesser, *European Cinema: Face to Face with Hollywood* (Amsterdam: Amsterdam University Press, 2005), 14.

5 Hilary Radner, "Hollywood Redux: *All about My Mother* and *Gladiator*," in *The End of Cinema as We Know It: American Film in the Nineties*, ed. Jon Lewis (London: Pluto Press, 2001), 72–80.

6 Mark Glancy, "The Hollywood Woman's Film and British Audiences: A Case Study of Bette Davis and *Now, Voyager*," in *British Women's Cinema*, ed. Melanie Bell and Melanie Williams (New York: Routledge, 2010), 49–61.

study of Spanish cinema and Almodóvar in particular: *Todo sobre mi madre* draws and reflects on an idiosyncratically accented (re)vision of Hollywood cinema deeply rooted in the personal biography of the filmmaker and his country's sociopolitical past.

Following the Civil War (1936–1939), Spain was a dictatorship under the rule of General Francisco Franco until 1975. The Francoist censor and the Catholic Church were more preoccupied with cinema than other media because Spain was a nation of dedicated filmgoers throughout the dictatorship period; as Alfonso Guerra, vice president from 1982 to 1991, notes in his autobiography, "The cinema was the university of life," one of the few places where young women were allowed to go unaccompanied and a potentially democratic art form in a fearful climate with high rates of illiteracy.[7] Period films set in the postwar period frequently make a point of how important the so-called seventh art (a term for cinema used far more frequently in Spanish than English) was to everyday Spaniards, something that often raised concern among the establishment.[8] A published treatise on youth problems by Father Aparicio Pellín expressed fears that, although cinema was a gift from God, "[t]he soul of the young, extremely impressionable and in a period of heightened sensitivity and passions, has to resist with force if he is a regular recipient of a cinematographic education."[9] Almodóvar would confirm the cleric's worst fears; his film *La mala educación* (*Bad Education*, 2004) clearly parodies such opinions to suggest that cinema provides a correlative and a corrective to the lessons learned through religious instruction. A hallmark of Almodóvar's oeuvre is characters watching films on the big and small screens: this technique generally performs an affective function and constitutes a privileged form of characterization. This is clearly the case in *Todo sobre mi madre*, where theater also comes to the fore. Esteban, unaware of his father's identity, lives with his mother, Manuela, a nurse in Madrid. They celebrate his birthday by attending a theatrical production of *A Streetcar Named Desire* (Elia Kazan, 1951) starring Huma Rojo, Esteban's favorite actress. Chasing after his idol's car for an autograph, he is run over and later dies in hospital, where his bereft mother grants permissions for his organs to be donated. Manuela returns to Barcelona, the Catalan capital from which she had fled when pregnant. She reencounters old acquaintances including her son's HIV-positive father—a transvestite given the birth name Esteban who goes by the name of Lola—and makes new friends including Rosa, a nun pregnant with Esteban/Lola's child, and Huma Rojo. The actress, now performing Tennessee Williams's play to critical acclaim in Barcelona, triumphs on the stage, but her personal life is in disarray as a result of tensions with her costar and lover, the increasingly drug-dependent Nina.

Although it is never explicitly stated in *Todo sobre mi madre*, Esteban's cultural tastes implicitly suggest that he is gay: his mother buys him a copy of Truman Capote's *Music for Chameleons*—a book originally dedicated to Tennessee Williams—for his seventeenth

7 Alfonso Guerra, *Cuando el tiempo nos alcanza: Memorias, 1940–1982* (Madrid: Espasa-Calpe, 2004).

8 See, for example, *El espíritu de la colmena* (*The Spirit of the Beehive*; Víctor Erice, 1973); *El sur* (*The South*; Víctor Erice, 1983); *Beltenebros* (*Prince of Shadows*; Pilar Miró, 1991); *El embrujo de Shanghai* (*The Shanghai Spell*; Fernando Trueba, 2002); and *Los girasoles ciegos* (*The Blind Sunflowers*; José Luis Cuerda, 2008).

9 Padre Aparicio Pellín, *Problemas de la juventud* (Madrid: Editorial El Reino del Corazón de Jesús, 1960), 269–297.

birthday, and they excitedly sit down to watch *All about Eve* (Joseph L. Mankiewicz, 1950) together.[10] As the opening credits roll, Almodóvar's script highlights the latent totalitarian kitsch of the dubbing of foreign films from the Francoist period that have remained extant in democratic Spain via television repeats: "When the adverts finish, the title of the film, *All about Eve*, appears on the screen. A grandiloquent voice in Spanish says, '*Eva al desnudo*.'"[11] Esteban comments that the translation of the film title into Spanish—*Eva al desnudo*—is incorrect: in his view it ought to be *Todo sobre Eva*. This is a fairly innocent example of potential linguistic slippage, but as Almodóvar has noted, the Franco regime attempted to control and distort at least some of the cinematic messages in an attempt to infantilize Spanish viewers.[12] In the case of *Eva al desnudo*, the line "Are you two lovers?" was dubbed as "¿Son ustedes amigos?" (Are you two friends?).[13]

In general, however, *All about Eve* experienced far more problems with censors in the United States than it did in Spain.[14] It premiered amid much fanfare at Madrid's central Callao on April 12, 1952. Mankiewicz, who himself began in the industry providing subtitles for the intertitles of foreign cinematic texts, has frequently remarked on the merits of his cinematic wanderings: "My films—particularly those I write as well as direct—seem to lose something in the original English."[15] Almodóvar effectively capitalizes on this humorous, off-the-cuff remark by incorporating not only the Hollywood film but also its European afterlife into *Todo sobre mi madre*'s intertextual universe. In Spain, *All about Eve* was screened for the first time in *versión original* (original version) with subtitles when it was given a high-profile rerelease in 1985; nevertheless, the dubbed iteration was screened on Spanish television the following year.[16] Beyond its continued popularity among cinephiles and the general public, the film—as in many other countries—accrued a loyal gay following.[17] On traveling to Paris for the

10 As Stephen Maddison notes of *Todo sobre mi madre*, it "is practically a lexicon of camp allusions and queer iconic references"; unlike earlier films, however, it is, to borrow a phrase from Patrick Paul Garlinger, "not a camp film but a film *about* camp." Maddison, "All about Women: Pedro Almodóvar and the Heterosexual Dynamic," *Textual Practices* 14, no. 2 (2000): 265–284; Patrick Paul Garlinger, "All about Agrado, or the Sincerity of Camp in Almodóvar's *Todo sobre mi madre*," *Journal of Spanish Cultural Studies* 5, no. 1 (2004): 117–134.

11 Pedro Almodóvar, *Todo sobre mi madre / Tout sur ma mère* (Paris: Petite bibliothèque des Cahiers du cinéma, Scénario bilingue, 1999).

12 See, for example, his discussion with Maria Delgado at the BFI on January 11, 2015, at the screening of a new print of *Mujeres al borde de un ataque de nervios* about how and why he made two of the central characters in the film specialists in dubbing. The best-documented source of information on this process is the following unpublished doctoral thesis: María del Camino Gutiérrez Lanza, "Traducción y censura de textos cinematográfico en la España de Franco: Doblaje y subtitulado inglés-español (1951–1975)" (PhD diss., University of León, 1999).

13 Alejandro Ávila, *La censura del doblaje cinematográfico en España* (Barcelona: Editorial CIMS), 80.

14 Sam Stagg, *"All about Eve": The Complete behind the Scenes Story of the Bitchiest Film Ever Made* (New York: St. Martin's Press, 2000), 52–57.

15 Gary Carey and Joseph L. Mankiewicz, *More about "All About Eve"* (New York: Random House, 1972), 99.

16 Ángel Fernández Santos, "El cine en la pequeña pantalla," *El País*, March 27, 1986.

17 In 1991, the director Juan Antonio Bardem was among the speakers at a high-profile Cinema and Literature summer course centered on the film, held in El Escorial. Fernando Trueba, the Oscar-winning director of *Belle Epoque* (*The Age of Beauty*, 1992), for example, has written the following: "In its day, *All about Eve* upped the mental co-efficient of cinema to levels that it had hitherto been unknown it could even aspire. If we compare it with the films that are now exhibited in any "civilized" city, the abyss between them is even more marked." Trueba, *Mi diccionario de cine* (Barcelona: Galaxis Gutenberg, 2006), 136.

first time to visit an older lover in the early 1960s, Terenci Moix—a cultural critic and Spain's self-elected custodian of camp—recalls that one of the most indelible discoveries was the ability to attend screenings of films from Hollywood's golden age. Singling out Mankiewicz's classic for special attention, he notes in his memoirs how "[t]he projection of *All about Eve* took place amidst the passion of the cinephiles and the delirium of the poofs fully committed to the worship of Bette Davis."[18]

The 1970 Broadway production *Applause*—based on the source text for *All about Eve*, Mary Orr's short story *The Wisdom of Eve*, because the rights to the latter were much cheaper than to the former—was, according to Bruce Kirle, "the musical most directly influenced by the Stonewall riots."[19] Staged in Madrid as *Aplausos* in Madrid in 1975, it was, alongside *Jesus Christ Superstar*, a popular phenomenon that firmly established the Anglo-American musical in Spain for the first time. Evidence of continued local inflection can, however, be detected in the choice of casting. The camp aesthete Addison Witt was played by Alfredo Mayo, whom filmmaker Carlos Saura had previously cast as a frustrated and brutalized middle-aged man in *La caza* (*The Hunt*, 1966), in part to deconstruct the actor's earlier heroic roles such as the figure representing the dictator in *Raza* (*Race*; José Luis Sáenz de Heredia, 1942), a film scripted by Franco himself. Conchita Márques—Eva Perón's goddaughter, whose mother was Concha Piquer, Spain's leading singer of *coplas* and who spent much of the early 1920s as a teenage Broadway star—took the role of the eponymous villain. Sharply attuned from a young age to the vagaries and connotations of popular culture, Almodóvar, who arrived in the capital from his native La Mancha in 1968, could hardly have been unaware of these various intertexts.

The pedagogical and psychological importance of cinema was one of the defining authorial stamps of Almodóvar's oeuvre from even before he made his first full-length film, *Pepi, Luci, Bom y otras chicas del montón* (*Pepi, Luci, Bom, and Other Girls like Mom*, 1980). In "Relato superficial de la vida de Miguel" (The Superficial Tale of Miguel's Life, 1975), an early short story contained in the collection *Relatos* (*Tales*) that predates his cinematic debut, "Miguel evokes his adolescence and a summer vacation with his relatives in a small village: a summer full of sex and films 'based on sordid tales from Tennessee Williams,' with Liz Taylor or Natalie Wood. He felt that they perverted him, little by little."[20] This prose homage to cinema is echoed in Almodóvar's subsequent labor in *Todo sobre mi madre*, as he himself notes: "The film is as autobiographical as any about a director from La Mancha who has just won an Oscar. *All about My Mother* even talks about the way I became a spectator, and about how I became a film-maker. I like to think that my education as a spectator was formed by films adapted from works by Tennessee Williams, notably *A Streetcar Named Desire*. Desire—'El Deseo,' in Spanish—is the name of our production company; it's the key word in the title of one

18 Terenci Moix, *El beso de Peter Pan* (Barcelona: Planeta, 2003), 610.

19 Stagg, "*All about Eve*," 284–290; Bruce Kirle, *Unfinished Business: Broadway Musicals as Works in Progress* (Carbondale: Southern Illinois University Press, 2005), 191.

20 Francisco A. Zurián, "Creative Beginnings in Almodóvar's Work," in *A Companion to Pedro Almodóvar*, ed. Marvin D'Lugo and Kathleen M. Vernon (Chichester, UK: Wiley-Blackwell, 2013), 39–58, 49.

of my films, and desire itself is present in all of the others."[21] *Todo sobre mi madre* also mimics the film adaptation of *A Streetcar Named Desire* in its resistance to fixity as regards translation across artistic media and national borders as Almodóvar reflects (on) how and why reception cannot be bracketed off from the ostensibly intrinsic meaning of a preexisting work. Kazan's film faced problems from both the censorship board of the Motion Picture Association of America (MPAA) and the Legion of Decency. Opinions vary as to the effect of the cuts both mandated, but it is a useful reminder that Francoist Spain was hardly an isolated example of censorship in the postwar period.[22]

Williams's play had been successfully staged in London and New York before Kazan decided to make a film adaption starring many of the same actors from the Broadway production. As in Spain, North American legislators subscribed to the philosophy that different rules pertained to the screen than to the stage. In Gene D. Phillips's account:

> The industry censor, Joseph Breen, was worried that a play that was quite acceptable on the stage would not be an appropriate film project. As the official administrator of the Code of the Motion Picture Association (MPAA), he wrote to Irene Mayer Selznick, who has produced the play on the stage and was considering the possibility of a movie version, that the provision of the Production Code presumed that "motion pictures, unlike stage plays, appealed to mass audiences, the mature and the immature." In fact, the Production code contained a section declaring that "everything possible in a play is not possible in a film" because motion pictures command a mass audience, and "the larger the audience, the lower the moral resistance to suggestion."[23]

The two major points of contention were Stanley's rape of Blanche and references to her ex-husband's homosexuality. Williams was willing to compromise on the latter, but not the former. Kazan attempted to circumvent the first objection by using ellipsis and symbolism to depict the rape; Breen was not satisfied, however, and insisted that Stanley be punished for his lust. Consequently, his wife leaves him in the film, whereas in Williams's play text, Stella, however perturbed by the situation, tacitly sides with her husband by allowing her sister to be taken away by doctors, presumably to an asylum.[24] Stanley responds to Blanche's departure by continuing to play cards before

21 Cited in Frederic Strauss, ed., *Almodóvar on Almodóvar*, trans. Yves Baignères, 2nd ed. (London: Faber and Faber, 2006), 204.

22 Ellen Dowling, for example, has written: "In my opinion, the censored version of *Streetcar*, while perhaps sparing some "innocents" from offense, does indeed "frustrate" the intelligent viewer." Dowling, "The Derailment of *A Streetcar Named Desire*," *Literature/Film Quarterly* 9, no. 4 (1981): 233–240. Although accepting that all the indications suggested this would be the case, Linda Constanza Cahir has argued precisely the opposite: "These cuts could have crippled the movie, reducing it to melodrama, diminished Blanche, and emptied characters of their most compelling and complex motivations. Instead, the film's . . . changes that Kazan and Williams knew to be painfully inappropriate, are worked to enrich the film by appropriately dislodging it from Williams's play." Constanza Cahir, "The Artful Re-Routing of *A Streetcar Named Desire*," *Literature/Film Quarterly* 22, no. 2 (1994): 72–77.

23 Gene D. Phillips, *The Films of Tennessee Williams* (London: Associated University Press, 1980), 81.

24 Phillips, *Films of Tennessee Williams*, 85. For a detailed account of the film's problems with the censor, see also Brian Neve, *Elia Kazan: The Cinema of an American Outsider* (London: I. B. Taurus, 2009), 33–45.

"he kneels beside her and his fingers find the opening of her blouse."[25] In other words, the play, unlike the cinematic adaptation, lays bare how and why Blanche is sacrificed to the perverse dictates of compulsive heteronormativity.

Kazan's film received a seal of approval from the Code Commission, but the Legion of Decency, which rated the suitability for its Catholic subscribers, advised Warner Bros. that *A Streetcar Named Desire* would receive a C (condemned) rating, and this led to a further twelve cuts, amounting to a total of four minutes.[26] In an example of the paternalism of Spanish censorial practices, a one-off screening of a cinematic adaptation of a play that had yet to be approved for the stage was allowed for an invited audience in 1951, but Kazan's film then faced serious problems when it was slated for a general release in 1952.[27] In his report, the censor José María Sánchez-Silva argued that "the extraordinary artistic and literary qualities of this film—provocative but not in my opinion immoral—have made me think that it could be shown in Spain if all due precautions are taken. It ought to be screened for over-eighteens only and with a warning that, EVEN IN THE HEALTHIEST COUNTRY IN THE WORLD it could be frankly dangerous for those spectators who do not fully grasp a plot about sick lives and souls. Nevertheless, it could be a good thing that Spanish viewers have the opportunity to contemplate certain aspects of life in North America."[28] In spite of this tentative individual approval, the general Censorship Commission decided upon viewing the film on June 30, 1952, that it should not be imported to Spain.

This was not the first time Kazan had faced problems with the Spanish censor. Despite being, or perhaps even because it was, the year's highest-grossing film at the North American box office, his *Gentleman's Agreement* (1947) had been banned on the charge of heresy; this caused controversy back home when the *New York Times* ran an article condemning Spanish attitudes. This, in turn, prompted a response from Spain's director general of cinematography, who, through the US embassy in Madrid, claimed that racism was not an issue in Spain and that they were not thus interested in such sordid aspects of North American life.[29] On the one hand, the censorship office were likely predisposed to view *A Streetcar Named Desire* with suspicion; on the other hand, the escalation of the Cold War, and the Franco regime's long-standing vocal opposition to communism, ensured that the US increasingly looked favorably upon Spain as a potential ally. An era of rapprochement was not without its tensions. In the cinematic realm, relations between the MPAA and the Spanish government entered a new, more conflict-riven phase between 1955 and 1957, as the former wanted to exert the kind of control over the type and number of Hollywood films released as it did

25 Tennessee Williams, *"A Streetcar Named Desire" and Other Plays* (London: Penguin Classics, 2000), 226.

26 Phillips, *Films of Tennessee Williams*, 87.

27 Román Gubern, *La censura: Función política y ordenamiento jurídico bajo el franquismo (1936–1975)* (Barcelona: Ediciones Península, 1981), 127.

28 Taken from reports contained in the administration's General Archive in Alcalá de Henares, box 36/03433. All translations are my own unless otherwise noted.

29 Eva Woods Peiró, *White Gypsies: Race and Stardom in Spanish Musicals* (Minneapolis: University of Minnesota Press, 2012), 3–4.

elsewhere in Europe.[30] Somewhat ironically, given the problems it had experienced at home, *A Streetcar Named Desire* would constitute a high-profile litmus test for North American soft power and Spanish malleability.

In a letter dated March 3, 1956, the film's distribution company, Warner Bros., implicitly threatened the Spanish government by stating that, taking into account the film's multiple Oscar wins, the continued prohibition of *A Streetcar Named Desire* could be interpreted as an attack on North American values. Offering a somewhat hypocritically anodyne interpretation of the narrative, they asked what possible objection could be leveled against "the story of a woman who becomes mentally disturbed as a result of losing her beloved husband and son in the war."[31] The argument was persuasive. A censorship board unanimously agreed it could be shown without cuts, despite noting that a censored version had been insisted on in both Canada and the Netherlands.[32]

Although no edits were made, dubbing once again allowed for a covert form of censorship. A note in a student film magazine, *Cinema universitario*, complained that "prostitute" was dubbed as "*extravagante*" (extravagant); the novelist Terenci Moix, who was first drawn into writing through translation, recalls how he "spent whole days translating Blanche DuBois's dialogue in an attempt to recuperate the original meaning that had been sequestrated by the censors."[33] As late as 1974, Hispanex's request to rerelease the film in Spain was conditional on admission being limited to adults and a dubbed, as opposed to a subtitled, version being screened.[34]

The belated opening of *A Streetcar Named Desire* only served to increase expectations and interest. According to the trade magazine *Cine asesor*, "The huge diffusion that this title has had in both magazines and newspapers alongside the names of the actors and the prestigious awards it has won, will be more than enough to ensure that the film's premiere will be eagerly awaited."[35] It was awarded the ecclesiastical rating of *3R Rosa fuerte* (Vibrant red), which indicated that the film was highly unsuitable for minors without entering into the *Grana* (Crimson Red) category, which would have meant it was unequivocally dangerous.[36] Its rating likely attracted at least as many spectators as it served to detract. Publicity materials sought to maximize the sensational shock value with proclamations such as the following: "At last, the most violent characters ever to be shown on-screen: at last, the seventh art's most vigorous and crushing actors. After playing her role in *A Streetcar Named Desire*, the famous actress Vivien Leigh needed help over a serious crisis of her nerves: that's how powerful her character is."[37] Spanish audiences experienced *A Streetcar Named Desire* on the screen before its arrival on the national stage, an instrumental factor in the play having an autonomous afterlife in

30 Pablo León Aguinaga, *Sospechosos habituales: El cine norteamericano, Estados Unidos y la España franquista, 1939–1960* (Madrid: Consejo Superior de Investigaciones Científicas, 2010), 297, 334.

31 Box 36/03433, General Archive.

32 Box 36/03433, General Archive.

33 "Aviso a la Real Academia Española," *Cinema universitario* 4 (December 1956): 3; Moix, *El beso de Peter Pan*, 318.

34 Box 36/04475, General Archive.

35 "*Un tranvía llamado deseo*," *Cine Asesor*, no. 1262 (1956), n.p.

36 Gutiérrez Lanza, "Traducción y censura de textos cinematográfico," 70.

37 "*Un tranvía llamado deseo.*"

Almodóvar's homeland in relation to its reception in the United Kingdom or United States. The first Spanish theatrical production of *A Streetcar Named Desire*, based on a translation by José Méndez Herrera and directed by Alberto González Vergel, premiered at Madrid's Reina Victoria in 1961. According to at least one contemporary review, it functioned as an antidote to the softened film version: "The Spanish stage has offered us an unrelenting version, which is very hard and has the asphyxiating whiff of a cloistered chamber."[38] This version did not, however, prove popular with audiences; it closed before reaching one hundred performances.[39] The play would not be revived for the professional stage until 1994; the production, under the direction of José Tamayo, would open at Madrid's Teatro Bellas Artes—perhaps not coincidentally the site chosen by Almodóvar for the Madrid production of the play in *Todo sobre mi madre*. This absence of a substantial performance tradition does not imply that Williams is not a canonical author in Spain.[40] Rather, the film version of *A Streetcar Named Desire*, which remains a popular classic, cast too heavy a shadow for Williams's play to have as much impact; as one review of the Tamayo production noted: "The bar was set too high and the celluloid version was so popular that nobody amongst us dared to stage it."[41]

Urban and Performance Palimpsests. At the time of writing, *Todo sobre mi madre* is the only Almodóvar film in which a departure from Madrid indicates a move to an urban as opposed to a rural setting—the international air space of *Los amantes pasajeros* (*I'm So Excited!*, 2013) notwithstanding. A challenge for a director with international ambitions—and indeed for a remarkably centralist national cinema—is that the Spanish capital lacks an iconic urban topography. The city's principal landmark, the Puerta de Alcalá, is no match for the Sagrada Familia, which, as Robert Hughes notes, "is to Barcelona what the Eiffel Tower is to Paris or the Harbour Bridge to Sydney: a completely irreplaceable logo."[42] If a kitsch recasting of Gaudí's unfinished masterpiece in *Matador* (Pedro Almodóvar, 1986) provides the backdrop for a postmodern diegetic catwalk in a Madrid-based fashion show, the architectural monument provides a privileged gateway in *Todo sobre mi madre* to the Catalan capital in both narrative and promotional terms. As Mariana Liz observes:

> Barcelona is introduced by a spectacular aerial view of the city. Ismaël Lô's "Tajabone" song begins as a soft guitar while the film's protagonist Manuela (Cecilia Roth) is on a train. As the harmonica is played and the music's

38 Ángulo, "Estreno de *Un tranvia llamado deseo* en el Reino Victoria," *La Vanguardia española*, January 20, 1961, 6.

39 Paloma Cuesta Martínez, *Comunicación dramática y público: El teatro en España (1960–1969)* (Madrid: Universidad Complutense de Madrid, Colección Tesis Doctorales, 1988), 102.

40 Other plays by Williams such as *The Glass Menagerie* and *Talk to Me like the Rain and Let Me Listen* have been performed with a certain regularity on the Spanish stage—it a sign of the playwright's standing in Catalonia that *Cat on a Hot Tin Roof* was chosen to reopen the refurbished emblematic Lliure theater in Barcelona's Grácia area. See Maria Delgado, "Relocations, Re-Workings, Re-Openings: Catalans in Madrid, Argentines in Barcelona," *Western European Stages* 23, no. 2 (2011): 13–30.

41 Enrique Centero, "Un mito americano," *Diario 16*, October 2, 1993. For example, I was unable to attend a large outdoor screening at the pop-up outdoor summer cinema at the Centro Conde Duque in Madrid in 2014 because I had failed to buy tickets in advance for the sold-out event.

42 Robert Hughes, *Barcelona: The Great Enchantress* (Washington, DC: National Geographic Society, 2004), 130.

> intensity increases, a helicopter shot shows Barcelona at night, seen from mount Tibidabo. In the following shot, a taxi drives through the Monument to Colón; the film then cuts to Manuela looking at . . . the Sagrada Familia Cathedral, from the taxi window. The music is moving and nostalgic, appropriate for someone returning to a place dear to them after a long absence; in this sequence, Almodóvar invests the city with a strong emotional charge.[43]

Both the subject and the tone of this description are symptomatic of the fact that, as Maria M. Delgado notes, the "iconography of Barcelona is bound up with performance."[44] Urban topography might remain, but the mise-en-scène and players have clearly changed irrecoverably over the course of the nearly two decades since Manuela was last in the Catalan capital, the urban development of which reveals much about the idiosyncrasies of Spain's transition to democracy.

Barcelona has become a "model for post-industrial reform" since the 1992 Olympics firmly put it on the international map.[45] As Edgar Illas notes, the transformation constituted "the articulation of a municipal political process that aimed to have an effect on each social sphere of the city while implementing a comprehensive urban renovation."[46] This process has not, however, met with universal approval: Manuel Vázquez Montalbán's *Barcelonas* and Manuel Delgado's *La ciudad mentirosa: Fraude y miseria del "modelo Barcelona"* (The Fabricated City: The Fraud and Misery of the "Barcelona Model") constitute bitter laments against ostensibly left-leaning technocrats who, in their view, sacrificed socialist ideals and the well-being of the working classes through the gentrification of areas such as the Barceloneta and the Raval required to turn the city into a chic global brand.[47] Even if the Olympics and the concomitant urban transformation were not necessarily the only or the best possible response, Barcelona in the 1980s was in desperate need of a fix: chronic drug dependency (possession of heroin was decriminalized in Spain in 1983, and the country went in the space of a decade from having one of Europe's lowest to one of its highest number of addicts) and rampant unemployment ensured that many of the city's most iconic areas around the central artery of Las Ramblas had become no-go areas; even left-leaning anarchist magazine *Ajoblanco* complained about the number of needles left in La Raval and the horrific violence unleashed by the presence of drug trafficking and foreign mafias.[48]

43 Mariana Liz, *Euro-Visions: European Contemporary Cinema* (New York: Bloomsbury Academic, 2016), 117. I thank Mariana for allowing me to see the manuscript before publication.

44 Maria M. Delgado, "Performing Barcelona: Cultural Tourism, Geography and Identity," in *Barcelona: Visual Culture, Space and Power*, ed. Helena Buffery and Carlota Caulfield (Cardiff: University of Wales Press, 2012), 173–192.

45 Gary McDonogh, "Discourses of the City: Policy and Response in Post-Transitional Barcelona," in *Theorizing the City: The New Urban Anthropology Reader*, ed. Setha M. Low (New Brunswick, NJ: Rutgers University Press, 1999), 342–376.

46 Edgar Illas, *Thinking Barcelona: Ideologies of a Global City* (Liverpool, UK: Liverpool University Press, 2012), 1.

47 Manuel Vázquez Montalbán, *Barcelonas* (Barcelona: Empúries, 1990); Manuel Delgado, *La ciudad mentirosa: Fraude y miseria del "modelo Barcelona"* (Madrid: Los libros de la Catarata, 2007).

48 Vicente Gracía, "'El Chino': Los chorizos autoctonos desbancados por los grupos extranjeros," *Ajoblanco* 2 (1987): 52–61.

Bypassing the collateral damage caused by Barcelona's recent history and the Olympic regeneration, *Todo sobre mi madre* constitutes a largely atemporal fairy tale, simultaneously poeticizing the transgressive energy of the past and the cosmopolitan gentrification of the present. Manuela is reunited with transsexual prostitute Agrado in an old haunt, a re-creation of Barcelona's infamous red-light district known by locals as the Via Litúrgica (a play on words based on the epicenter of the area being the Via Laeitana, a major road that originates in the Barceloneta port area to pass between the City Cathedral and the Picasso Museum to near the Plaça de Catalunya, traditionally considered the frontier between the city's bourgeois and working-class quarters).[49] She then rents a chic apartment—one that would be difficult for someone on a nurse's salary to afford—in the Plaça Reial, a square that, before gentrification, had "became a theatre for knife-fights and running battles between rival drug gangs."[50] From Agrado's flat, nestled between Las Ramblas and the Via Laeitana, the viewer can make out the pillars of one of the crowing achievements of Catalan modernist architecture, the Palau de la Música, and a photo on the lounge table is described in the script as follows: "It was taken at the beginning of the 1980s when the Barceloneta beach was a splendid display of beach bars and freedom."[51]

Todo sobre mi madre may be the first time that Almodóvar had shot a film in Catalonia, but, like Manuela, he has both personal and professional roots there. He appeared in a small role in *Un hombre llamado flor de otoño* (*A Man Called Autumn Flowers*; Pedro Olea, 1978) as a bitchy performer filmed in the dressing room of a transvestite cabaret in Barcelona, set in the 1920s during the Primo de Rivera dictatorship. More generally, as Alberto Mira notes, there are photographs of the young Madrid-based filmmaker with the leading lights of the post-Franco Catalan underground, a countercultural movement that predated *La Movida*, a drug-fueled explosion across the arts that put both Almodóvar and the Spanish capital on (inter)national cultural map(s) in the late 1970s and early 1980s.[52]

In temporal, aesthetic, and industrial terms, *Todo sobre mi madre* resides at the interface between *Ocaña, un retrat intermittent* (*Ocaña, an Intermittent Portrait*; Ventura Pons, 1978)—a

49 As Robert Hughes's description intimates, this is a Fellini-esque set(ting) in real life: "Unless they get into a cat fight, which sometimes happens, their dignity is vestal. . . . They stand widely separated, like idealized statues—carved from the gross and hairy male protein of their former selves, occasionally doing a circuit to mark off their territory, the older ones stalking and the younger ones teetering slightly in their high heels on the rutted surface. This one looks like Carmen Miranda, that like the young Anita Ekberg, a third like Veruschka, and a fourth, with an Egyptian wedge of frizzy hair, resembles Sonia Braga. But for a cache-sexe and some accessories—a feather boa, a leather bustier, or mesh stockings—they are naked, some with magnificent breasts that possess the artificial perfection of hothouse fruit, achieved like the grace of Saint Theresa through patient devotional mortification and self-denial: hormones, surgery, and much saving up to pay the doctors. . . . Most of the time they exhibit a regal indifference, a self-absorption within the strutting temple of the redesigned body that goes far beyond the ordinary narcissism of mannequins." Hughes, *Barcelona* (London: HarperCollins, 1992), 46.

50 Donald McNeill, *Urban Change and the European Left: Tales from the New Barcelona* (London: Routledge, 1999), 33.

51 Almodóvar, *Todo sobre mi madre / Tout sur ma mere*, 54.

52 Alberto Mira, "*Ocaña, Retrat intermittent / Ocaña: An Intermittent Portrait* (Ventura Pons, 1977); "The Mediterranean *Movida* and the Passing Away of Francoist Barcelona," in *Spanish Cinema, 1973–2010: Auteurism, Politics, Landscape and Memory*, ed. Maria M. Delgado and Robin Fiddian (Manchester, UK: Manchester University Press, 2013), 49–63.

semidocumentary about the eponymous protagonist, an Andalusian cross-dresser as prone to quoting Lorca as to exposing his penis to passersby along Las Ramblas—and the performative reiteration of Barcelona as global brand in subsequent English-language studio productions. If, as Edgar Illas notes, "foreigners find its fusion of European sophistication and Mediterranean lifestyle irresistible," then the simulation of this cosmopolitan cocktail is reminiscent of the Las Vegas model brought to the Old Continent: "Barcelona is a visible sign that European cities have become the real imitation of their imitation."[53] Although largely funded by European money, the employment of star casting and city branding in *Vicky, Cristina, Barcelona* (Woody Allen, 2008) and *The Gunman* (Pierre Morel, 2015) constitute a Disneylandization of the Catalan urban metropolis. Almodóvar's film adheres to a dominant cinematic tradition for sidelining the challenges faced by newcomers to Barcelona in having to negotiate a multilingual reality. The dialogue is somewhat improbably rendered exclusively in Castilian, but the film clearly pays homage to Catalonia's cultural specificity and reputed tolerance and openness. A cast of extras from around the world complemented by the aforementioned plaintive harmonica of the Senegalese "Tajabone" are instrumental to rendering Barcelona as what Samuel Amago terms the "centre of multi-cultural Spain" and the "capital city of globalized Spain."[54]

The film not only employs multiple intertexts but is also sharply attuned to performance intertextuality. In a reversal of what had happened before, during, and after the Civil War—when Latin American film and theater benefited immensely from the presence of Spanish Republican exiles—Manuel Palacio and Carmen Ciller have ventured to say that, from 1976 onward, "Spain was filled with actors, actresses and practitioners from Argentina. . . . The theatrical and cinematographic diaspora is the largest on record since the end of the Second World War."[55] Among the Argentine community in Madrid during the early 1980s was Carlos Gandolfo, an expert in Tennessee Williams who performed an important pedagogical role for the next generation of Madrid-based practitioners. Penélope Cruz is among the alumni of an acting school established in 1978 by Cristina Roto, another Argentine exile.[56] Genealogies of this kind weave into *Todo sobre mi madre*'s fabric, but in the words of Juan Carlos Ibáñez, "The most revealing connections with history are found in the margins of the text, in the subtle intertextual play established by Almodóvar between the character of Manuela and the biography of the Argentine-born actress Cecilia Roth."[57] Her father moved the family to Spain after his teenage son Ariel (who would go on to form hard-rock band Tequila) was threatened along with his friend Alejo Stivel. Alejo's parents were the filmmaker David Stivel and the actress Zulema Katz,

53 Illas, *Thinking Barcelona*, 1 and 168.

54 Samuel Amago, "Todo sobre Barcelona: Refiguring Spanish Identities in Recent European Cinema," *Hispanic Research Journal* 8, no. 1 (2007): 11–25.

55 Carmen Ciller and Manuel Palacio, "Cecilia Roth en España (1976–1985)," *Signa* 20 (2011): 335–348.

56 Carmen Ciller, "The Influence of Argentinian Acting Schools in Spain from the 1980s," in *Performance and Spanish Film*, ed. Dean Allbritton, Alejandro Melero, and Tom Whittaker (Manchester, UK: Manchester University Press, 2016), 110–121.

57 Juan Carlos Ibáñez, "Memory, Politics, and the Post-Transition in Almodóvar's Cinema," in *A Companion to Pedro Almodóvar*, ed. Marvin D'Lugo and Kathleen M. Vernon (Chichester, UK: Wiley-Blackwell, 2013), 153–175.

whose last film role was as the patient of the father of Sexilia—the character played by Roth in *Laberinto de pasiones* (*Labyrinth of Passion*, 1982), an almost documentary-like depiction of Madrid at the height of La Movida.

In a manner analogous to the way that the narrative of *Todo sobre mi madre* enables Manuela to reconnect with figures from her past, Roth's reappearance in an Almodóvar film (much like Carmen Maura's return to the director's fold in *Volver* [2006]) provided good journalistic copy, redisposing local viewers to be particularly attentive to cinematic and sociocultural palimpsests. The actress claims that, because of personal disagreements, the director punished her with small or nonexistent roles after *Laberinto de pasiones*; he, conversely, has suggested that she was simply one of the weaker actresses to perform in his film.[58] What reportedly changed his mind and convinced him that he wanted to reignite their working relationship was seeing *Martín (Hache)* (*Martin (Hache)*; Adolfo Aristarain, 1997), a Spanish-Argentine coproduction that, like *Todo sobre mi madre* and so many of its intertexts, is about the theater and highly theatrical but, somewhat counterintuitively, makes frequent use of the close-up, a quintessentially cinematic device.[59]

Roth's role in *Hache* is almost equidistant between Sexilia and Manuela: a drug-addled Argentine actress living in Madrid going out with a middle-aged self-absorbed Marxist filmmaker who took refuge in the Spanish capital fleeing repression in Buenos Aires. In *Todo sobre mi madre*, Almodóvar self-consciously bucks a trend by which, in spite of a strong tradition of intercultural exchange between his homeland and Argentina, the habit of dubbing has rendered Spanish audiences remarkably conservative in terms of the accents they expect in film.[60] Roth was dubbed in *Laberinto de pasiones*, an irony given that the name of her character, Sexilia, is an in-joke based on how the name Cecilia would be rendered phonetically in Peninsular Spanish if it were pronounced in an exaggerated Argentine accent. Roth's voice is, however, heard in *Todo sobre mi madre*, her accent employed as a source of humor and pathos for the attuned ear: in a morbid joke that is lost in translation, Manuela refers early on to someone being of blood type 0-positive or "cero-positivo"; because the Argentine accent renders *c*'s as *s*'s to the Spanish ear, this is rendered as "sero-positivo," which translates as "HIV-positive."

Performance intertextuality similarly takes on an important role as regards Spanish actors in the film. As Silvia Colmenero Salgado notes of the casting of Huma Roja, "Almodóvar created this role specifically for Marisa Paredes, totally in line with her

58 María Guerra, Elio Castro-Villacañas, Juan Zavala, and Antonio C. Martínez, *Cecilia dice . . . Conversaciones con Cecilia Roth* (Huelva: Festival de Cine Iberoamericano de Huelva, 1998), 80; Strauss, *Almodóvar on Almodóvar*, 19.

59 Guerra et al., *Cecilia dice*, 136. Although, for example, the influence of Rainer Werner Fassbinder is frequently detected in Almodóvar's work, an inherently cinematic approach to a theatrical(ized) text comes to the fore if, for example, one contrasts *Todo sobre mi madre* with *Die bitteren Tränen der Petra von Kant* (*The Bitter Tears of Petra von Kant*, 1972).

60 Complaints were, for example, aired about the supposed unintelligibility of the actor Viggo Mortensen, a Danish American actor who spent his teenage years in Argentina, when he appeared as the eponymous Spanish mercenary in *Alatriste* (*Captain Alatriste: The Spanish Musketeer*; Agustín Díaz Yanes, 2006). See Anne L. Walsh, "Spanish Stars, Distant Dreams: The Role of Voice in Shaping Perception," in *Stars in World Cinema: Screen Icons and Star Systems across Cultures*, ed. Andrea Bandhauer and Michelle Royer (London: I. B. Tauris, 2015), 92–103.

prior performances, in a kind of eternal prolongation of her reflected image."[61] Huma's dressing room contains what appear to be real-life photos of Paredes's stage performances, and the role marked the third time that the actress had appeared in an Almodóvar film as an exemplary and successful professional whose personal life is a mess, following starring roles as a bolero singer in *Tacones lejanos* (*High Heels*, 1991) and as a romantic novelist in *La flor de mi secreto* (*The Flower of My Secret*, 1995). Even in the case of Candela Peña, an actress who had never worked with Almodóvar previously, her role as Huma's much younger, lesbian, drug-addled lover evokes prior performances and roles, most notably as a heroin addict in *Días contados* (*Numbered Days*; Imanol Uribe, 1994).

If Almodóvar has always been attentive to performance, it is a habit he acquired when young. In interviews, he has claimed that it was watching his mother effectively lie that taught him about storytelling.[62] This disclosure provides one clue as to why motherhood and acting are so frequently conflated within *Todo sobre mi madre* while also contextualizing how and why critics are so divided as to whether the film ought to be considered a pro- or antifeminist text.[63] Broadly speaking, the former contingent—in line with, say, the work of Spanish feminist Victoria Camps—believes that qualities that have traditionally been denigrated as feminine ought instead to be celebrated.[64] The latter holds that the film is predicated on a remarkably essentialist and antiquated view of gender norms. One defense that can be wielded in Almodóvar's favor is the unfairness of an overly literal reading—that for him one of cinema's greatest gifts is the ability to transform as opposed to merely reflecting a preexisting reality.

In line with this conception, *Todo sobre mi madre* constitutes a salient case of Daniel Frampton's Deleuzian interpretation of "filmosophy": "It appears that film, in some of its forms, can rejig our encounter with life, and perhaps even heighten our perpetual powers. Cinema allows us to re-see reality, expanding our perceptions, and showing us a new reality. Film challenges our view of reality, forcing a phenomenological realisation about how reality is perceived by our minds."[65] Lourdes Estrada has carried out an analysis of *Todo sobre mi madre* along precisely these lines, and in a similar vein, Julián Daniel Gutiérrez-Abilla has suggested that Almodóvar not only reflects but goes beyond the theories of Judith Butler: "This ethical and aesthetic process of becoming a

61 Silvia Colmenero Salgado, *Pedro Almodóvar: Todo sobre mi madre* (Barcelona: Ediciones Paidós, 2001), 132.

62 See, for example, Javier Rioyo and Javier Ángulo, "Una pareja estable: Director y actriz de *Todo sobre mi madre*, Entrevista con Marisa Paredes y Pedro Almodóvar," *Cinemania*, April 1999, 8–11.

63 In terms of the anticamp, see Barbara Zecchi, "All about Mothers: Pronatalist Discourses in Contemporary Spanish Cinema," *College Literature* 32, no. 1 (2005): 146–164; and María M. Donapetry, "Cinematernidad," in *La mujer en la España actual: ¿Evolución o involución?*, ed. Jacqueline Cruz and Barbara Zecchi (Barcelona: Icaria, 2004), 373–396. Silvia Colmenero Salgado offers a detailed account of the pro-argument in her aforementioned book. Others who ascribe a feminist reading of *Todo sobre madre* include Leopoldo Alas, "*Todo sobre mi madre*: Un grado más," *Academia* 26 (1999): 72–77; Susan Martin-Márquez, "Pedro Almodóvar's Maternal Transplants: From *Matador* to *All about My Mother*," *Bulletin of Hispanic Studies* 81, no. 4 (2010): 497–510; and María R. Matz and Carole Salmon, "Facing Almodóvar's Vision of Spanish Contemporary Society: Women, Men and Everyone in Between," in *How the Films of Pedro Almodóvar Draw upon and Influence Spanish Society: Bilingual Essays on His Cinema*, ed. María R. Matz and Carole Salmon (Lewiston, PA: Edwin Mellen Press, 2012), 13–35.

64 See, for example, Victoria Camps, *El siglo de las mujeres* (Madrid: Cátedra, 1998).

65 Daniel Frampton, *Filmosophy* (London: Wallflower Press, 2006), 3.

'queer mother' makes us think of cinema less in terms of 'reflecting' an external reality or an external referent than as a means of producing theory itself."[66] Irrespective of whether we accept that this is an acceptable form of moral praxis, any genuine attempt to grapple with Almodóvar's creative universe does require the critic to at the very least attempt to engage with the filmmaker on his own terms.

In a manner akin to Aristotle's evocation of "poetic" as opposed to "historical" truths to rebuff Plato's dismissal of art as morally pernicious mimesis masquerading as reality, Almodóvar challenges mainstays of patriarchal discourse, such as the idea that women are prone to deceive, as *Todo sobre mi madre* reverses the traditional logic and reclaims this trait as positive as opposed to negative. Characteristics frequently denigrated in relation to women and female characters are venerated in *Todo sobre mi madre*. In *Persona* (Ingmar Bergman, 1966), for example, a nurse becomes psychologically unbalanced and a threat when her personality merges with that of the aging actress under her charge. By contrast, Manuela's ability to act and care for others moors her identity and constitutes an affective form of community service. That Sister Rosa frequently struggles to act and lie has a negative impact on her own psychical and physical well-being. She is truthful to a fault, but her mother, the film's only unattractive female character, is indelibly linked with copying rather than transforming reality through her occupation of forging Chagall paintings. She, in other words, has no desire to improve on a preexisting reality, the admirable vocation of actresses and mothers in Almodóvar's cinematic universe.

This moral (re)positioning is replicated through the reappropriation of a number of the intertextual references. Most of the women in *Todo sobre mi madre*'s source texts are engulfed by fantasy and ensnared by reality—or perhaps vice versa—but Almodóvar's protagonists are liberated and socialized through theater and fiction. He reinscribes a dominant tradition manifest in metatheatrical films produced before, and in fact after, *Todo sobre mi madre*—see, for example, *Black Swan* (Darren Aronofsky, 2014) and, to a lesser extent, *Clouds of Sils Maria* (Oliver Assays, 2014)—which suggest physical decline and female rivalry to be largely insurmountable obstacles for female performers, and arguably women in general, to negotiate as they advance into middle age. Unlike, say, the talented but lonely aging matriarch on the stage in *Bullets over Broadway* (Woody Allen, 1994), Huma is surrounded by a supportive network. As Gwynne Edwards notes, Huma, like Blanche DuBois, is mentally anguished, but the "latter lives in a world of fantasy, of gentleman callers, of imagined refinement and elegance, while Huma is a realist, toughened by hard work and accustomed to the triumphs and disappointments of life in the theatre."[67] Blanche's reported liaison with a seventeen-year-old boy costs her a job as a secondary school teacher in *A Streetcar Named Desire*. Huma's relationship with the much-younger Nina is dysfunctional but is neither grotesque nor humiliating.

66 Lourdes Estrada, "'La potencia de lo falso' en *Todo sobre mi madre* (1999) de Pedro Almodóvar," *Hispanic Research Journal* 15, no. 6 (2014): 530–546; Julián Daniel Gutiérrez-Albilla, "Becoming a Queer (M)other in/and/through Film: Transexuality, Trans-Subjectivity and Maternal Relationality in Almodóvar's *Todo sobre mi madre*," in *A Companion to Spanish Cinema*, ed. Jo Labanyi and Tatjana Pavlović (Chichester, UK: Wiley-Blackwell, 2013), 563–580.

67 Gwynne Edwards, "Almodóvar and the Theatre," *ALEC* 30, no. 1 (2005): 77–96.

This is both the product and cause of the fact that, unlike her North American predecessor, she can rely on the kindness of (female) strangers.

The scene in which Huma, Rosa, and Manuela sit on a sofa discussing sexual mores is self-consciously reminiscent of *How to Marry a Millionaire* (Jean Negulesco, 1953), but with the key distinction that homosocial bonding and life plans are not predicated on meeting a rich man. Male characters are, in fact, ostensibly incidental but nevertheless carefully crafted components in the film. As Mark Allison notes, the casting of prime-time television presenter Carlos Lorenzo as Mario—the character who plays Brando's role in the play-within-the-film version of *A Streetcar Named Desire* and whose macho demeanor does not prevent him from being obsessed with Agrado's penis—"not only increased media interest in the role, but also exploited the high-profile, high-masculine image of the actor."[68] The choice of Fernando Fernán-Gómez, an iconic and well-respected figure from Spanish television, theater, and cinema, in the role of an infirm old man with Alzheimer's alongside Toni Cantó, familiar to Spanish television audiences as a soap-opera heartthrob as Lola, are radically diverse tactics with a common aim: to keep the aegis of patriarchy at bay.

According to the film's press book, Manuela is "the anti-Eve Harrington." In *All about Eve*, Margo Channing is approaching forty—what David Thomson terms "that uninsurable accident for every actress"—and is increasingly insecure about both her career and her relationship with a man eight years her junior, echoing the pairing of an aging actress and her boytoy from *Sunset Boulevard* (Billy Wilder, 1950). Manuela's first meeting with Huma involves her helping the older woman find Nina. Manuela is later able to play Stella onstage because she had played the role as a young woman in an amateur production in which she appeared alongside Lola/Esteban; her aim is not to usurp Nina, but to provide much-needed support to Huma. *Todo sobre mi madre* closes with Huma and Agrado rehearsing an homage to Lorca. When Manuela pays them a visit, Agrado tells her that Nina is now married with an ugly child; as Almodóvar comments, "[t]he return to the village really is a failure, a goodbye to her life as an actress, to the *dolce vita*."[69] The wig Huma dons for the Lorca production is an intertextual wink to the one worn by both Eve and Margo in Mankiewicz's film, but the aging matriarch adopts a classical tragic grandeur rather than being subject(ed) to an unflattering comparison with a younger alter ego.[70]

Almodóvar provides an unusual and arguably unparalleled outlet for mature female acting talent; this distinction, however, carries its own dangers. If he holds the power to defend women from those who construe the aging process as a source of humiliation and shame, then his older female stars can also become typecast and dependent on his patronage. Antonia San Juan in *Piedras* (*Stones*; Ramón Salazar, 2002), for example, shamelessly and somewhat indignantly riffs on being best known for her role as Agrado. The casting of Verónica Forqué—a former *chica Almodóvar* who last collaborated with him in *Kika* (1993)—as the lead in *Enloquecidas* (Juan Luis Iborra, 2008)—an aging

68 Mark Allison, *A Spanish Labyrinth: The Films of Pedro Almodóvar* (London: I. B. Tauris, 2001), 86.

69 Cited in Strauss, *Almodóvar on Almodóvar*, 206.

70 David Thomson, *The Big Screen: The Story of the Movies and What They Did to Us* (London: Penguin Books, 2012), 260.

actress with a drinking problem, who describes her biography as being akin to that of a Tennessee Williams character, and whose current play is attended religiously by a spectator who never misses a performance because his dead parents were fans of *All about Eve*—is symptomatic of a second-rate attempt to unimaginatively ape the success of *Todo sobre mi madre*. These specific examples hint at a much-broader question to be addressed in the third and final part of this article: how best to forge an ethical and aesthetic appraisal of Almodóvar's skill at exploiting local talent for the international marketplace.

Lorca and Lesser-Known Intertexts. "Despite the sustained critique of the generalizations and abstractions of the apparatus theory, subsequent theorizations of spectatorship and/or audiences remain largely indifferent to the transnational experience of cinema and the specificities of the engagement of spectators with 'foreign' films."[71] This is both a symptom and the cause of the methodological challenge articulated by Michael Cronin in *Translation Goes to the Movies*:

> Students of modernity and globalization would be well advised to consider how film makers have handled translation issues within their narratives as a further angle to understanding how multilingual and multicultural concerns play out in a globally distributed medium. Though film scholars might be reluctant to dwell on language for fear of relegating image to a secondary position, or only consider translation in the context of the "technical" concerns of dubbing and subtitling, the issues raised by representations of translation are too important or persistent to be ignored in any attempt to understand the impact of cinema as one of the pre-eminent idioms of the modern age.[72]

The study of cinematic intertextuality is well suited to such a task, taking on board as it does multiple elements among which the verbal is not necessarily paramount. While, for example, Esteban quoting Truman Capote's *Music for Chameleons* is a verbatim transcription of the original, many of the secondary filmic references in *Todo sobre mi madre* are primarily visual: the appropriation, for example, of the running over of a seventeen-year-old fan by an actress's car on a rainy night from *Opening Night* (John Cassavetes, 1977), or the fetishistic dwelling on hospital drips and equipment rendered in a colorful mise-en-scène reminiscent of *Magnificent Obsession* (Douglas Sirk, 1954).

Federico García Lorca is both the film's primary autochthonous reference point and the only contemporary figure to rival the filmmaker's stature as a global ambassador for Spain. Almodóvar has cited Lorca as the starting point for *Tacones lejanos*, while *Volver* (2006) clearly references *La casa de Bernarda Alba* (*The House of Bernarda Alba*).[73] In *Todo sobre mi madre*, a cameo appearance by the theater director Lluís Pasqual is indicative of the fact that his dramatized anthology from 1996 of Lorca's rural tragedies, *Haciendo Lorca* (*Doing Lorca*), was an inspiration for *Todo sobre mi madre*. The affective and thematic

71 Dimitris Eleftheriotis, *Cinematic Journeys: Film and Movement* (Edinburgh: Edinburgh University Press, 2010), 180.

72 Michael Cronin, *Translation Goes to the Movies* (London: Routledge, 2009), xii.

73 Maria M. Delgado, *Federico García Lorca* (Abingdon, UK: Routledge, 2008), 8.

links become immediately apparent on reading a review of the earlier production, which starred Núria Espert alongside Argentine actor Alfredo Alcón; Eduardo Haro Tecglen remarks on the selective appropriation of Lorca's words:

> The theatrical talent of Lluís Pasqual selects, above all, words by Lorca's female characters: women from *Yerma*, *Bodas de sangre* and *La casa de Bernarda Alba*. The words of women without children, partner-less, or grieving the death of a man. I saw how some women in the stalls were crying (I went to the performance on Monday), and I suppose that it will be because of this, for women with a story to tell, childless or harbouring some tragedy: women penetrated by the word of a man who probably never knew a woman in the Biblical sense, and harboured some of their desires and frustrations, giving voice to them with unparalleled emotion.[74]

That four of the reviewer's six children had died from drugs, victims of La Movida's excesses, would perhaps have predisposed *El País*'s chief theater critic to home in on parental loss. Irrespective of subjective concerns, however, Lorca, a repository of cultural capital for both domestic and foreign audiences whose life was cut tragically short by fascist thugs at the outset of the Civil War, is a tragically apt fit for a film concerned with gay aesthetics alongside affective and physical rejuvenation through transplants and transposition.

In his discussion of critical moments in translator decision-making, Jeremy Munday identifies concepts that are "saturated with value in their culture" and "attitudinally rich epithets" as key.[75] Within the global translation and exchange of culture, branded figures such as Almodóvar and Lorca perform precisely this role: they are approached with what Munday terms an "invoked-associative" attitude.[76] Delgado's illuminating study of Lorca is effectively an attempt to provide an etymology for his present-day meaning(s), which she succinctly defines as follows: "More so than any other twentieth-century Spanish writer, he remains a paradoxical embodiment of the local, the national and the global. His life and work have become indelibly bound up in a process of mythification that has converted him into the ultimate countercultural icon—the gay, martyred seer and a taboo topic in Franco's Spain—and now the establishment face of the newly tolerant post-dictatorship Spain."[77] When an English-language version of *All about My Mother* was staged at the Old Vic in London, the references to Lorca and *Blood Wedding* (*Bodas de sangre*) were developed further than they had been in the original film.[78] This, along with the references to Sister Rosa's mother forging Picasso as opposed to Chagall paintings,[79] were the middlebrow equivalents to the

74 Eduardo Haro Tecglen, "Palabras en el espacio," review of *Haciendo Lorca*, *El País*, April 30, 1996.

75 Jeremy Munday, *Evaluation in Translation: Critical Points of Translator Decision-Making* (London: Routledge, 2012), 157.

76 Munday, *Evaluation in Translation*, 157.

77 Delgado, *Federico García Lorca*, 2.

78 Duncan Wheeler, "All about Almodóvar: *Todo sobre mi madre* on the London Stage," *Bulletin of Hispanic Studies* 97, no. 7 (2010): 821–841.

79 Wheeler, "All about Almodóvar," 829.

introduction of a female bullfighter and pseudo-flamenco rhythms into a subsequent English-language musical production of *Mujeres al borde de un ataque de nervios* (*Women on the Edge of a Nervous Breakdown*; Pedro Almodóvar, 1988).

In other words, "the multilingual and multicultural concerns" that Cronin identified in relation to a "globally distributed medium" such as cinema also pertain to older art forms. The genealogies and geographies of Lorca's canonization as a secular icon have been consistently mistranslated since his death. The Francoist state was unsurprisingly resistant to allow, let alone promote, productions of his works, although, by the mid-1960s, even the right-leaning *ABC* newspaper marked the thirtieth anniversary of his death with a commemorative edition, a symptom of a certain national(ist) reconciliation with the martyred poet that was both the cause and consequence of his works having been given professional revivals on the contemporary Spanish stage.[80] The first major postwar production of *Bodas de sangre* took place under the direction of José Tamayo at the Teatro Bellas Artes.[81] *Yerma* was staged at the Eslava theater by Luis Escobar in 1961. This precipitated a heavy police presence outside of the auditorium; there would likely have been reprisals were it not for the fact that Escobar was a well-connected aristocrat and had taken care to premiere the work abroad first—it represented Spain at the Spoleto Theatre Festival in Italy—and to invite his personal friend and General Franco's eldest daughter, Carmen, to an early performance, thereby preempting potential criticisms.[82]

From a logistical and legal perspective, this production established a precedent, because it ensured that *Yerma* had been approved for performance. The continued sensitivity of Lorca's work and the circumstances surrounding his death are well demonstrated by the challenges Argentine director Victor García faced in an elaborate staging of *Yerma* with set design by Fabio Puigserver and starring Núria Espert. This production toured Europe and was central to the international consolidation of Lorca's reputation, while the controversy in Spain exacerbated by the presence of theater practitioners openly critical of the regime led to frequent cancellations by the authorities on spurious grounds, which only served to heighten the renown and popularity of the production and Lorca alike.[83] A more significant and resilient barrier to the staging of his play than the Francoist regime, however, has been the Lorca estate.[84] This is especially marked in references to the poet's homosexuality, which he tried to keep secret from his family during his life.[85] Although Lorca's sister, Conchita,

80 Delgado, *Federico García Lorca*, 33.

81 Gwynne Edwards, "*Bodas de sangre* in performance," *ALEC* 22, no. 3 (1997): 469–491.

82 Luis Escobar, *En cuerpo y alma: Memorias* (Madrid: Temas de hoy), 205–209.

83 See Núria Espert and Marcos Ordóñez, *De aire y fuego: Memorias* (Madrid: Santillana Ediciones Generales, 2002), 143–149.

84 In the words of Maria M. Delgado: "Arbiters of, and financial beneficiaries from, the Lorca corpus, they authorize translations for staging, adaptation, and publication, approving or otherwise use of the writer's words for advertising, film, and television, and control reproductive rights over his drawings and illustrations. Theirs has been a grip as tight as that of the Beckett or Brecht estates." Delgado, "Memory, Silence, and Democracy in Spain: Federico García Lorca, the Spanish Civil War and the Law of Historical Memory," *Theatre Journal* 67, no. 2 (2015): 177–196.

85 In the words of Leslie Stainton: "He lived a compartmentalized life. With close friends he was open about his sexuality; with others—particularly his family—he was evasive." Stainton, *Lorca: A Dream of Life* (London: Bloomsbury, 1998), 392.

appeared in Escobar's production when staged in Italy, the director—himself a closet gay man—notes that his youngest sister, Isabel, was paranoid over any potential insinuations about her brother's sexuality while policing the production before its premiere in Spain.[86] As Javier Herrero remarks, more generally, "For almost half a century after Lorca's death there has been an almost impenetrable wall of opposition to . . . any [suggestion of] of his gayness."[87] Almodóvar—whose homosexuality is itself flagged and framed more positively abroad than at home—implicitly resists this tendency and effectively inscribes both himself and Lorca into a global gay canon alongside Tennessee Williams and Truman Capote, both of whom spent extended periods of time in Spain from the 1950s onward.[88]

In twenty-first-century Spain, Almodóvar is a far more contested figure than Lorca is.[89] The Manchegan director is frequently accused by critics, the industry, and the general public of offering an excessive, clichéd, and repetitive image of Spain and its culture for international consumption. This impression is, somewhat ironically, forged largely by the frequent recourse to national traditions and references likely to remain invisible to non-Spanish audiences. As Josetxo Cerdán and Miguel Fernández Labayen lament: "The persistent inability on the part of many Spanish critics to appreciate the multiple facets of the Almodóvar oeuvre is the product of a schematic vision that continues to evaluate forms of cultural expression in terms of high versus low and art versus folklore."[90] *Los amantes pasajeros* was, for example, readily dismissed by national critics for its ostensible frivolity in casting Cecilia Roth as an actress clearly intended to resemble Barbara Rey—a former glamour model, actress, and vedette, who is widely rumored to have had an affair with King Juan Carlos—and the inclusion of television heartthrobs Mario Casas and Hugo Silva in leading roles.[91] However, these domestic reference points and in-jokes—such as "agua de Valencia," which literally translates to "Valencian water" but is also slang for a specific kind of drugged cocktail—provided a challenge to the film's legibility in the international marketplace. The result was that the film failed to charm critics or audiences at home and abroad, albeit for different reasons.

86 Escobar, *En cuerpo y alma*, 208.

87 Javier Herrero, *Lorca, Young and Gay: The Making of an Artist* (Newark, DE: Juan de la Cuesta Hispanic Monographs, 2014), 131.

88 The former's *Suddenly Last Summer* references the bad treatment of homosexuals in San Sebastián.

89 While, for example, *Hable con ella / Talk to Her* (2002) won the Oscar for "Best Original Screenplay"—the first time a non-English-language film had won this category since *Un homme et une femme* (*A Man and a Woman*; Claude Lelouch, 1966)—it could not compete in the category of "Best Foreign Film" because the national Academy of Cinematographic Arts and Sciences put forward *Los lunes al sol* (*Mondays in the Sun*; Fernando León de Aranoa, 2002), a socially conscious drama about unemployment in Galicia—which failed to even secure an Oscar nomination—as the official Spanish candidate.

90 Josetxo Cerdán and Miguel Fernández Labayen, "Almodóvar and Spanish Patterns of Film Reception," in *A Companion to Pedro Almodóvar*, ed. Marvin D'Lugo and Kathleen M. Vernon (Chichester, UK: Wiley-Blackwell, 2013), 129–152.

91 For a more detailed discussion of the performances in the film and their reception by Spanish critics, see Maria M. Delgado, "*Los amantes pasajeros / I'm So Excited!* (2013): 'Performing' la crisis," in *Performance and Spanish Film*, ed. Dean Allbritton, Alejandro Melero, and Tom Whittaker (Manchester, UK: Manchester University Press, 2016), 252–269.

In terms of domestic reception, *Todo sobre mi madre* is, in many respects, the exception that proves the rule. It won six Goyas—the Spanish Academy Awards—and was put forward as the official Spanish entry for Best Foreign Language Film at the Oscars; as Marvin D'Lugo and Kathleen M. Vernon note of its subsequent victory, "The event confirms and celebrates the deterritorialization of Almodóvar's cinema beyond its presumed Spanish origins, a process that has been ongoing throughout the previous decade but which is now brought more dramatically into public light."[92] This "deterritorialization" was nevertheless instrumental in terms of domestic reception: references to Truman Capote, a more elite literary citation in the Spanish than in the Anglo-American cultural sphere, alongside the homage to Cassavetes, inscribe the Spanish filmmaker into an international cultural elite. *Opening Night* was not even given an official release in Spain; Almodóvar claims to have discovered it at a screening in Paris, which only serves to heighten the film's distinction in the eyes of Spanish critics for whom a little-seen work of a foreign director will almost invariably be construed to be a more commendable intertext than a homegrown television series.[93] *Todo sobre mi madre* can, in fact, be profitably construed as the antithesis of *Los amantes pasajeros*: national and international reference points are both legible and infused with cultural capital for domestic and foreign audiences and critics alike.

According to Marsha Kinder, Almodóvar's "films increasingly perform an evocation of earlier works (both his own and intertexts of others) that leads us to read them as an on-going saga and to regroup them into networked clusters."[94] Hence, for example, *Todo sobre mi madre* might be variously grouped alongside *La flor de mi secreto*—in whose narrative the motif of the transplant first appears—and *Carne trémula* (*Live Flesh*; Pedro Almodóvar, 1997) as part of a new mature phrase; the final part of a trilogy in which Marisa Paredes plays divas in various personal and professional guises; or as a refinement of the references to *A Streetcar Named Desire* and *All about Eve*, first sketched in the made-for-television short film *Trailer para amantes de lo prohibido* (Trailer for Lovers of the Prohibited; Pedro Almodóvar, 1985) and his prose alter ego, Patty Diphusa, respectively.[95]

Rewriting and improving on preexisting works of art is a habit that the filmmaker also picked up in the cinema auditoriums of his childhood; according to his brother, Agustín, he would take great delight in returning home and attempting to improve on the films he had just seen in his fictional retelling of the cinematic narratives.[96] This

92 Marvin D'Lugo and Kathleen M. Vernon, "Introduction: The Skin He Lives In," in *A Companion to Pedro Almodóvar*, ed. Marvin D'Lugo and Kathleen M. Vernon (Chichester, UK: Wiley-Blackwell, 2013), 1–16.

93 Almodóvar has mentioned this in multiple interviews. See, for example, his David Lean Lecture for Bafta in London in 2012. Available at http://www.bafta.org/film/features/pedro-almodovar-david-lean-lecture-2012.

94 Marsha Kinder, "All about the Brothers: Retroseriality in Almodóvar's Cinema," in *All about Almodóvar: A Passion for Cinema*, ed. Brad Epps and Despina Kakoudaki (Minneapolis: University of Minnesota Press, 2009), 267–294.

95 Pedro Almodóvar, *Patty Diphusa y otros textos* (Barcelona: Editorial Anagrama, 1991). In a text originally written in the early 1980s, Patty fantasizes about how she will go to Paris and make friends with Catherine Deneuve: "I'll become her right-hand woman, and, like Eve Harrington, take a great role from her when she least expects it" (145).

96 Maria M. Delgado recounted this from her conversations with Agustin in her plenary address at the Association of Hispanists of Great Britain and Ireland annual conference held in Exeter in April 2015.

anecdote goes some way to contextualizing what we might call Almodóvar's jouissance as opposed to anxiety of influence:

> I don't take it to be something passive. After you see a film, it leaves its mark, like a current that goes between you and the film. The film, then, is now a memory, it has become part of my experience, that is, the experience of having been present and having felt it all. At that point, it's no longer a matter of paying tribute or whatever; you become imbued with your conversations with your father, your mother, your brother, your fiancée, with what goes on in the streets, with what you read, but all that eventually becomes a part of you. Once you have experienced a feeling, that feeling is yours, and that's the one you'll remember. When I create a film, that's how I work, like something . . . well, the truth is, what I create is almost like a theft.[97]

There is, however, an ethical issue with this embodied approach to intertextuality and appropriation in a context where, for many spectators outside of Spain, Almodóvar has virtually patented the national cinema.

This issue is compounded by the fact that the filmmaker and academic commentary on his work are far from consistent in the attention and detail expended on acknowledging citations from different media and traditions. Paul Julian Smith, for example, persuasively notes that the influence of *How to Marry a Millionaire* on *Mujeres al borde de un ataque de nervios*—and to a lesser extent on *Todo sobre mi madre*—has been referred to much more regularly than that of Jaime de Armiñán's *Chicas de la ciudad* (*City Girls*, 1961), a domestic TV series.[98] In comparison with, say, Michael Keaton and Edward Norton in *Birdman or (The Unexpected Virtue of Ignorance)* (Alejandro González Iñárritu, 2014), international audiences are less likely to clue in to the conflation of actors and roles in *Todo sobre mi madre*, with the most recognizable performance intertextuality being Marisa Paredes's previous collaborations with Almodóvar. The dedication to Gena Rowlands at the end of *Todo sobre mi madre* is a recognition of her being an actress and mother, in addition to the film's indebtedness to her performance in *Opening Night*, especially in the ability of her face to communicate emotion through understated but highly affecting close-ups. Not all influences and genealogies are so explicitly credited.

In interviews, Almodóvar frequently refers to the influence of the white-faced man dressed in black in *The Seventh Seal* (*Det sjunde inseglet*; Ingmar Bergman, 1957) on the father's appearance at Esteban's funeral: "Lola makes quite an impression in that setting, descending the stone stairway of the cemetery as though a model on a fashion shoot."[99] It may be a remarkable coincidence, but there is an almost identical scene in *Más que amor, frenesí* (*Not Love, Just Frenzy*; Alfonso Albacete, Miguel Bardem, and David Menkes, 1996), a film little seen internationally that features a cameo appearance by

97 Qtd. in Paula Willoquet-Maricondi, ed., *Pedro Almodóvar Interviews* (Jackson: University Press of Mississippi, 2004), 147.

98 Paul Julian Smith, "City Girls II: Television's Urban Women, Pre- and Post-Almodóvar," in *Spanish Screen Fiction: Between Cinema and Television* (Liverpool, UK: Liverpool University Press, 2009), 38–64.

99 Strauss, *Almodóvar on Almodóvar*, 185–186.

Penélope Cruz and stars Bibiana Fernández, a real-life transsexual who goes by the stage name of Bibi Ándersen and was a regular *chica Almodóvar* up to and including *Kika*. The visual similarity between Lola's appearance and that of the transsexual star of *Una mujer fantástica* (*A Fantastic Woman*; Sebastián Lelio, 2017) in a narrative oriented around a death and a funeral predisposed viewers to identify the Chilean recipient of Best Foreign Film at the Oscars in 2018 as a direct heir to Almodóvar's gender-bending melodrama.

Deterritorialization can result in readings that are likely to be found both foreign and wanting by local audiences and practitioners. Almodóvar cast Antonio Banderas in his debut cinematic role in *Laberinto de pasiones* after the filmmaker and Cecilia Roth saw the young actor from Málaga in a production of Calderón de la Barca's play *La hija del aire* (*The Daughter of the Air*) in 1981.[100] Future scholars would do well to study how Banderas's early performance as Gaveston in a theatrical production of *Edward II* directed by Lluís Pasqual fed into the construction of the fragile masculinities embodied in subsequent screen appearances. Despite occupying radically different positions in the hierarchy of aesthetic forms, television and theater can both be rendered equally invisible to nonlocalized commentators. To cite another camouflaged genealogy from Spanish cinema, conventional wisdom among foreign and domestic commentators has it that the town mayor in *¡Bienvenido Mister Marshall!* (*Welcome Mister Marshall*; Luis García Berlanga, 1953) is a caricature of Franco that cleverly circumvented the censor.[101] Pepe Isbert—the actor who played the aforementioned role—appears completely unaware of this connotation in his autobiography, where he voices unconditional admiration and support for the dictator, noting that his performance, feted at Cannes, builds on a long-standing tradition in Spanish theater for buffoonish local mayors.[102]

Almodóvar's intuitive and studied awareness of multiple interpretive communities underpins a remarkable commercial and artistic vision. In 2006, the *Almodóvar Exhibition* opened at the Cinémathèque Française. The seventh part, titled "La vie spectacle," was dedicated to films the director has referenced in his own cinematic works; some were then screened as part of a season to coincide with the exhibition for which Almodóvar was one of the curators.[103] The sole Spanish entry was *El verdugo* (*The Executioner*; Luis García Berlanga, 1963), also starring Isbert. Later on, Almodóvar's inclusion of thirteen Spanish films that had inspired him as part of a British Film Institute (BFI) season dedicated to his works would suggest a shift in his public acknowledgment of his compatriots and a deliberate gesture to inscribe his work within a national canon. In addition to *El verdugo*, works included *El extraño viaje* (*Strange Voyage*; Fernando

100 Being well-versed in the Spanish classics came in useful as a quick-witted rebuff to Ricky Gervais at the 2012 Golden Globe Awards when Banderas responded to the British comedian's derogatory comment about the accents of Spanish-language actors in Hollywood by reciting lines from Calderón in Castilian at breakneck speed. See "Ricky Gervais volvió a hacer de las suyas en los Globo de Oro y criticó Salma Hayek y Antonio Banderas," *¡Hola!*, http://www.hola.com/cine/2012011656474/ricky-gervais-globo-oro-2012.

101 See Duncan Wheeler, "Spanish Films, 1992–2012: Two Decades of Cinematic Production and Critical Discourse," in *(Re)viewing Creative, Critical and Commercial Practices in Contemporary Spanish Cinema*, ed. Duncan Wheeler and Fernando Canet (Bristol, UK: Intellect, 2014), 7–34.

102 Pepe Isbert, *Mi vida artística* (Barcelona: Bruguera, 1969).

103 Javier Herrera, "Almodóvar's Stolen Images," in *A Companion to Pedro Almodóvar*, ed. Marvin D'Lugo and Kathleen M. Vernon (Chichester, UK: Wiley-Blackwell, 2013), 345–363.

Fernán-Gómez, 1964) and *Blancanieves* (*Snow White*; Pablo Berger, 2012), along with *Arrebato* (*Rapture*; Iván Zuleta, 1979) and *Jamón Jamón* (Bigas Luna, 1992), two films which the Manchegan director could previously have stood accused of appropriating from without due credit.

Almodóvar wrote on the BFI website, "Bigas Luna's film was Penélope Cruz's debut and the reason why so many directors, me included, dreamt about working with her some day. . . . *Jamón Jamón* is 'a genuine celebration of all things Spanish.'"[104] In a series of rants against what he perceives as the usurpation of his national cinema by foreign critics, Santos Zunzunegui argues that the targets of his attack have failed to pay sufficient attention to autochthonous traditions, what he terms "the richest, most original and creative vein of Spanish cinema."[105] In his view, the man from La Mancha provides an iconic manifestation of "the paradigm of transcultural reinscription":[106] "it is possible to contribute to the erasure of the postmodern cliché that, for example, has led foreign critics to turn Pedro Almodóvar into a mere fetish in order to situate him in his genuine terrain: that of an exemplary redresser of numerous aesthetic forms from the Spanish tradition."[107] There is a valid point to be made about critics not always paying sufficient account to Spanish intertextual sources, but the broader argument quickly collapses in several important respects. First, Almodóvar is clearly complicit in this process: his talent and success are predicated on his ability to factor in the contingency of reception so as to retain a degree of creative control while appealing to diverse audiences. Second, his relatively low critical standing at home is at least in part the result of domestic reviewers being unable to see anything in his films beyond recycled and frequently critically derided aesthetic forms. Third, the reification of national culture fails to address what music scholar and sociologist Motti Regev terms "the consolidation of aesthetic cosmopolitanism as the global cultural condition of late modernity," as Spanish imports as well as exports are subject to resignification.[108] The long Franco dictatorship delayed the onset of late modernity in Spain, but even then, a certain aesthetic cosmopolitanism was the cause and consequence of the appeal of Hollywood films; that this phenomenon is similarly not always taken into account is, for example, demonstrated by US-based critic Isolina Ballesteros attributing a feminist rewriting of *A Streetcar Named Desire*—in which Stella leaves Stanley—to Almodóvar, without taking sufficient account of the fact that Kazan's film is the more prominent antecedent than Williams's play text.[109] Fifth, foreign critics and approaches cannot so

104 Pedro Almodóvar, "Pedro Almodóvar: 13 Great Spanish Films That Inspire Me," *BFI Film Forever*, http://www.bfi.org.uk/news-opinion/news-bfi/features/pedro-almodovar-13-great-spanish-films-influenced-me.

105 Santos Zunzunegui, *El extraño viaje: El celuloide atrapado por la cola, o la crítica norteamericana ante el cine español* (Valencia: Eutopías, 1999), 100.

106 Zunzunegui, *El extraño viaje*, 63.

107 Santos Zunzunegui, *Historias de España: De que hablamos cuando hablamos del cine español* (Valencia: Generalitat Valenciana e IVAC, 2002), 15.

108 Motti Regev, *Pop-Rock Music* (Cambridge, UK: Polity Press, 2013), 9.

109 Isolina Ballesteros, "Performing Identities in the Cinema of Almodóvar," in *All about Almodóvar: A Passion for Cinema*, ed. Brad Epps and Despina Kakoudaki (Minneapolis: University of Minnesota Press, 2009), 71–100. As Stephen Maddison has explored, Almodóvar does nevertheless make one ostensibly small but telling departure from the film by not having Stella simply go upstairs but actually leave the stage, thereby implying a more definite rupture. Maddison, "All about Women," 266–267.

readily be coalesced into a homogeneous group, as they are not invariably unaware of cognitive and cultural limitations.[110]

Zunzunegui's argument would not warrant more than cursory attention if it were not for its resilience and influence in the domestic context. His most convincing line of attack homes in on cultural ownership and what he construes as the sequestration by Anglophile critics of Spanish cinema once it became established as an object worthy of study in universities around the world.[111] The problem, however, is that the chauvinistic reentrenchment in national paradigms and cultures is not only flawed methodologically but also unlikely to prove productive. Heuristic tools and cultural (re)appropriation change the meaning of films. This is as true of some Hollywood films as it is of ostensibly beleaguered European national cinemas. As Thomas Elsaesser notes: "What the auteur theory saw in them was not what the studios or even the directors 'intended,' but this did not stop another generation of American viewers appreciating exactly what the *Cahiers du cinéma* critics had extracted from them."[112]

Mapping international (and not necessarily universal) theories onto the films of Almodóvar can admittedly be suspiciously convenient: in the case of *Todo sobre mi madre* Ernesto R. Acevedo-Muñoz has, for example, rightly critiqued a reductive (re)appropriation of and recourse to the "use of theatrical situations as the locus of 'authentic' disclosures."[113] Agrado's monologue on authenticity and her various operations in her quest to become the perfect woman lend themselves to being interpreted as an iconoclastic and concise recapitulation of the major tenets of gender performativity, but that very directness can limit what can be gained from their application. In *Bodies That Matter*—the follow-up to the canonical *Gender Trouble*—Judith Butler argues against the ironically literal and reductionist reading(s) to which her most famous text has been subject(ed): "It would be a mistake to impose the same criteria on every cultural product, for it may be precisely the partiality of a text which conditions the radical characters of its insights. Taking the heterosexual matrix or heterosexual hegemony as a point of departure will run the risk of narrowness, but it will run it in order, finally, to cede its apparent priority and autonomy as a form of power. This will happen within the text, but perhaps most successfully in its various appropriations."[114] This is precisely the form of labor adopted by Almodóvar in his

110 Andy Medhurst has, for example, set out to explore "whether the specifically Spanish contexts of his comedy are lost on, or overlooked by, those international admirers (myself included) who revere Almodóvar as a totemic figure in queer culture." Medhurst, "Heart of Farce: Almodóvar's Comic Complexities," in *All about Almodóvar: A Passion for Cinema*, ed. Brad Epps and Despina Kakoudaki (Minneapolis: University of Minnesota Press, 2009), 118–138.

111 See Wheeler, "Spanish Films," 7–34. Marvin D'Lugo—coeditor of *The Wiley-Blackwell Companion to Almodóvar* and chief editor of *Studies in Spanish and Latin American Cinemas*—has, for example, referred to an essay by Antonio Francisco Pedrós-Gascón, clearly inspired by Zunzunegui's model, as "a mean-spirited chapter." See Antonio Francisco Pedrós Gascón, "¿Hacer cine como si Franco no hubiera existido?," in *How the Films of Pedro Almodóvar Draw upon and Influence Spanish Society: Bilingual Essays on His Cinema*, by María R. Matz and Carole Salmon (Lewiston, PA: Edwin Mellen Press, 2012): 137–156; and Marvin D'Lugo, "Review," *Bulletin of Spanish Studies* 92, no. 4 (2015): 634–635.

112 Elsaesser, *European Cinema*, 46.

113 Ernesto R. Acevedo-Muñoz, *Pedro Almodóvar* (London: BFI World Director Series, 2007), 230.

114 Judith Butler, *Bodies That Matter: On the Discursive Limits of Sex* (New York: Routledge, 1993), 19.

reappropriation of intertextual texts within *Todo sobre mi madre*. It therefore seems more fitting, and more radical, to carry out this task in relation to the film's reception as opposed to simply identifying those moments in the film that map most obviously onto Butler's worldview.

Conclusion. A celebrity in Japan, with bars and restaurants established in his honor in Australia, Almodóvar is a genuinely global phenomenon, unique among the select group of internationally feted Hispanic auteurs for having never shot abroad or in English. His ability to produce films that are simultaneously "culturally specific" and "open" is both a symptom and a cause of his cinematic genius. If *Todo sobre mi madre* means different things at home than it does abroad, then this is not exclusively or even predominantly the result of autochthonous reference points but can also be attributed to the contingencies of reception when Hollywood films are translated out of their original habitat. The recipient of the Oscar for Best Foreign Language Film at the 2000 Academy Awards is ideally placed to illuminate a transition away from what Stephanie Dennison and Song Hwee-Lim term "the iron grip of hierarchised binarism," by which anything not generically and geographically grounded in North American commercial cinema is automatically posited as Hollywood's "other."[115]

On the one hand, the resignification of performance intertexts ensures that meanings ricochet in ways that criticism can never exhaustively capture. Conversely, however, this does not imply that the desire to capture and analyze various iterations is futile, or that local commentators have a monopoly on the identification of sources of far from singular provenance. The translations and transfusions of *Todo sobre mi madre* resist reification and retreat into national paradigms or, for that matter, too sharp a division between text, theory, and performance. Future studies would be well advised to adopt a transnational approach at the level of both production and reception; films such as *Mujeres al borde de un ataque de nervios* and *Volver* have, for example, enjoyed sufficient international visibility to warrant the application of methodologies developed by the international *Lord of the Rings* audience project to study how this series of cinematic adaptations is never a closed book, remaining open to different readings in different geographical and cultural environs.[116]

Spain's most successful filmmaker is a cinematic cartographer capable of mapping different intertexts onto narratives that remained rooted in their domestic birthing pool but amenable to complex and contradictory adoption among different interpretive communities. As this article has sought to demonstrate, a holistic approach to his work requires the combination of local knowledge with a sensitivity to multiple inflections through a transnational sphere that "is not an anarchic free-for-all in which blissfully

115 Stephanie Dennison and Song Hwee-Lin, "Introduction: Situating World Cinema as a Theoretical Problem," in *Remapping World Cinema: Identity, Culture and Politics in Film*, ed. Stephanie Dennison and Song Hwee-Lin (London: Wallflower, 2006), 1–15.

116 For an overview of this project and some of the methodological issues it raised, see Martin Baker, "Envisaging 'Visualisation': Some Challenges from the International *Lord of the Rings* Project," *Film-Philosophy* 10, no. 3 (2006): 1–25.

deracinated postnational subjects revel in ludically mystified states of ahistoricity."[117] The outlandish masquerade of Almodóvar's cinematic output can frequently disguise the extent to which he is an ascetic Catholic consumer of myriad aesthetic forms; an appreciation of this requires viewing his oeuvre under different heuristic lenses as opposed to assigning his films according to preexisting categories. In undertaking this challenge, critics would be well advised to replicate his disciplined irreverence: cataloging various intertextual appropriations runs the risk of lapsing into academic pedantry, but reinscribing multiple performance intertexts also provides the possibility of tracing alternative genealogies and the opening up of new vistas onto the work of a remarkable Spanish filmmaker who has so successfully resisted standard taxonomies of national, European, and world cinema(s). *

117 Elizabeth Ezra and Terry Rowden, "General Introduction: What Is Transnational Cinema?," in *Transnational Cinema: The Film Reader*, ed. Elizabeth Ezra and Terry Rowden (London: Routledge, 2006), 1–12.

SCMS

The Pleasure of Mourning: Korean War Blockbusters in Post–Cold War South Korea, 1998–2008

by WE JUNG YI

Abstract: This article looks at the translation of memory in Korean War blockbusters produced during the decade of South Korea's Sunshine Policy (1998–2008). To trace how the nation's traumatic past has been reshaped as visual entertainment for the era of globalization, I examine three films of the genre: *Gongdong gyeongbi guyeok JSA* (*Joint Security Area*; Park Chan-wook, 2000), *Taegeukgi hwinallimyeo* (*Taegukgi: The Brotherhood of War*; Kang Je-gyu, 2004), and *Welkeom tu Dongmakgol* (*Welcome to Dongmakgol*; Park Kwang-hyun, 2005). As a popular platform for recalling and reworking Korea's division, the melodramatic spectacles of these films offer vicarious mourning, but only belatedly and from a distance, through the suspension of time or in a vision of death.

Korean War Blockbusters in the Era of Reconciliation (1998–2008). Of the numerous South Korean films that have dealt with the country's postcolonial division, *Welkeom tu Dongmakgol* (*Welcome to Dongmakgol*; Park Kwang-hyun, 2005; hereafter *Dongmakgol*) occupies an uncommon niche.[1] In revisiting the wartime period (1950–1953), the film presents an oddly pleasurable scenario. Set in a secluded, mountainous village called Dongmakgol, it features a group of soldiers who are unexpectedly stranded together: a US Navy captain, two South Korean soldiers, and three North Korean comrades. Gradually assimilating to the simple, peaceful life in Dongmakgol, the soldiers eventually form a fraternity with one another and build a strong bond with the villagers. But in the end, they leave the Arcadian community to prevent a bombing attack by the United States, and at the cost of their lives the "united force of Korean soldiers" completes their mission to defend the hamlet. In offering an enticing alternative to

1 In this article, Korean words are transliterated according to the Revised Romanization adopted by the South Korean government in 2000. Exceptions are names and terms that have gained currency in the English-speaking world, such as Pyongyang and Kim Il Sung. Asian names retain their order of family name followed by given name unless an author prefers given name first.

We Jung Yi is assistant professor of Asian studies at Vanderbilt University. She is completing a monograph that explores diverse forms of Korean War memories in the cultural history of South Korea. Her article "Melodramatic Tactics for Survival in the Neoliberal Era: Excess and Justice in The Heirs *and* My Love from the Star*" appears in the* Journal of Korean Studies *(March 2018).*

conventional Korean War narratives, which highlight the victimization of innocent civilians through the sudden attack of evil communists, *Dongmakgol* thus leaves the audience with a lingering question: how to apprehend Korea's division here and now. Since the Cold War has been declared over around the globe, do they form a new memory of the (inter)national conflict on the Korean Peninsula?

Indeed, South Koreans witnessed the explosion of Korean War memories onscreen at the turn of the millennium. The so-called Sunshine Policy, initiated by the South's liberal regimes of 1998–2008 to engage the North, not only promoted diplomatic and economic interactions between the two states but also reshaped the mnemonic landscape of the partitioned peninsula. In 1998, the founder of the Hyundai group visited the North, and this move toward inter-Korean economic cooperation was a spectacle as he herded hundreds of cattle across the Demilitarized Zone (DMZ). In June 2000, North Korean leader Kim Jong Il and South Korean president Kim Dae-jung met in Pyongyang, and this first inter-Korean summit led to a joint declaration for the nation's peaceful resolution of the reunification question. Against this backdrop, *Swiri* (*Shiri*; Kang Je-gyu, 1999), the urtext of the Korean War blockbuster, was a phenomenal success, as it took "a huge first step away from the master narrative of the Cold War" by portraying "for the first time . . . North Koreans as human beings."[2]

Released six years later, *Dongmakgol* further diverged from the Cold War–informed cinema of earlier periods and, through its unusual picturing of wartime Korea, even distinguished itself from Korean War blockbusters made during the Sunshine decade. With its phantasmic scenario that is at once comic and touching, the film brought another unprecedented success for the Korean film industry. By attracting more than eight million domestic viewers, the film broke the box-office record of *Swiri*. Produced without reliance on a star system or aggressive marketing, *Dongmakgol* was thus well received in the media as a cultural sign of the "postideological era."[3]

However, as indicated in the heroic but inevitable deaths of the allied Korean forces in its finale, the "postideological" sign emanating from *Dongmakgol* neither resolves the legacy of division at the symbolic level nor replicates in the field of visual entertainment the South's state-led initiatives toward the North. Rather, the film betrays both the absurdity of the nation's continuing division in the post–Cold War world and, at the same time, the uncertainties about a reunification that seemed to be moving closer under the Sunshine Policy. But did this indeterminate state between division and unification constitute a potent force that made the film a remarkable hit? In displaying ambivalences over inter-Korean rapprochement, *Dongmakgol* in effect worked to preempt, through the very lack of narrative closure, a potential trauma that might yet be inflicted by the postdivision process.[4] If what was at stake in watching

2 Michael Robinson, "Contemporary Cultural Production in South Korea: Vanishing Meta-Narratives of Nation," in *New Korean Cinema*, ed. Chi-Yun Shin and Julian Stringer (New York: New York University Press, 2005), 28.

3 See, for instance, Heo Ji-woong, "Gwangaek-deul eun wae *Welkeom tu Dongmakgol* e yeolgwang haneunga" [What Drives Audiences Crazy about *Welcome to Dongmakgol*], *Oh My News*, August 16, 2005, http://star.ohmynews.com/NWS_Web/OhmyStar/at_pg.aspx?CNTN_CD=A0000274799.

4 This potential trauma by Korea's *de*-division is reminiscent of what Michael Berry has noted in Sinophone literature and film in relation to the "anticipatory trauma" surrounding Hong Kong's handover. See Berry, "Hong Kong 1997,"

Korean War blockbusters in post–Cold War South Korea was how to manage both the crisis of imagining the nation's future and the confusion involved in recalling its past, *Dongmakgol* provided a stopgap measure *by deferring any resolution*, just as the war remained suspended in the era of reconciliation.

By teasing out the state of suspension found in Korean War blockbusters during the decade of the Sunshine Policy (1998–2008), this article seeks to articulate the relationships among memory, media, and cultural consumption in twenty-first-century South Korea. Taking note of the continued conflict between the two Koreas even after the Armistice, the "Korean War blockbuster" is defined here in a broad sense to include texts that wrestle with the symptoms and repercussions of the nation's postcolonial division, rather than being confined to those centered on the full-scale clash from 1950 to 1953. In this light, my analysis of *Gongdong gyeongbi guyeok JSA* (*Joint Security Area*; Park Chan-wook, 2000; hereafter *JSA*), *Taegeukgi hwinallimyeo* (*Taegukgi: The Brotherhood of War*; Kang Je-gyu, 2004; hereafter *Taegeukgi*), and *Dongmakgol* focuses on the ways these films reconstruct the multiple sites of the Korean War—from the battlefields of the 1950s to the DMZ in the 2000s. Ultimately, I show how the traumatic scenes reenacted in the films are inextricably tied to the postwar generation's apprehension about the region's unforeseeable future against the backdrop of post–Cold War dynamics and during a period of rapid globalization.

In exploring the transmission and transformation of mnemonic practices mediated by cinema, this article adopts a "transmemory" approach that incorporates insights from memory studies and translation theory.[5] This approach shares interests and concerns with scholarly works about the "post" generation's engagement with the past, including Marianne Hirsch's readings of "postmemory" texts by the descendants of Holocaust survivors.[6] But because the Sunshine decade's blockbusters about Korea's unfinished war complicate the notion of "postness" or indirectness in the making of memory by subsequent generations, the films call our attention to historical contexts under which traumatic knowledge is not merely transferred from the past but also transfigured in the present. In South Korea, inherited war memories invariably undergo a process of translation in negotiation with the geopolitical and material realities that sustain, even through alterations, the state of division. By connecting mnemonic practices to acts of translation, transmemory thus marks, echoing Homi Bhabha, "how newness enters the world" when memory drifts across genres, mediums, and periods.[7] In foregrounding transnational vectors that facilitate hybrid forms of remembering, my approach further reconsiders the films' spectacularization of Korea's division in the allegedly postnational, postideological era of globalization. By

in *A History of Pain: Trauma in Modern Chinese Literature and Film* (New York: Columbia University Press, 2008), 365–383.

5 I find this "transmemory" approach used in different contexts, including Agnieszka Bedingfield's comparison of Jewish and Chinese immigrant literatures in North America. Bedingfield, "Trans-Memory and Diaspora: Memories of Europe and Asia in American Immigrant Narratives," in *Sites of Ethnicity: Europe and the Americas*, ed. William Boelhower, Rocio G. Davis, and Carmen Birkle (Heidelberg: Universitätsverlag Winter, 2004), 333–346.

6 Marianne Hirsch, "Mourning and Postmemory," in *Family Frames: Photography, Narrative, and Postmemory* (Cambridge, MA: Harvard University Press, 1997), 22.

7 Homi K. Bhabha, *The Location of Culture* (New York: Routledge, 2004), 303–337.

reconfiguring the domain of Korean War spectacles as a political site that links the individual and collectivity, I uncover the pleasure of vicarious mourning in these works of transmemory, which function to unite their audiences by keeping them suspended between the nation's division and unification.

Laughter with Tears in *Dongmakgol*. The equivocal ending of *Dongmakgol* is a striking example of how the transitory unity of spectators is intensified through a suspension of vision, both perceptive and political, and through a division of roles in coming to terms with traumatic memories either returned or anticipated. Showcasing its genre-blending quality, the antiwar film often interweaves humor with pathos against the backdrop of its idyllic and dreamy imagery; this mixture reaches its ironic culmination as the main characters meet a valorous death in the midst of an air bombing. Shifting between long shots and close-ups of the united Korean soldiers, the camera records, in slow motion, a smile spreading over each of their terrified faces. The grins of the dying soldiers are then followed by the sound of children cheering in Dongmakgol, where the aerial bombardment is seen as spectacular fireworks. Cutting to the "repatriation" journey of Captain Smith of the US Navy, who had wanted to stay with his Korean comrades in the battlefield, the sequence ends with the foreign character's wail upon hearing the explosions from the site of operation (see Figures 1–3).

By inserting the contrasting reactions of the Dongmakgol children and the US captain to the combat beyond their range of immediate perception, this sequence illustrates the opposite poles of response to Korea's unfinished war during a time of rapprochement. At one end, the response is, like that of the innocent viewers in Dongmakgol, to "enjoy" the spectacle in the distance without knowing, or by misapprehending, what is taking place behind it. At the other end, the response is to "mourn" the death that remains invisible by becoming an active and empathetic listener as embodied in Smith. While the former display the blessing of misapprehension thanks to their alienation from the traumatic site, the latter manifests the pain of recognition, which involves feelings of powerlessness and responsibility. Juxtaposing these two ways of looking (back) on the war, the film also employs multiple divisions in the working of memory. The tears of Smith are better visualized and individualized

Figure 1. The "united force of Korean soldiers" smile in the midst of the falling bombs, in *Welkeom tu Dongmakgol* (Film It Suda, 2005).

Figure 2. Children in Dongmakgol cheer, watching the spectacular "fireworks" in the distance, in *Welkeom tu Dongmakgol* (Film It Suda, 2005).

Figure 3. US Navy Captain Smith breaks into tears, realizing that the Korean soldiers are dying in action, in *Welkeom tu Dongmakgol* (Film It Suda, 2005).

on the screen than is the communal laugh echoing from the mountain village. This audiovisual split, combined with the split between the collective and the personal, accentuates the already-existing gaps between the different types of survivors. The American captain is given more leverage—and hence more liability—than the Korean civilians in working through the unresolved past. Still, analogous to the Dongmakgol villagers, he is blocked from the site that bears the trace of the Korean hero-victims' deaths and is left to moan, incapable of articulating his grief. As a result of placing both the foreign mourner and the unenlightened mass at a distance from the field of operation, the film maintains a conflicted attitude toward the unmastered past of Korea. At one level, it separates the realm of everyday life from the history of division. By fantastically substituting that history with the prelapsarian world of Dongmakgol, the film prevents the necessity of coping with the issue of reunification; according to its alternative past, Koreans were never divided. At the same time, it makes a gesture that conjures up the traumatic memory of the Korean War, a gesture performed by both local and global bodies. Imagining the smiles of the dead on the one hand and demanding tears of grief from survivors on the other, the fantasy world of Dongmakgol thus at once commemorates and disavows what has been lost; by placing the site of battle beyond sight, the encounter with the traumatic loss is suspended.

To a certain extent, *Dongmakgol*'s configuration of invisible death and incomplete mourning inherits South Korea's Cold War aesthetics, which involved, as Theodore Hughes suggests, the "politics of what could be seen or spoken" in the divided nation.[8] The collapse of the international Cold War order, however, has further complicated the national frame of Korean War memories. Riding on the global flow of capital and technology, the hybrid format called the "Korean-style blockbuster" (*hanguk-hyeong beullokbeoseuteo*) has emerged as a popular platform for recalling and reimagining past events. By embracing the principle of speculation and intensity in postmodern culture, these films reenact the violent history of the nation in the form of spectacle and accommodate a new group of condolers—who will soon turn into consumers. Yet the mourning played out in the works suspends the moment of resolution, as shown in *Dongmakgol*'s spectacular ending.

What I emphasize here is the mode of translation that operates in Korean War blockbusters, thereby constituting "transmemory" as described earlier. If we approach these films as a site of memory production in which images of the past are rearranged and redistributed across generational and cultural boundaries, this leads

8 Theodore Hughes, *Literature and Film in Cold War South Korea: Freedom's Frontier* (New York: Columbia University Press, 2012), 3.

us to see how their translational practice draws up, again and anew, the previously forgotten or ungrieved. Without hiding its illusionary nature, the hybrid genre carves out a space in which contemporary viewers can make connections personally and affectively with those afflicted by Korea's long division. At once transnational and transgenerational, this cultural translation is transferential and transitional as well because the blockbusters' processing of the war trauma is achieved only through a surrogate witness or mourner, called over from the younger postwar generation both on and beyond the screen. And such working-through always remains fragmentary and incomplete because it limits responsibility for mourning at the personal level and demands reconciliation in only private terms.

Considering Korean War blockbusters as works of mourning in translation enables us to better trace the evolving perception in post–Cold War South Korea of what Paik Nak-chung has theorized as the "division system."[9] The salient actors in the cinematic rendition of the inherited system are the filmmakers who were dubbed the "386" generation; they were born in the 1960s, lived through democratization while in college during the 1980s, and entered their thirties at the time when the label was coined in the 1990s. Although this generation is often discussed in terms of their shared experience of political activism in the 1980s, it is seldom acknowledged that their memory of the (inter)national clash on the Korean Peninsula between 1950 and 1953 is not experiential but transmitted. Because they were born in an already-partitioned Korea and grew up learning about the war, their visualization of Korea's split and its aftereffects is bound up with a process of translation through which what is inherited becomes regenerated.

To elaborate on this multilayered translation of memory, the next section situates the production of Korean War blockbusters within the specific transnational networks that have driven the desire to screen—in a double sense—Korea's traumatic past. Locating the traffic of melodramatic affects and the family frame of the screen(ed) memory of the Korean War, the following analysis of *JSA*, *Taegeukgi*, and *Dongmakgol* explicates why their vision of border-crossing relationships inevitably accompanies the witnessing of the death of the beloved. These films do not merely repeat the impasse that was reached in earlier efforts during the Cold War period to reconnect across the thirty-eighth parallel; instead, their works of transmemory register the senses of shock, confusion, and anxiety in the new era of state-led inter-Korean cooperation. Noting how the roles of victim, survivor, and mourner are distributed or converge, my inquiry probes the ideological effects of the vicarious traumatization rendered by Korean War blockbusters and reevaluates the liminal position of the surrogate witness on the screen. Thanks precisely to their alterity in terms of gender, race, and generation, those characters are interpellated to mediate the Korean experience for the global audience. By demonstrating how inherited narratives and images of loss or lack morph through such a translational practice into a source of identity and unity at the moment of transition, I thus propose rethinking Korean War blockbusters in

9 In conceptualizing the "division system" (*bundan cheje*), Paik Nak-chung emphasizes the system's colonial origin and structural relationship to the world economy. Paik, "South Korea: Unification and the Democratic Challenge," *New Left Review* 197 (January–February 1993): 67–84.

terms of the pleasure of mourning. As their spectacle-charged forms suspend the time for melodramatic witnessing, their audiences are affectively moved to engage, and also disengage, from a safe distance with the legacy of Korea's division.

Spectacles of Memory and Specters of *Minjung* in the Age of Global Capitalism. The spectacularization of Korean War memories by the 386 generation's blockbuster filmmaking is interwoven with the spectralization of the *minjung* (the people), the collective identity that united South Koreans for the democratic uprising of 1987 and lingered with a ghostly aura afterward. With the arrival of consumer society and the spread of late-capitalist logic in postauthoritarian South Korea, the earlier social space of resistance has been realigned and appropriated under the neoliberal market reforms carried out during the administrations of Kim Dae-jung (1998–2003) and Roh Moo-hyun (2003–2008). Elected right after the 1997 Asian financial crisis, these two liberal regimes led by former political dissidents strove to revive the national economy within the changing geopolitical landscape of the Asia-Pacific region. In embracing the "world standard" imposed by the International Monetary Fund (IMF), the state also initiated engagement with North Korea and negotiation with the United States. Coinciding with the pan-Asian phenomenon known as *hallyu* (the Korean Wave), South Korea's globalization drive created a favorable environment for soft-power industries by advocating the importance of "information, knowledge, and culture" in the twenty-first century.[10] Against this backdrop, Korean-style blockbusters did not simply benchmark the Hollywood model for high-budget filmmaking. While aiming to appeal to the Americanized tastes of both domestic and overseas viewers, the Korean film industry often relied on national content. A signature brand of this hybrid format was the Korean War blockbuster. Through its conversion of the country's most traumatic scene into a special-effects-driven spectacle, the blockbuster evoked the nationalist desire to compete with Hollywood films, thereby challenging US hegemony in the region.[11]

At the same time, however, Korean War blockbusters in the 2000s resonated with the sense of disorientation that South Koreans felt at a time when both the statist Cold War propaganda and the *minjung* movement for national reunification appeared outmoded.[12] During the Sunshine decade, the democratic governments made efforts

10 Kim Dae-jung has stated, "The culture industry, which encompasses movies, databases and computer games, has a huge market which now dominates the globe." "Era of Universal Globalism Dawning," *Korea Times*, November 5, 1998, http://www.koreatimes.co.kr/www/news/nation/2013/02/116_50286.html.

11 Regarding the multilayered nationalist sentiments evoked by the "Koreanness" of Korean blockbusters, see Kim Kyoung Wook, *Beullokbeoseuteo ui hwansang, hanguk yeonghwa ui nareusisijeum* [The Illusion of the Blockbuster, the Narcissism of Korean Cinema] (Seoul: Chaeksesang, 2002).

12 In this reconstituted public sphere, the people, too, no longer appear to (care to) be the collective subject of history now that issues related to personal identity and well-being, and to private concerns and anxieties, are more important. Such changing needs of contemporary South Koreans eventually led to the success of well-made commercial films, thus creating a break from the new wave of critical realism that culminated around the turn of the 1990s. See Moon Jae-cheol, "The Meaning of Newness in Korean Cinema: Korean New Wave and After," *Korea Journal* 46, no. 1 (Spring 2006): 36–59. Under the tide of postmodernism, the increasingly corporatized film industry facilitated big-budget filmmaking, which daringly materialized the multifarious desires of the masses (*daejung*) celebrating their subjectivity as consumers. This "pursuit of and respect for 'the popular'" since the mid-1990s can be characterized as "a reorientation and/or an expansion of the cultural movement of the 1980s, with its focus

to correct historical injustices committed under previous authoritarian regimes. They acknowledged and compensated for the victims of state violence in the past, for example, through the activities of the Truth and Reconciliation Commission (2005–2010). Nevertheless, the remnants of the division system were not entirely expunged, and the National Security Law was maintained. The post–Cold War reorganization of East Asia has complicated rather than eased North-South Korean relations. The 386 generation and their children still encountered naval clashes and exchanges of fire in the West (Yellow) Sea, not to mention the nuclear crisis on the Korean Peninsula.

While the state-sponsored revision of national history increasingly blurred the old distinction between the official and oppositional discourses of Korea's division, the public memory of the Korean War remained contentious about, if not confounded by, the phase of cooperation endorsed from above. South Korean civilians were welcome to "enjoy" the shortened distance to North Korea, from the Kumgang Mountain tour to the Kaesong Industrial Zone; but this type of inter-Korean interaction was created only as an exception under strict control, while a new system of signification that could capably replace Cold War ideologies was yet to be formed. Furthermore, the long-awaited yet unprepared contact with North Koreans, including the growing number of defectors, took place at the very moment when South Koreans themselves were struggling to survive neoliberal restructuring. Produced under these social conditions, blockbusters dealing with Korea's division have, through their spectacular reenactment of that painful history, affectively deployed and temporarily deferred the tensions surrounding the globalization of the divided Korea(s) during the period of engagement.

Melodramatic Witnessing and Belated Mourning. The Korean War blockbuster of the 2000s makes generational and representational shifts in recalling the losses endured since the division of the country. As the spectacularized form of transmemory arranges a site of mourning on the screen, the younger generation of South Korea also convey their contradictory desires for an encounter with their violent history and for the closure of wounds from it. However, precisely because the Korean War is almost over, but not quite—as long as the peninsula is under armistice conditions—their failure to mourn is inevitable. Faced with this predicament, Korean War blockbusters during the Sunshine era tend to fill in the actual lack of resolution with what I call "melodramatic witnessing." Through this melodramatic witnessing, the spectators can, *only emotionally*, move toward "victims who are indeed deserving objects of mourning," only to then quickly and safely return to their everyday life.[13]

changing from *minjung* to *daejung* (the mass)," as Jinhee Choi puts it in *The South Korean Film Renaissance: Local Hitmakers, Global Provocateurs* (Middletown, CT: Wesleyan University Press, 2010), 27–28.

13 Dominick LaCapra, *Representing the Holocaust: History, Theory, Trauma* (Ithaca, NY: Cornell University Press, 1996), 214, qtd. in E. Ann Kaplan, *Trauma Culture: The Politics of Terror and Loss in Media and Literature* (New Brunswick, NJ: Rutgers University Press, 2005), 135. Although my idea of melodramatic witnessing is inspired by Kaplan, who elaborates on LaCapra's concept of working through in her reading of America's "trauma culture," I would like to emphasize that it is hard to separate what she calls the "ethics of witnessing" from "melodramatic attempts" (122, 22).

Given that traumatic memory is prone to breaking out of narrativity because of its sensory aspects or fragmented nature, film has an edge in reenacting traumatic events by virtue of its visuality and aurality.[14] Matching traumatic symptoms with cinematic mechanisms, E. Ann Kaplan thus pays attention to melodrama as "aesthetic forms . . . [that] emerge to accommodate fears and fantasies related to suppressed historical events." Her remark that "Hollywood's melodramas are arguably impelled to repeat the rent in the dominant fiction occasioned by historical trauma while at the same time seeking unconsciously to repair and reveal that rent" is useful in considering Korean War movies, for their screen memory also serves a similar sort of protective function.[15] The textual displacement of war trauma into a familiar—mostly familial—site is inexorable because, according to Kaplan, "for political or social reasons" it is "too dangerous" for the culture to recall the traumatic experience.[16] During years of reconciliation in still-divided Korea, by defusing such political or social dangers through displacement or death, Park Chan-wook's *JSA* recaptures the very site of confrontation in a melodramatic mode so as to simulate the virtual experiment of border crossing.

In blending mystery and thriller genre conventions, *JSA* fully employs the structure of flashbacks, a cinematic technique that fittingly displays the abrupt and fragmentary return of trauma on the one hand and the stranded relationship between the past and the present on the other.[17] Beginning with an unidentified gunshot fired in the DMZ, the camera follows the movements of Swiss Major Sophie Jean, an investigator assigned to the case of the shooting incident in the Joint Security Area. As the narrative unfolds, she plays multiple roles as a mediator—both spatially between the North and the South and temporally between the past and the present within the film, as well as between the diegetic world and the spectator beyond the screen. But Sophie's "superior" position, while allowing her exceptional traversals, ironically leaves her out of the core of the story. In interrogating the surviving Korean soldiers—who are at once the victims, suspects, and witnesses of the gunfight—she barely unlocks their memories, from which she is herself alienated. This marginalization of the authority figure from the outside is further complicated by her gender: the commanding woman in masculine society ultimately drives the male subjects to suicide.[18] Several feminist

14 In his study of war trauma, Jonathan Shay states: "Traumatic memory is not narrative. Rather, it is experience that reoccurs, either as full sensory replay of traumatic events in dreams or flashbacks, with all things seen, heard, smelled, and felt intact, or as disconnected fragments." See his *Achilles in Vietnam: Combat Trauma and the Undoing of Character* (New York: Simon & Schuster, 1994), 172.

15 Kaplan, *Trauma Culture*, 73–74.

16 Kaplan, *Trauma Culture*, 74.

17 Regarding traumatic memories and flashbacks in cinema, see Maureen Turim, "The Trauma of History: Flashbacks upon Flashbacks," *Screen* 42, no. 2 (Summer 2001): 205–210.

18 It is notable that the original novel, Park Sang-yeon's *DMZ* (Seoul: Minumsa, 1997), unfolds the story of Swiss Major Sig Versami, centering on the interiority of the male protagonist-narrator. This gender switch affects the entire power dynamic in the film. As discussed in detail in this article, the authority of Sophie as a member of the Neutral Nation Supervisory Commission is largely offset by the fact that she is "the first female staff in Panmunjom." The film adaptation also marginalizes the issue of language, a crucial part of both the suspenseful narrative and the identity crisis of the protagonist in Park's novel. The process of learning Korean is entangled with Sig's own trauma inflicted by his Korean father, and his fluent use of Korean often surprises Korean characters from both sides, as his personal background remains unknown until he discloses it. In contrast, Sophie's half-Koreanness

critics have thus keenly interpreted her as a vanishing medium sacrificed for the fulfillment of the male subjects' homosocial fantasy.[19]

What is often neglected about Sophie in *JSA* is that the foreign, gendered other stands in for histories that have no place, either in the past or in the present, and that this other acts for the spectators through her shifting roles. As Sophie gathers bits and pieces of the traumatic event in the Joint Security Area through cross-examinations about conflicting statements, she undergoes her own status change from a neutral investigator to an involuntary perpetrator (as her inference triggers suicide attempts by the two South Korean soldiers under interrogation), an underacknowledged victim (after one of the South Korean suspects attempts to strangle her over the fall of his subordinate), and eventually an empathetic witness to the tragedy of Korea's division. Embodying the translational and transitional features of transmemory, Sophie thus prefigures Captain Smith, the surrogate witness-mourner of the united Korean forces in *Dongmakgol*. Both characters are indispensable in these works of transmemory precisely because of their alterity. In certifying the successful globalization of Korean cinema, the foreign characters in their respective blockbusters introduce a perspective through which the audience of the 2000s can view the war on Korea from a distance.

Admittedly, Sophie's transnationality is entwined with her identity as the daughter of a North Korean prisoner of war (POW) who chose a third country after the cease-fire in 1953. However, Sophie is not simply mobilized to bridge the incompatible spaces of the North and the South, the past and the present, or the personal and the public. Granted with the exceptional ability to recover Korea's traumatic past in a transitory fashion, the in-between character rather inversely suggests the inability of the insiders to gain access to their volatile history. In establishing legitimate connections, Sophie's borderline position tactfully provides a safe way to manage the terror and loss that might be caused by crossing the DMZ. Accordingly, those who are not equipped with such a "protection device" cannot escape the punishment for their private contacts with the enemy of the state, as exemplified by the deaths of the two South Korean border guards who crossed "the bridge of no return."

Precarious Solidarity in *Joint Security Area*. Simply put, *JSA* depicts the cross-border friendship between North and South Koreans who have not experienced the war between 1950 and 1953 but have lived under the division system. Marked off from the firsthand memory of people who lived through the war, second-generation memory recalls the unexperienced, yet still haunting past through the re-creation of inherited discourses. This characteristic of what I describe as transmemory is acknowledged in

---

is abused, in combination with her gender minority status. Korean characters in the film not only take for granted communication in Korean but also express their superiority as native speakers. When she takes over the custody of the victim-suspect, a South Korean general gives her "advice," using the familiar form of Korean.

19 For example, Kim Soyoung, "The Birth of the Local Feminist Sphere in the Global Era: 'Trans-Cinema' and *Yosongjang*," *Inter-Asia Cultural Studies* 4, no. 1 (2003): 10–24; and "Hanguk-hyeong beullokbeoseuteo eseo-ui dongseong sahoejeok pantaji: *Telmiseomding* gwa *JSA*" [Homosocial Fantasies in Korean-Style Blockbusters: *Tell Me Something* and *JSA*], *Yeo/seong iron* 6 (July 2002): 151–178; Kwon Eun-sun, "'Hanguk-hyeong beullokbeoseuteo' *gongdong gyeongbi guyeok JSA* eseo-ui minjokjuui" [Nationalism in "Korean-Style Blockbuster" *JSA*], in *Gongdong gyeongbi guyeok JSA* [Joint Security Area JSA], ed. Yonsei Institute of Media Arts (Seoul: Samin, 2002), 61–85.

director Park Chan-wook's own comment on the comparison of *JSA* to Choi In-hoon's *The Square* (*Gwangjang*, 1960), the founding text of South Korea's "division literature": "Our generation is a generation fascinated with Choi In-hoon's *The Square*. I wanted to carry on such a beautiful tradition in a different genre. . . . [But] this film has nothing to do with the anguish of intellectuals. I just felt sympathy with individuals who are unable to choose either side."[20] Unlike the protagonist of Choi's canonical novel, the two young South Korean soldiers in *JSA*, Lee Soo-hyeok and Nam Sung-shik, traverse the demarcation line in search of pleasure. The central position of modern, postcolonial intellectuals in the earlier narrative of the divided nation is here replaced by these ordinary men (but not women) of contemporary South Korea who are, like postmodern consumers, otherwise anonymous entities.

The South Korean soldiers' transgressive border crossings lead them beyond the state ideology to discover the humanity of North Korean soldiers Oh Kyeong-pil and Jeong Woo-jin. Thereafter, the four soldiers foster dangerous but, thanks precisely to the risk, thrilling fraternal ties. Their secret brotherhood, mostly formed in a closed bunker during dark nights, goes on even when they encounter one another in a restricted military area during the middle of the day. In the scene in which Lee and Jeong confront each other while on sentry duty, they can hardly suppress their laughter as they spit across the line, as if to make a mockery of the arbitrary demarcation separating them. By framing them from the inside of Panmunjom first, the mise-en-scène here conveys an illusion of neutrality while simultaneously recalling the reality of division (see Figure 4). The following shot–reverse shots of the two soldiers spitting at the other side force the spectators to share their playful gaze, creating an impulse to cross the line. Uncannily enough, *JSA*'s intersection of the repressed desire in the dark, private room and the reclaimed ideology in the bright, public domain completely correspond to the absurdity of the rebonding of the two Koreas under the Sunshine Policy. The intimate utopia of the four soldiers cannot and must not be exposed to the "sunshine world" in which the military confrontation between the two states continues while the South offers economic and humanitarian aid to the North.

Figure 4. Establishing shot from the inside of Panmunjom that frames the two soldiers from the South (left) and the North (right) on sentry duty, in *Gongdong gyeongbi guyeok JSA* (Myung Films, 2000).

In contrast to the hierarchical relationship of realpolitik, these youths banding together underground seem to develop fraternity based on equality, averting the omnipresent gaze of the political fathers on each side. Most obviously, when the younger South Korean soldier takes a picture of the other three during their secret meeting on the North Korean side, he makes an effort to frame them excluding the

20 Interview in *Film 2.0* (a weekly movie magazine of South Korea), reprinted in *Gongdong gyeongbi guyeok JSA*, 166.

wall upon which hang portraits of Kim Il Sung and Kim Jong Il. As a counterpart, the South's dependency on American power—the neocolonial father—is pointed out when the junior North Korean soldier says: "Move your [South Korean] army. Then we can go head to head with those damned Yankees." It is worth underscoring that such a denial of the father's shadow constitutes a condition for the alliance of the North-South soldiers-cum-brothers in the movie. This fraternal connection across the DMZ is also differentiated from comradeship in the same system. To South Korean Sergeant Lee Soo-hyeok's request, "Can I call you brother? I've always wanted a brother," North Korean officer Oh Kyeong-pil responds, "After hearing 'comrade' all the time, it's nice to be called brother." Like a big brother, Oh strives to save his younger brothers from the South, even after an "accidental" gunfight in which he loses his comrade, Jeong Woo-jin, the youngest member of their alternative family. The private bond between the South and North Korean soldiers, which has trumped state-imposed camaraderie, leads to a catastrophic end. When their forbidden relationship is about to be disclosed, the South Korean soldiers elect to commit suicide, not only for fear that their transgressions will be discovered but also in self-reproach over the loss of the innocent Northern brother. The deadly closure opted for by the South Korean soldiers, however, neither abandons nor disavows their desire for reunion with the other; rather, it transfers their wish, along with a sense of guilt and responsibility, to the third party by transforming their authoritative interrogator into a proper witness (and, by extension, to the viewer behind the screen). Lee Soo-hyeok does not pull the trigger on himself until he sees that Sophie is looking down at him from the window. By setting up the melodramatic witnessing of Sophie, the audience's avatar, *JSA* stages an eerie site of vicarious mourning here (see Figures 5 and 6). After slowly rotating around the body of the dying man on the ground, the camera turns to Sophie, who is

Figure 5. Sophie stands at the edge of the traumatic scene, in *Gongdong gyeongbi guyeok JSA* (Myung Films, 2000).

arriving at the scene a step behind, and shows that the surrogate witness is barely able to move, aching with tears. In soliciting the viewer to mourn the victim only belatedly and from a distance, the Korean War blockbuster of the era of reconciliation, through the creation of such a suspended time, reveals the unfading effects of the war and, at the same time, counteracts the anticipatory trauma of Korea's postdivision process.

Figure 6. The moment of Sophie's melodramatic witnessing is framed in a close-up shot, in *Gongdong gyeongbi guyeok JSA* (Myung Films, 2000).

Gendered Strife and Deferred Remembering. The responsibility of the last witness, or the unintentional "accessory" to the deaths, is given to, not taken by, Sophie. With her Swiss citizenship and a JD degree, she initially stands in a higher position than the Korean soldiers involved in the gun battle in the DMZ. In contrast to their illegal border crossing at night, she lawfully enters the borderland in broad daylight. Nonetheless, her international authority hardly helps her surpass the invisible barrier constituted by the brotherhood between the South and the North. As a biracial female officer from outside, she can never understand the mysterious solidarity among brethren, however hard she strives to fit into the male world (e.g., cigarette smoking, physical training).[21]

Again, the bar that blocks Sophie's engagement is lifted by the male subject, just as her duties as the investigator-witness are assigned, or thwarted, by masculine dominance. Lee Soo-hyeok's last and most truthful confession is made only after he hears about her father—a former North Korean officer. Here, she neither resolutely denies nor openly embraces but rather suspends the signification of her father (in her family picture, the part with her father is folded down but not torn away). Perhaps she wanted to be reconnected with her father through this first visit of her life, but what is waiting for Sophie in her father's land, still divided, is her doubly negative identity.[22] Already marginalized by her gender, her agency is further undercut by her troubling origin.

Indeed, the power of the (dead, treacherous) father is exerted only on the female character in *JSA*. While the male soldiers, thanks to their lack of fathers, are tied together by an egalitarian brotherhood, the heroine cannot escape her father's shadow. Whereas the fatherless brothers are projected as self-made men who are entitled to build the (nation's) future, she is bound by the (nation's) past, as her status is, in the last instance, determined by her biological kinship. For the young men's

21 Regarding the existing interpretations of this double alienation of Sophie, see Kim Soyoung's and Kwon Eun-sun's works mentioned earlier.

22 This contrasts with Park Sang-yeon's original novel, in which the (belated) reconciliation between the male protagonist and his father represents one of the dual plots. Not coincidentally, this reconciliation between past and present in the original is also mediated by his wife—a woman from the Third World.

imagination of reconciliation, Sophie's intervention is dangerous in multiple ways, as other feminist scholars have noted.[23] Sophie brings in the law of the "foreign" father, the reality principle that permits her to cross the physical border, on the one hand, and the specter of the "forgotten" father, the returned past that helps her to transcend the psychological barrier, on the other. The daughter of the two fathers, however, is ultimately barred from the frame of fraternity constituted by the orphaned sons, who consciously leave out the image of the father in making their own vision. As implied by her folded family picture, Sophie hesitates about being detached from her father. After all, she is interpellated as a mute witness to the replayed tragedy of national division, not as a participatory subject in the male-centered fantasy of a reunited nation. There is no spot left for her in the fraternal imagination of the seemingly new, yet all-too-familiar community, as insinuated in the last scene. In the black-and-white photograph that the camera pans across and zooms in and out on, the young patriarchs of the divided nation reconvene at the very historical site of the division. It is as if they want to be remembered at the moment of their being together, even as their precarious solidarity is at once broken and sustained by death. But once again, precisely because Sophie is excluded from the site of contestation, her memory, including the one about her father, survives and returns; in this way, she represents the persistent appearance of the surrogate witness-mourner in Korean War blockbusters.

The Family before the Nation in *Taegeukgi*. Whereas *JSA* offers a close-up of the still divided Korean Peninsula in the post–Cold War world, *Taegeukgi* takes a trip back to the very moment the Korean War broke out. Leading an impoverished but cheerful life before the war, shoe shiner Jin-tae works hard to support his mute mother and younger siblings. His brother Jin-seok, the most intelligent and best educated among them, is the hope of the fatherless family. After the brothers are forcibly drafted into the South Korean Army, Jin-tae is determined to have Jin-seok discharged by earning a medal for bravery. But Jin-seok only feels alienated from Jin-tae, who is becoming a merciless soldier caught up in the madness of war. As the war progresses, the brothers are separated, and Jin-tae, believing his younger brother has been killed by a South Korean commander, becomes a North Korean sergeant full of vengeance. Thrown against their will into fratricidal war, the brothers in *Taegeukgi* replay the brotherhood suggested in *JSA*: the "Northern" elder brother, with a reliable character and a simple heart, is willing to sacrifice himself for the preservation or prosperity of the younger

23 In the critiques by Kim Soyoung and Kwon Eun-sun, Sophie is presented as a dangerous woman who thwarts the secret dream of reunification in alignment with a brother-centered family narrative, in which only two types of women exist: a second-rate family member like Su-jeong (Nam's sister and Lee's girlfriend) or the object of a male's sexual fantasies, such as Sung-shik's picture of South Korea's top actress. See Kim, "Hanguk-hyeong," 172–174; Kwon, "'Hanguk-hyeong,'" 73–77. If the absence of the father is the first condition of their companionship, their brotherhood is consolidated through the exchange of (pictures of) women. What has often been neglected in these previous criticisms is Sophie's agency—as implied in her tenacious effort to pursue the truth, even by suggesting a "deal" to the South Korean soldier—in other words, her performative power as a speaking subject. By refusing the woman's role as a silent image, she challenges the patriarchal order that governs both the national and international organizations she is involved with. Of course, her defiance is punished and she is left a mute witness, her voice lost.

brother in the South, who is more sophisticated and therefore suitable to become a modern subject.

As a corollary, *Taegeukgi* unfolds the tragic fate of the Korean family through the recollections of the surviving younger brother. Called in to an excavation site a half century after the Armistice, Jin-seok is finally "reunited" with his elder brother, but only to confirm Jin-tae's death. The belated encounter with the lost other actually occurs twice in *Taegeukgi*. Long before the remains of Jin-tae are found, the brothers face each other, alive, in the line of fire. Locating Jin-tae among the enemy, Jin-seok strives to galvanize his big brother, who is now trying to kill any South Korean forces around. As soon as Jin-tae recovers his senses, he urges his younger brother to escape the battlefield. Their brotherhood reaches its melodramatic climax as the camera alternates between the elder brother, who is fighting to the death in order to clear a way for Jin-seok, and the younger brother, who, with faltering steps, is walking away from the raining shells at his older brother's insistence. This momentary reunion of the separated brothers is compelling not simply because it takes place "too late," in accordance with the conventions of melodrama.[24] It is also compelling because the ending captures the paradoxical temporal structure of traumatic experience: belatedness and repetitiveness. Through its melodramatic witnessing, however, the Korean War blockbuster gives the nation's haunting past a burial too soon and contains the desire to mourn the loss of unity within the private realm of family.

The final reunion of the separated brothers in *Taegeukgi* is staged as a site of mourning in which the heir in the South is relieved of guilt as well because he has not only survived but also fulfilled the request of the dead. The successful modernization of the younger brother compensates for a sense of powerlessness rooted in the traumatic fratricidal past. At the same time, the flood of tears in the film's finale betrays an acknowledgment of the sacrifice of the others, without which there would have been no survival or success. The recovery of the lost brother, who is already presumed to have died in battle, by the surviving brother, who is also aged and waiting for his own death, is in effect all the more necessary for the post–Cold War generation as represented on the screen by Jin-seok's granddaughter (see Figures 7 and 8). By inserting into the frame of the present this young, empathetic audience proxy—who may feel less foreign than Sophie in *JSA*—*Taegeukgi* ably invites the spectators of the new millennium to become fellow mourners for those who lived through the war. In vicariously experiencing the history of loss, however, once again the audience participates in the rite of mourning only belatedly and only from a distance. Comparable to Sophie at the site (or sight) of suicide in *JSA*, the granddaughter in *Taegeukgi*, weeping in silence, stays in her place at the burial site, where a melodramatic witnessing overlaps with a belated mourning: that is, in her place just a step away from her grandfather, who kneels on the ground, wailing over the remains of his older brother. Watching the melodramatic resolution between the dead and the dying in this manner, the new generation are freed to move on, appreciating the benefits that are founded upon the sufferings of their forebears.

24 Linda Williams notes: "Melodramatic weepie is the genre that seems to endlessly repeat our melancholic sense of the loss of origin, the impossible hope of returning to an earlier state. . . . Origins are already lost, the encounters always take place too late, on death beds or over coffins." Williams, "Film Bodies: Gender, Genre, and Excess," *Film Quarterly* 44, no. 4 (Summer 1991): 10–11.

Figure 7. Called in to the excavation site where Jin-tae's body lies, Jin-seok is wailing on the ground, in *Taegeukgi hwinallimyeo* (KangJeGyu Films, 2004).

Figure 8. Next to Jin-seok, his granddaughter is mourning differently, in *Taegeukgi hwinallimyeo* (KangJeGyu Films, 2004).

This generational division of symbolic labor in *Taegeukgi* indicates a certain transition in the way of coming to terms with the legacies of the past, which I have discussed as a characteristic of transmemory. The motif of fratricide and the scene of reconciliation in death give a feeling of déjà vu, as these have been repeated in the tradition of Korean War narratives. One notable case can be found in Jo Jung-rae's *Taebaek Mountain Range* (*Taebaeksanmaek*, 1983–1989), which was read as an alternative history textbook during the *minjung* movement of the 1980s. In the ending of Jo's massive serial novel, the head of the decapitated elder brother, the leftist leader in postcolonial Korea, is reclaimed by his younger brother, the boss of a right-wing youth group. In iterating this kind of recovery of the older brother—who cannot be welcome in South Korea—only after his death, *Taegeukgi* marks a qualitative difference through its translation. Whereas the "original" *minjung* literature of the 1980s rehabilitates the nameless warriors of the partisan struggle by delineating a patrilineal genealogy of resistance that records them as "politically proud forefathers," the "derivative" Korean War blockbuster made in the post-*minjung*, post-IMF era retrieves the remains of the "politically innocent (grand)father" to remember his sacrifice for the well-being of the family. In registering the trauma of the "past" in the spectacularized form of transmemory, more than eleven million Korean viewers of the 2004 film might also have been processing the harsh realities of neoliberal capitalism that caused mass unemployment under the IMF system, realities that were more often than not emblemized by the phenomenon of the "jobless father's suicide."[25] If, as Rey Chow has stated, the cultural

25 Attracting 11.7 million moviegoers nationwide, Kang Je-gyu's *Taegeukgi* set a new record for the Korean movie industry in 2004. The waves created by the Korean War blockbuster, however, were more national(istic) than international. Despite its casting of *hallyu* (Korean Wave) stars, *Taegeukgi* drew an audience of less than 1 million in Japan, less than the record of its predecessors, *Swiri* (1.3 million) and *JSA* (1 million). See "Ol yeoreum ilbon gaebong hanguk yeonghwa ui heunghang seongjeokpyo" [The Transcript of Korean Films Released in Japan This Summer], *Cine 21*, August 25, 2004, http://www.cine21.com/news/view/mag_id/25794/p/1. In the United States, its gross income of $1.1 million fell short of Kim Ki-duk's *Spring, Summer, Fall, Winter . . . and Spring* (2003; $2.4 million), even though *Taegeukgi*, unlike Kim's art cinema, received the support of Koreans in America. "*Taegeukgi hwinallimyeo* miguk gwangaek daebubun i hangukgye" [Most of the American Audience of *Taegeukgi* Are Korean Americans], *Hankyoreh*, April 15, 2005, http://www.hani.co.kr/arti/culture/culture_general/26538.html.

translation that cinema engages with involves the twofold process of inscription and transformation, *Taegeukgi* intimately performs such an inscription-transformation in the context of a globalizing South Korea.[26] In morphing the verbal tradition of *minjung* onto the screen, the text of transmemory simultaneously inscribes the new generation's experience of the nation's violent incorporation into the neoliberal world economy through the very transnational medium of the blockbuster.

The Fantasy of Flight and Reunion in Death in *Dongmakgol*. The enactment of witnessing and mourning operates quite differently in *Dongmakgol* (2005), as discussed in the introduction. Set in a rural village that keeps itself away from the rest of the world, the fairy tale–like work dramatizes an unexpected encounter and coexistence between enemies during wartime. American Captain Smith is "dropped" from the sky, two South Korean soldiers desert from their barracks, and three North Korean comrades are cut off from their main force. Before ultimately forming a "united force," these maladjusted individuals from the combat zone are first reborn in the village of Dongmakgol, whose name means to "live carefree, like children." Reminiscent of Tao Yuanming's "peach blossom spring story," the carefree space is projected as a primordial community that might have continued to exist without contamination from the outside. Mesmerizing contemporary South Koreans with what has been lost through modernization, the film nostalgically reconstructs the homogeneous and harmonious social organism—or "the origin of the nation that . . . precludes heterogeneity," as Cho Hyung-rae puts it.[27] According to Cho, the assimilation process of the alien visitors is none other than retrogression to the phase of infancy in which the bodily matters of eating and excreting come first and foremost. The visitors live a second life as the "living dead" because they have already died once, as soon as they entered the "Imaginary Realm."[28]

Their "redemption" in the fantasy world of Dongmakgol is neither free nor harmless, however, because the presence of the strangers places the indigenous community in jeopardy. The outsiders therefore leave this utopia—where time has happily stopped—to meet death, which has been suspended during their stay in the village. Here, their cinematic journey from a supplementary life in the Imaginary Realm of Dongmakgol to a physical death outside of it seems to blur the distinction Slavoj Žižek makes about Antigone and the ghost of Hamlet's father, who are pitted against each other in a liminal position "between the two deaths."[29] Similar to Sophocles' Antigone, the symbolic death of the Korean soldiers—that is, their

26 Rey Chow's approach to Chinese cinema in terms of cultural translation distinguishes two types of translation: the cinematic "inscription" of "a generation, a nation, and a culture," and the "transformation of tradition and change between media," for example, from words to images. Chow, *Primitive Passions: Visuality, Sexuality, Ethnography, and Contemporary Chinese Cinema* (New York: Columbia University, 1995), 182. For an example of cinematic translation within the South Korean context, see Michelle Cho, "Genre, Translation, and Transnational Cinema: Kim Jee-woon's *The Good, the Bad, the Weird*," *Cinema Journal* 54, no. 3 (Spring 2015): 44–68.

27 Cho Hyung-rae, "Meokgo baeseol haneun sinche ro hoegwihara: *Welkeom tu Dongmakgol* saeropge ilki" [Return to the Body That Eats and Excretes: A New Reading of *Welcome to Dongmakgol*], *Cineforum* 8 (May 2007): 210.

28 Cho H., "Meokgo," 205–207.

29 Slavoj Žižek, *The Sublime Object of Ideology* (London: Verso, 1989), 135.

exclusion from the two Korean states—precedes their biological death. Also akin to Hamlet's father, their actual deaths are not registered symbolically in the diegetic space because their mission as a unified force is executed outside of the village after they leave it. However, the deaths of the allied Korean soldiers neither fill the gap between the two deaths with "sublime beauty" as in the case of Antigone, nor return as a "terrifying monster" in the way of Hamlet's father.[30] Rather, suspended in spectacle, as analyzed previously, their symbolic death remains to be signified by Captain Smith, the surrogate witness-mourner and foreign avatar for the global(ized) audience of the 2000s.

Ultimately, the second death of the united Korean forces, who choose to die with honor rather than live with shame, is arranged to transmit to the viewer the fantasy of an originary community that transcends divisive ideologies imported from outside. In forming an allied force against the US military, the ragtag group of losers (if not traitors) from each side of the divided Korea successfully prevents civilian casualties during the war. This imagined fulfillment of the wish for national autonomy expresses popular resentment against American imperialists, who are held accountable for massacres during the Korean War. Without a doubt, such a public critique of the US-related mass killings was made possible by democratic advances in the period of the Sunshine Policy, as noted earlier. In addition to a retroactive resentment of the foreign power, the narrative development of *Dongmakgol* also releases South Koreans from the burden of guilt about their own complicity in the massacres. The metamorphosis of Lieutenant Pyo, a runaway from the South Korean army, encapsulates such a working-through process. A "conscientious objector" who disobeyed an order to blow up the Han River bridge filled with refugees fleeing to the South, Pyo suffers from post-traumatic stress disorder, even in the utopian life at Dongmakgol. His trauma is not overcome until he gains the prerogative of the supreme command in the operation of the combined Korean forces.[31] In directing the mission to save the village, which remains undivided, the rebellious but powerless postcolonial subject is promoted to an autonomous and genuine leader of the united nation.

The irony of this imaginary solution in *Dongmakgol* lies in its modernized way of rescuing the premodern form of the nation. The primitive community consisting of innocent people cannot decide their fate for themselves; their survival rests in the hands of their "naturalized" members, who initially belonged to the civilized world at war. The power asymmetry between the traditional and the modern determines the relationship among the outsiders themselves. Although the Northerners outnumber the Southerners, they voluntarily follow the direction of the South Korean lieutenant, whereas their weapons and technology are supplied by the only member from the West, who resembles the benevolent missionaries who are assisting the modernization of the backward country(side).

30 Žižek, *Sublime*, 135.

31 Regarding South Korea's partial sovereignty over its military forces under the US-led Cold War alliance, see Kim Dong-choon, *Jeonjaeng gwa sahoe: Uri ege hanguk jeonjaeng eun mueot ieonna* [War and Society: What Was the Korean War for Us?] (Paju: Dolbegae, 2000), 344–345.

Innocence Must Be Defended. Arguably, the disarmament of the soldiers in Dongmakgol implies the death of the modern subject. At the same time, the dream life of the outsiders—or their life in a dream guided by butterflies—reaches a magical resolution of Cold War confrontations, even transcending racial and linguistic barriers. Although this dramatic settlement hardly deviates from the dominant narrative in the South of the Korean War (i.e., the "sudden invasion of the North"), it equally echoes the *minjung* imagination by dissociating the people from the state ideology. When South Korean Private Moon blames the North for having ruined his ambition to become a club manager, Taek-ki, the youngest North Korean soldier, is stunned into silence upon seeing his superior, High Comrade Lee, admit Moon's claim. But Taek-ki soon responds, "I just went to the South because they [the ruling power] told me to do so." In such a comical and satirical manner, the film also describes the absurdity and injustice of the war. For instance, upon hearing about the outbreak of war, the villagers conjecture it must be an aggression by the "Japs" or "Chinks." Unable to explain that the war is taking place between Koreans, Private Moon can only equivocate in response to the question raised by one of the villagers about whether it is fair for the North to fight against both the South and the United States.

The programmed animosity between the two Koreas is smoothed over in nonverbal ways in *Dongmakgol*, and such a presymbolic reconciliation is often heightened by the film's mise-en-scène and sound, which are evocative of Miyazaki Hayao's animation.[32] The first "military" clash between soldiers from the North and South ends in a spellbinding sequence: after a grenade is accidentally dropped and eventually rolls into the town barn, a stockpile of corn stored inside is blown up and falls down from the sky like popcorn. Foreshadowing the spectacular "fireworks" sequence in its finale, this scene, also in slow motion and with extradiegetic music, stretches time to establish a cease-fire and a momentary reconciliation between the divided Korean soldiers by placing them in the very state of suspension. Despite the fact that the explosion despoils all the provisions for winter, the troublemakers are not thrown out of the village but are instead treated to a plain meal. After sleeping in the same room, the former fighters gradually become accustomed to the natural life in Dongmakgol, where people are unfazed even when shouted at by someone with a gun. The soldiers finally create a basis for cooperation by working together to beat a wild boar that has been ravaging the crops that the farmers worked so hard to grow. In addition to delivering a lively thrill ride, the hunt scene alludes to an ideal way of solving a longstanding problem for Dongmakgol's agrarian society.[33] The youngest (North Korean) soldier has the pluck to fling a stone at the gigantic beast, which chases him until the altruistic (South Korean) officer pushes him out of the way and faces his own crisis. It is High Comrade Lee who knocks off the boar, by thrusting into the village enemy an improvised

32 Regarding "the absence of language" in the fantasmatic world of *Dongmakgol*, see Cho H., "Meokgo," 211–216. The soundtrack was composed by Joe Hisaishi, well known for his collaborations with Miyazaki Hayao, including *Mononoke Hime* (*Princess Mononoke*, 1997). For *Dongmakgol*'s Japanese animation–like traits, see Kyu Hyun Kim's review of the film on the website Koreanfilm.org, at http://www.koreanfilm.org/kfilm05.html#dongmakgol.

33 This hunt scene could also be seen as a parody of (or homage to) Miyazaki Hayao's *Mononoke Hime*, as noted in both Cho's and Kim's readings of the film. In this light, the scene exemplifies the transnational and translational features of *Dongmakgol* as a work of transmemory.

spear, namely, a crutch that is passed to him by Captain Smith. To be sure, the united front composed of the refugees from the modern world fixes the old headache of the country folk. But it is the civilized men who reap the most benefit from the big game; they enjoy a secret barbeque party that night and wonder why the village people do not know this taste.

Now the outsiders, shedding their military uniforms, are adopted as family members of the kinship community, or as honorary citizens who make great efforts to modernize the traditional society without harming the virtues of the simple life. Captain Smith now looks less like a member of the US Navy than a sympathetic "anthropologist" as he teaches the indigenous people American football and takes a motion picture of their festival. His affective connection with the Dongmakgol natives is distinct from the curious gaze of the foreign tourists who take photographs of Panmunjom in *JSA*, for instance. Carrying the oldest woman of the village on his back while she sleeps, just as a grandson would do for his own grandmother—or just as the new generation of the global era *should* do for their grandparents' generation—Smith says to himself, "That's life." Their communication does not require any linguistic intelligence then or when the wise "grandmother" simply applies soybean paste to the bee sting of the "grandson" who has dropped from the sky. Similarly, the harmony among the Koreans, both between the South and the North and between the old-fashioned and the newfangled, is achieved through the natural rhythms of their bodies, as crystallized in the festival scene. Private Moon sings a "boogie-woogie" song, which he might have picked up in a nightclub for Americans, with a percussion accompaniment played by the villagers. In blending seemingly incompatible elements in a marvelous way—or in a postmodern pastiche—*Dongmakgol* conveys more than an antiwar message. Inheriting *minjung* sensibilities, it also visualizes an alternative trajectory for Korea's postcolonial history: what if we Koreans were able to modernize ourselves without a foreign yoke?

Using wit and humor, this film made in 2005 provides its social commentary more lightly and comically than prior Korean War blockbusters. For example, when High Comrade Lee asks, "How is it that . . . you have such a hold on the villagers without ever raising your voice? What's the secret to your great leadership?," the village chief responds, "You just gotta feed them a lot." This unsophisticated yet pithy answer perplexes the young man from North Korea, a country suffering from mass hunger in spite of, or because of, their "great leader." The profound truth beyond the literal words thus touches on the issue of the North Korean famine and food shortage more subtly than does *JSA* (e.g., the North Korean officer's "dream . . . that one day, our republic will make the best damn sweets on this peninsula"). Nevertheless, like the other Korean War blockbusters, *Dongmakgol* reproduces, in its own subtle manner, the stereotypical image of impoverished North Koreans as nonresistant victims of a dynastic dictatorship. In contrast to their partners from the other side, the North Korean soldiers do not have traumatic flashbacks or secular desires; they are depicted as being so naïve that they just follow the orders of the state and as being simply lucky that they have survived thus far. Lacking interiority and historicity, North Korean characters in South Korean films often remain stuck in the past. Or they are merely imagined as belonging to the past precisely because their present is not accessible. In

Dongmakgol, although it may signal a shift in the Southerners' way of remembering the Korean War during the era of reconciliation, the trauma of North Koreans—perhaps located at the very core of their "submissive" subjectivity—has yet to be acted out, let alone worked through.

The Indispensable Other in the Formation of Our Family. Whereas North Koreans are always portrayed within the frame of a lost past, the American forces come from a future that will direct lives in South Korea, for good or ill. In *Dongmakgol*, the US Army represents modernity, mostly its detrimental side, from materialistic commercialism to rationalistic militarism. Aiming solely at a war victory, the American forces promptly decide to allow indiscriminate bombings, even in civilian areas and without further deliberation. They do not hesitate to abuse innocent people either, including children, women, and the elderly. The greatest irony of the massacre in the film is that the sudden attack of the United Nations paratroopers "helps" the heterogeneous members of the village become formally registered in the kinship community. The interpellation of power—or, more exactly, interrogation by torture—facilitates the construction of an undividable (pseudo)family. Taek-ki, speaking in a different dialect, is declared to be the son of a North Korean (Sergeant Jang) and a female native of the town. Comrade Lee, marked with a scar on his cheek, is identified as the father of a boy who is actually being raised by a single mother in the village.

This newly formed lineage in Dongmakgol is further solidified as the members witness the fall of the respectable village headman and, more melodramatically, the death of Yeo-il, a girl who embodies the innocence of the "carefree space," shot by the foreign invaders. While resonating with the anti-imperialist nationalism of the *minjung* narrative, the alliance forged in *Dongmakgol*, unlike the patrilineal genealogy from the 1980s, does not restore the authority of the father figure in a traditional way. Illustrating the double procedure of cultural translation, discussed earlier, that cinema performs, the 1980s *minjung* affect is altered in the 2000s, as hinted at in Private Moon's insistence on referring to Sergeant Jang, who is almost one generation older, as his elder brother. This "horizontal" fraternity between the North Korean elder brother, with his spiritual and physical superiority, and the South Korean younger brother, with a modern (capitalist) sensibility, is almost too familiar to South Korean audiences, as it has been repeated from *JSA* to *Taegeukgi*. Building up melodramatic sentiments, the banal but still powerful fantasy of brotherhood ultimately transforms the most cowardly and individualistic character into one of the selfless martyrs for their pristine community in crisis. Although he initially protests against the idea of becoming a decoy to divert the US-led bomb attack from Dongmakgol—"We're third parties. Even if it were my family, I couldn't do that"—Private Moon, in the end, meets a glorious, manly death on the battlefield, falling beside his elder brother from the North.

The familial bond that unites all Koreans in Dongmakgol is racially "purified" by returning Captain Smith to the US base, because the preservation of the utopian world depends in the last instance on his—the outsider's—report to the external world. In a Žižekian sense, the foreigner plays the role of the Other under whose gaze the Korean characters identify themselves as a unified national subject. What is critical here is that Smith is not only the survivor of the devastating war but also the witness to the sacrifice of the nameless warriors. When the American other sees a distant air raid on the joint operation area, he wipes away the tears rolling down his face as the sole mourner of the dying Korean soldiers. (This act of mourning from a distance is analogous to those performed by Sophie in *JSA* and Jin-seok's granddaughter in *Taegeukgi*.) In the meantime, the allied Korean forces smile as they stand up to the dropping bombs, as if they were watching spectacular fireworks over the sky, just like Dongmakgol children—or as if they know their deaths will not receive any signification from the national community, even though they have put their lives at stake for its existence.

The Korean War Blockbuster as a Site of Mourning. Inheriting the incomplete work of mourning from the previous era, the Korean War blockbuster in post–Cold War South Korea, in its hybrid form that incorporates foreign elements into the national imaginary, recalls memories of the dead, the forgotten, and the wounded from the division. Capitalizing on cinematic experience as an act of witnessing, the work of transmemory develops a visceral connection between the past and the present. Through the mediation of a surrogate witness and mourner, the films of the genre skillfully conjure apparitional subjects that could not be buried in the past and have therefore been haunting the present. In screening these ghosts who wander in the liminal space of the divided nation, the blockbusters discussed in this article project a longing for historical continuity during a time when the two Koreas are entering a new phase in their relationship amid the world's changing geopolitical climate. Such a longing, however, resonates with ambivalence, tension, and puzzlement. By imagining being reunited with the "brothers" across the DMZ only in the vision of death, the blockbusters intimately reveal South Koreans' apprehension and trepidation about their engagement with the North. Through cinematic techniques that suspend signification on the screen, the films thus prompt the audience to remember Korea's unfinished war in the era of reconciliation, on the one hand, and to simulate its postdivision process in a possible future, on the other hand.

This screened memory of the Korean War during the Sunshine decade also showcases how blockbuster filmmaking appropriates and refashions the nation's historical legacy and cultural traditions in its postauthoritarian and postmodern juncture. As a work of transmemory in the age of globalization, the blockbuster constructs a popular platform on which the incurred but not recorded losses can be reenacted in melodramatic spectacles and transferred to the next generation and beyond the national border. Through a vicarious witnessing of the unjust deaths of their innocent forebears, viewers come to indirectly mourn those who have been left unregistered in the existing symbolic order of the still partitioned Korean Peninsula. At the same time, the blockbuster's cultural translation of the violent past interlaces old fears with new anxieties, since the previous matrices of national collectivity, both the state's anticommunist discourse and the oppositional *minjung* narrative, are in transition. Straddling the nation's traumatic past and uncertain future, Korean War blockbusters in the 2000s thus respond to the lack of resolution in history with affects and fantasies. Through the cinematic experience, South Koreans encounter the lost members of their family in the North as a split self, but always too late or always from a safe distance. By evoking melodramatic witnessing in such a privatized and spectacularized way, the Korean War blockbuster operates as a site of mourning that remains to be completed by global audiences. *

I thank Brett de Bary, Michael Shin, Naoki Sakai, and Petrus Liu for their advice on the pursuit of this topic for my dissertation. This article benefited from feedback provided by Youngju Ryu, Charlotte Eubanks, Jonathan Abel, and Baek Moonim. I am also grateful to the journal's reviewers for suggestions.

IN FOCUS: Why Adult Film History Matters

Introduction

by David Church and Eric Schaefer

Film studies developed as an academic discipline in the late 1960s—roughly the same time that hard-core pornography emerged from under the counter and into the public sphere in bookstores and movie theaters. In its quest for legitimacy, film studies cast its gaze backward some thirty or forty years, largely focusing on classical Hollywood cinema. After their establishment in the late 1960s in small storefront theaters in the United States, pornographic movies also drew heavily on Hollywood's past, concentrating on narrative features, building a system largely based on bankable stars, and even mimicking Tinseltown with glitzy premieres for major releases. But even though film studies and pornographic cinema came of age at about the same time, the emerging discipline paid scant attention to adult film. Most academic work on adult movies at that time took place in the social sciences or legal scholarship. Although a few articles appeared in other journals earlier, it was not until 1988 that the first essay to deal exclusively with pornography was published in *Cinema Journal*.[1]

A year later, everything changed with the publication of Linda Williams's groundbreaking book *Hard Core: Power, Pleasure, and the "Frenzy of the Visible."*[2] *Hard Core* looked at pornography as a genre with its own distinct conventions and audience expectations—and served as a key intellectual intervention in the "porn wars" that had grown through the mid-1970s and into the 1980s as fundamentalist Christians joined with some feminists to rally against pornography as, respectively, a threat to traditional values and a manifestation of

1 Stephen Prince, "The Pornographic Image and the Practice of Film Theory," *Cinema Journal* 27, no. 2 (1988): 27–39.

2 Linda Williams, *Hard Core: Power, Pleasure, and the "Frenzy of the Visible"* (Berkeley: University of California Press, 1989).

patriarchal oppression. Notwithstanding the contributions of earlier work, Williams's book invited scholars to look at movies made for sexual arousal in a serious way. Articles in publications such as *Camera Obscura*, *Film Quarterly*, *Jump Cut*, and *Velvet Light Trap* multiplied through the 1990s and 2000s, as did monographs and edited collections. Papers on adults-only material also increased at conferences, no longer consigned to one-off events.

In the inaugural issue of the journal *Porn Studies* in 2014, Williams notes how the study of adult cinema has accrued its own sense of history as a subfield of film and media studies and is no longer in the perpetual state of "emergence" correlative to pornography's culturally suspect status.[3] While the movement to reclaim adult cinema as a worthy object of study has been partially won (although scholars may still be pigeonholed as their university's "porn person" for working in this area), a major reason for the subfield's provisional coalescence has been the difficulty of historicizing such a poorly documented and preserved corpus. Most scholars would be rightly skeptical of peers or filmgoers who dismissed any popular genre with a grand "seen one, seen them all" gesture or reduced a whole genre's appeal to one spectatorial purpose—yet this stigma against adult cinema has proved difficult to shake without a detailed accounting of historical diversity in production, representation, exhibition, distribution, and reception practices, not to mention sexual orientation and taste. As a corollary to pornography's reputation as an open secret (existing in the cultural shadows, widely viewed but seldom discussed in serious and dispassionate ways), adult cinema has been too often regarded as monolithic and largely interchangeable, a mass with little historical variation—but this presumption is precisely what the new wave of adult film historiography actively challenges.

At the 2014 SCMS conference in Chicago, Eric Schaefer called for the formation of the Adult Film History Scholarly Interest Group (SIG), citing the critical mass of scholarship that had developed. The mission of the SIG would be to "provide a forum for scholars working on adult film history to collaborate, share information and archival sources, debate issues within the field, and promote high caliber research"; to advocate for preservation of adult films; and to be "a liaison with scholars from other fields and other professional organizations."[4] The SIG is now thriving and continuing to grow.

The decision to eschew a name for the SIG like "Porn Studies" in favor of "Adult Film" was strategic, because as Walter Kendrick observed, "pornography names an argument, not a thing."[5] That word has been used to categorize everything from the novels of Zola and Spillane, to *Playboy* pinups and *Debbie Does Dallas* (Jim Clark, 1978). It offers no more precision than "smut," "dirty pictures," or "immoral film"—the latter once a designation employed by the New York Board of Censors. "Adult film," however, can refer to any time-based media designed to emphasize nudity and/or human sexuality and intended for viewing by adults, regardless of the time, place, or age at

3 Linda Williams, "Pornography, Porno, Porn: Thoughts on a Weedy Field," *Porn Studies* 1, nos. 1–2 (2014): 24–40.

4 SCMS Adult Film History Scholarly Interest Group Mission Statement, http://www.cmstudies.org/?page=groups_adultfilm.

5 Walter Kendrick, *The Secret Museum: Pornography in Modern Culture* (New York: Viking, 1987), 31.

which one is deemed to be adult. The flexibility afforded by "adult film" can encompass any moving-image medium and any sexual orientation and act. "Adult film" incorporates not only material designed strictly as entertainment or for sexual stimulation but also films that are educational, experimental, or made for other purposes. Finally, "adult" is the term used by the industry itself since the 1960s—from the trade group Adult Film Association of America to the industry publication *Adult Video News*. Although "pornography" continues to be an easy appellation, a shift to "adult film" could effectuate the integration of such material into the larger continuum of media history.

Adult film has historically been cordoned off from the rest of popular entertainment through censorship, alternative production and distribution channels, and separate physical spaces, resulting in historiographical challenges that are seldom confronted in other areas of media history. Yet adult cinema is a constitutive force in media history, with changing technologies for adult content serving as important drivers for the popularization of successive home-video formats, cable television, the internet—and, by extension, the increasingly hazy border between "cinema" and "media" that our larger field continues to explore.[6] Meanwhile, the evolution of feminism has drastically shifted the debate over adult content, with the once-dominant media-effects paradigm now supplanted by a sex-positive focus on equitable working conditions in production and distribution. An important implication of the upsurge in adult film historiography is a more ethical reconsideration of the labor of sex workers, including those from marginalized populations.[7]

Rather than rehashing textualist arguments over sexual representation that consumed earlier work on pornography, adult film history increasingly draws from the circulation-centered tactics of "new cinema history," including inspiration from audience studies, economics, urban studies, and especially media-industry and material-culture studies.[8] Privileging microhistories and ephemeral outliers as building blocks toward a history written with fewer a priori generalizations, this "trace historiography" enables adult film historians to sidestep wearied debates over the politics of representation and also provides tools for studying a genre in which many films from only a few decades past have already become inaccessible.[9] In this dossier, Elena Gorfinkel argues that examining a failed sexploitation film can reveal more about the avant-garde milieu of late-1960s New York City than writing that era's history in broad strokes. Indeed, much as new cinema history studies the social phenomenon of cinema without heavy

6 See Jonathan Coopersmith, "Pornography, Technology, and Progress," *IKON* 4 (1998): 94–125; Chuck Kleinhans, "The Change from Film to Video Pornography: Implications for Analysis," in *Pornography: Film and Culture*, ed. Peter Lehman (New Brunswick, NJ: Rutgers University Press, 2006), 154–167; and Peter Alilunas, *Smutty Little Movies: The Creation and Regulation of Adult Video* (Berkeley: University of California Press, 2016).

7 For examples, see Elena Gorfinkel, "The Body's Failed Labor: Performance Work in Sexploitation Cinema," *Framework* 53, no. 1 (2012): 79–98; Jennifer C. Nash, *The Black Body in Ecstasy: Reading Race, Reading Pornography* (Durham, NC: Duke University Press, 2014); Mireille Miller-Young, *A Taste for Brown Sugar: Black Women in Pornography* (Durham, NC: Duke University Press, 2014); Tristan Taormino, Celine Parreñas Shimizu, Constance Penley, and Mireille Miller-Young, eds., *The Feminist Porn Book: The Politics of Producing Pleasure* (New York: Feminist Press, 2013).

8 Richard Maltby, "New Cinema Histories," in *Explorations in New Cinema History: Approaches and Case Studies*, ed. Richard Maltby, Daniel Biltereyst, and Philippe Meers (Malden, MA: Wiley-Blackwell, 2011), 3–8.

9 Alilunas, *Smutty Little Movies*, 30.

reliance on texts themselves, adult film historians often find the contingencies of exhibition, distribution, and reception usurping the authority of textual coherence, as when the use marks left on surviving films (e.g., cuts and alternate versions made by distributors or theater owners) reveal local instances of censorship.

The surge in adult film history corresponds with a broad turn toward exploring archives (formal and informal) that track adult cinema's history of neglect, disavowal, and even outright destruction.[10] Aside from specialist archives on human sexuality and gay and lesbian community archives, however, few official archives openly accept or promote adult holdings. In one regard, the scarcity or lack of access to surviving films, paratextual materials, and industry personnel shares common ground with the orphan film movement's ethos of preservation.[11] Adult cinema's survival is also marked by loose, unofficial assemblages of material, including the idiosyncratic archives of desire seen in porn fans' personally curated collections and more instrumentally masturbatory "stashes."[12] With so much material in private hands, the need has arisen for initiatives like the Adult Film History Project (AFHP), which Peter Alilunas and Dan Erdman describe as a means of crowdsourcing adult film-related ephemera for digitization and open-access research. Although adult film's marginalization is obviously rooted in its sexual content, the AFHP nevertheless offers a model for how collaborative archival practices might benefit the study of other niche cinemas.

The state of adult film history differs from other underexamined areas of cinema because of the sheer proliferation of pornographies made available since the rise of the internet. Consider that the historical span and variety of pre-1990s adult cinema has been flattened into the catchall category "vintage" on porn "tube" sites like xHamster and PornHub, as if treating historicity as just another fetish for the clicking. Rather than a reliable archive, the fleeting nature and poor audiovisual quality of such online videos speaks to adult cinema's contingently uneven survival. Indeed, the adult film industry's early adoption of new technologies starkly contrasts with its lack of efforts to preserve, restore, or even retransfer films predating the DVD era. Such responsibilities have often fallen to for-profit video labels like Something Weird Video, founded in 1990. Since 2013 Vinegar Syndrome's highly professional preservation efforts have helped renew the aesthetic revaluation of adult cinema's historical texts, allowing their restorations to be programmed in repertory theaters. As historians uncover the details of adult cinema's past circulation, wider public reappraisal of adult film's cultural value has been aided by increased circulation of notable films returned from the private realm of home consumption into public spaces of shared appreciation.

10 See Thomas Waugh, "Archaeology and Censorship," in *The Fruit Machine: Twenty Years of Writings on Queer Cinema* (Durham, NC: Duke University Press, 2000), 272–296; Eric Schaefer, "Dirty Little Secrets: Scholars, Archivists, and Dirty Movies," *Moving Image* 5, no. 2 (2005): 79–105; Tim Dean, Steven Ruszczycky, and David Squires, eds., *Porn Archives* (Durham, NC: Duke University Press, 2014); David Church, *Disposable Passions: Vintage Pornography and the Material Legacies of Adult Cinema* (New York: Bloomsbury Academic, 2016); Jeffrey Escoffier, "Sex in the Seventies: Gay Porn Cinema as an Archive for the History of American Sexuality," *Journal of the History of Sexuality* 26, no. 1 (2017): 88–113.

11 Dan Streible, "The Role of Orphan Films in the 21st Century Archive," *Cinema Journal* 46, no. 3 (2007): 124–128.

12 On this distinction, see Katariina Kyrölä and Susanna Paasonen, "Glimmers of the Forbidden Fruit: Reminiscing Pornography, Conceptualizing the Archive," *International Journal of Cultural Studies* 19, no. 6 (2015): 601–603.

Along with this respectful treatment of adult films themselves by boutique DVD labels, unofficial archives of recent note include the blog *Rialto Report* (www.therialtoreport.com; created in 2013), which features well-researched oral histories and photo essays with adult cinema's pioneers. Yet the popular-academic divide lingers here, as adult film fans outside the academy alternately dismiss academic writing as highbrow theorization or gross oversimplification, whereas scholars may find limited value in such anecdotal evidence unless marshaled toward some greater level of (even microhistorical) generalization. Mariah Larsson's piece in this dossier draws on the *Rialto Report*'s in-depth interview with pornographer Lasse Braun while allowing her to make larger claims about how Braun's pseudonymous performance of pan-European identity allowed his early hard-core loops to travel transnationally.

The distinction between "fan-scholars" (nonacademics who perform scholarship) and "scholar-fans" (academics writing from a personal fan investment) is useful here, for these different types of researchers can learn from each other, even as they make different uses of their accrued knowledge.[13] Laura Helen Marks argues below that scholars should heed discursive shifts driven by porn fans, rather than ahistorically relying on shorthand terms (e.g., "gonzo") that continue to evolve in online forums.

Issues of fandom raise methodological questions about whether adult film history is explicitly written from a perspective erotically attuned to the films, or whether historical research into primary archival materials aims for "just the facts" neutrality in response to adult cinema's socially dubious status. Although some scholarship gracefully traverses these lines, the issue of whether historical research should foreground one's personal erotic investments hinges on where the researcher's own position falls in relation to the heteronormative status quo and the extent to which one's desires can be admitted within academic contexts.[14] Yet as John Paul Stadler's essay suggests, queer scholars of adult cinema have charted a historiographical path more closely attuned to the affective pull of the researcher's own desires, threading along queer theory's once-renegade, now-institutionalized status.

"Stop Reading Films!" shouts John Champagne's 1997 polemic against close textual analysis, arguing "the historical situation of the exhibition of gay pornography is of far more immediate pertinence than anything that can be said about any individual porno text." For Champagne, adult cinema's counterpublic spaces of consumption must be central to understanding its cultural specificity, whereas textual analysis unnecessarily "straightens" gay pornography by removing it from lived experiences of queer world making.[15] Although we might challenge Champagne that the historiographical project of evaluating adult cinema's texts is far from complete, his call to shift our disciplinary gaze beyond textual representation has proved remarkably prescient. Whitney Strub's essay, for example, explores how assaults on racial and sexual diversity intersect around

13 Matt Hills, *Fan Cultures* (New York: Routledge, 2002), 3–8.

14 On these broader implications, see Laura Kipnis, *Unwanted Advances: Sexual Paranoia Comes to Campus* (New York: HarperCollins, 2017).

15 John Champagne, "'Stop Reading Films!': Film Studies, Close Analysis, and Gay Pornography," *Cinema Journal* 36, no. 4 (1997): 77.

the gentrification of pornographic spaces in the historically African American city of Newark, New Jersey.

So why does adult film history matter? It is an integral—not separate—part of moving-image culture and a space where communities of many stripes form and dissolve. Adult films evidence attitudes, behaviors, and practices regarding sex from different times and different spaces, providing the opportunity to gain perspective through careful scrutiny and comparative analysis. They also serve as documents of places seldom captured in other forms or genres: skid rows, red-light districts, camera clubs, burlesque theaters, anonymous apartments, cheap motels, working-class bars, and nightclubs. Finally, adult film history matters because, as the following essays indicate, it is largely unexplored and has not yet become doctrinaire—thus providing opportunities to engage with a range of methods, to develop and mine new sources, and to intersect with other disciplines in meaningful ways. In short, adult film history is a vital space for experimentation and expansion in the field of film and media studies.

*****

This In Focus is dedicated to Chuck Kleinhans, associate professor emeritus of Northwestern University, who passed away as it was being completed. Most recognize Chuck as coeditor, founder, and publisher of *Jump Cut: A Review of Contemporary Media*, a passionate advocate for radical film and media, and a devoted teacher and mentor, for which he was recognized with the first SCMS pedagogy award in 2007. Chuck was also an ardent supporter of work on sexual representation and adult film as an editor and writer, and in the classroom. He was among the first to sign the petition for the creation of the Adult Film History SIG, and although "retired," he was an animating force in the group from its inception. The memory of Chuck's infectious enthusiasm, his humor, and his skills as a teacher, scholar, and editor will animate us over the years to come. *

Microhistories and Materiality in Adult Film History, or the Case of *Erotic Salad*

by ELENA GORFINKEL

> To my surprise, I discovered how important to me were, unknowingly, books I had never read, events and persons I did not know had existed. —Carlo Ginzburg

Writing more than fifteen years ago, Eric Schaefer detailed the state of the study of adult cinema in film studies in relation to the place of sex films in archives.[1] Many of the conditions he described exist largely unchanged. Master copies and source materials of adult films are not housed in any single archive, nor are they necessarily located at designated film archives (the UCLA film archive being one specific exception). Many adult films have been lost, but those that remain are found across varied locations and sold by for-profit video distributors.[2] Whereas producers and studios have been less likely to bequeath their collections to academic institutions, private collections of commercially released material have made their way to archives more readily, especially gay adult films.[3] It is not that adult film does not exist in archives; rather, it is collected, accessed, and framed a certain way, and thus assumes specific meanings. Adult films are rarely considered as cinema in their own right; they are treated as emblematic of their sexual content and their lowly status, as defined by public perception.

More recently established distributors such as Vinegar Syndrome, and private entities and collections such as the American Genre Film Archive, have made efforts to collect, restore, and circulate sex films on video. In many ways the fan and collector video market has long provided the preconditions for research on adult film and has shaped the kinds of questions and histories pursued. But a comprehensive

1 Eric Schaefer, "Dirty Little Secrets: Scholars, Archivists and Dirty Movies," *Moving Image* 5, no. 2 (2005): 79–105.

2 In addition to archives designated for film collections, adult films can frequently be found at sexuality archives, most prominently at the Kinsey Institute for Research in Sex, Gender, and Reproduction at Indiana University, Bloomington; in the video collection of the Institute for the Advanced Study of Human Sexuality in San Francisco, California; and in LGBTQ archives, such as the Canadian Gay and Lesbian Archives and the ONE Archives, among many others.

3 Lucas Hilderbrand, "Historical Fantasies: Gay Porn in the Archives," *Porno Chic and the Sex Wars: American Sexual Representation in the 1970s*, ed. Carolyn Bronstein and Whitney Strub (Amherst: University of Massachusetts Press, 2016), 327–348.

non–commercially driven archive of sex cinema is a pipe dream for most adult film historians. This fact sits in stark contrast to another incontrovertible reality: the sheer vastness and multiplicity of adult film and media in the twentieth and twenty-first centuries, a gargantuan volume of stuff that includes discarded analog media as well as digital material. Print-based and production records of historical adult film practices, when they exist, are spotty or held by private individuals—if they have even been saved at all—and are difficult to parse. More commonly they are not available or are poorly recorded. Box-office figures and industrial and economic details must be pieced together ad hoc through various industry trade sources, such as *Variety*, *Boxoffice*, and *Independent Film Journal*. Such approaches also presume accurate reporting of grosses by exhibitors.

This archival landscape presents many challenges. One difficulty is balancing local histories and case studies with broader trends and practices. As with all film history, adult films raise the question of the relationship between canonical or representative works and less typical, singular, or "anomalous" cases. But the persistently "disreputable" nature of adult material only catalyzes what can be said to count as a viable object of study. The idiosyncratic, disorderly, uneven nature of the adult film archive as a body of films—simultaneously opaque and voluminous—necessitates different strategies for scholarship. Adult film historians have to contend with how to choose a suitable object, one that might map practices most comprehensively. One of the processes of legitimation for adult film history has been evidenced in macroscale studies that look at adult films not at the level of individual text but as industry, movement, genre, and mode of production.[4] But in thinking about individual films that make up this broader history, do we choose and analyze typical or exceptional cases?

This question emerges from my research on sexploitation cinema—nonexplicit, feature-length sex films made in the decade before hard-core porn's public ascendance, and which featured female nudity and salacious situations. In the book that emerged from this research, *Lewd Looks: American Sexploitation Cinema in the 1960s*, I argue that sexploitation films foregrounded spectatorship as the mode's animating problem in a period in which cinema had not yet gone "all the way." At the time, I was attempting to ascertain the workings of a mode of production with a specific shape and period—US films made between roughly 1960 and 1972. False leads and dead ends were common. Smaller cases felt more like footnotes or divergences from the "main story" of more typical practices. My goal was to assert the legibility of a larger-scaled unit—of the 1960s sex film as mode of film practice—and to make it visible as cinema in its own right. There also did not seem to be a place for expanded analyses of lingering exceptions. As a graduate student at the time holding varied adjunct gigs, and with no more teaching assistantship funding available, I felt that such excursions into minutiae would be perceived as indulgent or not "major" enough to be valued by the field, especially if such research was to secure the legitimacy of my own scholarship.

4 See, for example, Thomas Waugh, *Hard to Imagine: Gay Male Photography and Film from Their Beginnings to Stonewall* (New York: Columbia University Press, 1996); Eric Schaefer, *Bold! Daring! Shocking! True! A History of Exploitation Films, 1919–1959* (Durham, NC: Duke University Press, 1999); and Peter Alilunas, *Smutty Little Movies: The Creation and Regulation of Adult Video* (Berkeley: University of California Press, 2016).

One such anomalous object illuminates the vital importance of doing and supporting microhistory in adult film and media history, as its singularity as a crossover between underground and sexploitation cinema asserts the valuing of in-depth analyses of individual sex films. In the early 2000s, I encountered a personal website for the film *Erotic Salad*, a sex film directed by Robert Robert (1969), whose real name I later learned was Robert Ringenberger.[5] Shot primarily in 1967, *Erotic Salad* was a one-off film, made by the artist as a sendup of the sexploitation and skin flicks playing then in Times Square. The film gives perspective on the ways that geographically proximate but artistically distinct areas of cultural practice—specifically avant-garde or underground filmmaking, the downtown scene, and sexploitation production—momentarily intersected and overlapped around sexual expressivity.

Ringenberger had studied visual art at Pratt University and in his twenties worked as a freelance graphic designer while living in New York City's SoHo. A habitué of the music and art scenes, he hung out at the Fillmore East and the Old Polish Meeting Hall, where an acquaintance, Fluxus artist Al Hansen, would stage happenings and performances. Ringenberger was keen on the rising star of Andy Warhol and the Velvet Underground; he also had an interest in animation.

Erotic Salad's narrative is structured around the fantasy life of Martin (Danny Landau), a wheelchair-bound photo hobbyist and aspiring peeping tom, who is henpecked by his wife. The film departs, Walter Mitty–style, into his fantasies, as Martin becomes the mod, hip fetish photographer "Martin Kleshay" ("cliché"). The film alternates between banal domestic squabbling, Martin's wife's quandaries of sexual dissatisfaction, and the fantasy world where Kleshay photographs nude models. While "peeping for his art," he records an illicit tryst that leads to a mafia shakedown. Scenes of nude women posing and bohemian pot parties draw on the standard tropes of sexploitation sensationalism. Fantasy and reality collide as Martin, now the browbeaten schmuck, discovers his wife in a tryst with an insurance salesman at an orgy. In its final segment the film shifts from black and white to color, as Martin performs onstage in front of a squad of naked men and women, camping for the camera in drag, with feather boa and velvet camisole. The film ends in a diffusion of boundaries between queer and straight, male and female, as intercut images of androgynous, futuristic-glam actors flicker in pink hue across the screen. A fevered Martin/Kleshay succumbs to group rapture as the nude performers engulf him. The end credits roll in black and white with Kleshay's secretary (Patti D'Arbanville), a cool young blonde with sunglasses on, saucily chewing gum and answering the phone while gazing at the camera.

Ringenberger had difficulty placing ads for nude models in the *Village Voice*, so he ended up casting mainly amateurs—friends and artists who had never acted professionally but were part of the downtown scene. The film also featured the actor and soon-to-be Factory grandee D'Arbanville, a SoHo neighbor of the filmmaker, in her first commercial film role, at age fifteen. Only one actor, Landau, was a professional and was acting in *Hair* on Broadway. Ringenberger borrowed a 35mm camera on

5 The *Erotic Salad* website has since expired, although some trace of it remains on a cached Internet Archive site, at http://archive.is/oUQJZ. The website was created by Ringenberger's friend Gary Schide, who lived in Maine and passed away in 2013. The subsequent information on this film and its production is derived from the author's interview with Ringenberger, conducted in July 2002 in his Greenwich Village apartment in New York City.

weekends from an exchange. Sound cameras were scarce on weekends, so all was shot without sound, with dialogue added in postproduction—a common practice of low-budget sexploitation films.

Needing funding to finish the film, Ringenberger approached theater owner and distributor Chelly Wilson, who was recommended by a friend from the downtown music scene. Wilson owned a number of skin-flick theaters in Midtown, including the Cameo and the Avon, and was known to invest in films. Wilson asked Ringenberger to add additional "anything goes" footage: more sexual content. (The film's title was also her invention.) Wilson saw him as a potential moneymaker, a young person affiliated with the art world who—perhaps like Warhol, then coming off successes including *The Chelsea Girls* (1966)—might bring a new, hipper, younger audience to the sex film. Ringenberger added the color footage of his all-nude cast frolicking at the Fillmore East. Landau improvised the drag performance, reappearing in costume while filming went on. Ringenberger had hoped to include an Al Hansen performance in which the artist wrapped his head in masking tape, but given the timing of the filming, it did not work out. The final cut of the film, with added nude footage, was exhibited for two weeks at Wilson's Cameo Theater in 1969, and there a month later for another two weeks, without much success. Wilson also attempted to show the film to a "straight" audience at the Cinema One Theater, a leading art-house theater in the 1960s, on 59th Street and Third Avenue, hoping that the film would attain highbrow cultural cachet; Ringenberger recalled that she was "laughed out the door."

The film mocked many of the conventions and scenarios of the sex film, from a youthful, ironic perspective. In general, the middle-aged makers of sexploitation films treated youth culture and young bodies with some circumspection, if also with a desirous gaze. Perhaps more than the sex film, *Erotic Salad* is inscribed with a familiarity with the aesthetic tropes and gestures of the New York underground and art scenes. A scene of a dancing woman posing for Kleshay is dynamized by slide projections being cast on top of her, likely influenced by Ringenberger's encounters with expanded cinema and Warhol's Exploding Plastic Inevitable. Another scene exhibits a naked woman getting into a bathtub filled with raw meat. As the water runs, she rubs her body as if with a sponge with various hunks of meat—a beef liver, a cow tongue, a whole chicken. The permeation of ideas from the world of downtown performance is a notable element of the film's pastiche; Carolee Schneemann's *Meat Joy* (1964) is a strong reference point, in its employment of meat and erotics in a live group performance. In several sequences, actors eat apples and celery as they talk, a device to mask the postsync sound additions and ease the addition of dialogue. Yet the eating becomes an aesthetic element that muddles the meanings of consumption in its erotic and alimentary varieties, also evoking strategies from avant-garde performance and underground film. Ringenberger also expressed admiration for Warhol's minimal works such as *Eat* (1963)—in which Robert Indiana eats a mushroom in extended duration—which he saw during a Velvet Underground performance.

The film likely floundered at the box office because of its transit between worlds that were illegible to each other, even though these were precisely the reasons that Wilson was initially interested in the project. The film's gambit of needling, if not deflating, the premises of sexual spectacle probably led to the film's poor reception;

it also earned Wilson's ire, as she had bought the film outright from Ringenberger for $3,000. Ringenberger screened the film once more for a weekend at the Bleecker Street Theater in 1970, sans promotion; it was not shown again. The filmmaker was able to get a 16mm reduction print for his own safekeeping, and this is the print from which in the early 2000s he made VHS cassettes. As a result of legal and copyright issues, the film did not circulate beyond this attempt at revival, in part because of lost evidence of signed performance releases from the actors. Additionally, Ringenberger worried that D'Arbanville and her lawyers would not want her name associated with it.

What might be drawn as the lesson of this unknown film? Looking back on my reluctance to use this work in my project on sexploitation, my regret now has a corrective dimension. It is clear in retrospect—perhaps because of the openness toward local and orphan histories as important sites for new film-historical research—that the example of *Erotic Salad*, however minor, makes visible the shared geographies of underground and sexploitation cinemas, even when the films themselves are difficult or even impossible to see. The film exposes a common phenomenon: the filmmakers who "dabbled" in making a sex film or two but did not continue on to viable careers in this cottage industry. It can illustrate how a less savvy player in the sexploitation world might have navigated the process of adult filmmaking while pursuing aesthetic aims that were at cross-purposes to the traditional sex film venue and audiences. *Erotic Salad* gives a view onto a broader environment of film experimentation in the context of a low-barrier-to-entry industry, as well as a consideration of networks of affiliation and circulation—and the limits to those networks—in works that did not necessarily succeed.

Erotic Salad's failure at the box office was not surprising given its position at the border of underground and sexploitation modes, as well as its filmmaker's inexperience and his lack of funds. Even if it does not necessarily illuminate the broader, generalizable practices of sexploitation cinema as a "legible unit," in its specificity an object like *Erotic Salad* allows us to reflect on the outliers at the border of a mode of production, the conditions of sexploitation's economic viability, and the porous site of practice that was the "adult film" in the 1960s. This case also invites us to consider doing adult film history as a shared project that might intersect with other areas of scholarship—in this case, with experimental or avant-garde film history—and in a more collaborative spirit, in which leads, hunches, and small discoveries can be networked and allow for the building of a wider and more sustained inquiry into historical film practices in the independent adult film scene. Of late, scholars have been using personal blogs or social media like Facebook and Twitter to discuss such small cases.[6] Nonacademic oral history sites also exist, such as the popular *Rialto Report*, which does not use scholarly methods or proper citation practices but presents itself as a journalistic "direct source" of primary research.[7] Some inroads have also indeed been made in themed academic journal issues, such as the "Canon Fodder" issue of the journal *Porn Studies*,

6 Whitney Strub, *strublog: everything is archival* (blog), https://strublog.wordpress.com; *Notches: (re)marks on the history of sexuality* (blog), http://notchesblog.com; Darren Kerr and Donna Peberdy, *Screening Sex* (blog), https://screeningsex.com.

7 *Rialto Report*, http://www.therialtoreport.com.

guest edited by David Church.[8] Yet this "margin work" needs more institutional and disciplinary venues of support, particularly for younger scholars who are testing the viability of new research areas and directions.

Our discipline must find ways to value the practice of going down the proverbial rabbit hole in pursuing stray individuals, footnotes, and minor films. Microhistories are a seemingly paradoxical, yet deeply materialist way to rise to the challenge posed by the overwhelming volume of adult moving-image media that we are confronted with cataloging and historicizing. Such close case studies can open out onto larger questions of the materiality of the film object and the film experience. Further, the field must attend to how failures, unfinished works, amateur works, and never-produced and illicit films are the majority of films that constitute the constellation we call *cinema* in its totality. If we strive to understand that totality, we need new ways of accounting for it. Consequently, the microhistorical allows a reexamination of the very matter of our methods and the nature of what "counts" as a viable object in film and media studies. *

Special thanks go to Lucas Hilderbrand for his insightful feedback on this essay and for years of conversation on sex, media, and archives.

8 David Church, ed., "Canon Fodder: Reappraising Adult Cinema's Neglected Texts," *Porn Studies* 4, no. 3 (2017).

The Adult Film History Project

by PETER ALILUNAS and DAN ERDMAN

Eventually, just about every adult film historian encounters a familiar, frustrating scenario. While conducting research, tantalizing traces of evidence—crucial contemporary press accounts, invaluable legal papers, or other primary documents—will come to light, only to vanish again, slipping through the historian's fingers as if they never existed. Generally speaking, the adult film industries did not create conventional paper trails, nor did they embrace their own long-term legacies.[1] In almost all cases, the bits and pieces they did leave behind have not been preserved or archived with conventional methods.[2] The result for historians has been a methodologically complicated landscape defined by particular challenges. In this essay,

1 For more on the reasons why, see Eric Schaefer, "Dirty Little Secrets: Scholars, Archivists, and Dirty Movies," *Moving Image* 5, no. 2 (2005): 79–105.

2 Prominent exceptions include the preservation done by Steven Morowitz of Distribpix, an early, prolific adult production outfit cofounded by his father, Arthur; and the efforts by Joe Rubin, cofounder of Vinegar Syndrome, to archive and preserve adult films and their legacies.

we describe the creation of the Adult Film History Project (AFHP), a crowdsourced, online repository of adult film–related materials with the goal of remedying at least some of these challenges.

The potential of this project—and particularly the linking together of personal collections—stems from the overwhelming scarcity of necessary research material. For example, a scholar researching the distribution and marketing of a non–adult film such as *E.T.* (Steven Spielberg, 1982) might be able to assemble, within hours and completely online, a thick dossier of advertisements, detailed box-office grosses, reviews, and trade discourses. A rich variety of physical archives and bricks-and-mortar libraries might also hold material applicable to the project. Should that same scholar research *E.X.* (Domingo Lobo, 1985), a hard-core parody of *E.T.*, they would struggle in vain to find any traces online and would likely find no more success in traditional libraries or archives. This shot-on-video production had no theatrical release, left almost no historical footprint, and was ignored by mainstream publications, as were tens of thousands of adult films.

Digging out the histories and contexts of adult films such as *E.X.* requires patience, creativity, a willingness to work (and occasionally compete) with collectors and dealers, and unflagging persistence and flexibility. These efforts still use time-tested historiographical methods, just applied in new directions and with new targets. Elsewhere, I (Alilunas) have described this process as "trace historiography," a method that examines fragments of seemingly disparate evidence in an effort to reconstruct a past that seems impossible to locate clearly in predictable and typical ways.[3] A crucial part of trace historiography is something that every historian—of adult film or any other kind—understands intimately: the construction of a personal archive. For the adult film historian, however, this personal archive often serves as the only option.

Traditional archives of material related to adult film's industrial histories do exist; the best known remains the Kinsey Institute for Research in Sex, Gender, and Reproduction at Indiana University, Bloomington, home to perhaps the most significant collection of sex-related materials in the United States. As Linda Williams, Thomas Waugh, David Church, and others have noted, however, the institute does not make its collection easy for scholars to access and employs confusing and perplexing metadata and filing protocols.[4] More recently, the Kinsey Institute has taken disturbing, politically motivated steps to make itself less public and less about sex.[5] A handful of

3 Peter Alilunas, *Smutty Little Movies: The Creation and Regulation of Adult Video* (Berkeley: University of California Press, 2016), 30.

4 Linda Williams, "'White Slavery' versus the Ethnography of 'Sex Workers': Women in Stag Films at the Kinsey Archive," *Moving Image* 5, no. 2 (2005): 107–134; Thomas Waugh, "Archaeology and Censorship," in *The Fruit Machine: Twenty Years of Writings on Queer Cinema* (Durham, NC: Duke University Press, 2000), 272–296; David Church, *Disposable Passions: Vintage Pornography and the Material Legacies of Adult Cinema* (New York: Bloomsbury Academic, 2016); Jennifer Burns Bright and Ronan Crowley, "'A Quantity of Offensive Matter': Private Cases in Public Places," in *Porn Archives*, ed. Tim Dean, Steven Ruszczycky, and David Squires (Durham, NC: Duke University Press, 2014), 103–126 (hereafter cited as *Porn Archives*).

5 Hellie Lieberman, "Desexing the Kinsey Institute," *New York Review of Books*, March 20, 2018, https://www.nybooks.com/daily/2018/03/20/desexing-the-kinsey-institute.

collections at other institutions focus on topics related to sex or adult film.[6] As with any type of archival research, there are barriers to entry: scholars must have the means and opportunity to travel, the time to work in them, and the general knowledge to quickly assess the collected material. That combination can be difficult even for senior scholars and often remains close to impossible for graduate students.

While this small group of "official" collections related to adult film exists, the truth is that extant material exists in all kinds of archives, often set aside in out-of-the-way shelves, uncataloged, ignored, or forgotten, as the archivist Dwight Sanson has described.[7] Scholars are often quick to attribute such laxity to prudishness on the part of the collection managers, but this neglect can occur for a variety of less exciting reasons. Many archives rely on grants and donations, and managers may be hesitant to upset the (real or imagined) sensibilities of their funders. Similarly, those at state-funded institutions are understandably cautious about attracting the attention of legislators or other political opportunists. But the more common, prosaic, and, frankly, depressing truth is that this material is often not a priority. It sometimes comes as part of a larger collection, often without clear connection to the archive as a whole.[8] Money, time, and personnel resources are at a premium in the best of cases, and committing these to processing material with no immediate relevance to the focus of the archive is often not an option.

For all these reasons, most adult film historians inevitably turn to the collector's market to construct an archive. Within this odd and freewheeling space, nonacademic historians, fans, performers, industry veterans, and disinterested capitalists maintain an ocean of historical material. That ocean can be arduous to navigate and its holdings difficult to acquire, if they can be found at all. It certainly does not operate as a lending library. This makes sense: for many, such materials are a source of income, a career legacy, or a lifelong passion. Navigating this market can be both rewarding and frustrating; it is, above all, a vital epicenter for trace historiography. Potential pitfalls loom, however: acquisitions often have no record of provenance (or none that is entirely trustworthy), casting doubt as to their authenticity and relevance. It is difficult to contextualize items available in such a haphazard fashion. With no clear sense of what other items were produced, for what purpose, in what kind of numbers, historians find their ability to make responsible historical generalizations compromised. Finally, constantly circulating is the nagging sense that more evidence exists but is too expensive to acquire or remains in private, inaccessible collections.

Virtual access to these materials would seem to be a potential solution. The growing adult film fan culture maintains a significant online presence. Many fan blogs host

6 For lists of these archives, see Linda Williams, ed., *Porn Studies* (Durham, NC: Duke University Press, 2004), 491–494; and Caitlin Shanley, "Clandestine Catalogs: A Bibliography of Porn Research Collections," in *Porn Archives*, 441–456.

7 Dwight Sanson, "Home Viewing: Pornography and Amateur Film Collections, a Case Study," *Moving Image* 5, no. 2 (2005): 136–140.

8 Lucas Hilderbrand writes about his experiences in gay archives across the United States, noting that "much of what constitutes their holdings is pornography" and that "such holdings often create an ambivalent affect of custodianship for the archivists, who may blush or boast, depending on the visitor." "Historical Fantasies: 1970s Gay Male Pornography in the Archives," in *Porno Chic and the Sex Wars: American Sexual Representation in the 1970s*, ed. Carolyn Bronstein and Whitney Strub (Amherst: University of Massachusetts Press, 2016), 329.

scans of paper material, and various social media groups post similar material. The pinnacle of this growing community is the *Rialto Report*, a blog and podcast operated by Ashley West and April Hall, adult film history fans who pay for interviews with industry veterans and occasionally display rare ephemera from their collection as part of their effort to document the so-called golden age of adult film from the 1970s and 1980s. Although we certainly appreciate these sharing efforts, these sites do not enable long-term, reliable access. Fan collections are hosted by proprietary, privately operated companies such as Facebook, WordPress, or Pinterest that devise restrictive, community-regulated content rules, making life difficult for the amateur adult film archivist. Facebook, for example, will remove any post featuring nudity upon receiving a single complaint, which inevitably happens even in closed, age-restricted groups set up explicitly for the purpose of preserving adult film histories. Beyond these regulatory frustrations lies a more basic concern: the complete and total lack of guarantees regarding longevity, leaving these collections—which might be the product of years of painstaking curating—susceptible to sudden and permanent disappearance.[9] As Linda Williams argues, "The lack of preservation of the pornographic heritage is appalling, and we cannot count on the hit-or-miss salvages of the Internet to do the job."[10] If the study of pornographic material is to progress, it is imperative that researchers find ways to overcome these technological limits.

As had many scholars, we observed the archival potential of the Media History Digital Library (MHDL) and Lantern, its search platform, created by Eric Hoyt, Carl Hagenmaier, and Wendy Hagenmaier in 2011.[11] For those without the means to travel to archives or to acquire the material themselves, MHDL offers invaluable search capability, with ready access to more than two million pages from classic media periodicals. We began to imagine something similar for adult film history and what effect that might have on our growing field. In 2014, Eric Schaefer founded the Adult Film History Scholarly Interest Group (AFH SIG) in the Society for Cinema and Media Studies. Since then, more than 150 members have joined, with presentations, panels, workshops, and seminars on adult film–related topics continuing to increase at the annual conference, and a dramatic increase in overall community building among scholars. In her recent assessment, Williams notes that, in addition to sustained, rigorous scholarship, journals, and conferences, an archive is a "crucial element necessary for the cultivation of a scholarly field."[12] The MHDL reimagines what that archive might look like, particularly given the complicated network of collectors, fans, and scholars making up the field of interested parties.

Concurrent with the creation of the AFH SIG in 2014, I (Alilunas) began thinking seriously about connecting these pieces. What if scholars and historians (including

9 The uncertain future of the music-streaming service SoundCloud illustrates these questions, as the potential disappearance of that company would consign the thousands of hours of user-generated material to oblivion. Jenna Wortham, "If SoundCloud Disappears, What Happens to Its Music Culture?," *New York Times Magazine*, August 1, 2017, https://www.nytimes.com/2017/08/01/magazine/if-soundcloud-disappears-what-happens-to-its-music-culture.html.

10 Linda Williams, "Pornography, Porno, Porn: Thoughts on a Weedy Field," in *Porn Archives*, 35.

11 See http://lantern.mediahist.org.

12 Williams, "Pornography, Porno, Porn," 35.

nonacademic allies) could be convinced to share their personal archives in a carefully maintained, searchable, and digital archive? What might happen to the field if this ocean of material was open to research and preserved in a more reliable manner? What histories could be uncovered? What new directions could the field go in if more material were easily accessible to more people? Rather than the occasional private network of sharing, as all academics do with one another and this particular field has long relied on, why not imagine something bigger that might also send a message about the value, validity, and legitimacy of this kind of work? There is certainly no doubt that part of the reason this material exists in the shadows is the cultural reluctance to accept it in the open. An online archive could serve not only as a research catalyst but also as a voice for the field's continued growth and development. These questions led directly to the creation of the Adult Film History Project (AFHP), which can be found at https://adultfilmhistoryproject.wordpress.com.

Early on, the Digital Scholarship Services Center (DSSC) at the University of Oregon, where I (Alilunas) am located, expressed interest in the AFHP. In many ways, this was the ideal scenario: a university-based partner, committed to research, and with the resources, equipment, staff, and experience to build, host, and maintain a digital archive (something it does very well on several other faculty-led projects). Yet over time, an impasse became clear: the DSSC was reluctant to serve as the host of this kind of material, despite understanding and supporting the archive's academic purpose. At that point, I (Alilunas) decided to seek out other opportunities and invited Dan Erdman to be a codirector of the project, given his archival expertise, academic background, and experience as an adult film historian. Despite the unwillingness of the DSSC to partner on the project, the University of Oregon has been supportive in other ways, providing funding and support for the initial research on the project. After the AFH SIG contributed a scanner, and an active collector and historian agreed to loan a significant collection of early sexploitation film–related periodicals from his personal archive, work began on assembling and testing the first pieces of the AFHP.

To address the issue of long-term sustainability, we have decided to house the AFHP at the Internet Archive, a large, nonprofit, legacy institution with broad support, a commitment to maintaining access to archival material, and no hesitation about adult content. As the archive takes root, we hope to find a university partner with a strong interest in building digital collections willing to accept a cosponsorship role alongside the Internet Archive, which would ensure the stability, access, and preservation of this vital material, as well as assisting in stabilizing and growing the field. After the fashion of the MHDL, much of the material we hope to make accessible will be in the form of publications, typically magazines and other ancillary material. (Films present other, more complicated challenges for online archiving.) As magazines and other documents tend to display the usual publication information (e.g., title, publisher, approximate date), they may be cataloged like any other published material. However, the ephemera of adult film history extends beyond bound, numbered publications and into such types of material as flyers, handbills, tokens, and myriad other elements that resist traditional definitions and offer representational and metadata-related challenges. The strategies devised by repositories devoted to material from sexual minorities have proved broadly useful to our effort and provide models from which to work. The Digital Transgender Archive, headed by K. J. Rawson, with its creative and innovative approach to metadata and spirit of collaboration, has been especially helpful to us as we envision possible archival systems.[13]

The Adult Film History Project is not something that can happen overnight. We envision it as a deliberately long-term project that can develop over time and with changes in the field, rather than as a static and immovable object stuck in an initial paradigm. We have built a system in which anyone, not just us, can scan and upload their collections to a linked space and have provided clear, easy-to-use instructions about metadata and other information that we can update and modify as necessary. This archive will obviously never be complete and is not a permanent solution. In some ways, that recognition reflects Eugenie Brinkema's argument that an archive, particularly one holding adult film–related material, can never fulfill our desires, but that its rough and unfinished nature can be a reward and opportunity rather than a limitation, allowing the archive to match the history it contains. "Let memory remain ragged," she writes. "Let history remain interrupted and uneven."[14] While we acknowledge these inevitabilities, the creation of the AFHP reflects our hopes to grow, stabilize, and solidify the field, and to continue to pull it out of the shadows and into a state of openness that will lead to rigorous, sustained, and serious scholarship. Given the archival structure that we have imagined, the AFHP can grow organically, in ways that reflect scholars' interests and pursuits, connecting them while also preserving for the future images of materials that have for far too long been hidden away or impossible to access. This potential future will require cooperation and trust among colleagues, and sincere outreach to include and collaborate with the nonacademic historians, fans, industry members, and others who often hold long-term skepticism and suspicion as to our motives. Part of the necessary reassurance will be demonstrating the value of an archive, not just as a vital requirement for the next step toward status as a thriving, stable, and evolved academic field, as Williams describes, but also as a repository for the preservation of history that serves interests beyond the small corners of scholarly activity.

Learn more about the Adult Film History Project and how to contribute at https://adultfilmhistoryproject.wordpress.com. *

13 See the Digital Transgender Archive at https://www.digitaltransgenderarchive.net.

14 Eugenie Brinkema, "Rough Sex," in *Porn Archives*, 281.

Oh Paris! The Journeys of Lasse Braun's 8mm Pornography

by MARIAH LARSSON

An easy way to challenge the concept of national cinema is by drawing on examples: if a Danish film director makes a film, set in the United States, funded by various European institutions and production companies, in Trollhättan, Sweden, bringing in an Icelandic singer as the star of the film as well as a French cinematic icon and American actors—how do we describe that film? Film journalists and critics have used the disparaging term "Euro-pudding" to mark such ventures, but as various recognized auteurs have come to exploit the possibilities of European funding, this type of transnational film production has become much more common and is not routinely disregarded anymore. The same kind of transnationality can be found in a 1970s porn context: if an Italian pornographer, with a production company at the time based in Copenhagen, makes a film in France with French and Vietnamese performers—how do we describe that film, in particular if the film surfaces in an American archive with an Italian title? Such is the case for the film *Hotel Amour* (Lasse Braun), of the Oh Paris! series from 1971 that also includes *Petite fleur* and *Magnifique!* Comparing *Dancer in the Dark* (Lars von Trier, 2000), described in the first instance, with *Hotel Amour* may seem far-fetched, but I would say that in terms of maverick transnationalism the two directors are not so different. The opportunistic transnationalism—that is, "responding to available economic opportunities at a given moment in time and in no wise about the creation of lasting networks or about the fostering of social bonds"—is evident in both cases, and in their respective contexts both are recognized as auteurs with distinct personal visions.[1]

The purpose of this article is not to compare Lars von Trier and Lasse Braun. Rather, I wish to point to and discuss some aspects of late 1960s to early 1970s pornography, using Lasse Braun and *Hotel Amour* to argue that adult film history provides a perspective on transnational film studies that contests received notions about how transnational films are produced and circulate. In fact, adult film and pornography in general challenge three traditionally strong conceptualizations of film history. First, because many such films were made in some

1 Mette Hjort, "On the Plurality of Cinematic Transnationalism," in *World Cinemas, Transnational Perspectives*, ed. Nataša Ďurovičová and Kathleen Newman (New York: Routledge, 2010), 12–33, at 19–20.

sort of transnational collaboration but were also often excluded from national film histories, they make evident the concept of national cinema as a clearly demarcated canon of films. Second, the history of adult film and pornography contests the notion of a world-dominant American (Hollywood) cinema, as the international diversity of productions on the internet and in the former "adult" sections of video stores demonstrate. Third, adult film and pornography defy the notion that popular European genre cinema and stars have difficulty traveling—that is, that European film stars often have to make a mark in a Hollywood film to be recognized in other European countries than their own.

Transnationality has become something of a buzzword within film studies—and, as Mette Hjort astutely observes, it seems to carry with it an intrinsic value in and of itself. Nevertheless, as Hjort goes on to point out, there are many different types of transnational cinema, and by distinguishing them, their ostensible value can be defined and measured.[2] In addition, one could argue that "transnationality" per se is a neutral term, simply referring to cross-border interactions. Outside of film studies, it is used in conjunction with both positive and negative issues, like transnational cooperation or transnational crime.

However, what is quite often disregarded in discussions of transnational cinema is the importance of nationality to making someone or something itinerant. Without any kind of acknowledged nationality, travel becomes difficult and may leave the traveler in a state of suspension, an eternal limbo, much like the stranded Viktor Navorski (Tom Hanks) in Steven Spielberg's *The Terminal* (2004), whose passport became invalid when his home country ceased to exist. Nationality, or at least an assumed nationality, is in fact a prerequisite for transnational interactions to take place.

Perhaps the most apparent example of the transnationality of pornography in the predigital era, and also, perhaps, the most famous 8mm pornographer, Lasse Braun, worked in various countries—among them Sweden, Denmark, the United States, and West Germany. Although he took a pseudonym with strong associations of Northern Europe (with the Swedish "Lasse" and the German surname "Braun"), the director was in fact Alberto Ferro, an Italian national born in Algeria. Described by the Finnish porn scholar Susanna Paasonen as a "markedly translocal operator . . . aiming to profile the productions as quality pornography with some narrative framing," Braun covered most of the world at the level of representation, from the exoticization and eroticization of Black bodies and tropical landscapes in his Trinidad films to the visual spectacle of rapist Vikings.[3] At the same time, through the distribution of his films by Reuben Sturman in the United States, Braun became as much a brand name as (American company) Swedish Erotica.[4]

Braun produced his 8mm films in series of three, with a unifying theme, often conspicuously branded by some kind of national characteristics: Scandinavia in the two series Vikings (1971) and Love in Scandinavia (1971), Spain and Italy in the series

2 Hjort, "On the Plurality of Cinematic Transnationalism," 14–15.

3 Susanna Paasonen, "Smutty Swedes: Sex Films, Pornography and the Figure of Good Sex," in *Tainted Love: Screening Sexual Perversities*, ed. Darren Kerr and Donna Peberdy (London: I. B. Tauris, 2017), 120–136.

4 Paasonen, "Smutty Swedes."

Top Secret (1970) (although shot in Málaga, Spain), Trinidad in the series Tropical (1969), and so on. Like art cinema, to some extent, adult film relies on the symbolic value of the national to make itself marketable abroad. By using various stereotypes (Vikings and natural landscapes, bullfighting, limbo dancing, palm trees and waves crashing on beaches), the geographical markers of Braun's films anchored them to the landscape of sexual imagination, providing an efficient point of departure for the brief and condensed narratives of his films.

Hotel Amour. The Oh Paris! series draws on the stereotypical conceptualizations of French sexuality: the cover of *Hotel Amour* features female buttocks, framed by black lace garters and stockings; and *Magnifique!* shows breasts, framed by a black and blue lace bra. *Petite Fleur* has a close-up of luscious lipsticked lips and the end of a Gauloises cigarette. The markedly staged and fetishized posing of the covers invites the spectator to gaze at an inactive object. These images associate Frenchness with a sinful sensuality, as well as an "observational" mode. As noted by Eric Schaefer, this mode is characterized by a kind of "voyeurism from a privileged vantage point" commonly connected to the notion of France as "sexy nation" in sexploitation films.[5]

In addition, illustrative of the transnational and transformative character of adult film, there seem to be at least two existing versions of *Hotel Amour*. One is released on the DVD collection of Lasse Braun films from Alpha Blue Archives. A copy of the other version can be found in the archive of the Kinsey Institute for Research in Sex, Gender, and Reproduction at Indiana University, Bloomington, under the title *Hotel Amore*. It is obviously the same footage and basically the same narrative: two women—one of them the Asian performer Ky-Sen, who performed in several Lasse Braun films—walk around in Paris, then go to a hotel room where they start to make love. A waiter appears with room service and joins in. However, the version at the Kinsey Institute is several minutes longer and contains an interesting interlude in which Ky-Sen attempts to penetrate the waiter from behind with a strap-on dildo while he is having vaginal intercourse with the other woman. He makes averting gestures with his hand, and she stops. On the one hand, penetrating or attempting to penetrate the male is something of an anomaly in straight pornography, so the interlude evokes issues of gender and agency, passivity and activity, subject and object, in a fascinating way. The man's reluctance also suggests issues of consent and nonconsent. On the other hand, none of these nonnormative aspects of sexuality or sexual imagination is very far off in any of Lasse Braun's productions, which abound with quirky suggestions, fanciful inventions, dark fantasies, and playful moods. "Exploring anal sex, double penetration, fetishes, bondage, domination and urination in close-up, the films were not confined to given notions of sexual normalcy but were in fact branded and marketed as deviations thereof," Paasonen observes.[6] One could easily place several of the sexual practices represented in Braun's films at the outer limits of Gayle Rubin's famous model of the sexual value hierarchy, where those sexual practices that are deemed

5 Eric Schaefer, "'I'll Take Sweden': The Shifting Discourses of the 'Sexy Nation' in Sexploitation Films," in *Sex Scene: Media and the Sexual Revolution*, ed. Eric Schaefer (Durham, NC: Duke University Press, 2014), 207–234.

6 Paasonen, "Smutty Swedes," 127.

normal and natural and therefore accepted by the dominant society are placed in the middle, in the "charmed circle," and those that are regarded as depraved, perverted, and abnormal are placed along the outer perimeter.[7] However, that this particular attempt at penetration is not included in the DVD version of the film is perhaps unsurprising, as the scene may have been intentionally omitted by a video label that otherwise specializes in straight pornography. The question is, rather, how the other version ended up at the Kinsey archive—is it an American release of the film, or is it a copy bought by an American during a trip to Europe, perhaps even to Stockholm or Copenhagen, the Scandinavian cities of sin?

Transnational Man of Mystery. Not only did particular films travel across national borders, the director-producer himself moved between nation-states. The biographical legend constructed by and around Lasse Braun places great emphasis on nationality, internationality, and travel. His father was a diplomat for the Italian government, working in Algeria when Braun was born in 1936. The family moved to Germany in 1939, then to Italy in 1940 and to Belgrade in 1942.[8] According to Braun himself, his venture into pornography started with bringing soft-core pornographic magazines into Italy from Monaco using his diplomatic passport and his car with diplomatic license plates.[9] Braun claimed that he entered into the pornography business because he wanted to change censorship legislation, and the first country he targeted was Denmark. Indeed, in Braun's words, it sounds as if, without him, pornography would still be forbidden in Denmark: "The best part of it was that we finally managed to overturn the ban on obscenity in Denmark. . . . In 1969, the Danish parliament passed a law legalizing the depiction of explicit sex in pictures and films. Pornography was finally legal there."[10] In the account of the Danish criminologist Berl Kutchinsky, however, the publication, prosecution, and acquittal of *Fanny Hill* (John Cleland, 1748) in 1965 was the significant event leading to the legalization of obscene material in Denmark. Braun is not mentioned in this context by Kutchinsky at all.[11] This, of course, does not necessarily mean that Braun was not involved. However, while attempting to subvert the Danish penal code on pornography, Braun lived in Stockholm, where his company, Beta Films AB, also was located, but he moved to Copenhagen in 1969.[12] Sweden decriminalized pornography in 1971. Although perhaps driven by the goal of subverting censorship and obscenity legislation, Braun's

7 Gayle Rubin, "Thinking Sex: Some Notes for a Radical Theory of the Politics of Sexuality," in *Pleasure and Danger: Exploring Female Sexuality*, ed. Carol Vance (Boston: Routledge & Kegan Paul, 1984), 267–320.

8 "Lasse Braun Interview—Part 1: The Early Years of a Trailblazer," *Rialto Report* (blog), March 1, 2015, http://www.therialtoreport.com/2015/03/01/lasse-braun-the-early-years-of-a-trailblazer-his-last-interview.

9 "Lasse Braun Interview—Part 1."

10 "Lasse Braun Interview—Part 1."

11 Berl Kutchinsky, "Pornography, Sex Crime, and Public Policy," in *Sex Industry and Public Policy: Proceedings of a Conference Held 6–8 May 1991*, ed. Sally-Anne Gerull and Boronia Halstead (Canberra: Australia Institute of Criminology, 1992), 43, http://aic.gov.au/media_library/publications/proceedings/14/kutchinsky.pdf. See also Isak Thorsen, "Family Porn: The Zodiac Film—Popular Comedy with Hard-Core Sex," *Journal of Scandinavian Cinema* 4, no. 3 (2014): 289–304.

12 "Lasse Braun Interview—Part 1."

frequent moves between different locations also seem to have been motivated by business opportunities and a sense of where the risk of his ventures might be low enough to be worthwhile. Consequently, Braun became a transnational pornographer.

Artistic Visions, Distribution, and Censorship. In crossing national borders—informally, through traveling tourists or business men bringing films with them back home, or formally, through distribution agreements—adult films encountered differences in national legislation and censorship. Sources date the US distribution agreement between Lasse Braun and Reuben Sturman to either 1971 or 1972.[13] Regardless, the Sturman connection provided a robust and profitable exhibition arrangement for what by then was called Lasse Braun Productions. With peep-show booths semiprivately showing loops to customers and Sturman's peep-show empire rapidly expanding, much film was needed. Paasonen argues that "along with the long-standing reputation of Swedish film, the peep show distribution of Braun's films contributed to the co-articulation of Sweden and pornography in North America."[14] In addition, Braun constructed himself as an auteur and marked his own films not only with his name (Beta Films AB eventually became Lasse Braun Productions or LB Productions) but also with his signature. Many are the 8mm films whose origins have become difficult to identify and the 8mm production companies that have disappeared into the great sea of unwanted history, but the Lasse Braun films are instantly recognizable (along with, for instance, films from Color Climax and Swedish Erotica). For the trained eye, their characteristic pacing and imaginative sexual scenarios would probably be possible to identify even without title cards and credits. The distinctiveness of a Lasse Braun film probably also accounts for his reputation and popularity. In Sweden, his films were strikingly often submitted to the National Board of Film Censors for review, compared to other labels, and when asked about films they remember from the 1970s, people mention Lasse Braun alongside the most prolific 8mm porn producer in the region, Color Climax, although Braun's output never matched theirs in quantity.[15]

Adult films were often pragmatically edited and released in different versions to fit the expectations, market conditions, and censorship protocols of different countries. Pornographic 8mm films were not always—not even most of the time—distributed formally, but rather bought privately by mail order, while traveling, or smuggled in large quantities together with magazines and card decks.[16] According to Braun, he traveled to the United States himself with the negatives of the films in his suitcase, hidden among the clothes, delivering them to Sturman to make copies. His only "non-negotiable term was that the films and the box covers would not undergo any changes. I didn't want my artistic vision to be changed."[17]

13 According to the *Rialto Report*'s interview, it was in 1972. Paasonen dates it to 1971. "Smutty Swedes," 127.

14 Paasonen, "Smutty Swedes," 127.

15 Mariah Larsson, *The Swedish Porn Scene: Exhibition Contexts, 8mm Pornography and the Sex Film* (Bristol, UK: Intellect, 2017), 116–119.

16 Braun describes how his films were sent discreetly "packaged in such a way that no one would know what was in the envelope." See "Lasse Braun Interview—Part 1"; Larsson, *Swedish Porn Scene*, 149.

17 "Lasse Braun Interview—Part 1."

This does not mean that 8mm films were not subject to censorship. In Sweden, when submitted to the National Board of Film Censors, Lasse Braun films were frequently banned or cut; for instance, the Oh Paris! film *Petite fleur* (censorship card 110 891) was cut for its "certain scenes in which dog or dogs participate in intercourse and similar."[18] In fact, the artistic vision of Braun was at times seriously compromised by the Swedish censorship, as in the case of *White Fantasies / Black Power*. In the last fourth of this film, two Black women who have had sex with a white man are abused and raped by two Black men who suddenly appear. The white man is tied up and finally killed. This part of the film was deleted, thereby radically altering the entire impression of the film.[19] The combination of sex and violence did not sit well with Swedish censors.[20]

This history might seem marginal, the microhistory of a sleazy pornographer who claimed to challenge obscenity law as an excuse to profit on sexually explicit material. However, as one of the pioneers during the early years of the burgeoning adult industry, Lasse Braun is an example of how the growing porn business in the late 1960s and early 1970s was a vital, creative, and shamelessly commercial activity exploring the potential of the new explicitness. The creativity involved concerns elements of fantasy, of objectification and agency, and a celebration of sexiness that might well diverge from mainstream prescriptions of beauty. Exploring society's limits of decorum, this early pornography employed racial and ethnic stereotypes juxtaposed in blatantly racist but also taboo-breaking and highly political constellations, and much more.[21] Beyond the level of representation, the exhibition contexts and patterns of viewing behaviors also provide a history of how people have interacted and related to issues of sexuality and the consumption of sexually explicit materials. More particularly for this brief essay, it says something about how the world is interconnected and how films can be transnational. Long before the internet connected porn producers and consumers across borders, adult moving-image material traveled easily, unlike many other types of film outside the dominant Hollywood cinema. *

18 These "certain scenes" show two dogs, leaping around playfully while a couple is having sex.

19 Mariah Larsson, "Lasse Braun, Rape Scenarios, and Swedish Censorship: A Case Study of Two 8mm Porn Films Featuring Rape," *Porn Studies* 4, no. 1 (2017): 23–34.

20 Sturman apparently also found that combination potentially disturbing to the audience and avoided distributing such films. See "Lasse Braun Interview—Part 1."

21 Laura Kipnis, "How to Look at Pornography," in *Pornography: Film and Culture*, ed. Peter Lehman (New Brunswick, NJ: Rutgers University Press, 2006), 118–129.

Porn Drift: Semantic Discord in the World of Gonzo

by LAURA HELEN MARKS

> Legal Porno is only one of a few fairly new studios from Europe that provides currently the biggest output on real old school gonzo porn. . . . And I'm talking here from gonzo porn that means scene contains: ATM, DP, DAP, TAP, Face Fucking, Balls Deep, Merry Go Rounds, SWALLOWING MULTIPLE LOADS, CUM GARGLING, ETC. Why can this work in Europe and not in US anymore? Otherwise I would suggest the American girls to visit Europe if they wanna experience some real hardcore poundings. —ultimate_sperminator, "US Porno is Softcore Compared to Legal Porno," *Adult DVD Talk*, October 11, 2015

While ultimate_sperminator, in the epigraph to this essay, is by no means the most articulate member of the fan forum *Adult DVD Talk*, and indeed was taken to task for the loosely defined terminology in this post, his query regarding Legal Porno handily elucidates the focus of my discussion here: the semantic drift in porn terminology. While many fans responded with questions about what he means by "gonzo," ultimate_sperminator's understanding of this term, among others, reflects a larger shift mobilized by industry and fans. Legal Porno specializes in extreme, hyperbolic sex acts—that is, double and triple anal penetration and other so-called circus acts. Not only do fans deploy "gonzo" in fluid ways; Legal Porno itself uses rhetoric in scene titles such as "Jessi Empera is back to Gonzo with DP, DAP & triple penetration [in scene] SZ1826."[1] Contrasting and ambiguous uses of "gonzo" are suggestive of an emerging attitude mobilized by fans and producers that replicates Justice Potter Stewart's infamous 1964 definition of hard-core pornography: "I know it when I see it."[2] Scholars often invoke this definition with wry humor when explaining the difficulties of defining pornography. Indeed, the history of pornography might be said to be a history of legal definitions, popular terminology, and social taste that shape and determine what

1 "Jessi Empera Is Back to Gonzo with DP, DAP & Triple Penetration SZ1826," *Legal Porno*, dir. Luis, August 13, 2017, https://www.legalporno.com/watch/32894/jessi_empera_is_back_to_gonzo_with_dp_dap_triple_penetration_sz1826.

2 *Jacobellis v. Ohio*, 378 U.S. 184 (1964).

constitutes the genre in a constantly evolving way.[3] Indeed, pornography highlights the intersection of genre, legal status, language, and consumption in a way that renders the study of adult film history an academic beacon for understanding the visual arts more broadly.

In the years since Stewart's decision, academics have comfortably settled on an understanding of hard-core porn rooted in industry and fan jargon—that is, constituting unsimulated sex, typically depicting penetration of orifices (whether by a penis, finger, or toy) and ejaculation (male or female, although it is male ejaculation that has come to be seen as a staple of hard core). Meanwhile, gonzo has traditionally been understood as a format popularized by John "Buttman" Stagliano in the late 1980s—a type of cinema verité porn in which the performer(s) acknowledge the camera and typically interact with the cameraperson or director.[4] Yet more recent fan and industry usage of the term "gonzo" indicates an understanding of this subgenre as a style—one that connotes extremity, hardness, and, to use antiporn scholar Gail Dines's phrase, "body-punishing sex."[5] For while the standard definition of "gonzo" porn is indeed simply the filmmaking form, the term is routinely deployed by porn studios, fans, performers, and (usually antiporn) scholars to signal a particular, heteronormative, and rather nebulous sexual aesthetic characterized variously as "hard," "extreme," or "nasty."

At some point over the past decade, fan and industry discourse has drifted away from static academic terms that at one time mirrored industry language. This drift has left an awkward chasm in which academics tend to retain a semantic definition rooted in the moment of the terms' origin while fans and industry producers are merrily conversing with a more flexible set of terms that carry a rather different meaning. The result is semantic discord in discussing pornography that reflects a larger anxiety over the distance between scholar and fan, between those inside and outside of the ivory tower. In this piece, I explore the semantic sphere of this discord with a specific focus on the changing meanings of "gonzo" in the Internet era. A meditation on the word "gonzo" might seem so myopic as to be irrelevant even to some porn scholars, let alone those in other fields—and yet consider the history of this single word, dating (at least in print) back to Hunter S. Thompson's 1971 *Rolling Stone* article "Fear and Loathing in Las Vegas."[6] There, it was used to describe a journalistic practice and aesthetic with no connection to pornography whatsoever; today, gonzo porn retains much of that original usage. In 1975, many years before "gonzo" became associated with the adult film industry, journalist John Filiatreau of Louisville, Kentucky, determined that "gonzo" "can only be defined as what Hunter Thompson does," adding: "It generally

3 Walter Kendrick, *The Secret Museum: Pornography in Modern Culture* (New York: Viking, 1987), 2.

4 John Stagliano's former wife, Tricia Devereaux, provided a definition of "gonzo" for *Adult DVD Talk*'s "dicktionary": "Gonzo can take on several different forms. It can vary from the cameraman (in adult, very often the director) interviewing the actors, or participating in the scene with dialogue and/or sex. It can also mean that the actors are simply acknowledging the fact that there is a camera shooting what they are doing. So, although in adult gonzo, the cameraman is usually somehow visible or audible, simply the actors playing to the camera constitutes a gonzo scene." See "The Adult DVD Talk Porn Dicktionary," *Adult DVD Talk*, https://www.adultdvdtalk.com/sextoys/dictionary.asp.

5 Gail Dines, *Pornland: How Porn Has Hijacked Our Sexuality* (Boston: Beacon, 2010), xi.

6 Hunter S. Thompson, "Fear and Loathing in Las Vegas," *Rolling Stone*, November 11, 1971.

consists of the fusion of reality and stark fantasy in a way that amuses the author and outrages his audience. It is Point of View Run Wild."[7] Such language uncannily echoes Justice Stewart, as well as both Buttman and Gail Dines. My interest in the complicated and conflicted uses of "gonzo" rests in such a conflicted merging of style, practice, and feeling, together with a concern over relying on ahistorical and inaccurate deployments of genre terminology—concerns that I suspect permeate many subfields of cinema and media studies.

Prompted by these concerns, I want to initiate discussion regarding what this semantic discord means not only for porn studies but also for the academic study of media genres, fan cultures, and participatory culture more broadly. Who sets the terms for media and genre discussion? What does it mean when academics resist the semantic drift of fan discourse, and what can the study of such drift do for porn studies and genre studies as a whole? Reflecting on the institutionalization of the phrase "porn studies," Linda Williams argues that such slippage from "pornography" to "porno" to "porn" risks "aligning our own work of scholarship too closely with the work of the pornography industry."[8] For Williams, "adopt[ing] the slang of an industry for the name of their object of study" weakens the legitimacy of an already-maligned field.[9] Yet if, as Zabet Patterson observes, "to interrogate Internet pornography, we must begin by considering the ways in which the organization of on-line pornographic discourses function to guide, if not overtly discipline, their targeted subjects," then it seems important to also consider the ways in which these discourses are guided by those very subjects.[10] Moreover, to resist semantic slippage in an attempt to legitimize academic discourse on disparaged subjects strikes me as a paranoid response to external skepticism.

The relationship between fans and academics is fraught with tension, particularly in connection to class, taste, knowledge, and authority. Upstart scholar-fans find themselves in what Jostein Gripsrud calls "cultural limbo," aware of their new higher standing in the academy while also eager to maintain and demonstrate that they are "one of the people."[11] Fans are often suspicious of academics, regarding them as elitist and Other, no matter how enthusiastic they are about the topic at hand. Matt Hills notes, "Academia is implicitly made other through a denigration of forms of knowledge which are divorced from passion and commitment, as well as through a distaste for the specialist jargon of the academic."[12] Yet at the same time, fans are specialists themselves who, "like the film elite (academics, aesthetics, critics), [are] particularly rich with 'cultural capital' and thus possess a level of textual/critical sophistication

7 Quoted in Martin Hirst, "What Is Gonzo? The Etymology of an Urban Legend" (2004), https://espace.library.uq.edu.au/view/UQ:10764, 4.

8 Linda Williams, "Pornography, Porno, Porn: Thoughts on a Weedy Field," *Porn Studies* 1, nos. 1–2 (2014): 34.

9 Williams, "Pornography, Porno, Porn," 34. By contrast, Rick Altman describes how slippages between industrial, critical or scholarly, and fan uses of generic terms are endemic to the ever-evolving process of "genrification." See Altman, *Film/Genre* (London: British Film Institute, 1999).

10 Zabet Patterson, "Going On-Line: Consuming Pornography in the Digital Era," in *Porn Studies*, ed. Linda Williams (Durham, NC: Duke University Press, 2004), 106.

11 Jostein Gripsrud, "High Culture Revisited," *Cultural Studies* 3, no. 2 (1989): 197.

12 Matt Hills, *Fan Cultures* (New York: Routledge, 2002), 7.

similar to the cineastes they construct as their nemesis."[13] Fans also create, deploy, and attempt to control their own jargon, which subsequently infiltrates the mainstream and the academy. This symbiotic relationship is vital to the study of popular culture.

A remarkably large part of the historical recovery, analysis, and discussion of porn has been initiated and disseminated by fans and industry workers.[14] Former producer, writer, and performer Bill Margold became one of the foremost historians of the industry, as did adult film director Jim Holliday, who wrote the widely respected *Only the Best: Jim Holliday's Adult Video Almanac and Trivia Treasury* (1986). Director William Rotsler wrote one of the earliest critical discussions of the genre, *Contemporary Erotic Cinema* (1973), and novelist Robert Rimmer turned his efforts toward adult film as a fan, painstakingly producing three volumes of adult film reviews and analysis, *The X-Rated Videotape Guide I–III* (1984–1993) that amount to the porn equivalent of *Halliwell's Film Guide*.[15] If we go back as far as the nineteenth century, we might also mention Henry Spencer Ashbee, bibliophile and erotic literature aficionado who, between 1877 and 1885, produced three massive bibliographies of obscene literature under the pseudonym Pisanux Fraxi. The intimacy of fan and scholar has intensified thanks to the development of online spaces. Fans such as Ashley West and April Hall of the oral history podcast the *Rialto Report*, film documentarian Jim Tushinski, film reviewer Dries Vermeulen, archivist and film restorer Joe Rubin of DVD label Vinegar Syndrome, vintage gay-erotica archivist Tim Wilbur, and Karl of the online "watersports" Tumblr *Yesterdays Erotic* are just a handful of fan-scholars producing labors of love that fill critical gaps in formal academic research—gaps that, while less gaping, surely exist in other fields and might helpfully be enriched by knowledge outside of the academy.

Online fan discourse readily indicates a shift in understanding of gonzo. Fan reviews of the 2014 *Riley Goes Gonzo* (Axel Braun), a showcase for former Digital Playground contract star Riley Steele, signal an interpretation of "gonzo" to mean "dirtier" and "harder" sex. In his review fu_q states, "Bursting through the 'contract girl' barrier with abandon, the blue-eyed, blond-haired beauty, Riley Steele, dispels the stereotypes and proves that she's far more dirty than she is dollish."[16] These discourses also reveal a merging of the terms "hard core" and "gonzo," here used to describe each other. In his review, Captain Jack observes that Riley "is going to be shooting more hard core scenes than she's used to!" though ultimately concludes that the film is, after all, "pretty ordinary and not very hardcore."[17] We also find some confusion in these

13 Jeffrey Sconce, "Trashing the Academy: Taste, Excess, and the Emerging Politics of Cinematic Style," *Screen* 36, no. 4 (1995): 375.

14 David Church, *Disposable Passions: Vintage Pornography and the Material Legacies of Adult Cinema* (New York: Bloomsbury Academic, 2016), 158.

15 Jim Holliday, *Only the Best: Jim Holliday's Adult Video Almanac and Trivia Treasury* (Van Nuys, CA: Cal Vista Publications, 1986); William Rotsler, *Contemporary Erotic Cinema* (New York: Penthouse/Ballantine, 1973); Robert H. Rimmer, *The X-Rated Videotape Guide* (New York: Arlington House, 1984).

16 fu_q, "*Riley Goes Gonzo*," *Adult DVD Talk*, December 31, 2013, https://www.adultdvdtalk.com/review/riley-goes-gonzo.

17 Captain Jack, "*Riley Goes Gonzo*," *Adult DVD Talk*, December 24, 2014, https://www.adultdvdtalk.com/review/riley-goes-gonzo-31615.

discussions. For example, in bono-ONE's review of *Riley Goes Gonzo*, he states: "It is a harder release than what we've been used to with Miss Steele or at least that's what I think they are going for here. Let's find out just how gonzo Riley gets here!"[18] Even when discussing older titles, produced in an era before gonzo porn was a twinkle in Buttman's eye, fans will describe content as "gonzo" whether due to style or form. For example, in his review of 1977's pseudo-documentary curiosity *Long Jeanne Silver* (Alex DeRenzy), Willie D remarks, "It's shot documentary-style where Jeanne introduces us to various experiences in her life. Each scene has a short intro, followed by some sex. Heck, this may be the first gonzo porno ever!"[19] In contrast, I recall a fan telling me that celebrated sexual dynamo Vanessa Del Rio was "gonzo before there was gonzo," signaling the heat, intensity, and authenticity of Del Rio's performances.

In her discussion of trending porn categories, Chauntelle Anne Tibbals expresses concern that "the term 'gonzo' is commonly misused," citing Dines's loaded use of the term in the latter's book *Pornland*.[20] Dines uses "gonzo" to describe a "genre" that "depicts hard-core, body-punishing sex in which women are demeaned and debased."[21] "Gonzo, however," Tibbals goes on, "is not a genre—it is a filmmaking form. Consequently, it is possible for any and all adult content to include moments of gonzo, the intensity of sex and/or genre notwithstanding."[22] Tibbals's concern is understandable, considering the bad-faith application of the term "gonzo" in Dines's book. The danger of Dines's conflation of form and genre is that "subjective assessments regarding the nature of sex depictions" obscure a more complex discussion of production and consumption trends.[23] Dines does not objectively analyze sex styles and positions. Instead, she applies a value judgment of degradation and misogyny as though hyperbolic sexual athleticism were inherently degrading to women. Yet her use of the term "gonzo" has less to do with understanding it as a filmmaking form and more to do with shallow and subjective applications of taste-based politics to particular sexual acts.

Angela White attends to the complex politics of porn terminology in the marketing behind her 2016 self-directed release *Angela Loves Gonzo*. White's video and its surrounding discourse are useful in parsing the shifting, nebulous terminologies of pornography and the way these terms are politicized, weaponized, and deployed in the industry, in fandom, and in academia. Moreover, her commentary indicates the importance of directly engaging with these drifting terminologies. With this title, White signals a stylistic change, shifting away from the more cinematic approach she typically takes to one that breaks the fourth wall and utilizes point of view (POV). At the same time, she is also signaling that she has produced a series of scenes that amp

18 bono-ONE, "*Riley Goes Gonzo*," *Adult DVD Talk*, January 20, 2014, https://www.adultdvdtalk.com/review/riley-goes-gonzo-29654.

19 Willie D., "Long Jeanne Silver (1977)," *XXX Porn Talk*, April 25, 2007, http://forum.jerkoffzone.net/ubbthreads/ubbthreads.php?ubb=showflat&Number=240619.

20 Chauntelle Anne Tibbals, "Gonzo, Trannys, and Teens—Current Trends in US Adult Content Production, Distribution, and Consumption," *Porn Studies* 1, nos. 1–2 (2014): 129.

21 Dines, *Pornland*, xi.

22 Tibbals, "Gonzo, Trannys, and Teens," 129.

23 Tibbals, "Gonzo, Trannys, and Teens," 129.

up the sexual action from vanilla to something more intense. In the text accompanying the scene's release on her website (text that is also used in promotional materials and press releases), White explains the film as a direct engagement with the politics of "gonzo": "As a genre, gonzo has had an onslaught of attacks from conservative and anti-porn feminist campaigners for being the most degrading and misogynistic type of pornography. I wanted to release a gonzo DVD that challenges the assumption that women cannot or should not enjoy rough sex."[24] White explicitly positions her use of the term as a political act, one that attempts to redefine our perceptions of "gonzo," particularly in connection to women:

> Releasing *Angela Loves Gonzo* is a political statement as well as being another step in my sexual exploration through porn, . . . but another thing I wanted to make clear with this release, and what I think most critics of the genre miss, is that gonzo can also be one of the most intimate and authentic genres. By removing the crew and the artifice of scripts and storylines, gonzo allows performers to focus on connecting with each other. I always find that authentic chemistry is showcased most effectively in gonzo porn and while *Angela Loves Gonzo* features consensual rough sex, it includes an equal amount of genuine intimacy, light hearted jokes, tenderness and mutual affection between performers.[25]

This marketing rhetoric both circulates and challenges several popular understandings and characterizations of "gonzo": that it is a shooting format (POV), that it is altogether "hard" or "rough," and that it is associated with misogyny and degradation of women. White's hopes for redemption are directed toward two maligned categories: women and gonzo. On the one hand, White hopes to show that women can enjoy rough sex, and on the other hand, she hopes to show that gonzo can be intimate and affectionate. In addition, the rhetoric surrounding White's film signals the extent to which "hard core" has drifted from its standard definition—unsimulated penetrative sex—toward a space simultaneously occupied by gonzo. Hence, White promises "four gonzo scenes that do away with camera crews and professional lighting to focus on real, raw hardcore action," blurring the format-based understanding of gonzo with a stylistic understanding that is "hard core."[26]

In response to what can appear to be an alarming dissolution of concrete meaning, Enrico Biasin and Federico Zecca articulate gonzo style as a logical development arising out of the gonzo format. That is, "the effacement of narration gives way . . . to the expansion of the sexual act."[27] In this way, it makes sense that fans might linguistically understand "gonzo" to mean both a format and a descriptor that signals hyperbolic sex acts—a type of pornography that, because of its format, privileges sexual athleticism

24 "Angela White Stars in New Showcase DVD 'Angela Loves Gonzo,'" *Adult Video News*, May 27, 2016, https://avn.com/business/press-release/video/angela-white-stars-in-new-showcase-dvd-angela-loves-gonzo-668025.html.

25 "Angela White Stars."

26 "Angela White Stars."

27 Enrico Biasin and Federico Zecca, "Contemporary Audiovisual Pornography: Branding Strategy and Gonzo Film Style," *Cinema & Cie* 9, no. 12 (2009): 143.

as the main attraction. Fans, along with the industry, have thus arguably mobilized this dual meaning to the point where it is verging on an institutionalized meaning.

The rapidly proliferating field of porn studies, like many an academic field, tends to retain the concrete definitions of old or steadfastly refuses to deviate from definitions that serve a political or scholarly purpose. Against this backdrop, the vocabulary of fandom and industry rhetoric offers a fruitful site for complicating and shaking up scholarly investigations of pornography. It is important to ask what porn fans and industry workers know that we academics do not; to ask how terms that we might believe are set in stone are being redefined, reshaped, and put to work to discursively navigate the bewildering terrain of pornographic media; and to ask how and why we might attend to this semantic drift in a way that informs and strengthens our scholarship. *

The Queer Heart of Porn Studies

by JOHN PAUL STADLER

In a field retrospective, Linda Williams historicizes the development of porn studies under the tutelage of film and video studies. Williams notes that, in hindsight, porn studies might also have thrived under "history, anthropology, cultural studies, or the then-developing queer studies."[1] Following this supposition, I want to explore what queerness can teach us about the study of adult film.[2] The familial resemblance between porn studies and queer studies suggests that their coemergence was perhaps not coincidental at all but resulted from sex-positive feminist and nonstraight scholars who, amid the culture wars (and the rise of neoliberalism), took that indeterminate site of power—sexuality—as their primary object of study. Both epistemological projects are deeply indebted to Foucauldian thought, poststructuralist methodologies, and unabashed interest in perversion. Both emerged in dissent to and reconfiguration of second-wave feminism, both share an objective to denaturalize sex and uncover its social constructions, and both agitate against the patriarchal processes of normalization.

To map their similarities, I turn to queer theory, which inaugurated the development of queer studies in the 1990s. Gayle Rubin's 1984 essay "Thinking Sex" laid the groundwork for queer theory by asking why feminism had not yet "critically thought" the sexual practices that

1 Linda Williams, "Pornography, Porno, Porn: Thoughts on a Weedy Field," *Porn Studies* 1, no. 1 (2014): 25.

2 I am invoking here Lauren Berlant and Michael Warner's pedagogy-themed essay "What Does Queer Theory Teach Us about X?," *PMLA* 110 (1995): 343–349.

fell outside of "the charmed circle" or that imagined division between "good" and "bad" sex.[3] In her diagram, pornography and homosexual sex acts both unsurprisingly exceeded the circle's normalizing boundary. Rubin was responding in part to the infamous 1982 Barnard Conference on Sexuality that had tumultuously brought together bristling factions of antipornography and anticensorship feminists. Porn studies, too, emerged out of that tumult, for early porn studies scholars had to defend themselves against the media-effects debates of antiporn feminists.[4] But whereas Rubin wanted to "think sex," Linda Williams in *Hard Core* sought to "speak sex," a distinction that highlights the enunciatory imperative for sex to produce discourse. For Williams, pornography holds the vexed position of being "on/scene," where "a culture brings on to its public arena the very organs, acts, bodies, and pleasures that have heretofore been designated obscene and kept literally off-scene."[5] The tension of on/scenity positions pornography as an open secret, one that its scholars would need to negotiate carefully, often from the starting position of defensiveness. On/scenity also reveals the arbitrary line between the unacceptable and acceptable, signaling the importance of context. A medical diagram of the naked body in the doctor's office isn't pornography, but in a different space it could be. That slipperiness is something to which queer theory was no stranger.

In the essentialist versus constructivist debates surrounding homosexual origins, queer theory faced a debate with no positive outcome, a dilemma that resonates with the media-effects debates in porn studies—the ones that go something like, "Does pornography cause X?"[6] Eve Sedgwick speculated that the political desire to locate an etiology for homosexuality, regardless of one's position, distressingly revealed the desire for the eradication of homosexuality, and not the attempt to understand it better.[7] Rather than engage ad nauseam with the question of adult cinema's presumed causal effects—which similarly reveal the desire for eradication rather than understanding—porn studies chose a different set of questions to consider, starting with complications to visuality. Williams famously articulated the latter in the expansion of Jean-Louis Comolli's concept of the "frenzy of the visible," where tropes like the "money shot"

3 Gayle Rubin, "Thinking Sex: Notes for a Radical Theory of the Politics of Sexuality," in *Pleasure and Danger: Exploring Female Sexuality*, ed. Carole S. Vance (Boston: Routledge & Kegan Paul, 1984), 267–319.

4 See, for instance, Laura Kipnis, *Bound and Gagged: Pornography and the Politics of Fantasy in America* (Durham, NC: Duke University Press, 1996); Thomas Waugh, "Men's Pornography, Gay vs. Straight," *Jump Cut: A Review of Contemporary Media*, no. 30 (1985): 30–35; Linda Williams, *Hard Core: Power, Pleasure, and the "Frenzy of the Visible,"* 2nd ed. (Berkeley: University of California Press, 1999).

5 This definition comes from Williams's introduction to her anthology *Porn Studies*, but she first coined the term in the added epilogue to the second edition of *Hard Core*. In fact, she has revealed elsewhere that *Pornographies On/Scene* had been her preferred title for the anthology that would become *Porn Studies*. See Williams, introduction to *Porn Studies*, ed. Linda Williams (Durham, NC: Duke University Press, 2004), 5; Williams, *Hard Core*, 282; and Williams, "Pornography, Porno, Porn," 34.

6 In the 1980s, the "X" of this formula stood for rape, violence, and misogyny, but more recent media-effects debates have come to treat pornography as a (mental) health crisis. "X" in the latter case can be seen to mean any number of things: erectile dysfunction, lowered libido, heightened libido, depression, anxiety, antisocial behavior, addiction, or—classically—the demise of a relationship.

7 Here I reference Eve Kosofsky Sedgwick's queer critique: "There currently exists no origins or development of individual gay identity that is not already structured by an implicit, trans-individual Western project or fantasy of eradicating that identity." Sedgwick, *Epistemology of the Closet* (Berkeley: University of California Press, 1990), 41.

stand in as constructions of desire's so-called truth.[8] The political stakes for porn studies have, then, largely centered on obscenity and censorship. For queer theory, they have concerned contestations of heteronormativity, a validation of socially illegible subjects, and an aspiration for alternative social structures.[9]

Although there are resonances between porn studies and queer theory, the two do not always map onto each other neatly. When the term "queer" travels within porn studies, it often fails to denote queer theory's inaugural desire to evade culturally legible sexual-identity categories. In her 1993 essay "Queer and Now," Eve Sedgwick wrote that "same-sex sexual object choice" remains the definitional center of queerness; simultaneously, she called for "queer" to signify more than same-sex attraction.[10] The tension of making same-sex object choice central while simultaneously refusing to limit queerness to an identificatory understanding of "gay" can also be seen in Sedgwick's development of a universalizing versus minoritizing framework. Sedgwick uses the latter concepts to destabilize and ultimately disrupt the long-standing nature-versus-nurture debates, but this tension also reveals the scales at which her vision for a queer discourse operated: with the universalizing project of coming to terms with myriad forms of sexual "difference" existing beyond discrete identity categories on the one hand and, on the other hand, the minoritizing project of supporting gay men during the AIDS crisis.[11] In other words, the "queer" of queer theory often served, at least in its earliest articulations, as a concept whose referent refused capture, and as such it was imagined to offer a radical hermeneutic for disrupting received knowledge.[12]

The "queer" of queer theory, then, initially sought to undermine reference to and question the construction of identity structures, whereas the broader "LGBTQ studies" was more likely to codify identities into discrete and legible categories to further the pursuit of civil rights and recognitions.[13] "Queer" within porn studies often follows a more identity-centered approach to "queer," adopting a usage fairly synonymous with "gay" and "lesbian." Film scholars Thomas Waugh and Richard Dyer were foundational to the study of gay pornography in the 1980s.[14] Their scholarship

8 Williams, *Hard Core*, 36, 112–113; Jean-Louis Comolli, "Machines of the Visible," in *The Cinematic Apparatus*, ed. Teresa De Lauretis and Stephen Heath (New York: St. Martin's Press, 1980), 122–123.

9 Lauren Berlant and Michael Warner's notion of heteronormativity, José Muñoz's understanding of disidentification, and Michael Warner's use of counterpublics give a rough sketch of the rich concepts developed under queer theory. See Berlant and Warner, "Sex in Public," *Critical Inquiry* 24, no. 2 (1998): 547–566; José Esteban Muñoz, *Disidentifications: Queers of Color and the Performance of Politics* (Minneapolis: University of Minnesota Press, 1999); Michael Warner, "Publics and Counterpublics," *Public Culture* 14, no. 1 (2002): 49–90.

10 Eve Kosofsky Sedgwick, "Queer and Now," *Tendencies* (Durham, NC: Duke University Press, 1993), 8.

11 In an interesting bridging of praxis and representation, the pornography industry was one of the first cultural institutions to heed the call of queer activists by incorporating safer-sex protocols and disclaimers into the gay pornography of the era. See Cindy Patton, *Fatal Advice: How Safe-Sex Education Went Wrong* (Durham, NC: Duke University Press, 1996), 118–138.

12 Sedgwick, "Queer and Now," 8.

13 "Queer theory" has not been able to fend off implications of being an umbrella term for minority sexual-identity categories, but I want to follow its initial desire to do precisely that.

14 See Thomas Waugh, *Hard to Imagine: Gay Male Eroticism in Photography and Film from Their Beginnings to Stonewall* (New York: Columbia University Press, 1996); Thomas Waugh, "'Men's Pornography, Gay vs. Straight': A Personal Revisit," *Porn Studies* 4, no. 2 (2017): 131–138; Thomas Waugh, "Homosociality in the Classical American Stag Film: Off-Screen, On-Screen," *Sexualities* 4, no. 3 (2001): 275–291; Richard Dyer, "Male Gay

engaged in the feminist "sex wars" by taxonomizing gay pornography in order to distance it from heterosexual "smut" and in turn legitimize gay and lesbian porn scholarship. From the 1990s onward, gay and lesbian porn scholarship experienced a veritable explosion of scholarly writing.[15] Williams observes that the "queer and 'queering' approach has perhaps flourished the most" in the field of porn studies. She goes on to explain that the "growing field [of] studying gay pornography . . . can be expected to flourish because the scholars who write about these pornographies have found them crucial to their identities as gays or queers."[16] Williams presents the terms "gay" and "queer" alongside each other, almost interchangeably, but also as constitutive of identity. While the importance of pornography to gay culture and identity is undeniable, the way in which "queer" signifies here—as if "covering all the bases"—diverges starkly from queer theory's hope to disrupt these very identities.[17]

Porn studies has recently begun to reflect more rigorously on its critical lineage and approach, toward which this In Focus dossier also contributes.[18] Not only is porn studies beginning to trace its own field formation; it has expanded its methodology into something of an interdisciplinary constellation: in addition to textual analysis, methodological approaches include cultural studies, historicism, archival studies, industry studies, fan cultures, and ethnography. John Champagne's early polemic "Stop Reading Films!" gives just one example of discursive reflection, when he calls for scholars to leave behind the textual analysis component in gay porn studies for a more contextual analysis of the sexually fluid reception and exhibition practices.[19] Here,

---

Porn, Coming to Terms," *Jump Cut: A Review of Contemporary Media*, no. 30 (1985): 27–29; and Dyer, "Idol Thoughts: Orgasm and Self-Reflexivity in Gay Pornography," *Critical Quarterly* 36, no. 1 (1994): 49–62.

15 An abbreviated overview: Heather Butler, "What Do You Call a Lesbian with Long Fingers? The Development of Lesbian and Dyke Pornography," in *Porn Studies*, ed. Linda Williams (Durham, NC: Duke University Press, 2004), 167–197; José B. Capino, "Seminal Fantasies: Wakefield Poole, Pornography, Independent Cinema and the Avant-Garde," in *Contemporary American Independent Film: From the Margins to the Mainstream*, ed. Chris Holmlund and Justin Wyatt (New York: Routledge, 2005), 155–173; John R. Burger, *One-Handed Histories: The Eroto-Politics of Gay Male Video Pornography* (New York: Hayworth Press, 1995); Jeffrey Escoffier, *Bigger than Life: The History of Gay Porn Cinema from Beefcake to Hardcore* (Philadelphia: Running Dog Press, 2009); Richard Fung, "Looking for My Penis," in *How Do I Look? Queer Film and Video*, ed. Bad Object-Choices (Seattle: Bay Press, 1991), 145–168; Tan Hoang Nguyen, "The Resurrection of Brandon Lee: The Making of a Gay Asian American Porn Star," in *Porn Studies*, ed. Linda Williams (Durham, NC: Duke University Press, 2004), 230–270; John Mercer, *Gay Pornography: Representations of Sexuality and Masculinity* (London: I. B. Tauris, 2017); Cindy Patton, *LA Plays Itself / Boys in the Sand: A Queer Film Classic* (Vancouver: Arsenal Pulp Press, 2014); Cherry Smyth, "The Pleasure Threshold: Looking at Lesbian Pornography on Film," *Feminist Review* 34, no. 1 (1990): 152–159.

16 Williams, "Pornography, Porno, Porn," 26.

17 Queer theory has itself also been taken to task for failing to mean more than "gay and lesbian." See, for instance, Susan Stryker, "Transgender Studies: Queer Theory's Evil Twin," *GLQ: A Journal of Lesbian and Gay Studies* 10, no. 2 (2004): 212–215.

18 The metadiscursive analysis of pornography studies is limited but beginning to grow. See Williams, "Pornography, Porno, Porn"; Tim Dean, "Introduction: Pornography, Technology, Archive," in *Porn Archives*, ed. Tim Dean, Steven Ruszczycky, and David Squires (Durham, NC: Duke University Press, 2014); Kipnis, "How to Read Pornography," in *Bound and Gagged*; and Frances Ferguson, *Pornography, the Theory: What Utilitarianism Did to Action* (Chicago: University of Chicago Press, 2004).

19 John Champagne, "'Stop Reading Films!': Film Studies, Close Analysis, and Gay Pornography," *Cinema Journal* 36, no. 4 (1997): 76–97. José B. Capino, Rich Cante, Angelo Restivo, and Samuel Delany have each undertaken reception studies of adult cinema that carry forward Champagne's call.

then, we see a branch of porn studies that took a demonstrably queer approach—in the sense that it distanced itself from the dominant mode—to apprehend adult cinema's social meanings.

Contemporary online pornography lends insight to another form of queerness through its expansive naming and categorization processes. One might think this proliferation would codify a host of paraphilias into identity structures. (If you can think it, there is porn for it, the internet meme "Rule 34" tells us.)[20] Indeed, writing in 1999, Williams notes that she could not do justice to the variety of pornographic forms that had emerged since the 1980s, although she still compiled a list that includes sadomasochism, yuppie, gonzo, amateur, fetish, bondage and discipline, instructional, "real" lesbian, bisexual, fat, enema, spanking, transvestism, transgender, and racial and ethnic pornography.[21] Against this proliferation, though, she noted that "unitary categories of identity begin to cross and blur."[22] To her list, we can add feminist porn and queer porn, ready for more ethical consumption, as well as newer digital forms with more complicated ethics: cam shows, revenge porn, dick pics, and so on.[23] In *Carnal Resonance*, Susanna Paasonen echoes Williams's suspicion that proliferating categories might codify identities, and she insists that "sexual depictions and activities need to be considered outside the framework of fixed identity categories. A queer orientation to pornography involves analytical curiosity and openness that does not start from or resort to binary models."[24]

What exactly would a queer orientation to porn studies look like, though? If we treat pornography with less familiarity, and instead estrange our understanding of its formal incitation of rhythms, durations, tropes, forces, and structures, we might open up what Eugenie Brinkema calls the radical formalism of pornography.[25] Because porn studies has so aptly deconstructed the fictive representations of female pleasure in the "frenzy of the visible" and "the money shot," a deconstructive approach to pornography's rendering of sexual identity would seem fitting. For Whitney Strub, queerness links to questions of both methodology and content. He argues, for example, that the impoverished adult cinema archive has led "porn studies scholars to miss the enormous queer drifts of early hardcore."[26] An answer, then, to locating a queerer orientation to pornography might require first a methodological answer to the question, How do we locate our objects when they are under threat of vanishing? It would seem that the temporal uncertainty and urgency undergirding queer praxis (and

20 Williams, *Hard Core*, 301–303.

21 Williams, *Hard Core*, 301–303.

22 Williams, *Hard Core*, 304.

23 See Tristan Taormino, Celine Parreñas Shimizu, Constance Penley, and Mireille Miller-Young, eds., *The Feminist Porn Book: The Politics of Producing Pleasure* (New York: Feminist Press, 2013).

24 Specifically, Paasonen seeks to disband binary thinking about pornography posed in terms of "us and them, in and out, gay and straight." See *Carnal Resonance: Affect and Online Pornography* (Cambridge, MA: MIT Press, 2011), 153.

25 Eugenie Brinkema, "Irrumation, the Interrogative: Extreme Porn and the Crisis of Reading," *Polygraph*, no. 26 (2017): 130–164, https://polygraphjournal.files.wordpress.com/2017/12/polygraph-26_eugenie-brinkema.pdf.

26 Whitney Strub, "Sex Wishes and Virgin Dreams: Zebedy Colt's Reactionary Queer Heterosmut and the Elusive Porn Archive," *GLQ: A Journal of Lesbian and Gay Studies* 23, no. 3 (2017): 363.

life!) amid the AIDS crisis in the 1990s might also inform the object of pornography, viewed here as expendable, undervalued, and in need of care.

In this brief sketch, I have traced homologies that suggest a strong affinity between queer theory and porn studies, but their complementarity reflects their particularities as well. For while queer theory and porn studies appear increasingly to intersect, they also leave impressions on one another, which I have tried to make explicit. Linda Williams's suggestion that porn studies might have flourished under queer studies invites us to consider the ways that queer theory—queer studies' instantiating hermeneutic—can reorient our understanding of adult cinema. To study pornography continues to require a rigorous defense—what I call "the disclaimer"— of the critical value of the very object before the analysis we hope to pursue can begin, much as queer theory did in its early days.[27] Meanwhile, porn studies can learn from queer theory to be more promiscuous, interdisciplinary, capacious, and reflective of itself. Lee Edelman notes the homologue I have been tracing as follows: "Like pornography, queerness occupies the space of what resists the advances of knowledge, what conceptualization can't domesticate by way of its will-to-identity. As such it never coincides with itself, never quickens into form."[28] It is in this resistance to a preset knowledge that queerness and pornography seem most alike, most challenging, and most productive. *

27 In an ironic turn, it is contemporary queer theory that now appears to be more institutionalized and less in need of a defense.

28 Lee Edelman, "Unbecoming: Pornography and the Queer Event," in *Post Porn Politics: Queer-Feminist Perspective on the Politics of Porn Performance and Sex-Work as Culture Production*, ed. Tim Stüttgen (Berlin: b_books, 2009), 38.

No Sex in Newark: Postindustrial Erotics at the Intersection of Urban and Adult Film History

by Whitney Strub

No masterpiece of pornography by most standards, *Newark Penn Station Pt 1: Dude Fingering My Musty Booty* (neaneal4, 2015) consists of fifty-six seconds set in a restroom that foreground a man's thrust-out ass. We peer up into it from below, as another man sitting on a toilet in an adjacent stall reaches under the divide to, indeed, finger it. The man being fingered shoots the scene from his phone camera, held in one hand as he strokes himself with the other, leaving us with a shaky and constrained view. Just before the minute mark, it abruptly stops.

Fortunately for viewers left disoriented or seeking narrative or sexual closure, our cruising pornographer, known only as neanea14, posted a short sequel to his XTube channel. In the caption to *Newark Penn Station Pt 2* (2015), he explains, "i went to the urinals and we went into the stall to finish what we started at the urinals. my dick was musty as fuck. hope you enjoy."[1] This fifty-seven-second scene brings the video to an orgasmic conclusion, as the two men, now standing inside one stall, jack themselves and each other off to completion, ejaculating in turn into the toilet bowl. In the next stall, a man stands to pee and flushes, seen only by his feet.

We never see faces in the two videos, which afford us mere snippets of the men at play: black, with tight athletic abdomens, dressed casually in sweatpants, jeans, and sneakers. From neanea14's profile, we get an expanded sense of an attractive twentysomething very interested in public sex, public masturbation, and the act of recording himself. Much of his erotic circuit seems to follow the route of the northern New Jersey Port Authority Trans-Hudson (PATH) train itinerary, with similar encounters recorded at the Journal Square stop in Jersey City and elsewhere.

Much could be said of the sometimes charming, sometimes troubling erotic subjectivity that neanea14 charts over the course of his fifty short videos, all posted to XTube between approximately 2013 and 2016. As a proud versatile bottom and self-identified Christian, his stated turn-ons include mustiness and men of all varieties, with the exception of "fat guys and Caucasian men." As an exemplar of Black queer autopornography, he represents do-it-yourself (DIY) culture work of the sort that still receives too little scholarly attention.[2]

The work of neanea14 also points toward the ways pornography proves useful at the intersection of urban history, film studies, and the history of sexuality, especially when traditional archives fail us. Both the production and the exhibition of porn offer rich resources for documenting precarious postindustrial erotics that too often go overlooked. Notably, neanea14's "hit me up" geography does not include New York City—a mere three stops and ten minutes past Journal Square on the PATH, and so easily accessible for him. Instead, it comprises a North Jersey nexus of Jersey City, Bayonne, Newark, Hoboken, and East Orange. Nor is neanea14 the only DIY pornographer working in this space; XTube user deesoul87 offers *Penn Station Head* (2011), seventy-five seconds of blow-job footage riskily shot on an elevator inside Newark Penn Station.[3]

Clearly, Newark affords space for pleasure and desire. One would not know it from the existing scholarship on the city, however. In the dominant national symbolic economy, Newark remains an overdetermined metonym of urban decay, eternally trapped in the shadow of 1967's long hot summer and its incessant renarrativization everywhere from PBS to Philip Roth novels.[4] When anthropologist Ana Ramos-Zayas

1 The profile of neanea14, with links to his videos, can be found at https://www.xtube.com/profile/neanea14-3759531.

2 Indeed, Black gay porn in general needs and deserves more critical analysis. See Terry Rowden, "The 'Top' of the Heap: Race, Manhood, and Legitimation in *My Life in Porn: The Bobby Blake Story*," *Black Camera* 2, no. 2 (2011): 80–99.

3 deesoul87, *Penn Station Head* (2011), https://www.xtube.com/video-watch/penn-station-head-1260146.

4 See, for example, *Revolution '67* (Marylou Tibaldo-Bongiorno, 2007); Philip Roth, *American Pastoral* (New York: Vintage, 1998).

studied how Newark was rendered legible to Brazilian and Puerto Rican immigrant communities, she found that blackness registered as an affect, defined through aggression, which in turn became the "meta-narrative of emotion in Newark."[5] In this reading of the city, otherwise-marginalized groups partook of hegemonic consensus.

Indeed, postindustrial blackness seems to foreclose the sort of urban erotics bestowed on other cities. To pluck from eclectic historiographies for effect: eighteenth-century Philadelphia begins with *Sex among the Rabble* and grows into the postwar *City of Sisterly and Brotherly Loves*; New York gets both *Licentious Gotham* and *Prurient Interests*; San Francisco, simply *Erotic City*.[6] Even Kansas gets *Sex in the Heartland*; Minnesota, *Land of 10,000 Loves*; and Arkansas, the enticingly queer *Un-Natural State*.[7] Yet when it comes to Newark—and this could easily be Gary, Flint, Cleveland, or Baltimore—urban history flattens into a familiar but desexualized arc of immigration, redevelopment, riots, Black Power, and urban decay. *No Cause for Indictment* is the connotative apotheosis, a self-declared "autopsy" of the city.[8] Tellingly, when Kevin Mumford wrote a book about Newark in between his pioneering history of interracial sex districts and his field-defining Black gay history monograph, he attended carefully to gender, but even he saw no sex.[9]

Amateur pornographers such as neaneal4 and deesoul87 thus importantly articulate an urban eros otherwise insufficiently recognized: the simple fact that Newark, like other postindustrial Black and Latino cities, is as sexy as any other place, yet defined through a general absence of the whiteness that corresponds uncomfortably with eroticism in dominant narratives. That said, a representational charting of desire can take us only so far. While scholars of urban film history have generally failed to account for the central role of pornography in both depicting cities and mapping sexuality, recent work has taken up the challenge, from Elena Gorfinkel's investigation of grindhouse historicity in sexploitation's recursive reliance on Times Square footage to Jeffrey Escoffier's argument for 1970s gay hard core as "homorealism."[10] In my own

5 Ana Ramos-Zayas, *Street Therapists: Race, Affect, and Neoliberal Personhood in Latino Newark* (Chicago: University of Chicago Press, 2012), 41.

6 Clare Lyons, *Sex among the Rabble: An Intimate History of Gender and Power in the Age of Revolution, Philadelphia, 1730–1830* (Chapel Hill: University of North Carolina Press, 2012); Marc Stein, *City of Sisterly and Brotherly Loves: Lesbian and Gay Philadelphia, 1945–1972* (Philadelphia: Temple University Press, 2004); Donna Dennis, *Licentious Gotham: Erotic Publishing and Its Prosecution in Nineteenth-Century New York* (Cambridge, MA: Harvard University Press, 2009); Andrea Friedman, *Prurient Interests: Gender, Democracy, and Obscenity in New York City, 1909–1945* (New York: Columbia University Press, 2000); Josh Sides, *Erotic City: Sexual Revolutions and the Making of Modern San Francisco* (New York: Oxford University Press, 2012).

7 Beth Bailey, *Sex in the Heartland* (Cambridge, MA: Harvard University Press, 1999); Stewart Van Cleve, *Land of 10,000 Loves: A History of Queer Minnesota* (Minneapolis: University of Minnesota Press, 2012); Brock Thompson, *The Un-Natural State: Arkansas and the Queer South* (Fayetteville: University of Arkansas Press, 2010).

8 Ronald Porambo, *No Cause for Indictment: An Autopsy of Newark* (New York: Holt, Rinehart and Winston, 1971).

9 Kevin Mumford, *Interzones: Black/White Sex Districts in Chicago and New York in the Early Twentieth Century* (New York: Columbia University Press, 1997); Mumford, *Newark: A History of Race, Rights, and Riots in America* (New York: New York University Press, 2007); Mumford, *Not Straight, Not White: Black Gay Men from the March on Washington to the AIDS Crisis* (Chapel Hill: University of North Carolina Press, 2016).

10 Elena Gorfinkel, *Lewd Looks: American Sexploitation Cinema in the 1960s* (Minneapolis: University of Minnesota Press, 2017); Jeffrey Escoffier, "Sex in the Seventies: Gay Porn Cinema as an Archive for the History of American Sexuality," *Journal of the History of Sexuality* 26, no. 1 (2017): 88–113.

work, I have examined Pat Rocco's groundbreaking gay soft-core films as acts of place-claiming in late-1960s Los Angeles, as well as the ways both straight and gay hard core narrate the purported urban crisis of the 1970s.[11] The intersection of adult film and urban history remains fertile ground for further analysis, and yet the overwhelming preponderance of this material was shot in three cities. We can find scattered stand-alone examples in Memphis, Seattle, and elsewhere—Detroit's *Hot Summer in the City* (Gail Palmer, 1976) is one striking bit of porno-urbanism. However, other noncoastal cities have even sparser filmic records. New York, Los Angeles, and San Francisco dominate the history of hard core, at least until the San Fernando Valley and to a lesser extent Las Vegas begin their ascent (in both cases largely without the rich location shooting of 1970s porn). Beyond the internet-era tube-site videos, I can locate only two adult films shot in Newark, both thanks to the copious documentation at the *Rialto Report*: *Love Lords* (Bob Mason, 1972), a soft-core crime thriller with some vivid location shooting that was later spiced up with inserts and revived as the hard-core *Saturday Night Special* (Sam Bloch, 1976), and *Joy* (Harley Mansfield, 1977), a primarily New York–based film that concludes with a scene at Newark Liberty International Airport. Neither engages with desire embodied in a specific urban setting the way neanea14's videos do.

But if we turn to exhibition, pornography returns us to urban histories of film and sexuality largely unrecorded. During the 1970s and into the 1980s, publicly screened hard-core films defined the urban landscape. Samuel Delany's *Times Square Red, Times Square Blue*, which brilliantly blends personal memoir with sociological analysis, inevitably stands as the canonical citation for describing the cross-class, multiracial (yet generally homosocial) public sphere of democratic sexuality enabled by pornographic space, in which men seeking to fulfill "needs that most of our society does not yet know how to acknowledge" also forge community and solidarity in porn theaters.[12] Delany's depiction, loving yet carefully nonutopian ("humane and functional" is his precise description), seems broadly applicable to other spaces of smut.[13] But what does it mean to extricate adult theaters from the already-sexualized space of Times Square to the less preemptively eroticized terrain of a place like Newark? Where does this intense, concentrated, complicatedly queer space fit into the narrative of postindustrial Black (and later, Latino) cities?

Newark still hosts the Little Theatre, which has outlasted every porn theater in Manhattan and nearly all in the New York City metropolitan area.[14] To date, no scholar has paid heed to the venue, but if we take it seriously as a sexual institution, it points

11 Whitney Strub, "Mondo Rocco: Mapping Gay Los Angeles Sexual Geography in the Late-1960s Films of Pat Rocco," *Radical History Review* 113 (2012): 13–34; Strub, "From Porno Chic to Porno Bleak: Representing the Urban Crisis in 1970s American Pornography," in *Porno Chic and the Sex Wars: American Sexual Representation in the 1970s*, ed. Carolyn Bronstein and Whitney Strub (Amherst: University of Massachusetts Press, 2016), 27–52.

12 Samuel Delany, *Times Square Red, Times Square Blue* (New York: New York University Press, 1999), 90.

13 For a rare look at heterosexuality in contemporary adult theaters, see David Church, "'This Thing of Ours': Heterosexuality, Recreational Sex, and the Survival of Adult Movie Theaters," *Media Fields Journal* 8 (2014), http://mediafieldsjournal.squarespace.com/this-thing-of-ours.

14 All that remain of the classic adult theaters in New York are the King's Highway, deep in Brooklyn, and the Fair Theatre in East Elmhurst, Queens.

toward further ways adult film history can enrich our current stories of sexuality, race, and urban history. Moreover, researching the Little Theatre leads one immediately to the perpetual archival crisis of pornography, in which traditional documentation remains elusive. When I interviewed Danny Ganota, who ran the three-hundred-seat theater from approximately 1966 to his death in 2017, I asked what sort of records he had. He told me they all went out in trash bags years earlier.[15] Material in the National Board of Review of Motion Pictures records at New York Public Library establishes the theater's early years as a white ethnic haven with second-run Hollywood movies interspersed with films in German, Yiddish, and other languages. We can learn what the opening-night screening was in March 1930 (the 1928 Indian film *Shiraz* [Franz Osten]) but not much about the theater's later sex culture.[16]

The Little Theatre followed a standard trajectory for midsized venues, shifting to frolicsome nudie films by the late 1950s, grittier sexploitation in the 1960s, and finally hard core in the early 1970s, which it has shown ever since, switching to video projection sometime in the 1980s and digital by the early twenty-first century.[17] Around the mid-1980s it opened an "all-male" screen, located at the top of a tight, winding stairwell and consisting of a large flat-screen television and about twelve chairs. Behind the screen, a small unlit room allows for both sex and conversation. A purported third screen noted on the ad board at the ticket counter merely consists of two small elevated televisions at opposite ends of the main hallway, playing the same video, often louder than the muffled audio on the main screen.

The exhibition histories of such theaters are familiar to adult film scholars, although the Little Theatre's longevity is noteworthy. Framed from another angle, however, the Little Theatre points toward urban sexual geographies less recognized than those of such iconic neighborhoods as Greenwich Village or the Castro. From interviews at the Queer Newark Oral History Project (which I codirect at Rutgers–Newark), we know that the theater was part of a thriving public sex culture as far back as the 1950s, when John, an Irish-Catholic born in 1938, turned tricks with older men as a teenager there, in between his purely for-pleasure dalliances elsewhere across the city.[18] Later, as the sexual revolution was inscribed on the urban landscape, the theater became something of an anchor for downtown Newark's small but robust red-light district, which included two more porn theaters by the 1970s and the Lincoln Motel, where prostitution and in-room adult movies sat alongside Zanzibar, a mixed straight and gay disco and a crucial site for New Jersey house music.

By this point, Newark's demographics had shifted, as it became a Black-majority city around 1965, and the first major East Coast city to elect a Black mayor, Kenneth Gibson, in 1970. Black Power politics, under whose aegis Gibson had run (but would

15 Danny Ganota, author interview, June 15, 2016, Newark, NJ.

16 Invitational flyer, March 14, 1930, box 150, folder 1, National Board of Review of Motion Pictures Records, New York Public Library.

17 Sources for this paragraph can be read in more detail at Whitney Strub, "The Sticky Floors of History at the Little Theater (Pornography in Newark, Part 4)," *Strublog* (blog), September 18, 2016, https://strublog.wordpress.com/2016/09/18/the-sticky-floors-of-history-at-the-little-theater-pornography-in-newark-part-4.

18 John, oral history, August 3, 2016, Queer Newark Oral History Project, http://queer.newark.rutgers.edu/interviews/john.

not always serve), broke with the old white machine politics of Newark in many ways but shared much with the sexual and gender conservatism of the Catholic and Jewish ethnic groups whose power it otherwise displaced. From Amiri Baraka's deeply traditionalist gender politics to the inability of civic leaders and local schools to openly confront the intersectional issues at stake in the 2003 murder of masculine-presenting fifteen-year-old Black lesbian Sakia Gunn, Newark remained beholden to what Zenzele Isoke, in her study of Black women and the politics of resistance, labels "black heteropatriarchy."[19]

Certainly the social violence of heteropatriarchy was felt, in Newark as in all US cities, in a multitude of ways. And yet under Gibson and his successor, Sharpe James (who consecutively governed from 1970 until 2006), Newark showed virtually no propensity for the sort of porn-busting fervor that periodically flared up in ostensibly more socially liberal New York from mayors John Lindsay through Rudy Giuliani. The regulation of sexuality in Newark was enforced not through the moral politics traditionally implemented via vice squads, raids, and zoning laws, but ultimately, instead, through gentrification and redevelopment, embodied in mayor Cory Booker, harbinger of Newark's devolution from Black Power politics to Twitter-based neoliberalism. Still, even when the Lincoln Motel met its end in 2007, eagerly bulldozed by the then recently elected Booker, an amused *New York Times* noted the Cameo Twin Theater down the street, "whose cinematic delights appeal to those of all sexual orientations."[20]

The Cameo closed in 2010. Danny Ganota passed away in May 2017, and a For Lease sign went up on the Little Theatre the following week. That year brought changes—the disappearance of the two video-game consoles in the hallway, an admission charge raised from ten to twelve dollars—but as of this writing in April 2018, the Little Theatre remains defiantly open. It is a relic, to be sure, anachronistic in the era of Grindr and tube sites, but also a thriving sexual public sphere to the bitter end, inhabited largely but not exclusively by men of color. Its clientele skews middle-aged but includes a sizable contingent of younger men. A typical weekday afternoon might find a dozen men scattered throughout the theater; on a weekend, there are sometimes several dozen. Almost no one sits and watches the films, which lurch erratically from glossy French porno noir to scenes from GirlsRimming.com, from the work of queer feminist director Nica Noelle to such random curios as *Gotcha!* (2008), directed by golden-age performer Paul Thomas. Rather, it is the pornographic space itself that enables the sex culture, which transpires in the seats, bathroom, upstairs backroom, and screen-adjacent exit hallway (which offers no exit, the door to outside being locked).

Again, none of this is exceptional to Newark. But it is important to consider given contemporary queer theory's New York–centric eagerness to mourn the "ghosts of public sex" after Disney killed Times Square and the Metropolitan Transportation Authority locked the bathrooms.[21] That spirit is alive and well a few miles away, not

19 Zenzele Isoke, *Urban Black Women and the Politics of Resistance* (New York: Palgrave Macmillan, 2013).

20 Andrew Jacobs, "Newark Loses Unwanted Landmark as Lincoln Motel Goes," *New York Times*, October 8, 2007.

21 José Esteban Muñoz, *Cruising Utopia: The Then and There of Queer Futurity* (New York: New York University Press, 2009).

centered on white men, and visible in no small part through pornographic space and production. Consequently, Newark's underappreciated urban erotics and queer history offer a compelling argument for the importance of adult film history beyond the niche of porn studies. *

Sadly, the Little Theater abruptly closed on June 25, 2018. Public sex in Newark, however, lives on.

Contributors

Peter Alilunas is assistant professor of cinema studies at the University of Oregon. He is the author of *Smutty Little Movies: The Creation and Regulation of Adult Video* (University of California Press, 2016). His work on adult film history appears in *Film History*, *Television & New Media*, *Creative Industries Journal*, *Post Script*, and *Porn Studies*.

David Church is a lecturer in cinema studies in the Department of Comparative Cultural Studies at Northern Arizona University. He is the author of *Disposable Passions: Vintage Pornography and the Material Legacies of Adult Cinema* (Bloomsbury Academic, 2016) and *Grindhouse Nostalgia: Memory, Home Video, and Exploitation Film Fandom* (Edinburgh University Press, 2015).

Dan Erdman is an archivist and writer living in Chicago. He has worked in a variety of institutions, including Chicago Film Archives, the American Genre Film Archive, and the New Museum. He has also written articles for *Moving Image*, *Hyperallergic*, *Los Angeles Review of Books*, *Indiewire*, *Senses of Cinema*, and *Public Books*. He is currently working as the video preservation specialist at Media Burn Archive.

Elena Gorfinkel is senior lecturer in film studies at King's College London. She is the author of *Lewd Looks: American Sexploitation Cinema in the 1960s* (University of Minnesota Press, 2017) and coeditor of *Taking Place: Location and the Moving Image* (University of Minnesota Press, 2011) and *Global Cinema Networks* (Rutgers University Press, 2018).

Mariah Larsson is professor of film studies at Linnaeus University. Among her recent publications are *The Swedish Porn Scene: Exhibition Contexts, 8mm Pornography and the Sex Film* (Intellect, 2017) and *Swedish Cinema and the Sexual Revolution: Critical Essays* (coedited with Elisabet Björklund; McFarland, 2016).

Laura Helen Marks is a professor of practice in English at Tulane University in New Orleans. Her work has appeared in *Sexualities*, *Phoebe*, *Salon*, and *Porno Chic and the Sex Wars* (University of Massachusetts Press, 2016) and is forthcoming in *Menstruation Now*, *Porn Studies*, and *Feminist Media Studies*. Her book, *Alice in Pornoland: Hardcore Encounters with the Victorian Gothic*, is forthcoming from the University of Illinois Press.

Eric Schaefer is professor of visual and media arts at Emerson College in Boston. He has been publishing and presenting research on aspects of adult film history for thirty years. He is the author of *Bold! Daring! Shocking! True! A History of Exploitation Films, 1919–1959* (Duke University Press, 1999) and the edited collection *Sex Scene: Media and the Sexual Revolution* (Duke University Press, 2014).

John Paul Stadler received his PhD from the Graduate Program in Literature at Duke University, where he completed a dissertation titled "Pornographesis: Sex, Media, and Gay Culture." His publications include "Introduction to 'Pleasure and Suspicion'" (with Rachel E. Greenspan; *Polygraph*, 2017); *Prehistoric* (*Cupboard Pamphlet*, 2016); and "Dire Straights: The Indeterminacy of Sexual Identity in Gay-for-Pay Pornography" (*Jump Cut*, 2013).

Whitney Strub is an associate professor of history, director of the Women's & Gender Studies Program at Rutgers University–Newark, and codirector of the Queer Newark Oral History Project. He wrote *Perversion for Profit: The Politics of Pornography and the Rise of the New Right* (Columbia University Press, 2011) and *Obscenity Rules:* Roth v. United States *and the Long Struggle over Sexual Expression* (University Press of Kansas, 2013), and coedited *Porno Chic and the Sex Wars: American Sexual Representation in the 1970s* (University of Massachusetts Press, 2016).

BOOK REVIEWS

edited by LAURA ISABEL SERNA

Ghostly Desires: Queer Sexuality and Vernacular Buddhism in Contemporary Thai Cinema

by Arnika Fuhrmann. Duke University Press.
2016. $94.95 hardcover; $24.95 paperback; e-book available. 272 pages.

reviewed by MASHINKA FIRUNTS HAKOPIAN

In *Ghostly Desires: Queer Sexuality and Vernacular Buddhism in Contemporary Thai Cinema*, Arnika Fuhrmann materializes the apparitions summoned in Thai cinema after 1997, recoding spectral protagonists as figures of nonnormative desire who resist both doctrinal Buddhism and the state regulation of minoritized sexuality. Fuhrmann revisits sites of cinematic haunting and horror to assemble their specters under the rubric of "Buddhist melancholia," a term denoting the Buddhist-coded tendency to eroticize loss in Thai cinema. Across Fuhrmann's five dazzling case studies, apparitions surface as queer, feminist, and trans-identity avatars whose posthumous desires refuse prescriptive heterofamilial structures of longing.

Spanning a heterogeneous array of works, each chapter of *Ghostly Desires* is devoted to a discrete genre of cinematic production. The heritage genre is examined through Nonzee Nimibutr's *Nang Nak* (1999); Hong Kong–Thai coproduced horror through Danny and Oxide Pang's *The Eye* (2002); independent cinema through Apichatpong Weerasethakul's *Tropical Malady* (*Sat Pralat*, 2004); video art through Araya Rasdjarmrearnsook's corpus; and queer documentary through Thunska Pansitthivorakul's *This Area Is under Quarantine* (2008). While these works are demarcated from one another by distinct generic boundaries, they each foreground counternormative longings that either issue from or direct themselves at bodies exceeding the category of the human. In the process, they trouble recent nationalist policies seeking to articulate notions of citizenship through narrowly defined models of sexual personhood. As Fuhrmann compellingly argues, it is here that ghostly cinema's critical possibilities lie: in the attempt to "redefine frameworks of resolution for cases of minoritarian injury, and reimagine trajectories of attachment."[1]

A broad spectrum of disciplinary discourses is brought to bear on this subject matter, each deployed with virtuosic deftness. To chart the intersections of recent cinematic narratives with Buddhist ontologies, Fuhrmann turns to the newly instantiated national emphasis on "sufficiency" as an instance of Buddhist-coded economic policy.[2] Theravadin soteriology also figures prominently within the text, a salvation doctrine that uses the image of the female body's decomposition as a pedagogical aid to admonish against worldly attachment. Fuhrmann extends this examination to consider how female, queer, and *kathoey* (translated by Fuhrmann as transgender or trans-identity) subjects are accorded a karmically assigned "diminished personhood" in the contemporary Thai imaginary, echoing a vernacular Buddhism fused with liberal political formations in what Fuhrmann calls a Buddhist-liberal synthesis.[3]

A particularly incisive example of this phenomenon is furnished in the first chapter's analysis of *Nang Nak*, whose ghostly protagonist continues to experience desire for her lover beyond the event of her own death. Although the legend of Nang Nak serves as source material for more than two dozen filmic adaptations, Fuhrmann identifies Nonzee Nimibutr's 1999 adaptation as distinct in its dual focus on the themes of desire and Buddhist detachment. In Nimibutr's version, Nak alternately appears as an emblem of Thai feminine ideality and a cadaver in the process of decay. Fuhrmann links this latter manifestation to the Buddhist story of Vāsavadattā, a courtesan whose "desire for pleasurable equity" was denied in a narrative that culminated with her bodily dismemberment.[4] Advancing a feminist reading of Nang Nak, Fuhrmann considers Buddhist object lessons regarding the "repulsiveness" of feminine corporeality in a national context marked by the Ministry of the Interior's programmatic surveillance of women's bodies.[5]

As this example illustrates, *Ghostly Desires* is also crucially concerned with tracing the shifting landscape of social and cultural policy in Thailand following the financial crisis of 1997. As Fuhrmann describes it, in the post-1997 milieu of state disciplinary programs, "bodies became a last national good . . . and sexuality became an increasingly central component of citizenship."[6] Attending to recent practices of "cultural monitoring" undertaken by the Ministry of Culture, Fuhrmann shows how the state's performance of discipline, prohibition, and regulation unofficially banned

1 Arnika Fuhrmann, *Ghostly Desires: Queer Sexuality and Vernacular Buddhism in Contemporary Thai Cinema* (Durham, NC: Duke University Press, 2016), 22.

2 Quoted in Fuhrmann, *Ghostly Desires*, 34.

3 Fuhrmann, *Ghostly Desires*, 34.

4 Fuhrmann, *Ghostly Desires*, 77.

5 Quoted in Fuhrmann, *Ghostly Desires*, 70.

6 Fuhrmann, *Ghostly Desires*, 192.

queer desire from certain public spheres, to be haunted by them anew in the realm of cinema.[7] More broadly, *Ghostly Desires* engages a genealogy of haunting in cinema studies, in dialogue with scholars from Bliss Lim to Avery Gordon.[8] Queer and affect theory, ranging from Lauren Berlant's conception of the politics of pain to Lee Edelman's formulation of queer negativity, serve as theoretical ballasts and departure points in the text.[9] In a deviation from the latter, Fuhrmann's formulations explore the fissures inherent to seemingly totalizing systems of negativity.

The third chapter of *Ghostly Desires* begins with the description of a scene from Weerasethakul's independent film *Tropical Malady*. In the scene in question, an erotic encounter unfolds between two men, Keng and Tong, on a depopulated road. They lick each other's hands with vigor against the backdrop of two flags: one, Thailand's national flag, and the other, a flag evoking Buddhist iconography. After describing this embrace, Fuhrmann carefully unravels what it means to "kiss for the nation" (as Weerasethakul describes the scene) in a national context where vernacular Buddhist discourse and state policy combine to generate anxieties around precisely such erotic encounters.[10] Rather than prioritize straightforward representations of political resistance, Fuhrmann pinpoints *Tropical Malady*'s radical possibilities in the ordinariness of how it renders same-sex desire. It is this ordinariness that enables the film's crucial deminoritizing of queerness. By jettisoning cinematic tropes associated with queer trauma and shame, Fuhrmann proposes, *Tropical Malady* also models a refusal of neoliberal subjectivity. In other words, it is the seeming banality of Keng and Tong's coupling early on that suffuses Thai "social environment[s] with highly public queer intimacies" and "same-sex relations in everyday life" to sketch a queer utopian fantasy.[11]

Fuhrmann plots the radicalness of Weerasethakul's gesture against the disciplinary mechanisms of the Thai state and the vernacular Buddhist discourses that partially undergird them. Returning to the Ministry of the Interior's social ordering campaign, the chapter accords attention to the public relations texts produced in service of the ministry's program. In these texts, Deputy Minister Pracha Malinond narrates his account of the bar raids executed under the auspices of social ordering, with individual vignettes bearing sensationalist titles like "Sexy Nights Gay Bar." As *Ghostly Desires* outlines, a Theravadin Buddhist–coded view of gay and transgender identity as denoting ontologically and karmically diminished personhood undergirds the rhetoric of these texts. They explicitly seek to stigmatize queer and transgender bodies, and to evict them from Thai public space. For this reason, Fuhrmann incisively argues, the ordinariness of same-sex desire in *Tropical Malady* represents a crucial intervention. In

7 Quoted in Fuhrmann, *Ghostly Desires*, 24.

8 Bliss Cua Lim, *Translating Time: Cinema, the Fantastic, and Temporal Critique* (Durham, NC: Duke University Press, 2009); "Spectral Times: The Ghost Film as Historical Allegory," *positions: east asia cultures critique* 9, no. 2 (2001): 287–329; "Queer Aswang Transmedia: Folklore as Camp," *Kritika Kultura* 24 (2015); Avery F. Gordon, *Ghostly Matters: Haunting and the Sociological Imagination* (Minneapolis: University of Minnesota Press, 2008).

9 Lauren Berlant elaborates her concept of the politics of pain in "The Subject of True Feeling," *Transformations: Thinking through Feminism* (New York: Routledge, 2000), 33; Lee Edelman, *No Future: Queer Theory and the Death Drive* (Durham, NC: Duke University Press, 2004).

10 Quoted in Fuhrmann, *Ghostly Desires*, 122.

11 Fuhrmann, *Ghostly Desires*, 128.

lieu of portraying queerness as an exceptionally marked category of personhood—as the social ordering campaign would have it—the film "centers on homosexual desire to such an extent that queerness exemplifies the human (and creaturely) as such."[12]

Turning to the genre of video art, the final chapter preceding the coda of *Ghostly Desires* takes up the recoding of female death and desire ventured in its first case study. Here, Fuhrmann addresses the contested oeuvre of Araya. Across a thematically linked set of performance and video works, the artist stages intimate encounters with the bodies of the dead. In *The Class* (2005) and *Death Seminar* (2005), these encounters take a pedagogical tone as Araya endeavors to instruct the deceased about death. Assuming the role that Jacques Rancière calls an "ignorant schoolmaster"—an educator who refuses a position of mastery over his students—the artist delivers lessons to a group of pupils who bear greater degrees of expertise about the subject being taught.[13] Elsewhere, in *Reading for Male and Female Corpses* (1998), Araya recites a "scene of flirtation" to a row of gurneys, positioning them as potential objects of nonnormative desire. In doing so, the artist unravels the sovereign subject as the locus of desire, instead offering a desiring "female self oscillating between disintegration and survival."[14] Here, Araya casts the dead as interlocutors within a discursive exchange. Fuhrmann turns to this set of works to draw out what it might mean to pivot from a Theravadin understanding of the decaying female body as an object lesson, or "privileged pedagogical tool," toward an understanding of that body as a participant in a pedagogical exchange.[15]

As methodologically rich as it is precisely argued, *Ghostly Desires* draws from a robust set of archives and modes of data gathering. Beyond citing print and visual ephemera, the text builds on ethnographic research conducted from 1999 to 2015 in Thailand, participant observation, and interviews with a wide range of figures and practitioners. Notably, the study also reflects data culled from involvement in the activism of the group Anjaree, whose organizing focuses on policy change related to queer and transgender rights in Thailand. These sources give the text political urgency, far removed from the abstraction of exclusively theoretical or formal analysis. The effects of this expanded approach are keenly evident in the nuanced texture and vitality of the study's argumentation, For instance, Anjaree's lobbying against the branding of queer and transgender identity as a mental disorder by the Department of Mental Health inflects Fuhrmann's account of how the state's classificatory criteria palpably code desire in the national context.

Across its spectrum of case studies, *Ghostly Desires* entreats viewers to cast their glance anew in the direction of cinema's apparitions, mapping spectral desire along previously undetected coordinates of queerness and counternormativity. Its interdisciplinary orientation renders *Ghostly Desires* an essential contribution to scholarship across cinema studies, Southeast Asian studies, queer and affect theory, Buddhist studies, and beyond. Fuhrmann's is a provocative and illuminating study rendered in a register no less haunting than its subject matter. ✻

12 Fuhrmann, *Ghostly Desires*, 156.

13 Jacques Rancière, *The Ignorant Schoolmaster*, vol. 1 (Stanford, CA: Stanford University Press, 1991).

14 Fuhrmann, *Ghostly Desires*, 182.

15 Fuhrmann, *Ghostly Desires*, 163.

Hokum! The Early Sound Slapstick Short and Depression-Era Mass Culture

by Rob King. University of California Press.
2017. $34.95 paperback; open-access e-book available. 253 pages.

reviewed by HENRY JENKINS

James Agee summed up a whole tradition of thinking about American film comedy in his influential essay "Comedy's Greatest Era" when he asserted, "The only thing wrong with screen comedy today is that it takes place on a screen which talks."[1] Agee's assertion defined how sound-era screen clowning has been discussed, much as the essay established the canon of silent comedians deemed worthy of studying. Gerald Mast's *The Comic Mind: Comedy and the Movies* preserves the idea of a breach between silent and sound comedy, shifting from a focus on silent clowns to screwball comedy with the entry of talking pictures, a move that oversimplifies the history of both subgenres.[2]

Continuing a project begun with his own earlier book *The Fun Factory: The Keystone Film Company and the Emergence of Mass Culture*, Rob King's *Hokum! The Early Sound Slapstick Short and Depression-Era Mass Culture* seeks to reassess the historical evolution of screen slapstick, here digging deeper into what happened as this comic tradition entered the sound era.[3] In the process, King provides a rich illustration of how to bring a deeper historical understanding to an essential film genre. Agee, Mast, and Walter Kerr's *The Silent Clown* represents the masterpiece tradition at work, writing a history focused on exceptional works by essential artists, largely isolated from larger developments in

1 James Agee, "Comedy's Greatest Era" (1949), reprinted in *Agee on Film* (New York: Perigee Books, 1958), 1:4.

2 Gerald Mast, *The Comic Mind: Comedy and the Movies* (Indianapolis, IN: Bobbs-Merrill, 1973).

3 Rob King, *The Fun Factory: The Keystone Film Company and the Emergence of Mass Culture* (Berkeley: University of California Press, 2008).

the genre, leaving aside the film industry or a broader mediascape.[4] King's approach is thoroughly revisionist, a genre history as grounded in the archive and the trade press as it is in the screening room, one that seeks to dramatically expand which films matter. His primary contribution here involves a recentering of the history of sound shorts, which have received very limited attention compared to what has been written about the silent shorts of Mack Sennett and Hal Roach. To do so, he has to reconstruct the industrial history of 1930s short-film production, including some rich material on the ways shorts were being positioned as a desirable alternative for audiences apt to be too weary to watch double features. He traces key producers, including Earle W. Hammons's Educational Pictures and the Jules White unit at Columbia, as they seek to differentiate themselves in a crowded marketplace. Well-known performers such as Laurel and Hardy and the Three Stooges are discussed at some length here, but so are those less likely to be recalled today, such as Andy Clyde or Clark and McCullough.

King is attentive to the discourses that framed these shorts and, in particular, the responses of exhibitors in the trade press that offer an indication of regional and class divides in terms of what forms of comedy proved desirable. Here, he does identify some signs that slapstick bore a "stigma" during the early sound period. As one critic recalled, "Sound came along and out went the pies."[5] The book's opening paragraph also signals a shift in the meaning of the word "hokum" during this period. A *New York Times* reporter notes with surprise that a piece of stage slang which originally meant surefire material now more often referred to "hooey, tripe, apple-sauce, blah and bologna."[6] The instability in how slapstick was read during this transitional period remains a core concern across the book. King shows the continued popularity of slapstick across the decade, especially outside of the major metropolitan areas.

King draws on Raymond Williams's model of cultural dynamism (of emergent, dominant, residual, and archaic cultural practices) and Pierre Bourdieu's field of production models to account for several shifts in the status of slapstick across the 1930s.[7] As King explains, these comic shorts emerged from "a sui generis network of interpersonal, professional and institutional relations radiating out of the studio gates into the fields of vaudeville, burlesque, circus and even literary humor within which hierarchies of comedic value—and slapstick's place within them—were defined."[8] Tracing that network of connections is the book's central project and represents a productive approach to understanding how genre operated across performance sites during this era.

With the dawn of the talking picture, the broad humor of the silent slapstick comedy was temporarily replaced by East Coast stage performers—but they were

4 Agee, "Comedy's Greatest Era"; Mast, *Comic Mind*; Walter Kerr, *The Silent Clowns* (New York: DaCapo Press, 1975).

5 Peter Vischer, *Exhibitors Herald-World*, March 1930, as quoted in Rob King, *Hokum! The Early Sound Slapstick Short and Depression-Era Mass Culture* (Berkeley: University of California Press, 2017), 59.

6 Frank J. Wilstach, "How 'Hokum' Declined from Its High Estate," *New York Times*, July 8, 1928, 96.

7 Raymond Williams, *Marxism and Literature* (New York: Oxford University Press, 1977); Pierre Bourdieu, *The Rules of Art: Genesis and Structure of the Literary Field*, trans. Susan Emanuel (Stanford, CA: Stanford University Press, 1996).

8 King, *Hokum!*, 6.

later displaced, often by silent screen stars in their declining years, as a consequence of the broadening of the audience for sound films to include more hinterland filmgoers. Here, the short-subject units followed a path that I had identified in feature film production over this same time frame, although King prefers the period-specific and more particularized term "cuckoo school" over what he sees as my own too-broad formulation of the "vaudeville aesthetic" to describe the nonsense style associated with these performers.[9] His mapping of the "cuckoo school" across literary magazines and stage reviews represents a real contribution here, as does his tracing of Robert Benchley from Algonquin Club wit to American everyman across the decade. The "vaudeville aesthetic" was intended to be a broad set of norms encompassing a range of different kinds of performances, comparable to norms associated with classical Hollywood cinema, whereas the "cuckoo school" helps us identify a more precise set of traits shared by a smaller cluster of performers at a particular historical juncture, both generative ways of thinking through these changes.

King also understands the pushing aside of slapstick during this initial phase as a consequence of technical shifts—the inability to undercrank in production and project at a faster speed—which had consequences for timing and tempo, key concerns for comedy producers. Of course, the term "slapstick" refers to a sound-making device used in earlier popular theater traditions, and King offers compelling examples of how dialogue, noise, and music were gradually embraced in comic short films, as slapstick was able to reassert itself again. After this initial period of "metropolitan" comedy, King documents the "banalization" of slapstick—in some ways, reversing the movement of silent clowns from shorts to feature films, as the clowns who survived the period, including Buster Keaton and Harry Langdon, returned to the production of shorts, many of which were more popular with 1930s small-town audiences than they are with today's viewers.

In a third phase, King discusses a shift in slapstick's affective status as the genre was perceived with nostalgic welcome as "good old fashioned" or "old time" comedy. This last phase paved the way for the nostalgia industry around slapstick comedy that was shaped by critical essays like Agee's, the sale of these shorts to early television, the rise of a Super 8 collector's market and various compilation films, and so forth, all of which have tended to reaffirm the idea that the coming of sound led to the slow, lingering death of slapstick comedy. While reading about the nostalgic rediscovery of slapstick in the late 1930s, I could not help but think about the reassessment of 1980s film and television currently taking place, as a similar nostalgic return to sometimes disreputable works released several decades prior. Might we understand the same impulses as producing *Hollywood Cavalcade* (Irving Cummings and Malcolm St. Clair, 1939) and *Stranger Things* (Netflix, 2016–)?

This focus on the cultural status of slapstick helps to inform several important reassessments, including a focus on the operetta films of Laurel and Hardy on the one hand and what King describes as the "plebian populism" of the Three Stooges on the other. He wants us to look at these films from a new perspective—literally, in

9 Henry Jenkins, *What Made Pistachio Nuts? Early Sound Comedy and the Vaudeville Aesthetic* (New York: Columbia University Press, 1992).

fact, since he includes QR code links to several rarely seen shorts—but his goals here are more focused on making causal claims than interpretive ones. For a recent book that offers some rich critical insights into the early sound era's comedian comedy, let me strongly recommend Scott Balcerzak's *Buffoon Men: Classic Hollywood Comedians and Queered Masculinity*, which draws on contemporary theories of gender and sexuality to explore how such performers as Eddie Cantor, Jack Benny, Wheeler and Woolsey, and W. C. Fields pushed against the era's masculine norms.[10] Read side by side, the two books represent the efforts of a new scholarly generation to reclaim the value of largely neglected film comedies of the early 1930s.

Several decades ago, Kristine Brunovska Karnick and I called for a new kind of genre history in the introduction to our AFI reader, *Classical Hollywood Comedy*.[11] We wanted a history that deployed more rigorous research methods and sought to understand the historical evolution of the genre as a whole rather than the artistic development of individual artists; we wanted to situate screen comedy in a larger history of popular humor, including comparisons across media; we argued for an expansion of the corpus to include average rather than exceptional works; we urged a shift toward a more institutional and industrial context; we advocated greater attention to the conditions of reception; and finally, we suggested more attention to comedy's relationship to other screen genres. By all these criteria, *Hokum!* is a triumph! King demonstrates what happens in an era of expanded access to archival texts that are now more widely available on DVD, the digitization of trade press reports, and the ongoing refinement of film historiography. At the risk of ending on an unapologetically bad pun, comedy has a new King. *

10 Scott Balcerzak, *Buffoon Men: Classic Hollywood Comedians and Queer Masculinity* (Detroit: Wayne State University Press, 2013).

11 Henry Jenkins and Kristine Brunovska Karnick, "Introduction: Golden Eras and Blind Spots—Genre, History and Comedy," in *Classical Hollywood Comedy*, ed. Kristine Brunovska Karnick and Henry Jenkins (New York: Routledge, 1995).

Melodrama: An Aesthetics of Impossibility

by Jonathan Goldberg. Duke University Press.
2016. $89.95 hardcover; $23.95 paperback; e-book available. 204 pages.

reviewed by ANUPAMA KAPSE

An understanding of affect as an index of the political has been vital to the resurgence of scholarly interest in melodrama. As an affective mode par excellence, at least in the last two decades, melodrama has been associated with the ability to amplify the emotions of marginal and disadvantaged groups.[1] Analytically, in cinema studies the challenge has been to uphold melodrama's capacity to posit individual problems as larger, more complex indices of a desired social imaginary. Jonathan Goldberg's *Melodrama: An Aesthetics of Impossibility* attempts to offer an interdisciplinary account of melodrama's political possibilities by returning to its musical roots. Goldberg attempts to retrace melodrama's original meaning of "drama to which music has been added." More provocatively, he approaches melodrama as a musical-temporal mode that can incorporate queer desire into its form outside the progressive register of teleology.

Such a project necessarily presents itself as a book for advanced readers. Wasting no time on rehearsing arguments, Goldberg simply assumes the reader's familiarity with the key conventions and debates of melodrama.[2] By and large, following Peter Brooks's foundational work *The Melodramatic Imagination: Balzac, Henry James, Melodrama and the Mode of Excess*, scholarship on melodrama has foregrounded

1 For detailed accounts of white supremacist iterations of melodrama, see in particular Linda Williams, *Playing the Race Card: Melodramas of Black and White from Uncle Tom to O. J. Simpson* (Princeton, NJ: Princeton University Press, 2002); and Elisabeth Anker, *Orgies of Feeling: Melodrama and the Politics of Freedom* (Durham, NC: Duke University Press, 2014).

2 Especially useful for understanding Goldberg's problematic are Christine Gledhill's "Rethinking Genre," in *Reinventing Film Studies*, ed. Christine Gledhill and Linda Williams (London: Arnold, 2000), 221–243; and Thomas Elsaesser's "Tales of Sound and Fury: Observations on the Family Melodrama" (1972), in *Imitations of Life: A Reader in Film and Television Melodrama* (Detroit: Wayne State University Press, 1991).

victimhood as the primary site of expression and intervention.[3] Goldberg privileges a dense, poetic mode of writing: eschewing an overly rationalistic road map of his chapters, he complicates the existing meanings of melodrama as a hyperbolic form to be "explained" away. The style of the book is essayistic—symmetrically arranged readings and fine-grained analyses are themselves presented lyrically instead of being organized chronologically.

Part 1 examines opera and cinema. Part 2 focuses on the novel and cinema. The four chapters in these two parts include an eclectic and often canonical range of examples that are read noncanonically: Beethoven in chapter 1 and Douglas Sirk, Rainer Werner Fassbinder, and Todd Haynes in chapter 2. The third chapter is titled "The Art of Murder: Hitchcock and Highsmith." The fourth and final chapter, "Wildean Aesthetics: From 'Paul's Case' to Lucy Gayheart," looks at Willa Cather's novels through a melodic lens. Featuring astute readings of the nonverbal, Goldberg uses musical metaphors to "listen" to queer meanings and otherwise invisible emotional parameters. Whether it is Beethoven's *Fidelio*, Alfred Hitchcock's *Strangers on a Train* (1951), Luchino Visconti's *Ossessione* (1942), or Willa Cather's *Lucy Gayheart* (1935), he aims to find the "queer lever[s]" that "ignit[e] sites of desire at . . . places of crossing" (xiii).[4] These chapters foreground affective intersections, over and above any clear examples of moral certitude. Putting relationality over identity, Goldberg begins with Beethoven's opera *Fidelio* (1814), an example of how "for male to become female is not to become woman but to enter into the differentially shared space of self-division."[5] Similarly, Todd Haynes's melodramatic "remakes" of Sirks and Fassbinder's films enact (or reenact) a "disengagement of the term *woman* from its referent "woman" setting into motion a "homo-aesthetics" vis-à-vis the politics of a similarity-in-difference.[6]

Fidelio functions as the book's analytic center: it is an opera about a cross-dressed protagonist who switches voice, pitch, gender, and tonal registers that are dependent on an identity that collapses as soon as he/she retrieves his/her husband from jail and lapses back into being Leonore. As such, "the thrill of hearing Leonore's voice ascend into soprano range has a great deal to do with its escape from confinement to the alto register [as Fidelio]."[7] As Fidelio descends into the depths of prison to help dig the grave of an unjustly imprisoned man, Beethoven interrupts the separation of the speaking voice and music, joining melos and drama together in a moment the score names technically, formally, as "Melodram."[8] The central argument depends not only on the interpenetration of identities but also on the Melodram as the point at which music and speech begin to coexist as two coresponsive entities. Representing the interval—that point in the narrative that is about neither Fidelio nor Leonore but

3 Peter Brooks, The Melodramatic Imagination: Balzac, Henry James, Melodrama and the Mode of Excess (New Haven, CT: Yale University Press, 1976).

4 Jonathan Goldberg, *Melodrama: An Aesthetics of Impossibility* (Durham, NC: Duke University Press, 2016), xiii.

5 Goldberg, *Melodrama*, 31.

6 Goldberg, *Melodrama*, 31 and 30.

7 Goldberg, *Melodrama*, 97.

8 Goldberg, *Melodrama*, 156.

their cusp—Beethoven's Melodram helps Goldberg to theorize an intermediality that interrogates the social and the real.

"'Is he Musical?' we know, can be an oblique question about sexual identity," writes Goldberg: in Patricia Highsmith's Ripley novels *Ripley's Game* (1974) and *The Boy Who Followed Ripley* (1980), "music plays [a] central role [where] musical distinctions, and their attachments to achieved identity are explicitly refused."[9] Similarly, the second chapter, "Identity and Identification: Sirk-Fassbinder-Haynes," analyzes Rock Hudson as a preferred Sirk star because he epitomizes the in-between, a middle that is neither "effeminate or delicate" but "ambiguous" and "masculine."[10] Hudson's star persona blurs race and class oppositions, dissolving them into the sexual. Further, the star telescopes the sexual into a wider orchestration of setting, lighting, and musical montage that amplifies the melos of *All That Heaven Allows* (1955).

The meanings melodrama yields when it is understood not as one medium but at least two, neither music nor drama but relationally both, are suffused with critical insight. Building on the aural as a polemic, Goldberg insists that melodrama has always been predisposed to hybridity and intermediality: "Music is literally elusive. Unlike what the camera invites us to see, music cannot be located. . . . [We can] shut our eyes, but . . . we cannot shut our ears. . . . It enters us."[11] Truth, if any, is something that defies articulation; it is best felt by our ears, at an embodied level. "Aesthetic form does not simply mirror the social. . . . Aesthetics and the social may mirror each other, but ideology is not secure enough to be able to repress what it suppresses. . . . [M]elodrama is a complex mix of repudiation and identification. . . . [M]elodrama [may] unveil the social, but only, finally, to see it as a site of willed, if limited, coercion and domination."[12] Goldberg untethers melodramatic value not only from the constraints of identification but also from compulsions to locate excess. Such questioning is itself a manifestation of the social as an imaginative crisis that melodrama must wrestle with at any given historical moment, musically or otherwise.

The thrust is to tease out modalities that cannot be pinned to a transparent ideological register such as gender, race, or sexuality as placeholders of moral legibility: "In considering the not-to-be-named . . . I do not mean to arrive at some truth allied to (homo)sexual identity; rather, by way of contradictions—in race, gender, and sexuality; in formal and historical situation—I aim to relocate the impossible place that Brooks occults yet glimpses. . . . Like Lauren Berlant, I have 'a commitment to maintaining contradiction.'"[13] To this end, Goldberg frames truth, especially that tied to identity, within a politics of impossibility. Implicitly rather than explicitly, he attempts to queer melodrama by releasing it from liberalizing explanations of excess. Attuned to melodramatic foreclosure, he positions the queer in the interstice, in moments that implode rather than explode. The political—in this case the centrality of queer desire and expressivity—can be found in only subtle, ineffable articulations.

9 Goldberg, *Melodrama*, 121, 120–121.

10 Goldberg, *Melodrama*, 46.

11 Goldberg, *Melodrama*, 97.

12 Goldberg, *Melodrama*, xiii.

13 Goldberg, *Melodrama*, xi.

Musical signification deliberately alludes to aspects that known iconographies of liberty, equality, and fraternity fail to communicate. An aural that can penetrate the visual represents a claim to include feelings as the province of the political but without the guarantee of liberal recognition or justice.

Goldberg understands absolutes as manifestations of liberal imperatives. Arguing instead for the messy interdependence of principal roles—man-woman, good-evil, white-black, left-right, straight-queer—his work problematizes not only the determinism of truth but also frames of reference that position identity as a stable, reliable sign of political enfranchisement. Relationality presides over Manichaean dichotomies. Melodramatic intersectionality, so to speak, complicates neat divisions among race, class, age, and gender: their tenuousness embodies the multipronged, socially interwoven aspects of citizenship as a grid on which victim and aggressor are not opposite each other but can shade into each other, depending on the moment. This is the case in Fassbinder's *Ali: Fear Eats the Soul* (1975), where Emmi "may appear to be victimized, but she has strong desires to identify with those who victimize her. . . . Emmi's complexity could be summed up in her relationship to Nazism; Ali's in his relationship to a Morocco he idealizes and yet has fled."[14] Emmi and Ali fail to represent nation, race, class, or gender in the singular. Instead, they embody the exchangeable, volatile nature of everyday selfhood.

Methodologically, Goldberg's sensitivity to the hybridity of identity opens up a critical space for addressing stereotypical connotations of evil.[15] In *Ripley Underground* (1970), a painting defines Tom's relationship with Heloise as an object that can "reach out and touch someone [like a] telephone, telepathy . . . [with] unheard melodies. . . . When Tom reflects on his relationship to her, Heloise's material opacity as an object of desire and bafflement is summed up this way: 'She was like a picture on the wall'"—the focus is on an appeal that remains outside the protagonist's reach.[16] The novel, Goldberg argues, "fails" to affirm the "purity" of Ripley's heterosexuality or his queerness.

Ekphrasis, the art of making pictures speak, gestures aurally not toward the surety of knowledge but toward access to "sameness and relationality."[17] Oscar Wilde's epigraph "I think I would more readily die for what I *do not believe* than what I hold to be *true*. . . . [T]he artistic life is a long and lovely suicide" provides a metaphor for "murder and untoward sexuality [as] the means": violators of the accoutrements of class and social identity that make room for "aesthetic pleasure."[18] Ripley's homoeroticized "villainy" can thus be melodramatically parsed as a sign of his aesthetic *talent.* Likewise, in Willa Cather's *Lucy Gayheart*, music is the privileged site of self-realization. Lucy's very existence depends on music, for she lives and dies "in song." She comes alive when she

14 Goldberg, *Melodrama*, 64–65.

15 Nor should we ignore the racial connotations of melodramatic villains as dark moors. See, for example, the revisionist and postcolonial interventions of Jonathan Dollimore and Alan Sinfield in *Political Shakespeare: Essays in Cultural Materialism* (Ithaca, NY: Cornell University Press, 1994); and Ania Loomba in *Shakespeare, Race, and Colonialism* (London: Oxford University Press, 2002).

16 Goldberg, *Melodrama*, 458.

17 Goldberg, *Melodrama*, 126.

18 Goldberg, *Melodrama*, 132 (my emphasis).

imagines her innermost desires as aesthetic ekphrases born from a Schubert recital.[19] The image is secondary; music is the primary object of discussion. Taking his cue from Thomas Elsaesser, Goldberg focuses on "*how* music and drama are to join together. . . . There are rules of composition and of harmony, to be sure, but the music for drama is not usually a sustained piece of composition. It is interrupted, played for effect. . . . [T]he indeterminations of the remediated nature of melodrama allow for the possibilities in the impossible."[20]

An impetus to parse melodrama's sonic landscapes is an impetus to queer melodrama by discovering likeness over binary oppositions in musical interludes. Beyond queer aesthetics in Western media, a dedicated attention to music can map the harmonies and dissonances that generate the complex representational regimes of non-Western cinemas. Take, for example Japanese film, where a Benshi could be called on to provide ekphrastic musical accompaniment at the very moment of cinema's inception. *Melodrama: An Aesthetics of Impossibility* represents a serious engagement with music as a core melodramatic operator, not mere accompaniment. Prior familiarity with music and queer theory is highly recommended. Goldberg's vocabulary is drawn not from film but from literary and music theory that centers queer aesthetics vis-à-vis opera, the novel, and film. His key premise is to attend to same-sex expressivity through the interdependence of music and image to find "a way beyond words" that can see beyond straight iconography.[21] Last but not least, this is a book whose intellectual vitality resides in the pathways that demand an understanding of melodrama as an intersectional mode. *

19 Goldberg, *Melodrama*, 144–145.

20 Goldberg, *Melodrama*, 156.

21 Goldberg, *Melodrama*, 167.

Spectacular Television: Exploring Televisual Pleasure

by Helen Wheatley. I. B. Tauris.
2016. $135.00 hardcover; $28.00 paperback; e-book available. 276 pages.

reviewed by Emily Saidel

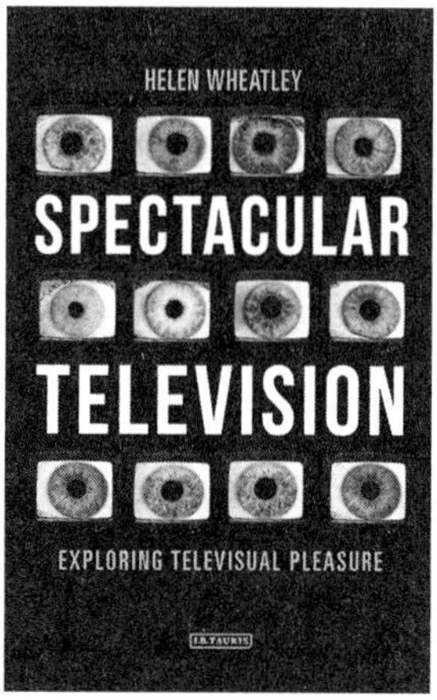

Helen Wheatley embarks on an ambitious project in *Spectacular Television: Exploring Televisual Pleasure*. She focuses on visual pleasure as an always-present component and competitive strategy of television that has been foregrounded by the turn to digital technologies. Wheatley is responding to two theories prevalent in television studies: medium specificity and John Ellis's glance theory, which positions television as a medium of distracted viewing.[1] Medium specificity posits a taxonomy contrasting cinematic style with televisuality. Wheatley introduces site-specific, large-scale "public television" as a "third category" of moving image, distinct from both home broadcasting and cinema.[2] She examines examples of this hybrid medium throughout the book from television exhibitions of the 1930s–1950s to the BBC's *Blue Planet Prom in the Park* (BBC, 2002), in which visuals from the television program were accompanied by live music, and finally with the public viewing of *London 2012 Olympic Opening Ceremony: Isle of Wonder* (BBC, 2012). Wheatley's category of "spectacular television" simultaneously encompasses a genre of programming, a historical movement, and a broader style of programming, all of which contribute to intentional and intensive, rather than distracted, viewing. These definitions refute Ellis's argument that viewers only glance at the televisual image by emphasizing the allure and attraction of looking at the television screen. *Spectacular Television* builds on John Caldwell's notions of televisuality but rejects Caldwell's periodization and link between visual style and affluent demographics.[3] Instead, Wheatley argues that "television schedules have

1 John Ellis, *Visible Fictions: Cinema, Television, Video* (London: Routledge & Kegan Paul, 1982).

2 Helen Wheatley, *Spectacular Television: Exploring Televisual Pleasure* (New York: I. B. Tauris, 2016), 37.

3 John Thornton Caldwell, *Televisuality: Style, Crisis and Authority in American Television* (New Brunswick, NJ: Rutgers University Press, 1995).

incorporated the spectacular throughout the medium's history" and that it "is not solely produced to appeal to a particular viewer demographic."[4] Finally, Wheatley dismisses the notion that spectacular television is necessarily cinematic and asserts instead that both film and television can be equally spectacular.

Spectacular Television is divided into three parts: the historical launch of television in the United Kingdom and the subsequent launch of color television; the visual pleasure of landscape and nature programs; and the body on television as erotic, freakish, or abject. Notably during this modern era of what FX network's CEO John Landgraf called "peak TV" and more than four hundred scripted programs per year, Wheatley largely turns her gaze beyond prime-time drama and uncovers televisual pleasure in other parts of the spectrum.[5]

Informed by industrial documentation and critical reception, Wheatley's initial case studies focus on midcentury exhibitions: the Festival of Britain, the National Radio Show, and the Ideal Home Show. These events cumulatively positioned television as part of the spectacle of modernity, emphasizing the materiality of the electronic and glass device and the audience's participation in the televised spectacle itself through closed-circuit broadcasts. Programs, production files, and listing guides lead the analysis of the entrance of color to the British television system. Recognizing that perceptions of color are both individually and culturally specific, Wheatley brackets her personal experience viewing early color programs with an acknowledgment that the tuning of each television receiver could produce different experiences with color. The BBC's contemporary rhetoric emphasized avoiding the perceived garishness of the American color system by focusing on realistic or faithful colorization. At the same time, against the backdrop of more than a decade of the normalization of black-and-white broadcast, color television necessarily became a vivid, visual spectacle. This chapter complements recent work on the introduction of color television around the world while also offering a distinctly British and comparative perspective on the foremost industrial concerns during the visual transition.[6]

Part 2 focuses on television landscapes as spectacle and is the longest part, comprising three chapters. A close reading of 1950s safari programming featuring Armand and Michaela Denis in the East African Protectorate (now Kenya) extends arguments about the television as a window onto the world and the domesticating properties of home viewing. The following chapter draws from John Street's work on

4 Wheatley, *Spectacular Television*, 4–5.

5 Lacey Rose and Marisa Guthrie, "FX Chief John Landgraf on Content Bubble: 'This Is Simply Too Much Television,'" *Hollywood Reporter*, August 7, 2015, https://www.hollywoodreporter.com/live-feed/fx-chief-john-landgraf-content-813914.

6 For additional works on the transition from black and white to color, see Oren Soffer, "The Eraser and the Anti-Eraser: The Battle over Color Television in Israel," *Media Culture and Society* 30, no. 6 (2008); Andreas Fickers, "The Techno-Politics of Colour: Britain and the European Struggle for a Colour Television Standard," *Journal of British Cinema and Television* 7, no. 1 (2010); Jonathan Sterne and Dylan Mulvin, "The Low Acuity for Blue: Perceptual Technics and American Color Television," *Journal of Visual Culture* 13, no. 2 (2014); Dylan Mulvin and Jonathan Sterne, "Scenes from an Imaginary Country: Test Images and the American Color Television Standard," *Television & New Media* 17, no. 1 (2015); Susan Murray, "Never Twice the Same Color: Standardizing, Calibrating, and Harmonizing NTSC Color Television in the Early 1950s," *Screen* 56, no. 4 (2015); and Susan Murray, *Bright Signals: A History of Color Television* (Durham, NC: Duke University Press, 2018).

aesthetics and Charlotte Brunsdon's 1997 work on quality television to examine the alignment of beauty, quality, and the reverence for nature in such programs as *The Blue Planet* (BBC, 2001) and *The Frozen Planet* (BBC, 2011).[7] On television, Wheatley asserts, beauty is a democratic value that "is understood as both pleasurable treat provided by extraordinary television and as part of the ordinary, everyday pleasures of the medium, with visual pleasure repeatedly expressed as part of the quotidian viewing experience of television."[8] Using in-person interviews and an online survey, Wheatley concludes that audiences consistently classify these technically audacious programs as both beautiful television and quality television.

Despite the concerns of BBC officials of an earlier era that the "merely pretty" spectacle of color television would distract from the art of performance, Wheatley finds that, rather than overwhelm the spectator, the visual beauty of these nature programs simultaneously delights and conveys concern for the potential loss of these spectacular environments.[9] Part 2 of *Spectacular Television* concludes by contemplating how travel programming, through its association with heritage and national identity, has been buoyed by the transition to high-definition broadcasts in the 2000s. This chapter has contemporary resonance as a result of the recent broadcast of *Planet Earth II* (BBC, 2016), which continued the series' history of innovation in the capture of nature footage with the integration of cameras on drones, high-speed and infrared videography, and the latest generation of motion stabilizers.

In the final section, Wheatley splits her analysis of the human body on television into chapters on the medicalized spectacle and the erotic spectacle. The body genres of television that Wheatley highlights are not those of melodrama, horror, and pornography (pace Linda Williams), although each of these finds its place on the schedule, but instead educational, surgery, and autopsy shows. Here Wheatley puts Linda Williams's work on pornography into dialogue with Michel Foucault's *The Birth of the Clinic*.[10] From factual entertainment in the 1950s to documentaries enhanced by computer-generated imagery of the 1990s and 2000s, Wheatley finds that the human body has been objectified, interrogated, and penetrated by cameras. In these spectacular medical examinations, the body becomes alien, uncanny, and something to be mastered. Next Wheatley turns her attention to intentional and accidental erotic spectacles provided by British and American prime-time dramas.[11] From close readings of the "sexposition" of *Game of Thrones* (HBO, 2011–2019) and the research sequences on *Masters of Sex* (Showtime, 2013–2016), and her analysis of a snowball questionnaire with primarily female respondents, Wheatley concludes that the depiction of sex is

7 John Street, "Aesthetics, Policy and the Politics of Popular Culture," *European Journal of Cultural Studies* 3, no. 1 (2000): 27–43; Charlotte Brunsdon, *Screen Tastes: Soap Operas to Satellite Dishes* (London: Routledge, 1997).

8 Wheatley, *Spectacular Television*, 118.

9 Quoted in Wheatley, *Spectacular Television*, 68.

10 Linda Williams, "Film Bodies: Gender, Genre, and Excess," *Film Quarterly* 44, no. 4 (1991): 2–13; Michel Foucault, *Birth of the Clinic: An Archaeology of Medical Perception*, trans. A. M. Sheridan Smith (New York: Routledge, 2006).

11 Wheatley, *Spectacular Television*, 191.

spectacular in that it is intended to be watched but is simultaneously rendered ordinary through its domestication on television.[12]

Spectacular Television is an eminently readable book with strong examples that support its fundamental argument that visual pleasure is intrinsic to television aesthetics and practice. Yet one can sense the origins of most of the chapters as previous publications, as some of the book's conceptual through lines are not sustained evenly throughout the text. For instance, some chapters offer fascinating contemplation of spectacular environmental landscapes, yet Wheatley does not connect these arguments to her later discussion of representations of the human body, even while describing it as "a spectacular, navigable landscape" and "a terrain, clean, smooth and pulsating red."[13] These limits do not detract from Wheatley's comprehensive research and articulate analysis. Instead, each part speaks to a different aspect of the abundant visual pleasure available on television. *

12 Wheatley, *Spectacular Television*, 199.

13 Wheatley, *Spectacular Television*, 165, 166.

Stealing the Show: African American Performers and Audiences in 1930s Hollywood

by Miriam J. Petty. University of California Press.
2016. $34.95 paperback; $65.00 hardcover; e-book available. 320 pages.

reviewed by Samantha N. Sheppard

In 1976, James Baldwin published "The Devil Finds Work," a nonfiction blend of autobiography and film criticism.[1] Detailing his own cinephilic perception, the essay critically interrogates the visual economy of race in American cinema. "It is scarcely possible," Baldwin notes, "to think of a Black American actor who has not been misused: not one has ever been seriously challenged to deliver the best that is in him."[2] Describing the stunted careers of Paul Robeson and Ethel Waters, Baldwin suggests that "what the

1 James Baldwin, "The Devil Finds Work," in *James Baldwin: Collected Essays* (New York: Library of America, 1998).

2 Baldwin, "Devil Finds Work," 554.

black actor has managed to give are moments—indelible moments, created, miraculously, beyond the confines of the script: hints of reality, smuggled like contraband into a maudlin tale, and with enough force, if unleashed, to shatter the tale to fragments."[3] In *Stealing the Show: African American Performers and Audiences in 1930s Hollywood*, Miriam J. Petty skillfully mobilizes Baldwin's observation to mine the cinematic fragments and figures of American cinema. Focusing on the semiotic meanings of Black "protostars"—specifically Hattie McDaniel, Bill "Bojangles" Robinson, Louise Beavers, Fredi Washington, and Lincoln "Stepin Fetchit" Perry—Petty magnifies the indelible moments, the unforgettable impacts on- and off-screen, of these "picture stealers" and details how Black audiences claim, critique, praise, interpret, and grapple with these figures and their attendant discourses.

Stealing the Show, recipient of the Society for Cinema and Media Studies' 2017 Best First Book Award, provides a necessary recalibration of American cinema's studio era. A corrective to simplistic, broadly drawn readings of 1930s Black performers, *Stealing the Show* deftly balances nuanced readings of Black stereotypes, cinematic moments, extracinematic dynamics and discourses, and self-fashioning and spectatorial politics. In doing so, Petty demonstrates the substantial and, often, subversive ways that "Black entertainers and audiences expressed agency and negotiated ideas about their lives and identities through acts of performance and discourse that incorporated and exceeded the cinematic frame."[4] Focusing on widely known performers and performances, Petty pushes beyond a superficial reading of Black representation in the 1930s, encouraging a more thoughtful account of the import and impact of the roles these pioneering, beleaguered stars played.

In the past decade, scholars have shifted the historical, theoretical, and critical conversations around American cinema and African American filmgoing, specifically attending to the on-screen figures, critical discourses, and spectatorial practices during early cinema and the studio system.[5] Film historians have delved into the complex and often fraught performative practices of African American entertainers and the varied and sometimes contradictory discourses produced by Black audiences. Petty's smart and engaging study is a significant contribution to this body of scholarship. With evocative and well-argued prose, her interrogation of the acclaim and visibility of Black actors and actresses as well as the problematic nature of Black stardom in the era of social and cinematic Jim Crow is both rich and easily digestible. With deep archival research buttressed by detailed textual analysis, Petty's historicist impulse masterfully contextualizes the cinematic and cultural significance of the cadre of Black performers that make up the book's case studies.

3 Baldwin, "Devil Finds Work," 554.

4 Miriam J. Petty, *Stealing the Show: African American Performers and Audiences in 1930s Hollywood* (Berkeley: University of California Press, 2016).

5 See Charlene Regester's *African American Actresses: The Struggle for Visibility, 1900–1960* (Bloomington: Indiana University Press, 2010); Cara Caddoo's *Envisioning Freedom: Cinema and the Building of Modern Black Life* (Cambridge, MA: Harvard University Press, 2014); Allyson Nadia Field's *Uplift Cinema: The Emergence of African American Film and the Possibility of Black Modernity* (Durham, NC: Duke University Press, 2015); and Ellen C. Scott's *Cinema Civil Rights: Regulation, Repression, and Race in the Classical Hollywood Era* (New Brunswick, NJ: Rutgers University Press, 2015).

Stealing the Show's sophisticated and expansive conceptual framework can best be understood by unpacking the idea conveyed in the book's title. Like the performances, public personae, and discourses of the stars profiled, the notion of stealing the show is a multilayered, rhetorical maneuver. For Petty, "stealing the show" describes and lauds the ways in which Black performers captured viewers' attention in a film, scene, or sequence. Shifting the gaze from the putative center of attention—meaning away from the top-billed (white) stars foregrounded on screen to the margins and, thus, the marginalized people in the cinematic frame—"stealing the show" denotes a performative act that pulls focus and makes Black actresses and actors visible in new and consequential ways. In doing so, the phrase also captures the complex racial and cultural politics embedded in the discussions of these scene-stealing stars in the African American and mainstream press.

While "stealing the show" involves performance, ability, and audience, Petty purposefully revises the terms of the phrase itself to show how Black entertainers "create performances that are bounded by the strictures of American racism, yet that resonate and Signify in ways that exceed these same boundaries."[6] Drawing on an excerpt from Toni Morrison's 1987 *Beloved*, Petty replays the story of the slave Sixo, who is accused of stealing a pig—a shoat—by his white master. When caught having partially eaten the shoat, Sixo explains that he was not stealing the pig but merely improving his master's property. Aware of the sonic similarities and wordplay of "show" and "shoat," Petty astutely uses the fable to illustrate how "'stealing the shoat' acts as a kind of shadow figuration for 'stealing the show'—it is always there, undermining the phrase's celebratory connotations and reminding one of the specific social, political, cultural, and historical terms of Black cinematic performance."[7] Thus, I read the ellipsis of the introduction's title ("Stealing the show . . . or the shoat") as a tether, tying the performative praise heaped on "picture stealers" to questions of identity, craftsmanship, perspective, and curtailed opportunity for Black actors and actresses in Hollywood, then and now.

Stealing the Show's four chapters put familiar, scene-stealing figures in a new critical (spot)light. Beginning in the book's first chapter with Hattie McDaniel and the iconic image of "Mammy" in *Gone with the Wind* (Victor Fleming, 1939), Petty manages to reveal new depths of this overdetermined cinematic figure while addressing the actress's artistry on-screen and the promotional tactics she used to appeal to Black audiences who condemned and celebrated her Academy Award–winning portrayal. Petty is precise in her scrutiny of how McDaniel, as Mammy, "embodied a historical and cultural myth of slavery and its interpersonal racial relations, as well as a contemporary social reality: the post-slavery predominance of domestic work as the way many African American women earned a living."[8] Providing a close reading of McDaniel's signature performance in the film's somber staircase scene, Petty beautifully mines the sequence's textual and contextual significance to make the case for McDaniel's landmark performance as "monumental." Her exemplary close

6 Petty, *Stealing the Show*, 9.

7 Petty, *Stealing the Show*, 5.

8 Petty, *Stealing the Show*, 27.

reading of the scene should be used as a template for rigorous textual and contextual analysis. Systematically digging into the scene and McDaniel's performance, Petty excavates the ways in which the mammy figure, a racist fiction and amalgam, becomes not only an emblematic symbol of race, class, and gender but also a cipher and site of ideological struggle. Petty concludes by reflecting on McDaniel's attempt to reframe herself within and outside of her on-screen monumental image by "tying her role as Mammy to a history and legacy that directly contradicted the notion of her character as the 'faithful slave' immortalized in Mitchell's novel."[9] The chapter renders clear McDaniel's unprecedented promotional work and the progressive discourse she used when speaking to Black presses and audiences in her attempt to "steal the show" from Mammy's racist taint.

Stealing the Show continues this critical reshaping of our understanding of familiar Black female performers. The book's third chapter addresses how actresses Louise Beavers and Fredi Washington took center stage on the screen and in popular debates. Calling them "the perfect double act," Petty explains that Beavers's and Washington's respective characters, Delilah and Peola in John Stahl's *Imitation of Life* (1934), upstage and eclipse the white mother-daughter acting duo in the film. Although there is an extensive body of scholarship on Stahl's film as well as Douglas Sirk's 1959 remake, Petty's chapter ostensibly "steals the show" in terms of critical debates about *Imitation of Life*. She argues that the two characters and actresses are Janus-faced figures that play out the gendered constructions and intraracial politics of the "Old Negro" and "New Negro" paradigm. "As Delilah and Peola," Petty explains, "Louise Beavers and Fredi Washington were subject to varied, interconnected readings by African American audiences. As stars and characters, they embodied key aspects of what it meant to be Black, female, urban, modern, dark- or light-skinned, politically progressive, racially loyal, and respectable in early twentieth-century America. . . . Their show stealing enabled and facilitated this dialogue in unique ways."[10] This chapter demonstrates how both figures signified for Black audiences, a meaning-making process that was "tied to skin color, hair texture, and what each symbolized socially, culturally, politically, and historically."[11] The oppositional visual poles that Beavers and Washington represent evoked critical debate about the film and the actresses among Black audiences, with moviegoers interpreting their interconnected performances and personas in complex and contradictory ways.

Stealing the Show's attention to Black audiences' negotiation of cinematic texts vis-à-vis Black stars grounds the book's ample and compelling textual analysis. Petty's chapter on Bill "Bojangles" Robinson perhaps provides the most ambitious theorization of spectatorship in the book. As she pans out from Robinson's performance with his pint-sized costar Shirley Temple in *The Little Colonel* (David Butler, 1935), Petty raises questions about "the relationship between Robinson and Black children as both spectators and performers, and perhaps most provocatively, about the kinds of looking relationships that Black children forged when they went to the movies in the 1930s and

9 Petty, *Stealing the Show*, 58.

10 Petty, *Stealing the Show*, 171.

11 Petty, *Stealing the Show*, 131.

1940s."[12] In doing so, she provides an original interrogation of Black children's cultural reception of Robinson and other screen idols. Working through popular theories of spectatorship from bell hooks, Manthia Diawara, Anna Everett, Jacqueline Stewart, and Patricia White, Petty explores, more generally, how the movies operated as "one of the places in which African-American children were both implicitly and explicitly instructed about the existence and limitations of the racially exclusionary social order that organized and circumscribed their lives."[13] Drawing on a range of literary sources both fictional and nonfictional, Petty, like Stewart, imaginatively "recover[s] and describe[s] dynamics of Black spectatorship," putting to us the question of "what kinds of 'evidence' can we mobilize to understand" past moviegoing experiences of Black youth.[14]

Stealing the Show's pedagogical possibilities and pairings are as exciting as they are refreshing. This book should be used in American cinema classes broadly and should serve as a requisite text for African American cinema classes. Not only will the chapters illuminate discussions of the actor's filmographies; Petty's book will be a powerful grounding text when paired with more contemporary films and figures. For example, I can imagine teaching excerpts of Petty's book alongside Robert Townsend's 1987 satire *Hollywood Shuffle*. As Petty's text culls the weighty implications of Black stardom and the politics of representation, the dialectical exchange between Townsend's film and, say, the book's final chapter on Lincoln Perry and his Stepin Fetchit persona, would be generative and far-reaching. Reading Townsend's famous "Black Acting School" scene against the narrative of Perry's problematic stardom can reveal the historical consequences of characterizations that "steal the show." Petty soberly reminds us that "Stepin Fetchit is perhaps the most lucid example of the way that race limited the opportunities for Black performers to occupy a conventional Hollywood model of stardom in the early twentieth century, and to some extent in the contemporary moment as well."[15] This nod to the present in *Stealing the Show* invites readers to consider the broad scope of Petty's arguments and the "critical questions about the nature of stardom as inflected by American racial ideologies" in and beyond the 1930s.[16] There is so much that this excellent book says about Black stars and audiences today in what Kristen J. Warner calls the "time of plastic representation" in Hollywood.[17] *Stealing the Show* should inspire cinema and media scholars to expand on this stunning contribution to the field by looking back at the roles of other "picture stealers" in the studio era and thinking forward to their modern-day counterparts. *

12 Petty, *Stealing the Show*, 73.

13 Petty, *Stealing the Show*, 98.

14 Jacqueline Najuma Stewart, *Migrating to the Movies: Cinema and Black Urban Modernity* (Berkeley: University of California Press, 2005), 95.

15 Petty, *Stealing the Show*, 213.

16 Petty, *Stealing the Show*, 26.

17 For more on the contemporary politics of Black stars and audiences, see Kristen J. Warner's "In the Time of Plastic Representation," *Film Quarterly*, 71, no. 2 (Winter 2017): 32–37.

Contributors

Mashinka Firunts Hakopian is a doctoral candidate in art history at the University of Pennsylvania. She is a member of the media and performance group Research Service and a coeditor of Present Tense Pamphlets, a series devoted to score–based performance, released through Northwestern University and the Block Museum of Art.

Henry Jenkins is Provost's Professor of Communication, Journalism, Cinematic Arts, and Education at the University of Southern California. He has published seventeen books, including *What Made Pistachio Nuts? Early Sound Comedy and the Vaudeville Aesthetic* (Columbia University Press, 1992).

Anupama Kapse is associate professor of film studies at Loyola Marymount University. Her research and scholarship situate moving-image melodrama within a wider cultural history of the body, affect, ethics, and citizenship, with a focus on South Asia.

Emily Saidel is a doctoral candidate in communication studies at the University of Michigan. Her research areas include television studies and paratextual studies, with a focus on the representation of American government in fictional television programs.

Samantha N. Sheppard is the Mary Armstrong Meduski '80 Assistant Professor of Cinema and Media Studies in the Department of Performing and Media Arts at Cornell University. She writes extensively on race in film and television.

UNITED STATES POSTAL SERVICE® Statement of Ownership, Management, and Circulation (All Periodicals Publications Except Requester Publications)

1. Publication Title: Cinema Journal	2. Publication Number: 0009-7101	3. Filing Date: September 12, 2018
4. Issue Frequency: Quarterly	5. Number of Issues Published Annually: 4	6. Annual Subscription Price: $264.00 Inst.
7. Complete Mailing Address of Known Office of Publication (Not printer) (Street, city, county, state, and ZIP+4®): University of Texas Press, 3001 Lake Austin Blvd. Ste. 2200, Austin, Travis County, Texas, 78703-4210		Contact Person: Christopher Farmer Telephone (Include area code): 512-232-7620

8. Complete Mailing Address of Headquarters or General Business Office of Publisher (Not printer)

Same as 7.

9. Full Names and Complete Mailing Addresses of Publisher, Editor, and Managing Editor (Do not leave blank)

Publisher (Name and complete mailing address)

Same as 7.

Editor (Name and complete mailing address)

Caetlin Benson-Allott - Georgetown University, New North 306,
3700 O Street, NW, Washington, DC 20057

Managing Editor (Name and complete mailing address)

Caetlin Benson-Allott - Georgetown University, New North 306,
3700 O Street, NW, Washington, DC 20057

10. Owner (Do not leave blank. If the publication is owned by a corporation, give the name and address of the corporation immediately followed by the names and addresses of all stockholders owning or holding 1 percent or more of the total amount of stock. If not owned by a corporation, give the names and addresses of the individual owners. If owned by a partnership or other unincorporated firm, give its name and address as well as those of each individual owner. If the publication is published by a nonprofit organization, give its name and address.)

Full Name	Complete Mailing Address
Society for Cinema and Media Studies	640 Parrington Oval
	University of Oklahoma
	Wallace Old Science Hall, Room 300
	Norman, Ok, 73019

11. Known Bondholders, Mortgagees, and Other Security Holders Owning or Holding 1 Percent or More of Total Amount of Bonds, Mortgages, or Other Securities. If none, check box → ☒ None

Full Name	Complete Mailing Address

12. Tax Status (For completion by nonprofit organizations authorized to mail at nonprofit rates) (Check one)
The purpose, function, and nonprofit status of this organization and the exempt status for federal income tax purposes:
☒ Has Not Changed During Preceding 12 Months
☐ Has Changed During Preceding 12 Months (Publisher must submit explanation of change with this statement)

13. Publication Title: Cinema Journal

14. Issue Date for Circulation Data Below: Cinema Journal 57:4

15. Extent and Nature of Circulation			Average No. Copies Each Issue During Preceding 12 Months	No. Copies of Single Issue Published Nearest to Filing Date
a. Total Number of Copies (Net press run)			3977	4030
b. Paid Circulation (By Mail and Outside the Mail)	(1)	Mailed Outside-County Paid Subscriptions Stated on PS Form 3541 (Include paid distribution above nominal rate, advertiser's proof copies, and exchange copies)	1890	552
	(2)	Mailed In-County Paid Subscriptions Stated on PS Form 3541 (Include paid distribution above nominal rate, advertiser's proof copies, and exchange copies)		
	(3)	Paid Distribution Outside the Mails Including Sales Through Dealers and Carriers, Street Vendors, Counter Sales, and Other Paid Distribution Outside USPS®	758	235
	(4)	Paid Distribution by Other Classes of Mail Through the USPS (e.g., First-Class Mail®)		
c. Total Paid Distribution [Sum of 15b (1), (2), (3), and (4)]			2648	787
d. Free or Nominal Rate Distribution (By Mail and Outside the Mail)	(1)	Free or Nominal Rate Outside-County Copies included on PS Form 3541	12	12
	(2)	Free or Nominal Rate In-County Copies Included on PS Form 3541		
	(3)	Free or Nominal Rate Copies Mailed at Other Classes Through the USPS (e.g., First-Class Mail)		
	(4)	Free or Nominal Rate Distribution Outside the Mail (Carriers or other means)		
e. Total Free or Nominal Rate Distribution (Sum of 15d (1), (2), (3) and (4))			12	12
f. Total Distribution (Sum of 15c and 15e)			2660	799
g. Copies not Distributed (See Instructions to Publishers #4 (page #3))			1317	3231
h. Total (Sum of 15f and g)			3977	4030
i. Percent Paid (15c divided by 15f times 100)			99.5%	98.5%

* If you are claiming electronic copies, go to line 16 on page 3. If you are not claiming electronic copies, skip to line 17 on page 3.

UNITED STATES POSTAL SERVICE® Statement of Ownership, Management, and Circulation (All Periodicals Publications Except Requester Publications)

16. Electronic Copy Circulation	Average No. Copies Each Issue During Preceding 12 Months	No. Copies of Single Issue Published Nearest to Filing Date
a. Paid Electronic Copies		
b. Total Paid Print Copies (Line 15c) + Paid Electronic Copies (Line 16a)		
c. Total Print Distribution (Line 15f) + Paid Electronic Copies (Line 16a)		
d. Percent Paid (Both Print & Electronic Copies) (16b divided by 16c × 100)		

☐ I certify that 50% of all my distributed copies (electronic and print) are paid above a nominal price.

17. Publication of Statement of Ownership

☒ If the publication is a general publication, publication of this statement is required. Will be printed in the November 2018/ Fall Issue issue of this publication. ☐ Publication not required.

18. Signature and Title of Editor, Publisher, Business Manager, or Owner: Journals Manager — Date: 09/12/2018

I certify that all information furnished on this form is true and complete. I understand that anyone who furnishes false or misleading information on this form or who omits material or information requested on the form may be subject to criminal sanctions (including fines and imprisonment) and/or civil sanctions (including civil penalties).

Forthcoming

- Caroline Ben, The Diptych in Narrative Cinema: Medial Transubstantiations and Generic Paradox in *Grindhouse* and *Death Proof*
- Carmela Garritano, Living Precariously in the African Postcolony: Debt and Labor Relations in the Films of Mahamat-Saleh Haroun
- Paul Haacke, The Melancholic Voice-Over in Film Noir
- Justin Remes, Brakhage and the Birth of Silence
- Ben Rogerson, "Nobody Knows Anything": Professionalism and Publics in *The Great Waldo Pepper*
- Avi Santo, Retail Tales and Tribulations: Media Industries, Transmedia Brands, Consumer Products, and the Significance of Shop Talk